Writer's Block

by L.A.Smith

Dedication

Dedicated to all the souls who believe that they are not worth it.
You are.

Thank the Lord for giving me such wonderful talents, and for the ability to connect with other people. I've got to spread my thanks to my parents who supported me when I had nothing left, to Christa, for putting up with all my questions, and to Carrie and Bek, who not only pushed me into finishing, but helped to read through and edit, and even help to create my cover art for the book.

You have all of my love and gratitude.

L.A.Smith is a student just trying to get by. She is a published artist, writer, and actress, wanting nothing more than to fill the world with meaningful stories, be they written or watched. She hopes to one day own her own company in order to do so, but until then, she'll keep on working towards that goal one step at a time.

In a parallel universe, true love is unquestioned as each soul finds its mate.

First Chapter

"You want me to run for president?" Taylor asked.

"You've got the skills for it," Miss Hart went on. "You're talented, responsible, likable-"

"Now I *know* you're lying," the teen smirked. Miss Hart frowned at her student, head cocked to the side with her fists balled at her hips, giving her signature look of annoyance.

"Look, all I'm saying is that you are the one I would pick to lead the group if I were away for whatever reason. I trust you, Taylor, and I can see great potential in you if you would just take a chance." Taylor plopped his stuffed backpack onto his desk and began filling it even more with his books.

"Next year will be your last year here. It won't be the same without you, and if you can't train an apprentice to be almost as good as you before you leave, I'm stuck teaching all the idiots who can't tell the difference between a shift bar and caps lock."

"Miss Hart." Taylor shouldered his backpack and began walking out the door before continuing. " It's not that I can't lead the computer club. It's that I *can't* lead the computer club. I don't have the time. Between school, home, and always looking for work, I'm swamped."

"Yes, but this could give you more jobs."

Taylor stopped mid-step out the door, paused for a moment, then turned to look at his teacher. Miss Hart smiled to herself. Now she had him hooked.

" *'Head of Riviera Computer Technology Class.'* Has a nice ring to the resume`. More people outside of class and tutoring will seek you out. I guarantee it." Taylor furrowed his brow, not speaking; but Miss Hart was not done.

"Did I mention that it would also look great on your college entrance papers?"

she asked with a smirk of her own. Taylor sighed, annoyed at how glamorous it was all starting to sound, and knowing that Miss Hart knew she had reeled him in with that. After a while of smoldering, he finally muttered "I'll think about it," and bid his farewell for the evening, leaving Miss Hart grinning from ear to ear.

Taylor was a good kid of sixteen years. He was quiet, a hard study and usually alone, but the most remarkable thing about him was his intelligence. Often, when someone's computer had crashed or needed repairs, they would turn to Miss Hart for help, who would then refer them to Taylor for hire.

Unknown to many, he was one of the best technologists in the entire town- and an even better hacker. Miss Hart liked Taylor, and tried to help him as much as she could. She knew he was worth it because to her, he *was* a good kid. She also knew how desperate he was to earn as much as he could before graduating, and computer repairs, programing and tutoring just wouldn't cut it. Not if he wanted to study abroad like he planned. Dangling more work in front of him to get what she wanted was just plain dirty. Today, though, there was no work to be done, so it was time for him to head home.

Taylor walked down the halls of his school, not really in a hurry to be going anywhere. Truthfully, he was debating whether or not to go home at all; at least for a few hours. As much as he didn't like it, his father knew of Taylor's erratic work schedule. One message on the chat-line would alert his father to his absence for the evening and he would be free to do whatever he wished until dinner.

Dinner.

The realization that he needed to cook with no ingredients slowly crept into him with this one word. "*Crap,*" he thought. Last he checked, there wasn't anything edible enough to make a proper meal unless he wanted to serve beer and popcorn. With nothing decent in the fridge, Taylor decided it would be best to leave straight away in order to get enough to whip up a meal, and his pace quickened at the thought.

As Taylor rounded the corner, he could hear rowdiness going on behind the large, rounded stairs set in the middle of the grand entrance hall. He stopped, recognizing the voices, and groaned inwardly as he peeked around the staircase. Sure enough, it was him: Team captain Kaleb Evans and his group of moronic lackeys from the football team.

Kaleb was tossing a football between himself and two other friends, whose names Taylor couldn't quite recall at the moment. One started with a 'J', perhaps? The other was facing away from him, so he couldn't quite see his face. They were being rather rough with each other, and with any luck, Taylor thought to himself, they were preoccupied enough for him to slip by unnoticed. The blonde boy flipped his hood over his head, removed his ever-present headphones from around his neck, and shoved them into his backpack. Then, once he was sure he had a chance, he stepped out from the staircase and made a beeline for the exit just past the rambunctious boys.

Taylor held the boys within his peripheral vision but kept his head down, hands shoved in his pockets, mostly listening for any signs of danger to be as inconspicuous as possible. About halfway, his hood blocked the boys from sight completely and he had to rely solely on his hearing, but it wasn't too long before he reached the doors. Just as his hand touched the handle-

"Hey! Look who it is, guys!"

So close.

Taylor pushed forward through the first set of doors, not yet running, but not at the same pace as before either. By the second set of doors a few steps away, the boys had caught up with him.

"Hold up, there, Tommy."

This was in reference to Taylor's last name, Thompson; though it didn't please him in the slightest to be called this. Rather than correcting them, however, Taylor continued on, ignoring the athletes entirely. Kaleb wouldn't have it. He grabbed Taylor's backpack, pulled it off his back, and from this action, forced Taylor to step back or fall to the concrete beneath his feet. Before Taylor could regain his balance, Kaleb used his unsteadiness to wrap his arm around Taylor's neck in a choke hold to keeping him just above his knees; a move he particularly favored to use on Taylor.

"Hey, now," Kaleb spoke, mouth right above Taylor's head. "Daniel here was trying to talk to you. It's a little rude of you to ignore him like that, don't you think?"

Daniel, *that's* what his name was. Upon closer inspection, Taylor noticed the faces of the lackeys grinning down at him as he struggled to get some air space between Kaleb's arm and Taylor's neck. That's when he noticed the '*J*' boy.

The other boy had to be Gerrit, yet another teammate. Taylor mentally smacked himself for not noticing sooner, as Gerrit was not only Kaleb's best friend, but was the team's best running back because of his size. His tiny stature allowed him to be agile and fast as he ran past giants to the end of the field. He was easily recognizable, even off the field. Aside from this, though, he was more memorable to Taylor because of his horrible attitude.

"I think Tommy might need a little refresher course on manners," Daniel said, crossing his arms as he spoke.

"I agree." Gerrit smirked. "After all, Mommy's not home to do it."

Kaleb glared at his friend, but said nothing. It wouldn't have done any good anyways because Gerrit ignored this, and bent down to face Taylor to murmur to him.

"Off across the Great Waters, right?" He faked an obnoxious frown. "Guess she couldn't stand being around you anymore, huh?" Taylor said nothing, but the glint in his eyes were full of fury, and his grip tightened on Kaleb's forearm. Gerrit shrugged, and stood back up.

"You did this to yourself, really."

Taylor trudged home, alone on the sidewalk, listening to his music as loud as his headphone speakers would allow. He was glad to have known to hide them away in his backpack before the goons attacked, otherwise they most likely would have either been broken from the rough treatment they gave him, or stolen altogether.

For the past year, this was the norm for Taylor. Neither Kaleb nor Gerrit had ever forgiven Taylor for publicly humiliating Gerrit halfway through the previous school year, and neither had the rest of his friends. With Taylor's technological skills, however, it was simply too easy. Since then, Kaleb's crew had been tormenting Taylor on a daily basis, and Kaleb did nothing to stop it. Worse still, because of his first attack, Taylor couldn't rebuttal any of their attacks with his own unless he wanted to be suspended; thereby losing any chance of getting out of that crummy town on a scholarship.

The 'punishment' the boys had spoken of, was to test out the new stink bombs the Alchemy club had created. After tossing him around a bit, they threw disgusting little pouches full of foul chemicals at him, each exploding on contact, just as they were created to do. And to finish it off, Daniel took whatever cash Taylor had in his wallet after Kaleb and Gerrit had started to leave, despite the smell. Now Taylor was retreating back home, empty handed and trying not to retch from his own stench.

As he stepped up to his front porch, he paused a moment to rid himself of whatever layers of clothing he could before he was considered a stripper, and laid them over the handrails surrounding his porch to air out as much as they could before he brought them in the house to be washed. Once that was done, he unlocked the door and stepped inside to find the television blaring, and he could hear his father snoring in his recliner before it.

Quietly, Taylor closed the front door and checked on his father. Asleep in his chair, beer in one hand, the remote in the other. He slipped the remote out of his father's fingers and lowered the volume without a word, then made his way to the kitchen.

Taylor didn't expect to find much. Beer, noodles, eggs, hot dogs; not much to work with at all, really. However, Taylor was used to getting creative, and started boiling water to make a buttered pasta dinner for the night. Some herbs and seasonings he found hidden in the pantry would make it a bit more desirable. A quick shower was needed before he could really start cooking though, lest the stink bomb chemicals seep into the food. With that fear in mind, Taylor left the water to boil on the slowly heating stove, and headed off for a much needed cleansing.

Taylor shed whatever clothing he had left while in the bathroom. For a moment, he stilled long enough to inspect himself in the mirror. He was a skinny boy indeed, but hardly frail. His muscles peeked out here and there, which was really the only proof of him being older than twelve. Save for his smooth chest, his body hair was so light and fair, the other boys would often tease him, and accuse him of shaving his legs. The hair on his head was only slightly darker, but still light in color all the same; this helped to highlight his bright blue eyes.

All of this went unnoticed, however, as Taylor was more focussed on the bruises left on his skin. They were scattered about his body, carefully hidden beneath layers of clothing, and scarcely seen, even to himself. The only constant visible blemish, however, was a small, but deep scar just below his right eye. Taylor turned away from the mirror, sighing to himself, and turned on the shower, hoping to wash away the ugly black and blue splotches on his body.

"What have I told you about ragging on moms?" Kaleb growled at his friend.

"Sorry, man, it's just easy material," Gerrit replied. They were walking home after their little test run on Taylor. Daniel lived on the other side of the neighborhood, and had already made it home, leaving Gerrit and Kaleb to walk the rest of the way to their own homes alone. This gave Kaleb the best chance to reprimand his friend without anyone else seeing them argue.

"That's no excuse," Kaleb grumbled. "Would you want me talking about your mom? No. She's got nothing to do with it, so leave it."

"Alright, alright," Gerrit groaned. "I'm sorry. Quarter, already."

Kaleb frowned at his friend for using such an old apology, but knew that was the best he could get out of him, and let the issue drop. He looked ahead, tossing his football in the air every so often while the two boys tried to find something else to talk about when he remembered the first game of the season.

"You ready for next week?" Kaleb asked, squeezing a smile out of his smaller friend.

"Yep. Fast as ever." Gerrit gave a little in-place sprint to prove his point, which caused a laugh to leak out of the giant walking next to him.

Kaleb was the complete opposite of Gerrit. His black hair sprang up naturally into a short, curt cut that spiked easily with a bit of bed-head after a good nights sleep. His brown eyes were much darker than his skin, but he was tan all the same from all the hours training in the sun. Most importantly, though, he was big, strong, and broad: perfect for a football player- unless you were Gerrit.

Gerrit was just about half the size of Kaleb width-wise, and just barely scraped under his shoulder in height. He was super skinny, but heavily muscled, and almost just as tan as his taller friend. His brown hair was cut short as well, and dangled just above his ears. Far below his bangs, if you looked close enough, you could see that his eyes were a muddy green, and full of mischief.

Kaleb and Gerrit grew up together in the little town of River Hill side by side; an easy task with their houses across the street from each other. How these two became friends was a mystery even to them, but they clicked naturally, and you couldn't find two closer companions in town. The size difference didn't even bother them.

They would play into it fairly often, with many a quick remark. Sometimes, as a joke, Kaleb would carry Gerrit atop his shoulders and run around screaming battle cries, searching for opponents to challenge them. Other times, they would slander each other; Kaleb walking around on his knees while Gerrit climbed up on a bench or a chair of some sort to imitate the other without any real repercussions. No one would think it strange because that's just how they were. No one would take them seriously either, because they knew how closely bonded the boys were.

They always looked after each other, just as real brothers would. So when an embarrassing video of Gerrit was broadcast schoolwide on Riviera High's morning announcement channel, it was Kaleb who tracked down the culprit, Taylor. No matter the case, if something bothered the other, they were sure to fix it.

As the two friends neared their houses, they went their separate ways, laughing still at their own jokes and conversations. Kaleb on one side of the street, Gerrit on the other, just as it has always been.

Taylor slurped up the last of his noodles from his bowl as he logged off of his favored chat room and onto his school-issued web account. He had just finished a comforting conversation with his closest friend online, and now he needed to get down to business. He clicked his inbox link and searched for any unread e-mails. Nothing. He slumped a bit, annoyed at the fact that he was, yet again, jobless.

Throughout the school district, there was an online education plan set up for tutoring and the like. It was a monarchy of sorts, run by the school board to help to teach the students about business and trade early on at a primitive stage, while also helping to improve their studies. Only the highest marked students were allowed to become tutors and receive payment for their efforts, and luckily, Taylor was one of those few students.

Today, though, his message box was empty. Taylor sighed heavily, and checked Riviera High's 'help wanted' site just in case, but found nothing. He then decided to look through other campuses to see who may require his services- he even went so far as to look through middle and elementary schools. River Hill was a small town, with little to no business for him at all. Often times, he would find more work in the few cities surrounding the little town. A fifty coin ride on the trolley to other cities was well worth his efforts when he earned some work. Still, there was no work for him to find.

Groaning, he logged off, completely irritated. Taylor listened for his father downstairs, hearing nothing but the television and the faint tapping of silverware on diningware as his father ate. Thankfully, he had woken from his sudden slumber in a good mood, and went directly for his dinner once he saw it waiting for him on the side table next to him, leaving his son on his own.

Taylor closed his eyes, took a deep breath, held it, then released it slowly as he leaned back in his chair, his head dangling off the back of it. He opened his eye to the ceiling, staring at nothing in particular. "Just a little while longer," he mumbled. He stayed like this for a few minutes, not really focusing on anything. Then, without any prompting, he stood up from his chair, stretched, and moved to ready himself for bed.

Yet another pea crashed into Taylor's lunch tray, this time getting stuck in his barely-touched mashed potatoes. A few others rolled away and off the table when two more peas came crashing into a collected pile beside the tray, and another one soon followed after it. Taylor flicked his hair from his eyes, ignoring this one as well to focus on his writing, when a new pea bounced off his scarred cheek. He couldn't help it, his eyes rose up without his face, glaring from beneath his brow at his assailants.

Kaleb was sitting with his friends at a table not too far from Taylor's, each boy proud of their captain's most recent shot and snickering uncontrollably along with him. Every boy had tried to shoot their projectiles properly with Taylor as their target for practice, but it was Kaleb who had concocted a catapult of sorts out of his spoon and someone else's lunch tray.

Taylor was surrounded by the peas that had been tossed haphazardly around him and his lunch tray, all failed attempts at reaching Taylor spot on. He rolled his eyes at the table full of boys, then returned to his notebook with an irritated sigh. Kaleb turned back around to his table, whispering to his friends, but Taylor was back in his own little world, too immersed in his writing to care.

For a few minutes, Taylor was left alone in his world. His words flowed from his pen like a river running through rough rapids, each word tumbling through his mind in desperation to reach his paper. As they landed, homes were placed, battles ensued, and characters were created, dancing through life before the next plot twist. The heroine, a half-blooded warrior of sixteen, was making a fantastic breakfast to share with her teachers and whomever else would share a seat with them. All were in a glorious stupor, even singing and dancing around the table to old songs born of their heritage.

His warrior was giddy in the arms of one of her teachers, twirling around their meal in a rare sense of absurd silliness. She was passed on to another warrior in training, equally as happy, yet lighter on his feet as they danced through the room. Laughter accompanied the singing that filled the room, and the smells of all the food that had been prepared mingled with it in a harmonious mixture.

Their meal covered the entire table with very little room for personal plates. Several different pitchers were placed around the table, each filled separately with a surplus of coffee, juices and teas. Each serving plate and bowl was overflowing with different colors and choices; fruits, and vegetables, eggs and grains, several different kinds of baked bread and -*splat*- mashed potatoes...

Taylor nearly jumped out of his skin when the kamikaze spuds landed on his journal, just as his pen had come up from a word and was settling down to form a new one. He did, however, jump up from his seat at his lunch table. He snatched the journal and tried to wipe off the creamy substance from his pages as quickly as he could. The laughter he heard across from him could only be the previous attackers, but he was too worried about his work to bother with them at the moment.

When he did look up, or, moreover, *glare* up, he saw the same boys and a few other onlookers laughing insanely. Some were holding their sides, some slapping the table and each other, and some rolling into their knees and along the edge of the table. The other people watching were a bit more subtle, merely snickering or just laughing without the dramatic flares. Kaleb, the mastermind who had landed the fatal shot, was stifling his laughter behind a hand and wide eyes, but his shaking shoulders betrayed him. Taylor grabbed his things and left the scene, disgusted by another one of Kaleb's power-plays.

"Wait, wait! Tommy!" Kaleb wheezed, but his laughter left him immobile. Taylor wouldn't have let him speak anyways. He readjusted his backpack on his shoulders as he left the cafeteria, inspecting his journal for any permanent damage. A bit of gravy had smudged some of the words in the middle of the page. It would be hard and sticky for the next few days until it completely dried up and broke off- even then, the paper wouldn't be as flexible anymore.

Though the damage was little, he was still fuming. The cafeteria food was toxic enough to Taylor himself, his work didn't deserve this kind of torture too. He scraped at the plasticy residue again, trying to remove whatever evidence of 'food' there was left, but to no avail.

"What do they *put* in that stuff?" Taylor murmured to himself.

Overhead, the bell rang, signaling the end of third-year's lunch, and the five minute window given to get to their next class. Taylor closed his journal and buried it within the confines of his bag hanging off his shoulder. The day was almost over, and it wouldn't matter to anyone else if his journal had been destroyed- save for his readers. He made his way through the growing crowds to his next class without a hitch, and sat quietly in his seat until the bell rang. He just wanted the day to hurry up and be over with.

Taylor waited on Mrs. Rose while everyone else chatted with one another. She was a large woman with curly, dark red hair, not unlike Miss Hart's; though this was due to the fact that they were sisters. Mrs. Rose had found her soul mate early on, and had married soon after. Miss Hart, however, was a fiery woman, who preferred a steady career first. She had become a teacher many years before Mrs. Rose, though it didn't bother her as much as people had thought.

Mrs. Rose was a lovely woman with a charming personality to match it, but it was her adorable ignorance to things that really set her apart from her sister. Taylor craved her accidental stupidity more than anything at the moment. If anything, it would help to lighten his mood. Instead, a scrawny, middle-aged, balding man approached the class.

"Hello class, I am Mr. Sutherland, your substitute teacher for the day," said the man. A student in the back raised a hand.

"What happened to Mrs. Rose?"

Mr. Sutherland sighed, slightly annoyed. "Please wait to be called before speaking," he droned. "Unfortunately, Mrs. Rose is sick. I may be here tomorrow as well while she rests over the weekend. It's last minute, but we have a video lesson set up." He looked towards the first student to his left and asked, "Pass around the attendance sheet while I set this thing up," he ordered, handing her a sheet of paper.

A few days had passed since the run-in with Kaleb and his goons, and life went on as usual for Taylor. He sat nonchalantly at his desk, watching the substitute teacher fumble with cords and wires, trying desperately to make the machine work. The attendance sheet rounded the room, each student signing their name as it passed through their hands, and Mr.Sutherland was still trying to 'make the damn thing work.' He muttered under his breath, cursing only loud enough for those closest to hear him, yet he was getting nowhere, despite his efforts. The class was becoming restless from the wait, and their chatter soon turned into a dull roar, making things more irritating to their substitute.

"Settle down, everyone," he nearly yelled in annoyance. Taylor sighed, and stood from his desk. He walked over to the machine without a word, and despite Mr. Sutherland's irritated flusters to have him return to his seat, he fixed the damage the substitute had done, and had the video running on screen within a short few minutes.

"Thank you," Mr. Sutherland grumbled as Taylor took his seat. Taylor said nothing, but nodded instead.

"Cocky asshole," muttered one of the other students, whom Taylor recognized as another one of Kaleb's friends.

The movie played on without any problems, just ending by the time the bell rang. Taylor gathered his backpack and started out the door when he felt a hand roughly land on his shoulder.

"Hey, Tommy." It was the boy who muttered before, Dylan. Taylor flicked his attention away once he noticed that he had also been one of the boys from lunch. "So, I hear you're good with the homework. Good enough to register as a tutor."

Taylor shrugged off Dylan's hand, but listened in for a chance to earn some money. "You heard right," he responded, walking as he spoke.

"Perfect, because I've got this paper-"

"I'm free this afternoon if you want to meet up before the game tomorrow," Taylor interrupted. "Otherwise, you'll have to wait until next week."

"Well aren't we cocky?" Dylan grinned. "You think you can finish my paper by then?" Taylor stopped. He gave Dylan an irritable, incredulous look.

"Excuse me?"

"You think you can write my paper by this afternoon and make it sound good," responded Dylan. "S'that what you're saying?"

Taylor shook his head. "No, absolutely not."

"Yeah, I didn't think so," Dylan smirked. Taylor shook his head again.

"No, I mean, *no.*" Taylor looked Dylan square in the eye when he spoke. "I offer tutoring, *not* homework. If you want that paper done, you're going to have to do it yourself. I won't waste my time doing it for you."

"Excuse me?" Now it was Dylan who was incredulous, following after him. "I don't have time to do this paper, I've got the game." Taylor wouldn't have it, he continued down the hall, not bothering to stop when he spoke this time.

"If you can have time for the game, then you can have time for your school work. I don't do extra homework." It was only then when he stopped long enough to smirk at Dylan. "I thought you guys would've figured it out after Gerrit, but I guess I gave you too much credit."

The two boys stared each other down, waiting for the other to waver, but neither willing to back down. A good thirty seconds passed by with no decrease in stubbornness, until a new voice entered the conversation.

"There a problem here, Dylan?" Daniel and another boy from the team stepped into the conversation. Dylan sighed and threw on a grin.

"Nothing a little persuasion can't fix."

Taylor's blood ran cold. One idiot he could handle, but when they flocked together like this, they could very well rule the world.

"Why don't we go somewhere a little more quiet?" Dylan motioned towards the men's room to his back. Taylor didn't move. He knew better. Dylan's friends, however, stood up right behind him. "I insist."

Corny as they were, they were dangerous- and infuriating. Taylor never ceased his glare on Dylan's; cursing the football team's tight knit friendships, and at the moment, Dylan in particular. He knew if he ran now, he would never stop running. Even if he succeeded in escaping that moment, they would find him sooner or later, and then it would be worse.

Taylor kept up his glare on Dylan as he walked through the swinging door, both out of anger and keeping up his fearless facade. Once inside, Dylan walked along the stalls, checking to see if anyone were using one at the moment. When he decided it was clear, he started speaking again.

"Now, see, we've got a problem here," he said, rubbing his mouth as he spoke. "If I don't finish this paper, I won't pass this class." He looked up at Taylor. "And if I don't pass, I don't play." Taylor said nothing, so Dylan continued on. "The team needs all of its members, Tommy. We've all gotta 'stick together,' in a sense. So I'll make this simple." Suddenly, with a look from Dylan, his friends each grabbed an arm from behind Taylor and held him in place. "If I don't play, you don't walk out of here."

Taylor's glare was still glued to his face, and still, he said nothing. To this, Dylan found his answer and shrugged. "Okay." He turned away from Taylor, then, with full force, swung his fist into the blonde's gut, earning a resounding guttural groan from Taylor's mouth. This cued the other two boys to throw their target to the ground and start beating on him as well.

Taylor did his best to protect himself from each blow, knowing full well he could have avoided this all together had he just accepted Dylan's offer. However, with the school's honorary code, if he had been caught, he would never be eligible to attend college- let alone study abroad. He was already on thin ice because of the scheme he pulled on Gerrit the year before for the same thing. He just couldn't take the chance.

After a while, the athletes grew tired of their efforts, and left the battered blonde alone on the bathroom floor while they left just as the one minute warning bell rang. Taylor rolled over and uncurled his body as much as he could, trying hard to breath normally. Slowly, he was able to stand with the help of a nearby stall, and caught a glimpse of himself in the mirror.

Once again, they were careful to avoid any areas that would end up being visible to the public, although, when he lifted his shirt, he could see the bruises beginning to form already over the old ones. Taylor huffed, dropping his shirts, and shouldered his backpack again. He did one more once over in the mirror, then exited the bathroom with one fleeting thought:

"This is just not my day."

Chapter 2

"Come on, Mr. G," Kaleb groaned. "We learned all of this in junior high. Do we really need to go over the birds and the bees again?" A handful of other students accompanied his complaints, but Mr. G continued on.

"I know, I know," he said, waving his students down. "But, it's part of the lesson plan, so sit down and shut up. Maybe we'll see something good on the video later." A chuckle rippled through the room along with Mr. G's own smile.

"Now." He clicked on a little handheld to the next projection picture of a topless woman turned away from the camera. "Here is a woman who hasn't found her soulmate yet. How do we know this...?" He hummed a bit, looking for a person to answer before choosing. "Jason?"

"Her soul crest is still on her back," Jason answered.

"Exactly; right between the shoulder blades." Mr. G moved to the next slide of a man in the same situation as the woman before him. "This guy hasn't found his soul mate either. Poor schmuck." More giggling.

"The soul crest is like that of a tattoo that you are born with, usually black in color, and always in various designs." Mr. G went on, droning as he read from the lesson plan. "Tell me, somebody, how do we know when the soulmate is found?" Mr. G pointed to a young, blond girl.

"When your soul crest combines with another person's crest," she answered.

"That's right, Allison, but who can give me another answer?" Mr. G wandered about the room some more, debating which student to pick, but Kaleb piped up before he could choose.

"When your crest moves from your back to your chest."

"Ah, yes, but you didn't raise your hand," Mr. G commented. "Lightning round. Ready?" Kaleb grinned a deep, toothy grin and shifted in his seat, leaning forward as though he were ready to pounce out of it. An excited hush fell over the other students as Mr. G shook his own shoulders, and after a moment of staring down his opponent, began his assault with the first attack.

"When does one's crest first begin to show?"

"Born with it, but it's not fully complete until the first year."

"Which two crests are exactly alike?"

"Trick question- no two souls are the same; not even twins."

"Once you've met your match, how do you know your crests have bonded?"

Kaleb scrunched up his face. "Psh, they combine, of course."

"Nope. That's after. Three second recall, hurry."

"Wha- uh…" Kaleb stumbled.

"Three, two…" Mr. G looked to his student.

"I don't know," Kaleb sighed.

"Then you should raise your hand next time and ask." Mr. G smiled, and the rest of the class laughed along at the response. Kaleb leaned back and covered his face in defeat, groaning; not entirely embarrassed, as Mr. G always won in lightning rounds no matter how much anyone studied. A hand raised towards the front.

"What happens if something happens to your mate before you can find them?"

Mr. G's eyes lit up and he whirled around to hold a finger up to his inquisitive student. "Ah! Excellent question." He slapped his hands together for a rub. "Have you ever felt sad for no reason at all? Maybe even sick?" Around the room, the students nodded randomly. "From birth, you are connected to your mate through your crests. When they are upset, you feel it- and vice versa." Another hand rose.

"What if you've already bonded and the other one dies?"

The teacher whipped around to face the new question. "Sadly enough, you live on," he answered. "However, your crest moves back to your back, and you're given another chance at love with someone else." He shrugged. "Most of the time, your crest will change slightly to accommodate with the new soul, but it mostly stays the same."

The bell rang, signaling the end of class, and the students gathered their belongings to leave on to their next class. "Remember, anatomy exam tomorrow." Mr. G spoke over the scraping of chairs and moaning, disappointed students. "And if you cheat, I can't take a nice picture of you before you 'mysteriously' go missing because my camera's broken, so study hard or the picture they use for the milk carton will be from your crappy yearbook." Kaleb chuckled at his teacher's crude humor, shoving his binder under his arm. Before he could leave, though, he needed to find out what the correct answer was to his failed lightning round.

"Hey, Mr. G?" Kaleb asked. "How *do* you know when you've bonded?" Mr. G turned to his student with his usual grin.

"Ah, see," he raised a finger. "When you've met together in a moment of passion, something amazing happens."

"What?" Kaleb stepped in closer, gripping his pocketed fists in anticipation. Mr. G wiggled a finger to have his student lean in closer, to which he abided. Mr. G looked around from left to right before leaning in close to Kaleb's ear and whispering. "We'll go over that next time."

"Teaser!" Kaleb shoved his teacher's shoulder, who was laughing heartily at his little joke. "You're such an imp, I swear."

"I wouldn't have to be if you kids weren't so easy," responded the older man. Then, "Hey, study group after school today still good?"

"Yeah," Kaleb nodded, then with a smile. "No worries, G.G."

Mr. Gregory Goodson chuckled once more as Kaleb left for his next class, shaking his head at his playful student, and began preparing for his next class period.

Kaleb wandered down the packed hallways of his school, smiling, laughing, and greeting almost every face he walked past. As captain and star of the football team, he was easily the most well known boy in school. Each person greeted him in return, some even giving him high fives and shaking his hand as he walked by. He slowly made his way to his next class, but not before bumping into Taylor coming out of the men's room.

"Hey, Tommy, my man!" Kaleb slapped him on the back, then grabbed him by the shoulders, squeezing him a little harder than he meant to. "Thanks for helping out with the stink bombs the other day," he said with a wink. "How'd it wash out, by the way?"

Taylor said nothing, but glared at him instead. Kaleb's grin widened. "What's that look for? It's a serious question." Taylor shrugged off Kaleb's grasp and walked on. "Poor sport!" Kaleb called after him, but did not follow, knowing that they both needed to get to class.

Something about how off-putting Taylor was to everyone around him didn't sit right with Kaleb. In fact, it rather annoyed him. Taylor was quiet, and too good at ignoring people; as though he felt that he were too good to talk to them. Whenever he saw Taylor, it angered Kaleb to see how poorly he treated Kaleb's friends.

"He may be smart," Kaleb thought, *"but that doesn't make him better than everyone else."*

There were other things about him as well, like how he would scowl at people who bothered him, like he did to Kaleb not thirty seconds prior; or how he refused to tutor a select few- mostly Kaleb's friends in particular, but the worst of them all was how he could use his skills against people for no good reason, just as he did to Gerrit the previous year.

Kaleb prided himself on spreading and keeping up with the idea that friends should stick together, and Taylor only helped the idea to grow further. He made it easy to be hated. Kaleb stood there staring after Taylor, stewing over every little thing that bothered him about the strange boy until he was abruptly interrupted by someone calling his name.

"Kaleb!" He turned to see his friend Kara, who was walking towards him. "I need your help on a project later," she said. "Got a day to spare?"

"Not with the game this week." Kaleb shrugged. "How about after the weekend? After school?"

"Perfect. Four o'clock, usual place." With that, Kara left Kaleb and entered a nearby classroom. Kaleb watched after her, muttering to himself as he headed for his own class.

"Usual place."

"Alright, let's go! Knees up! Knees up!"

The team was shoving in one last hard practice before the game the next day, and neither Kaleb nor coach Abernathy would accept anything less than their best. At the moment, the boys were practicing zig-zags; an agility training technique that worked their feet around cones in rapid, miniature steps on their toes. They took turns rounding the lined up cones as quickly as they could. "Move!" Kaleb shouted. "Let's see some hustle out there!"

"Evans!"

Coach Abernathy called to Kaleb, to which he responded with a quick "Yes, coach!" The athletics teacher, not wanting to bring more attention to himself, nodded over his team captain, waiting to speak until he had reached him. "I need to leave for a bit," he said, pausing a moment to silently tell the nearby Gerrit to turn and leave with the swirl of a finger. "Keep them busy until I come back."

Kaleb nodded. "Yessir, coach." He didn't bother asking what it was that needed his coach's attention, knowing full well that there was no point. He would get an earful of rage before being told to do his duty again, and in the end, that's all he would get. Coach was a simple man, really. It didn't take Kaleb very long to figure out his quirks at all. Follow orders, and life would be peaceful. Simple.

"Alright, boys." Kaleb trotted back to his position overlooking his teammates during practice, with Gerrit close behind. "Hustle, hustle! Heads up!" One after another, the boys basically tip-toed their way around each cone, tagging the next boy in line for his turn as they finished. Things were going smoothly. A little too smoothly for Gerrit's taste.

"Dude, this is so boring," he murmured to Kaleb. "Why don't we rile things up a bit?"

"Coach gave me my orders," Kaleb said.

"I heard him," Gerrit responded. "He said 'keep them busy;' that's what he said."

Kaleb cocked a brow at this revelation. "Go get some more cones," he murmured with a smile, and Gerrit quickly complied with a grin of his own. "Alright," Kaleb stepped forward, addressing his team. "Who wants a race?" Cheers from the boys came and went as they abandoned the current loop and split into two lines once given the order. Gerrit returned with the extra cones, and after a word from Kaleb, set them up identically next to the first set, then lined up with the others.

"Fastest team to zig-zag through the cones completely, wins," Kaleb explained. "And losers have to clean up the equipment while the rest get first showers." The boys hooted their approval of the terms, riling themselves up even more. Kaleb stood to the side, grabbing a stopwatch from off a nearby bench. "Ready?" Kaleb rose his hand high for all to see, then dropped it to signal the start. "Go!"

The head of each line bolted forward to the first cone, then slowing to rapidly tip-toe through the line. Once they reached the last cone, they rounded back, only running once they had tip-toed past the first cone again to tag the next boy in line, starting the process all over again. Kaleb watched intently, looking for any mishaps. Seeing his teammates work for the win, even a small win, put a sense of pride deep inside his chest.

"Eyes forward, heads up!" he shouted.

They were three boys in on either side, and Gerrit was next in line for his team. The other team groaned in disappointment when they realized the mistake of not having Gerrit on their side, and shouted to their boy to hurry him up. Gerrit grinned his wicked grin, crouching forward in preparation of his turn.

He burst forward once Daniel slapped his hand upon returning, and flew past the other teammates as though they were moving in slow motion. He reached the first cone in no time, racing on his toes, quick as ever. One cone, two cones, three, four, left, right, left; he rushed through the process as though he were actually running. His knees whirred up and down in a blur, looking almost as though he were vibrating.

"Keep your head up!"

The boys in Gerrit's line were whooping with joy as Gerrit rounded the last cone and started tiptoeing right back the way he had come from, while the other team's boy had only reached the middle cone in his line. By now, coach Abernathy had returned, but no one bothered to notice. They were all too preoccupied with the win to care.

They were so focussed on Gerrit and the task at hand, that Kaleb had decided to take the opportunity for a lesson of his own. With the approval of the coach, he grabbed a football, and was aiming within seconds. He threw the ball full force at Gerrit. He had meant for it to hit his gut, but Gerrit was crouched so low over his legs, that the ball hit his knee, which ricocheted it right into his face.

Gerrit fell flat on his back, holding his face, while everybody else burst into laughter. "Son of a *bitch*!" Gerrit yelled.

Kaleb only yelled back, arms wide. "Riled up enough for you?" He turned to the rest of the team. "That's why you gotta keep your head up!" Gerrit scrambled back up to finish his round, but everyone was laughing too hard to finish the race. Even Gerrit, after rubbing away some of the pain, found himself laughing at the trickery of his best friend.

"Dude!" Daniel ran forward, pointing to Gerrit's chin. "You left the lace marks on his face!" More laughter ensued at this discovery, and Gerrit, being the sport that he was, ran around trying to find someplace to see his reflection so that he could laugh too.

"Did he really? Lemme see!"

"Alright, ladies, you've had your fun," Coach interrupted, surprising some of the boys who hadn't noticed his return. "Let's get back to work." Gerrit threw a glance at Kaleb, receiving a shrug. Even without words, he knew what was being said.

"You asked for it."

Gerrit also sent a silent message to his friend.

"You're next."

Kaleb could only chuckle at this, knowing his friend meant no threat, and held up his rounded out fingers to mouth out "quarter," earning a snicker inducing glare. Whatever tricks they pulled, whatever games they played, in the end, they were still best friends who never held a grudge. Kaleb knew Gerrit wasn't angry. He knew he would have taken this as a joke; one for them to laugh about later as they always did. Kaleb took comfort in this fact, as he knew Gerrit was the only other person he could always do this with.

The two boys dropped their silent conversation and headed off to their respective training areas. Some of the boys were still giggling about the scene that had just played out, but were soon quieted down with more drills to run by order of their coach. Kaleb entered the practice field with a smile on his lips, ready for whatever came at him next. As for Gerrit, he stayed with the zig-zag cones, this time, keeping his head up.

"Finally the weekend," Taylor sighed, stretching his arms high above his head before flopping them down in relief. The final bell had rung some time earlier, but Taylor still sat in his seat. Out of habit, he stayed long after the last bell had rung to avoid the mass hysteria of students leaving school; more importantly, Kaleb and his friends. Today was different, though. Today was the last day of school before the weekend: game day.

He was glad that he could finally relax for the moment. With the big football game later on in the evening, he wouldn't have to worry about running into trouble until school started up again. Although he wasn't a huge fan of the game himself, he was glad that it was scheduled weekly, so that for this one day at the end of each week, he could walk home in peace. Everyone else was too busy preparing for the game to concern themselves with him.

Taylor strolled along the sidewalk, taking his time, enjoying his music provided to him through his large, white headphones and feeling the warmth of the sun on his skin. Not a cloud in the sky, it was a beautiful sunny day, and he planned on enjoying it to the fullest. Starting with something he would always look forward to. With his mother in the country of Lori, Taylor would visit the post office at the end of every week in hopes of receiving a crisp, new letter.

"Hello, Hector," Taylor said as he walked through the door.

"Hey, Taylor." Hector waved to him as he entered. "Got a big one for you today." The old postman wandered to the back of the building to retrieve Taylor's package, all the while calling out to the young teen waiting behind the counter. "You're gonna share it with me if it's food, right?"

"Don't know about that, Hector," Taylor shouted back. "We'll have to wait and see."

Taylor liked Hector. He often got along with adults more than people his own age, but Hector was different. Every week, Taylor was greeted with smiles upon arrival, and he was never disappointed when he left; even if it was empty handed.

Hector Sabat had a way with people that, simply put, made others want to be just as friendly as he was. Well past the age for retirement, no one really pushed him to leave because they enjoyed his presence as much as he enjoyed theirs. Not to mention, he was as stubborn as a mule. From work to play, it had to be Hector's way. Even as an elderly man, he insisted on being called by his first name rather than Mr. Sabat.

"Mister is too old," he would say, then smile and add, *"Besides, why waste such a beautiful name my mother gave me?"*

Taylor could hear the shuffling of Hector's feet coming closer, and soon enough, saw him coming around from behind the wall holding a medium sized box before his chest. "It's nice and light," Hector said with a chuckle. "If anything, it might be cake, or candy or something."

"Then I'll be sure to share it with you." Taylor couldn't help but grin. Hector's smile was far too contagious.

"Got your stamps and an extra envelope for you." The postman carefully laid the items atop the box. "Usual fee, son."

"Thanks, Hector. Be back in a minute." Taylor paid his due, then gathered up his things to leave.

"I'll be here!" Hector waved Taylor goodbye, his delightful smile still plastered on his face.

Coach Abernathy banged on a locker behind him for every athlete's attention before speaking, his usual scowl burned across his face. "Alright, ladies, you have two hours. You can go home, you can eat, whatever, but if you're not back by the time the bus is loaded and ready to go, we're leaving without you. First game of the season and I want to start it right, and on schedule. Understood?"

"Yessir, coach!" the team roared in unison.

Kaleb nudged Gerrit with his elbow. "Up for a burger?"

Gerrit frowned. "Out of money, dude."

"No worries." Kaleb stood to leave. "I'll spot you." Gerrit's frown turned into a smile.

"Thanks, man. Next one's on me."

Kaleb and Gerrit, and every other teen in River Hill, were used to walking wherever they needed to go. It was a small town, having everything within walking distance. Cars and busses were mainly used by adults to leave for work, supermarkets, or sporting events at rival schools. More often than not, anyone without a license either walked or used a small boat down the river- though carrying it back upstream was too much of a chore for many. It was a rarity to see a teen driving in or out of town unless they were working, and even then, there was the trolley.

The two boys talked along the way to the diner, their usual jokes and pointless conversations entertaining them as they walked. Kaleb and Gerrit were regulars at Tammy's Diner, but so was everyone else in town. So when they arrived, it was smiles all around. They sat at their designated table, laughed along with the other men's teasings, and greeted Tammy with a huge smile when she stopped by their table for their order.

"Tell you what, boys," Tammy said. "Win this game, and you've got yourselves a milkshake on me next time."

"I'll hold you to it!" Gerrit was always on the lookout for free stuff. By the time their meals came, Kaleb spotted something odd through the front window. It was Taylor, leaving the post office just across the street, with a package in his hands and walking towards the diner. Kaleb tapped Gerrit's shoulder for his attention, then gestured to Taylor coming in through the front door.

"Oh, no," Gerrit grumbled, wiping some ketchup off his lip. "Can't even eat in peace."

Kaleb frowned at his best friend. "Dude, come on."

"What are you even looking at him for? You've got more important things to worry about," Gerrit argued. "Focus on the game- and you can start with a full stomach."

"Yeah," Kaleb murmured.

He dug into his food to appease his smaller friend, but couldn't help but notice

Taylor off in the far corner. Again, he was alone, choosing to be by himself, and when Tammy stopped by his table, he merely nodded. He, like Kaleb, was more interested in the box.

Kaleb watched as Taylor slit open the top and pulled out a soft looking flannel blanket. This sincerely confused Kaleb. With Taylor's reputation, Kaleb figured that the package would be full of technological tools and toys. The contents of the box was surprising to Kaleb, but what really caught him off guard, was the fact that he saw Taylor smiling.

Kaleb almost dropped his burger from shock. This had to have been the first time he saw Taylor without a foul disposition. No scowling, no rude remarks, nothing to suggest his usual behavior. Kaleb could hardly believe it to be true. He watched as Taylor checked inside the package for any other contents. He quickly pulled out an envelope from the bottom of the box and began reading it, a small smile still hiding in his eyes.

Tammy stopped by his table again a minute later to drop off a soda. Taylor only stopped reading long enough to nod to her again, then returned to the paper in his hands. Once he had finished reading the letter, he carefully folded it up along with the blanket and place them back inside the box they came in. Next, he pulled out a notebook and pen from his backpack and began writing; most likely a response. Kaleb couldn't help but marvel at such a sudden change in attitude. He was so enamored by it, he didn't even notice Tammy trying to talk to him.

"Sorry, what?" He dropped his burger onto his plate and started searching for something to clean the ketchup that dripped off it from off his fingers.

"I was asking if you were doing okay. Refills? More napkins, maybe?" Tammy whipped out a handful of napkins from her apron and handed them to the messy boy, who accepted them eagerly.

"Thanks," he murmured.

"You look like you just stuck your head in on the girls bathroom," Tammy snickered. "What's got you so worked up?" Kaleb became flustered at the older woman's reference, unable to speak without stammering. Luckily, Gerrit was there to speak for him.

"That guy in the corner over there gives us a lot of problems at school."

"Taylor?" Tammy said, completely shocked. "You're kidding me!"

Now Kaleb was even more confused. "What do you mean?"

"Well, he comes in here every week," Tammy answered. "He stops by Hector's first, comes here to read his mail, then goes back to Hector to send it off before he goes home. He's always been really sweet, same order every time; never been a problem." Tammy looked to the boys again. "You sure that's the right guy?"

"Oh, yeah," said Gerrit with a frown, but Kaleb shook his head.

"Don't worry about it, Tammy," he said. "It's just stupid stuff." As he was saying this, Taylor had finished his drink and his letter, and was leaving the diner for Hector's, never paying any attention to the two athletes who despised him so.

"Alright," Tammy said uncertainly. "Just be sure to keep it out of the diner, you hear me?" Kaleb turned away from watching Taylor in the middle of the street and smiled at the waitress.

"Yes ma'am."

"Dude, come on." Gerrit tapped Kaleb on the arm. "We gotta get going." Kaleb emptied his wallet of the necessary papers plus a little extra for a tip and left them on the table for Tammy to retrieve later.

"Good luck, boys!" Tammy called, and the rest of the diner crew cheered on after them as they set out back to school to catch the bus.

Taylor carried his package under one arm, and his grocery sack on the other. Thanks to Miss Hart, he had gotten some work again and was able to shop with his earnings afterwards. Whatever money he had left, he would stash away in his lock box under his bed.

Taylor had saved a substantial amount so far, almost to the point of needing another lock box. Most of the papers inside were single bills, but it didn't stop him from feeling as though he had accomplished something. Later in the weekend, he would gather his money and try to trade the smaller papers for larger ones, but for now, he held on to the bit of pride he had for collecting so much already.

Although he had his groceries with him, Taylor still wasn't ready to go home just yet. He had one more stop to make before he could even consider going home, and that was to someone else's home- his only friend in town, Bubbie. Taylor made it a point to make it a daily visit, as Bubbie was always happy to see him. Today especially, since, at least on this day, Taylor had new goodies to hand out.

Hidden away under brush and foliage along the creek bed, there was a worn out, man-made cave of sorts out of rectangular concrete chutes. The chute was large enough to stand in, and almost twice as wide. Long ago, it was used to navigate parts of the river water to the creek bed beneath it, which helped to fill the water reserves. However, with the building of a new dam just outside of town, the waterway was long since abandoned. It was the perfect hideaway for any uninvited guest to live in- such as Bubbie, and occasionally, Taylor himself. He whistled to Bubbie, alerting him of his presence, and in a flash, a sheep herder rushed out from hiding to greet him.

"Hey, boy," Taylor muttered through a smile, glad that his friend was so happy to see him. Bubbie barked his greeting in return, circling Taylor as he neared the old concrete den to settle in. "I know, I know." Taylor pushed the rambunctious shepherd's nose out of his grocery sack and dug in himself. Bubbie's tail was already wagging furiously, but the sight of the dog treats in Taylor's hand caused his entire body to quiver with anticipation.

"Dinner first," Taylor scolded, and Bubbie, having learned what 'dinner' meant, rushed deep inside the chute to where his bowl lay. Taylor followed the mutt inside, lighting a lantern as he entered, and couldn't help but smile at what he saw: Bubbie, sitting patiently next to his bowl, tail wagging and ears perked when he entered. Taylor shook his head, then went on to feed his beloved friend.

While Bubbie was chowing down, Taylor set to work ridding himself of the few items he wished to keep in his second home; the flannel blanket being one of them. He emptied the package of his mothers gift and placed it atop his sleeping bag rolled up beside the far wall. His heart softened at the sight, reminding him of what his mother had written.

"It's almost Winter, so bundle up and keep warm!"

Taylor took the letter that came with the blanket and locked it away in a box filled with letters exactly like it, each one with a new story about her week, and how she was doing. Each one telling him how much she missed him. Each one telling him how much she loved him. Taylor patted the box gently, and returned his attention to Bubbie, who had finished his dinner and was waiting for his dessert.

"Quick as ever," Taylor mumbled. "I'm surprised you don't get sick." Bubbie only huffed at him, still waiting for his treat. "Alright," Taylor said, dipping into the treat bag for a beef stick. Then, while Bubbie was inhaling his reward, Taylor picked up a tennis ball and tossed it in the air, catching it before it could escape.

"Want to play?"

"Want to play, big guy?" Kaleb taunted the enormous linebacker across from him. His response was, more or less, a guttural sound that vaguely resembled an animal's roar. "I'll take that as a yes." Kaleb smirked.

The play was called, the ball was tossed, and a flurry of uniforms, sweat and muscle collided within a single instant. The announcer calling the play-by-play on the overhead speakers could hardly be heard over the fans. The crowd cheered the players on as loud as they could, no prompting needed from the cheerleaders who were screaming just as loudly.

The game was tied, 42-42, only minutes left to the finish, and the Riviera Trouts were running out of steam. The Highland Rebels were also exhausted, but did just as well to hide it from their opposing team. Kaleb, though drained of energy, did his best to keep his teammates pumped up with his taunts. The others, sensing his efforts, did their best to comply, with Gerrit being the most supportive of course.

A new play was called and put into action, the ball flying high in the air, taking its time before landing in the arms of a Trout. It was Daniel who had the ball now; he was rushing to the endzone, desperate to reach the goal line, but was eventually chased out of bounds by a very brutish pair of opposing players. There was a unified displeasing cry from the crowd, causing Daniel to drop his head in his own disappointment.

"No worries, Dan!" Kaleb shouted, running to the huddle. "We've got them on the run." Kaleb, and a few other players, removed his mouth guard to speak to the rest of the team clearly.

"What's the plan, boss?" Daniel asked.

"Gerrit," Kaleb said curtly. "No matter what, get the ball to Gerrit."

"Are you sure, Cap?" another team member, Dylan, asked. "I mean, he's almost been crushed by these guys, like, six times already. They don't hold back." Kaleb nodded.

"He can do it." Then, turning to his friend, "No holding back either this round, buddy."

Gerrit grinned. "You got it."

"Watch his back, guys," Kaleb ordered. "Ready?"

"Break!" The team clapped the huddle's closure and set up the play. Both teams were ready for their last showdown. Kaleb shouted out his same orders to his team mates in code, offering support to each other, all the while knowing this was their last shot at winning the game.

The ball snapped into play, thrown directly to Kaleb who immediately searched for Gerrit. Kaleb took a few steps back, avoiding the aggressive players in front of him, then spotted his friend. Gerrit had bolted across the field and was only a few yards away from the goal line. He was looking to Kaleb as he ran, expecting the ball. Kaleb ducked down, rolling an opposing player off of his shoulder before he could tackle him. Then he stood tall, and threw the ball as hard as he could to Gerrit.

Gerrit rushed after it, dodging giant after giant, always keeping his eye on the ball. With one outstretched hand, he snagged it right out of the air, clutching it with everything he had and running as though his life depended on it to score a touchdown. The crowd roared with delight as Gerrit ran over the last line of fine powder just as the final gun rang out, winning the game for the Trouts.

Gerrit and the rest of the team were equally ecstatic at their victory. They charged after him at the end of the field, screaming and throwing him atop their shoulders once they reached him. Every team member, that is, except for Kaleb.

Through the confusion, it was only the opposing team who had noticed him lying on the grass, gripping his leg in agony. It was the player who had tackled him down after he threw the ball that stayed by Kaleb's side. Clearly seen through his body language, he was panicking after realizing he had hurt Kaleb, and desperately waved over to the sidelines for help. Only after the rest of the Trouts noticed the crowd gathering around in the center of the field did they notice their missing captain, and it was only then that they understood what was happening.

Taylor stepped through his front door without a word. Once he had discovered his home to be empty, he continued on to the kitchen to empty the last of his grocery sack. After this, he rushed to his bedroom to rid his wallet of any papers remaining. With more work lined up over the weekend, he was sure he would be visiting the box again soon, but he didn't want a repeat of the stink bomb incident.

He shoved his papers in as much as he could before locking the box, and had decided to count his money later that night, after his father had gone to bed; if he even came home at all. For now, he needed something else.

Taylor quickly closed and locked his bedroom door, then snatched his laptop from his backpack, placed it on his desk, and turned it on. He dug out his charger as well and plugged it into the wall as well as his device while he waited for it to boot up, and once it did, he logged on to his one haven.

```
Dallas_Lori has logged on.
DragOnBreath282:Omg, HI DALLAS!
MillyLillyLotusBitty:Dallas! Hi!
MlkH8rll: lng tym no c bby
Grammar_Soldier: @Dallas_Lori= Do you have a new chapter
for us? Oh, /PLEASE/ say you do!
boomBoomBOOM: Up for a chat?
Hotstuff94:Noooooooo chat with meeeeeeee!!!!111
```

Taylor smiled at the warm welcome. Online was different from real life. Here, he could be himself with no one knowing how different he really was. He could be accepted, and look like something he wasn't without anyone caring: normal. Everyday, Taylor marveled at the difference between his two lives, and was constantly amazed and curious as to why this was so.

He gave his friends' list a quick read through, not seeing whom he really wished to speak with, then leaned in to respond to the others who were logged on.

```
Dallas_Lori: Hey guys, it's been a while, good to see you.
I do have a new chapter, but I have to type it up. Give me
a few?
Grammar_Soldier: @Dallas_Lori= Good grief, hurry! I can't
```

34

wait to see what happens next!
HotStuff94:lolz, sure babe. but stay and chat a bit? iv
missd you!!!
CraZeeNDaHed: YES! YES! YES! PLEASE TYPE!
MlkH8r11: ya
Drag0nBreath282:How ya been?

Taylor stayed onsite to speak with his admirers in between typing a fresh chapter onto a new document page from his notebook. More people logged on and off during his time online with them, but not the one who he was waiting for. Then, out of nowhere, she appeared.

Hacker_Nekko has logged on.
HotStuff94: NEKKOOOOOOOOOOO!!!!11
BabyGurl565: Hi!
Hacker_Nekko: Sup, guys?

Taylor minimized the current chat room, and sent Hacker_Nekko a private chat request. She quickly accepted, and her smiling face appeared on Taylor's screen within seconds.

"Hey, Tee, what's up?" she asked with a smile.

Taylor ticked his mouth back at her and responded with "Typing up a new chapter."

"Yes!" she hissed, pumping a fist.

They went on talking back and forth for over an hour, bantering a bit here and there, talking about their day and what all was going on in their lives at the moment, only pausing shortly in between to respond to the other chat room goer's inquiries.

Hacker_Nekko, or Rebekah, in real life, was Taylor's first online friend. She was the first to talk to him, to get him to start speaking out more and build him up, and it was she who insisted that he post his writing online after prompting him to read what he was always scribbling down in his notebook.

She was also the first woman to tear him a new one when he called her by her real name after she first gave it to him. It wasn't personal in the least, Rebekah simply refused to be called "Rebekah" by any of her friends. She insisted that they call her by any other name, and Taylor was more than happy to oblige after the skin-crawling verbal beat-down he had received.

"You sound like my mother," she would snarl.

Despite all this, Taylor couldn't ask for a better friend than Bekah, and he really didn't want any other besides her- not as his best friend, at least. She understood him, same as he did her, and though they lived mountains apart from each other, they were still the closest of friends.

Taylor, along with many other men, considered Bekah to be a good looking young woman. She wore glasses over her pale green eyes, and her smile was so crooked that her eyebrows had to follow into a sheepish grin. Her straight brown hair was shoulder length, but the orange kitty hat that never left her head covered whatever bangs she may have had except for the tips, which flared out over the thick rims of her glasses. Her signature look was a striped sweater with the kitty beanie, and it was a rare sight indeed to see her without them. Taylor, however, was one of the very few who had.

"How are the bruises coming along? Nothing new, right?" she asked when she noticed him wincing at his arm.

"No, not since Kaleb," he lied, refusing to bring up his meeting with Dylan the day before. "Their bombs stunk more than they hurt, but it still stung, you know?" He chuckled. Bekah didn't.

"I don't understand why you're so cool with this," she muttered.

"I'm not," Taylor replied. "I'm just used to it."

Bekah pouted angrily away from her screen and grumbled. "Well you shouldn't be."

"Beck," Taylor smirked. "Don't worry about me. I'm a big boy, I can handle it."

She whipped back to face him. "But you shouldn't have to face this alone!"

"I'm not alone," he said. "I have you."

Bekah rolled her eyes and hung her head. "Uhg, that's not the same." Taylor chuckled at his friend before speaking again.

"I don't have much longer to go. Once I graduate, I can get out of here and cross the Great Waters. Until then, I can hold on a little longer." His smile softened. "You still with me?"

Bekah smirked too. "Duh. I may not live out in the great little town of 'Happyville' like you do, but I certainly don't want to be here either. To Lori I go."

"To Lori I go," Taylor repeated.

The two friends shared a smile, and for a moment, just enjoyed the sight of it. They had a common goal, and though their reasons were different, they would work together to get it, no matter what.

"Ready for that next chapter?" Taylor asked.

"Oh, my soul, yes!" she responded, and immediately went looking for Dallas_Lori's latest update on his webpage.

Chapter 3

"You know," Gerrit said slyly. "When they say 'break a leg,' they normally don't mean that literally."

"Not *broken*," Kaleb grumbled, tossing a used napkin at his friend. "Dislocated. And it's my knee, not my leg." Kaleb was resting on his hospital bed, just finishing his lunch. He had his leg raised up on a armful of pillows, encased in a removable cast for protection. Surrounding his room could have been a garden from all the different flowers he had been given, complete with balloons and get well cards.

"What are you in such a bad mood for?" Gerrit asked. "You're getting out today. You can go home and play sick for as long as you want. Your parents are putty in your hands, dude."

"I don't *want* to play sick," Kaleb replied. "I'm dying of boredom in here; I *need* to get out and do something."

Gerrit took on a stupefied grin. "You need to?"

"I have a mighty need," Kaleb said in a deep, throaty voice, gripping the air before him and shaking his fists.

Gerrit shook his head. "Why do I hang out with you?"

"Because I am awesome." Kaleb used the same, powerful voice as before- this time flexing his muscles. Gerrit laughed, shoving Kaleb's elbow enough to drop his arms from his ridiculous pose. "Ah!" Kaleb feigned, holding up his arms in defense. "Quarter! Quarter!" Just then, a nurse knocked on the door frame and entered Kaleb's room.

"Hello, gentlemen. How are we doing today?" the nurse asked with a smile. Gerrit raised his eyebrows at Kaleb, grinning a wicked grin.

"Hey Stephanie, we're doing fine." Kaleb smiled right back at her, ignoring Gerrit, who had left the room with nothing but a wave. " Ready to get out of here."

"I bet," said Stephanie. "Your parents are almost done with your paperwork, and I've sent for a wheelchair to escort you downstairs. So, you're all set as soon as you finish your lunch."

Kaleb pushed away his tray. "Done and done, but do I have to use a wheelchair? I could use the practice with the crutches?"

Stephanie gave Kaleb a coy, but condescending look. "Hospital rules." With that, Kaleb flopped back into his bed in defeat, and Stephanie went about checking Kaleb's vitals one last time. "You could open up a flower shop with all the goodies you've got in here," Stephanie went on.

"No need to buy them from me, you can have them." Kaleb propped back up. "In fact, why don't you just take them all?"

"Well aren't you bold?" Stephanie said with yet another smile.

"That's not it." Kaleb threw her a grin so as not to hurt her feelings. "It's just, they'll die if I take them home. They'll die either way, but this way, at least I wouldn't have to clean up after." Then a thought hit him. "Why not give them to the other patients? I'm sure they'd appreciate them more than me."

Stephanie beamed. "I think we can make that work."

Kaleb smiled at the idea. "Cool, but, just one thing." He pointed to the largest vase in his room. This particular arrangement came from Connor, the boy who had tackled Kaleb in the first place. It was full of irises, baby's breath, beaded ribbons and at least three different kinds of roses. It took up an entire corner in his room, and no matter how many times Kaleb tried to say that he didn't blame him for his injured knee, Connor still insisted on Kaleb keeping the enormous arrangement.

The pollen from it, however, bothered his father's nose constantly, and the smell was overpowering. Really, he only kept it to keep Connor from giving him anything else. Beautiful as it was, there was no way Kaleb would force that on any other sick person-especially with such small rooms to begin with. Aside from that, though, more than once he had caught Stephanie admiring it, and heard her talking to the other nurses about how beautiful it was.

"Save that one for the nurses' station."

"I'm sorry."

Kara wasn't saying anything at all. She merely crossed her arms and stared down her friend, unamused. "You're *late*," she said.

"I was in the hospital!" Kaleb rebuttled, but Kara wouldn't have it.

"Not only late, a week late."

"I was *in the hospital*!"

"You could have sent a chat."

"I said I was sorry!"

"No excuses, Kaleb!" Kara kept her firm gaze upon her taller friend for a moment longer while he floundered for answers, finding nothing. Then, "Are you doing any better?"

"Yes," Kaleb sighed, massaging his temples. "I'm doing just fine."

She jerked her chin at his removable cast. "How much longer 'til that comes off for good?"

He looked down to look at his leg unconsciously when she motioned to it. "About five more weeks, I guess."

Kara gave a curt nod. "Good. I guess I'm going to have to get creative until it does." She grinned darkly. "I do love a challenge."

Kaleb groaned, rubbing his face in annoyance. "You've got a weird way of caring, you know that?" Kara only cocked a brow and grinned her special grin in reply. Kaleb hobbled along to a stool closer to Kara's work station on his new crutches, clicking with each step.

"What did it feel like?" Kara asked as she walked to her cubby for her belongings. Kaleb only rolled his eyes.

"It felt like someone pulled my leg off."

"Technically, he did," she pointed out, and Kaleb shook his head, but she went on. "What'll you do in the meantime?" The sound of her voice slightly echoed off the walls of the small enclosure. "You certainly can't play on your broken bones."

"Not broken. Dislocated," Kaleb repeated. "I don't know, maybe visit practice. You know, get the guys going."

"Because the entire school would shut down if they didn't have Kaleb Evans around to rule the field." Kara pried her attention from her routine for a moment to look him dead in the eye. "You know, you *can* do more than just football. The town won't hate you, I promise."

Kaleb cleared his throat and turned away, wanting to change the subject. "What about you? What are you working on now that your star model has gone off duty, Kar?"

"I am not an unintelligible vehicle," she puffed.

The golden boy grinned at his success. "At least I don't call you-"

"Don't you even dare." She whipped around to point a rigid finger at him. He giggled at her, his grin sealing away his words. Kara huffed, still staring daggers at him, but continued on with her work. She had already pulled down her paints, brushes and shawl from her cubby, and was hauling a canvas almost as large as herself over to her work station. "It started out as abstract," she told him. "You know, just to get the juices flowing. Then it started to turn into a garden of sorts." She placed the canvas upon her easel, giving Kaleb a chance to really see it.

It was a flurry of different colors. Reds, blues, greens, they all burst about the painting as though they had blown up like a paint bomb. It was rampant, and excitable with no clear pattern, though the long brush strokes indicated a mind at ease. Nothing was black or white, but all warm, vibrant shades. It was the perfect base for what lie atop the explosion of color.

Bordering the painting's edges were flowers of different exotic breeds blooming along the top middle of the canvas, progressively getting smaller as they grew down the right hand side. Little spritz of different colored circles littered most of the bottom right corner and thinned to its left, while a large, bright blood-orange hibiscus flower reigned over the entire top left corner, it's leaves and vines dripping beneath it.

"Wow," Kaleb breathed as he stared, dumbstruck, at the work before him. "I don't know how to say it without sounding weird, but it's just like you."

"I'll take that as a compliment," Kara stated, and Kaleb nodded. He lost himself in the painting as he thought. Truly, the painting was like Kara; an extension of herself in more ways than one. Colorful, beautiful, different. Not something you see everyday, and most certainly more out of the box.

As far as Kara went, she was different. Her skin was the color of melted chocolate, and her short, black hair was so wiry and stiff that she almost always had it sticking straight back in a scarf, defying the laws of gravity as well as giving her a signature style that no one could copy. There was a time when she would garnish herself with long, flowy fabrics; though, after many an argument with her mother, she switched her favor for tighter, more natural shirts. Her sleeves never ventured past her elbows, even in the Winter, so that no paint may ever dare stain her clothing again.

Kara was a fiery young woman. She was the very definition of a free spirit. Passion drove her far more than any other person in the school. Everyone who knew her, knew that she would never back down from any bullshit. Any injustice in the world would be met with Kara's iron fist. She even rebelled against her mother, who insisted that she become a lawyer over an artist. Her grades, due to her mother's nagging, were stupendous, but it was her artwork that really drove her. From her look, to her personality, there was nothing common about Kara Osborne.

Kaleb enjoyed Kara's company and often visited her when he needed problem-solving of the therapeutic nature. In return, she would have Kaleb pose for her while she painted. With Kaleb's leg, though, this would put a damper on their arrangement.

At the moment, Kara was busy tying her shawl around her waist; a gift from her father. The poor piece of fabric was completely stained from years of use in preference to an apron, as it covered her legs better. Whenever her fingers became too caked with color, she would absentmindedly wipe them along the side of her jeans. Her father bought the shawl to keep from replacing all of her ruined pants- and to appease her mother. Today, it would be put to work once again.

"There's something missing," Kara muttered. "I just haven't figured it out yet." Kaleb tuned out of his dreamy trance and shook his head, declining her of the idea.

"I like it just the way it is. What could be missing?" he asked. Kara shook her head as well, though this was due to her not knowing. Kaleb scoffed. "Artists. Don't know talent when it sits there in front of them."

"It wouldn't be art if the artist didn't hate it."

Kaleb rolled his eyes at her response, but Kara merely sighed. She stared at her mural long and hard, leaning her head so far off to the side, it practically laid on her shoulder.

"Nope," she murmured, taking the painting off her easel and setting an empty canvas in its place. "It just won't do." With a fresh image in her mind and a new backdrop to set it on, Kara picked up her brush, and began her work creating another masterpiece.

Kaleb sat silently watching her, knowing full well not to disturb her, even if he had the ability to do so. It took little to no effort for Kara to enter a zen-like state once her creative juices began flowing from her fingertips. It never took her long at all to kick out the distractions of the world and immerse herself in her work. He watched as her eyes constantly darted across the canvas, seeing her mind spinning with ideas and plotting her next move with the paintbrush. This technique effectively covered the white cloth board with mystifying beauty every single time.

Time passed by with ease while Kara worked the board; neither party speaking a word, nor any word need be said. Kaleb took comfort in the silence after the uproar of his return. Within the week of his absence, stories spread like wild fire. Kaleb surrounded by worried onlookers, the ambulance rushing to the football field, the paramedics stealing away their beloved captain- it was all too much excitement for the little town of River Hill, and became the source of much gossip.

Some claimed to have seen Kaleb's leg turned completely round when he was placed on the stretcher, others say his mother fainted at the sight of blood. Someone even spread the idea of the ambulance rushing onto the field without any care for the civilians and nearly ran over a few people- "skid marks and all."

The worst of all of them, however, was that he had died. Thanks to Gerrit and his horrible sense of humor, on the day before his return, half the school believed that Kaleb had died at the hospital. The students held a memorial service with candles, and many girls cried loudly through the entire thing, while the guys tried to hide their emotions.

The reaction paired with Kaleb entering his first class that morning, was a mixture of shock, happiness and fear. One girl fainted, another screamed, the rest of the students were either too stunned to speak, or crying tears of joy over his resurrection while they climbed over one another to hug him. Gerrit, on the other hand, was laughing hysterically while Kaleb fumbled to try and make sense of the confusion.

Since then, Kaleb couldn't get a moment's peace. People were always questioning him for how he felt, what he wanted, how he was doing, "how can we help?" Trying to do something on his own would be impossible, even if he was discreet with whatever it was he was doing. A fallen notebook would be back on his desk before he could bend over, his drinks were always open for him, and his stomach was alway full thanks to people shoving snacks at him.

Once, Gerrit and two other boys were walking by when they noticed him struggling to get up the stairs with his crutches. With one look to each other, and a nod from Gerrit, the two bigger boys each grabbed an arm on either side and hoisted Kaleb up the stairs. Gerrit snagged Kaleb's crutches from beneath his arms and lugged them over his own shoulder, following the bigger boys. Not a word was spoken, and their actions swift, despite the verbal declining from Kaleb himself. They soon had him on the second floor, and though he was slightly embarrassed, Kaleb couldn't help but feel impressed with his friends for this effective action.

When he went to descend the stairs, later, the boys followed Kaleb all the way to the edge of the railing. He stopped them when he turned to them, smiled, then hopped onto the hand railing and slid down to the halfway curve where the stairs flattened for a semi-circle platform. He then hobbled to the other end of the platform for the second set of stairs with minimal effort, all the while enjoying the shocked looks on everybody's faces.

With everyone hovering over his shoulders, the solitary calmness of Kara's work station was refreshingly pleasant. With only the sound of her paint brush on canvas, Kaleb could finally find peace. It wasn't that he was ungrateful, the students were simply trying to help, but their helpfulness was becoming too overbearing with the first hug. Aside from this, though, Kara's presence soothed his weary mind, even in the quiet.

After about an hour of lovely silence, Kaleb rose from his seat. It was time for him to have a visit with coach Abernathy and the team before heading home for the night. He didn't bother stopping Kara in the middle of her work- she would have bitten his head off if he did- but simply muttered a goodbye as his crutches clicked out the door.

Taylor packed away Bubbie's food and ball for the day, and gave him one last good rub on his neck and ears. Bubbie knew this meant his friend was leaving, and began to whine and paw at Taylor. "I know," Taylor murmured, causing Bubbie's tail to wag. "I wish I could stay too." He pushed his backpack straps onto his shoulders and stood up to leave, making Bubbie's attempts advance.

"Down, Bubbie." Taylor gently pushed away the shepherd and headed out of the cave, with Bubbie following close behind. "Sit." The dog obeyed quickly, but whimpered all the same. Taylor gave him an apologetic look. "Sorry, boy. You've gotta stay here." He gave his friend one last glance over his shoulder as he trudged over the creek-bed, both pleased and disheartened at the same time to see that his friend was sitting in the same spot, watching Taylor leave with the same, sad face.

After a bit of a hike over stony terrain, Taylor finally climbed through a bundle of bushes, brush and trees at the top of the creek. With a quick look, he checked the area for any onlookers, and, seeing no one, went ahead through the wall of vegetation. He shuffled off some spare leaves that had snagged onto him, then headed over to the barren sidewalk for home.

After a few moment of walking, Taylor grew tired of the silence and dug out his headphones from his pack. As soon as the clunky white plastic covered his ears, a sense of peace had already begun to lay over him. The music started to play, and it drowned out the rest of the world as Taylor's spirits began to lift.

He passed through the park, and soon after crossed the bridge that covered the creek below it. His eyes momentarily lingered in the direction of the cave as he walked, but the music helped to smother the guilt of leaving Bubbie alone. Again.

If his father wouldn't throw an abominable hissy-fit with Taylor ending up thrown through the roof- and quite possibly not coming back down until the end of the year- he wouldn't hesitate a single breath before bringing Bubbie home for good. Taylor hated leaving him out as a stray when he wasn't a stray at all. He was Taylor's dog. Taylor's friend. He loved Bubbie, and if he had asked his father any previous year, Mr. Thompson would surely have accepted the dog with open arms. Friedreich Thompson, however, hadn't been himself ever since he had returned from the war.

On the island of Akenya, South-West of the Alterian Colonies and far beneath River Hill, the war on the hot desert lands raged on for several years. There had been tension between the two lands for many years previous, but it was a visit from one of their princes that finally tipped the scales. Unknown to the people of the city, he had gotten himself into trouble and ended up in jail. There, he had wronged the wrong man in the same cell, and ended up with a knife in his neck. With the combination imprisonment and death of one of their princes, the Akenian-Alterian War finally broke out.

Every Akenian of age ran head-first to fight the northern lands all in the name of vengeance, wiping out an entire major city and a few smaller towns surrounding it with their first attack. Every man, woman, child and beast who called that area home was dead within twenty-six hours. It took all of one day for Alteria to decide to fight back.

Being a small, desert island compared to the Colonies, Akenia's military was not very large, but the citizens were a proud race, and their tactics effective. This was the only reason why they were able to hold off the Alterians in the slightest for fifteen years running. Shortly after they invaded, the Colonies pushed them back to their deserts, and the battles raged on there instead. For fifteen long years, Akenian sands soaked up the blood of fallen soldiers from both sides.

For four of those years, Friedreich fought on those same sands for his home. He fought valiantly, day in and day out, defending his fellow troops, his land's honor, and most importantly, defending his own life. Letters would come to him periodically to boost his spirits and let him know that his family still thought of him every day, but the scarcity of paper on the battlefield forced his responses to be non-existent, and it was his commanding officer that alerted his family of his return.

Friedreich had finally come home from the battlefield for good just before Taylor's fifteenth birthday. It wasn't a grand reunion. He simply walked through his front door, surprising both Taylor and his mother. He refused any physical contact from either of them, then locked himself in his and Mrs. Thompson's bedroom alone. He wouldn't come out until later that evening, prompted by the smell of dinner, though not a word was drawn from his lips.

Friedreich's eyes were glued to his plate as he crammed as much food as he could into his mouth, and when offered seconds, he grabbed the serving bowl and took it with him to the bedroom once again. Mrs. Thompson slept in the guest bedroom that night, and for the next two nights that followed before Friederich started to loosen up again.

It took a few days for him to start speaking as well. Small single-word responses at first, slowly growing into short sentences by the end of the month. When asked about what was bothering him, though, he would clam up and leave the room. They soon learned to keep away from the topic of the war and anything associated with it if they wanted him to stick around. They were patient with him, understanding with him as much as they could be, but the nightmares were too strong for them to comprehend. Friedreich just wasn't the same, and he wasn't coming back.

Taylor remembered a completely different man from his childhood. He remembered smiles and laughter. He remembered him being silly just to make Taylor and everyone else grin. He remembered a happy man, without a care in the world.

This was not that man. Taylor was convinced that his father's very soul had changed- and he had physical proof to back the theory up. He had only caught a glimpse through his parent's cracked doorway, but he saw it nonetheless.

Friedreich was getting dressed after coming out of the shower, and hadn't noticed the door being slightly ajar. There, Taylor saw that his father's soul crest had changed from it's original form. Since his birth, Friedreich Thompson's soul crest had been a perfect match to his wife, Sarah's. Together, they formed a beautiful stain-glass-like rose for a bonded soul crest; Sarah having the unbloomed rose, and Friedreich with the outer petals and stem.

The crest on his chest now, however, was mangled into jagged pieces. The stem still stood, but its form had changed. The traditional black inked look of the skin now had a tint of white inside the stem where it cracked in various places. Throughout the entirety of the crest were cracks, and along the outer edges, red veins spewed out of it as though it were inflamed. The sight of his father's new crest terrified Taylor, making him run back to his room and lock his door, tightly hugging a pillow and trying to hold back his shivers.

It took all of four months for the drink to finally take him too far. With the dangerous combination of liquor and his flashbacks, Friedreich let his hand fly, and his wife was the unfortunate victim. One evening, it happened after dinner. Taylor tried to intervene, but Sarah wouldn't have it. She would shove Taylor away before he could get hurt too, but by then, Friedreich was over his fit and had already moved on. This would happen at least once a week. In the beginning.

"Please, mom," Taylor would plead. "Leave this place before it goes too far."

Taylor begged his mother to leave everyday, convincing her that his father would not hurt him if he kept away during a flashback. He promised to stay careful and to follow her soon after, as long as she built a safe home for them to live in while his father figured out how to live with his horrendous nightmares. Once that was done, then they would come back and be a real family again, but until that happened, he couldn't bare to see her in pain anymore.

"Once I finish school, I'll be right there with you. You just have to wait a little."

As much as he begged, Sarah Thompson refused to leave her son with such a dangerous man. They could barely afford sending one of them away, and if she could help it, she would stick with her child until the bitter end. Taylor kept at it though, throwing reason and convincing arguments her way until finally, he eventually wore his mother down, telling her that a separated family is better than a dead one. They snuck off in the middle of the night, carrying everything she would need in their new home, wherever it may be. Once at the train station, she bid her son a tearful goodbye and promised that they would soon be reunited just as Taylor had planned.

It was unheard of for soulmates to part. So naturally, when news of her disappearance spread, the Thompsons were shunned from society. Taylor refused to let his mother hear of this, as her departure was hard enough on her already. She didn't need any more guilt. Instead, he wrote to her as soon as he received her first letter, and hadn't stopped since. She had crossed the Great Waters and gone East, choosing to live in the rolling lands of Lori; arguably one of the best educational cities on the maps. If Taylor would be living with her after he graduated, Sarah wanted to make sure he would be schooled properly at least.

Now, Taylor was more eager to reunite with his mother than ever. He was sick of this godforsaken town and all its gossip, tired of the gossiper's children using him as a punching bag and no one caring, tired of hearing his father's screaming from his nightmares and drunken rampages. More than anything, he wanted to finish this year without anyone bothering him, and go to his mother as soon as his graduation letter hit his hands. He was ready to leave; nothing tying him down- except for Bubbie.

Taylor spent some nights lying awake in his bed, trying to figure out what would be best for the dog. Of course, he wanted to take Bubbie with him to Lori, but transferring an animal across the ocean would be fairly difficult, both in physicality and mentality for humans and animals alike. Not to mention from the description of the place Sarah had found to live, there wouldn't be much room for him to play and be happy- even if the manager did allowed pets. If Bubbie were to go to Lori with Taylor, Sarah would have to move all over again.

Leaving Bubbie here alone would be heart-wrenching, it took Taylor all he had now not to pack all of his belongings and move into the cave to be with his friend. Leaving him in River Hill, however, seemed to be the best option. The travel alone would be too hard on him. This was his home, not some tiny apartment in a far-off land.

Another trouble was that there was every possibility that Taylor would be returning to River Hill. After his father cleaned up his act and learned to live with his demons, the Thompsons had every reason to go back to being a family again. There was no reason to uproot the dog from his lifestyle twice. So, with a heavy heart, Taylor decided to leave his best friend behind for the moment. Should anything give him a reason to change his mind though, he would take it in an instant.

Taylor rounded a corner, getting closer to his neighborhood with each step. A new song had begun, and he turned up the volume on his headphones to enjoy it more. He bobbed his head to the beat, humming ever so slightly as he listened. Music was an escape for Taylor. A way for him to ignore the whispers and the finger pointing, to forget the name-calling and teasing that the other students so very much enjoyed. He focused only on the song that echoed in his mind, listening intently to the lyrics, the instruments and the vocals.

Now, walking up to his front porch, Taylor stopped to finish the latest song, waiting to enter his house. The music played its last chords, and a ghostly whisper was left in its wake, leaving only a memory of its existence. Quietly, Taylor turned off and gently placed his headphones back into his backpack before standing back up, and heading inside.

"I am so screwed." Dylan sighed despairingly into his hands. He, Gerrit, and just hobbling in, Kaleb, were hanging out in the locker rooms talking while everyone else had already gone home.

"What's wrong, man?" Kaleb asked, sitting down on the bench opposite of him. Dylan shook his head with his hands still stuck to his face.

"I'm failing literature," he mumbled through his fingers. "If coach finds out, I'm on the bench with you, gimpy." Kaleb yanked a towel out from under Dylan's butt to get back at him, causing him to fall forward from off the bench.

"Now how did that happen?" Kaleb grinned, but Dylan wasn't in a very playful mood.

"Dude, this is serious!" he said. "I failed an essay paper and now my grade is in the toilet." He scowled, making a face as though he had eaten something bitter. "This is so stupid. None of this would'a happened if that stupid Tommy kid had helped me out like I asked."

This caught Kaleb's attention. "He turned you down for tutoring?" he asked, and Dylan threw up his hands.

"I asked him to help me finish this paper, and he flat out refused. He said, and I quote, *'absolutely not,'* then avoided me like I had a virus or something."

Now Kaleb's face turned sour. "That's not right."

"I know," Dylan agreed. "I failed that stupid paper because of him. Mr. Rodenberg said I could re-do it and make it up, but I have no idea what he wants. If this one screws up too, there's no way I'll be able to play. I gotta play, I just have to."

"Chill, man," Gerrit chided. "I can hook you up." Both Dylan and Kaleb gave Gerrit a look of suspicion.

"*You* know literature?" Dylan asked in a tone that Gerrit didn't care for.

"*No,*" he replied in a mocking voice. "but I do know someone who can help."

"You do?" Dylan lit up.

Gerrit nodded. "Sure do. C'mon. I'll introduce you." Dylan rushed over to Gerrit's outstretched arm and went along with the smaller boy, his smile burning bright.

"See you later, captain!" he called out, Gerrit only waving over his head as they left Kaleb alone in the smelly room. Kaleb offered a wave as well, then stood up to leave, looking for Coach Abernathy. He found him in his office looking over some papers that had piled up on his desk.

"Coach?" He knocked on the door frame.

"Evans," Coach grunted when he saw who had asked for his attention. "What do you want?" Blunt as ever. James Abernathy was not a man who trifled with demeaning things such as small-talk or subtlety.

"Just wanted to let you know that I'm back," Kaleb said.

"There's no way I'm playing you, Evans," Coach quipped, flipping through more papers.

"Of course, sir, I wasn't asking-"

"Then what *are* you asking, Evans?" Coach interrupted, not even bothering to drop his paperwork.

"I was going to let you know that I'll still be around at like, practice and stuff. You know, cheering the guys on, boosting morale, go team." He kept his voice monotone through the entire ordeal, though a fist pump was needed for the last part.

"No you will not."

Kaleb blinked. "What?"

"I said no." Coach finally dropped his papers and looked to Kaleb. "We don't need any dead-weight hanging around holding us back. No fooling around, no side tracks- strictly football."

"But coach, I wouldn't-"

"Do I need to repeat myself, Evans?" Coach asked.

"No, sir," Kaleb said.

"Look, you're a good kid," Abernathy went on. "Once your leg is back in place, you can come back. But until then, I don't need you coming around messing with everyone's heads. They need to concentrate."

"Yes, sir," Kaleb said, this time more defeated. Coach Abernathy gave a curt nod, turning back to his paperwork. "Good. See you at the next game, then."

"Yes, sir."

Chapter 4

"He came back today." Taylor took a sip from his drink before setting it down on his knee, pressed up against the desk's edge.

"So he's alive, then?" Bekah responded.

"Yeah, he is." Taylor scratched the scar on his cheek. "I didn't really believe it anyway; would have made it all over town instead of a handful of kids." Taylor was locked away in his room again, video chatting with Rebekah- though if he were to call her by name, he would get a thorough tongue-lashing. They were busy telling each other about their day, and of course, Kaleb became a topic of interest.

"I guess you're right," Bekah replied. "So how did they handle it?"

"Horribly," Taylor snickered, setting his drink on his desk. "There was a big mess about it too, I heard some girl fainted when she saw him come in. Everyone else went right on bowing down to their king."

"I'd have given anything to see that," Bekah snorted.

"Right?" Taylor chuckled again. "Poor, defenseless fangirl falls to the floor while everyone else tramples one another to touch the prince."

"I hear a plotline brewing." Bekah smiled broadly, with Taylor following along with a smirk of his own. He lowered his legs from off his chair, looking to the ceiling and biting his lip as he came closer to the screen.

"Far away, in the poor, pathetic, little village of River Hill, a poor, pathetic airhead falls faint when she sees the ghost of her beloved idol, the poor, pathetic Prince Douchebag," Taylor started, making Bekah snicker. "Then in a flurry of intense idiocy, the children of the village sprang forth to dance and frolic in his presence- 'Huzzah!' they sang, 'Huzzah! Let me touch you!'"

By now, Taylor had her hunched over her desk in muffled laughter, trying desperately to be quiet with her hand clamped tightly over her mouth. With the time change between them, Bekah's mother was napping in the room next over, and she didn't want to alarm her. Meanwhile, Taylor acting out his story in his chair wasn't helping matters at all.

"What ho? Pray tell, what is this?" he went on with one of the most idiotic voices he could muster. "The poor, pathetic prince is broken? No matter, we shall carry him. Come along, your royal douchiness, step on my back as I walk along the ground like a dog. I worship the very idea of being your carriage."

"Stop it!" Bekah hissed a loud whisper through her hands. "My mom will hear!" Taylor could only smile at his friend, still struggling not to giggle so loudly at his silliness.

"You asked for a script," he told her flatly. All she could muster was an annoyed glare from her eyes, as her mouth was preoccupied with a smile, which was preoccupied by her hand. She shook her head playfully at him, throwing off his nonsense with a great breath to remove her giggles.

"I must be tired," Bekah admitted. "That shouldn't have been that funny." Taylor gave her an inquisitive look.

"How can you be tired? You're usually up much later than this."

"Yeah, but I usually sneak a nap in at tech," Bekah replied. "Today, we had a sub- and she was *mean*. Always going on about proper etiquette and how computers are tools for the privileged and blah, blah, blah, blah, blah." She shrugged. "Long story short, I didn't get my nap today."

"Suck," Taylor said, knowing that there was no real need for her to be awake during that class anyhow. As good at technology as Taylor was, Bekah held on par with him. Her username, "Hacker Nekko," was literal, as hacking into technology of any sort was her strongest skill. They often traded secrets and ideas on how to fix things during a job, and they taught each other a great deal more than either of them had known alone.

Sometimes, when Bekah was feeling devious or had misbehaved in class, she would hack into her school network to take a peek at her records, or change a few grades. She was constantly out to find new hacks, and was desperate to get Taylor's school's system cracked as well so that she could change his records, though Taylor refused every attempt.

"Hey, what should I make for dinner?" Taylor asked. She shrugged again.

"I don't know, mom made pasta with tomatoes and veggies." She looked to him. "Any of that sound good?" Taylor shook his head.

"Have the vegetables, but I ran out of pasta last week. Forgot to buy it." He thought for a moment. "I have rice, though- and the chicken from yesterday."

"Meat-eater," Bekah mumbled.

Taylor gave her a smug look. "I'd be more sorry if it didn't taste so good."

Bekah recoiled in her seat. "Manners, good sir, you have none!"

Taylor could only chuckle. "Chicken soup it is, then."

Bekah shook her head, in a mockingly sneering manner. "Yeah, you eat that soup and you think about how that bird died for your taste buds." He threw her a grin.

"I'll enjoy every bi-"

Crash!

A commotion downstairs stopped Taylor mid-sentence, shocking both he and Bekah, with eyes growing wide at the realization that his father had returned home from whatever soulless pits he had run off to. More clanking and banging came as Friedreich fumbled about the lower level of the house, and unintelligible shouting and growling echoed along the walls. For a moment, things went silent, and the tension stilled. Then, after a resounding curse, Taylor could hear the thudding of footsteps upon stairs.

"I gotta go," Taylor whispered, not meaning to. Bekah leaned in close to her camera, hurriedly speaking before they parted.

"Let me know you're okay."

"I will," Taylor tried to promise when halfway through, a bang came across his door, so forceful that it shook the very frame surrounding it. Taylor slammed his laptop close, trying desperately to shove it into his backpack without properly shutting it down. A rageful cry came from behind the wooden door, as the handle jiggled, trying to be opened with the lock in place.

"I'm coming, hold on!" Taylor shouted, but the door burst open before he could reach it. There, in the doorframe, his father stood, holding a lamp lengthwise at the height of his eye as though it were his gun, and drunk as the day is long.

"Don't move!"

Kaleb trudged down the sidewalk alone with his thoughts, only the clicking of his crutches could be heard. *"What am I going to do now?"* he wondered. He hadn't wanted to go home just yet, as no one would be there. Mr. and Mrs. Evans both worked in the medical field, and wouldn't be home until dinner time. He didn't like the idea of being home alone, so he decided to clear his head with a walk through the neighborhood. The problem with this, however, is that he couldn't walk, so halfway through the western side, Kaleb grew tired, and needed a rest.

Gingerly, he sat down on the curb, adjusting his protected knee so as to sit somewhat comfortably. The wind playfully rustled his hair as he rested, and in the distance, he could hear the coo of a morning dove. As he sat, he enjoyed the silence the afternoon brought, and was once again sedated by the lack of people trying to 'help' him. The slowly dying sunlight warmed his face, bringing a smile to his lips. No one was out to talk to him. No one was near to bother him. It was just Kaleb and the sound of life around him. Until he heard the screaming.

Behind him, inside the house he was resting in front of, there was crashing and thumping and screaming. Gradually, the noises got louder as they moved closer to the front of the house, and suddenly, they burst out with the screech and bang of a screen door opening and closing shut quickly; the screaming voice chasing after. With his chunky cast in the way, Kaleb couldn't turn around completely to see what all was going on. When he tried, someone tripped over him entirely, clunking him over the head with a shoe.

Kaleb rubbed the back of his head, trying to get a visual on the person who had knocked his head around, but his vision had gone loopy, and all he saw was a blurry body scrambling up from the sidewalk and running down the street and out of sight. The screamer, much to the disappointment of Kaleb's throbbing head, had stayed on the porch, yelling after it.

"Piece of shit! Get back here!" A man in his mid-forties was screaming so hard his face was red. "I said get-! Fine! Run away, coward! Don't expect-!" He stopped short when he noticed Kaleb staring at him. The man stared him down just as Kaleb did to him, though it was due to the fact that he couldn't look away.

"What are you looking at?" the man growled. Kaleb shook his head, not wanting any trouble. "Then get off my property."

With that, the man retreated back inside his house. Kaleb wasted no time in doing as he was told. He hobbled down the street as quickly as he could, heading home. *"What was that all about?"* Kaleb wondered. He had never seen anything like it before, and if he did, he had surely forgotten it by now. He pondered all the questions and possibilities about the scene that had just unfolded before him all the way home. By the time he had made it to his front porch, Kaleb was thoroughly shaken, and a bit irritated.

" *'Then get off my property,* '" Kaleb mimicked in an annoyed tone. "Jerk." He laid his crutches up against the wall by the front door as he entered his home, then headed for the kitchen. He heard a welcoming mew before he saw Skitters come running to him and jumping up on the kitchen table in greeting. "Hey, kit-cat," he muttered, giving the silky cat a rub from her ears to the tip of her tail as he walked. Skitters followed him, jumping down from the table only to jump up onto the bar sectioning off the kitchen and living room.

"Hungry?" Kaleb asked when he saw her empty bowl. Skitters mewed in response, having learned a few human words and knowing that 'hungry' meant food. He dragged out her food from the cupboard and filled Skitters' bowl, soon to be accompanied by Skitters herself. "There you go." He replaced the bag in the cabinet, then set out to bew himself something to drink. "What do you think; mint with honey?" he asked his feline friend, however, she was too concerned with her meal at the moment to give him any thought. He chuckled, then prepared the ingredients to make his tea.

"Ah, well," Kaleb muttered, calming down. "Just some guy having a bad day, I guess."

Bubbie was ecstatic. Taylor was back again, twice in one evening- could it be his birthday? If dogs did celebrate such a day, he would surely have explained it as so. He rushed out to see his friend, running circles around him and, having learned not to jump on him after the last accident, bounced around his feet in desperate attempt to get closer to him. He whined a happy, excited whine, and his tail blew away fallen leaves it wagged so fast. Taylor rubbed his friend's ears in greeting, just as happy to see Bubbie as he was to see Taylor.

"Looks like I'm staying the night after all."

"Day two," Kaleb playfully thought to himself. *"and the natives still insist on bidding grace on my every will."* He smiled at his own joke, replaying his first class as though it were a documentary. The students acted weird enough around him, they just made it too easy. Now he was out, and active. People threw smiles at him as he clicked down the hall to his next class, parting left and right to give him room for his crutches.

"The wild River-Hillians flee, baring their teeth in terror before the mighty Kaleb-Evansapian as he marches forward; fearful of his deadly, second set of silver, titanium legs." Kaleb's smile grew as the joke proceded, until he spotted Taylor.

"Behold!" His grin grew, turning his thought loose to the world. "A wild Grouch-a-lottis has appeared!" Taylor didn't completely register what had been said, but when he noticed Kaleb staring at him with that ridiculous grin, he rolled his eyes and walked on. Some students who had heard Kaleb laughed, not knowing what he was talking about entirely until they saw him pursuing Taylor.

Kaleb was now right behind Taylor, rushing after him closely, and commentating aloud just like he had in his head. "This Grouch-a-lottis appears to be a male, though you really have to look close in order to know for sure." Taylor continued to ignore Kaleb as he spoke. "The Grouch-a-lottis is just as it sounds, grouchy in nature and a major kill-joy. It is a rare, extremely dangerous endangered species in the urban lands of River Hill, as it is a mutation of the regular River-Hillians, who are much happier and nicer than this strange creature." More students were laughing now, catching on to what Kaleb was doing.

"Watch as he broods." Kaleb crouched as low as he could over his mobile crutches while he stalked the smaller boy. "Fascinating." Now, Taylor was too irritated. He stopped quickly and turned around to face Kaleb, who almost bumped into him. "He's angry!" Kaleb shouted, backing away a few steps. "Run for your lives- don't make eye contact!" Kaleb slapped his hands over his eyes, faking a horrified scream that brought about more laughter. Taylor simply watched, miffed at the taller boy's stupidity.

After a few death moans, Kaleb split his fingers apart to peek at his target, glaring at him as always, though with more annoyance than anger. To be honest, Kaleb liked this face better. Taylor's single raised eyebrow and flat mouth was a much better reaction than fiery, hate-filled eyes. Kaleb hated Taylor's glares for that reason alone. It didn't matter if his hatred was valid, feeling all that malice sent chills down Kaleb's spine, and left a sour taste in his mouth for the rest of the day. This face was a nice change of pace for once. He smiled at Taylor from behind his fingers, hoping to catch a similar reaction from the smaller boy, but with no luck. Taylor simply blinked at Kaleb, not saying anything, then:

"Don't you have anything better to do?"

This took Kaleb by surprise. Taylor rarely ever spoke to him, just ignored him and moved on. Now he was actually engaging a conversation.

"Not really," he replied, grinning. "Haven't had much to do since the whole 'breaking off my leg' thing. Everybody else does it for me."

"You poor thing," Taylor droned, rolling his eyes as he turned away to walk to his class again.

"Hey!" Kaleb wanted to follow him again, but the warning bell rang, and he needed to get to his own class instead. Begrudgingly, he turned and left as well.

"You *shithead!*" Bekah hissed, trying to be quiet again. "I was up all night worried sick about you, you stupid- stup-pi-pid- shi- *asshole!*" She tended to swear more, and trip over her words and stutter a bit when she got angry, which she had every right to be.

"I'm sorry," Taylor whispered back. "I dropped my laptop at home when I was leaving. Besides, there's no connection in the chutes."

Bekah was one of the few people who knew about Taylor and Bubbie's home, but she wasn't about to excuse him for that reason alone. Taylor rubbed down his hair after running a hand through it.

"I really hope it didn't get crushed," he murmured, thinking of his neglected computer. Bekah merely groaned in frustration.

True to her word, she had stayed up most of the night hoping to hear back from Taylor. Her thoughts were grim, and off and on in the small bits of sleep she could get, she would have nightmares of never seeing him again. She had given up hope of hearing from him until after his schooling; was dressed and ready to go to her own school, when she heard the chime of her chat alert ringing. Sure enough, there sat Taylor in a classroom, using an outdated computer to talk, but looking just fine.

Bekah ran her hands over her eyes and through her hair, sighing in relief. "Jack ass," she whispered, mostly to herself. Taylor had snuck into the computer classroom in order to speak with his friend before she headed off for class, and though he knew she would be relieved to see him, he also knew that he was in for a guilt trip. If he could get out now, there wouldn't be a need.

"Look," he started. "I need to get back, and you need to get going, so why don't-"

"Yeah, yeah, say no more," she huffed. "Run away." Taylor felt a pang of guilt in his gut with those two words. *"How do women do that?"* he wondered. He sighed as well, and the two friends made eye-contact as he rest his chin on his hand, both feigning a small, fleeting smile as if to say everything would be alright.

"I'll try to see you later," he said after a few minutes of silence.

"'Kay," she muttered, then added, "Later. Ding bat."

"Yeah, you too," he said. "Dummy."

It was the last class of the day, and the only possible explanation as to how Kaleb got ahold of a straw was either that he had brought it from home, or saved it from lunch earlier that afternoon. Either way, it was effectively shooting spitballs at the back of Taylor's head.

This was the one class that he had with Kaleb that, by whatever cruel hand of fate that had been given, Taylor had ended up sitting in front of him. As usual, he ignored Kaleb's antics, not wanting to give in to his will or cause trouble, and as usual, Kaleb kept right on bothering Taylor until he got any sort of reaction from him at all.

Taylor sighed to himself. Another spitball whizzed past his cheek, plopping down onto his desk and rolling across his paper. He wiped it onto the floor, reuniting it with a few others that had missed him. They were small, about the size of a grain of rice, never bigger than a bean, but they were irritating nonetheless. Taylor ruffled the hair on the back of his head, making sure there weren't any stuck in between a few strands, when another one shot into his hand.

"Ow!" Taylor hissed, trying to be quiet, but grabbing the attention of his teacher anyways.

"Is there a problem, Mr. Thompson?" he asked. Just his luck, it was Mr. Sutherland again, subbing for Miss Hart after she caught her sister's bug- and even worse, he remembered Taylor.

"No, sir," Taylor said.

Mr. Sutherland was about to drop the issue and move on until he spotted the balled up paper bits on the floor around him. "What are those?" he asked, beginning to walk over to Taylor's desk. Taylor quickly looked down at the mess. "Pick those up. Don't be a slob."

"Oh, sorry." He bent down to pick them up, and as he did so, his hood flipped over onto his head. Normally, this wouldn't be a problem- except that it was full of the spitballs that had hit his head and fallen into his hood. Dozens of spitballs rained down over Taylor's head, falling to the floor. This action brought a laugh from all who saw, except for Taylor, and unfortunately, Mr. Sutherland.

"Now, I know you didn't do that yourself," the teacher grumbled. He looked around for suspects, effectively spying Kaleb trying to write without any ink while trying to casually hide some ripped paper.

"Aha!" Kaleb couldn't help but snicker at Mr. Sutherland's outburst, which didn't help the man's already rotten attitude. "Give me that." He snatched the weapon from Kaleb's hands and inspected it. The straw that Taylor had originally believed it to be, turned out to be a gutted pen. Even Taylor was a little impressed, but Mr. Sutherland's face turned a violent shade of red, making it even harder for Kaleb to keep his snickering down.

"Very clever," Mr. Sutherland admitted. "But also very stupid." He confiscated Kaleb's pen, walking to the teacher's desk and pulling out a pink paper slip. "You've just earned yourself detention. What's your name?"

"Myanal Holehurts," Kaleb grinned.

"My...an... al..Hole-" Mr. Sutherland murmured the name as he wrote, but stopped once he realized it was a fake. His reaction, once again, brought laughter to the room. "That's disgusting" he hissed, Kaleb only shrugged.

"Hey, blame my parents, it was their idea."

Taylor slowly sunk deeper into his chair as Mr. Sutherland furiously scratched out the name on the pink slip before realizing he could rip it out and tear it up. From the irritation in the substitute's eyes, Taylor could see trouble brewing, and Mr. Sutherland was all too happy to oblige in the premonition. "Two weeks now, young man."

"That's a bit extreme, isn't it?" Kaleb said quietly, and the rest of the class quieted as well.

"Want to make it three?"

"That would be unfortunate."

"Three it is!"

"What for?"

"I can go all day!"

"But-"

"Don't tempt me."

Taylor noticed that Kaleb had lost his playfulness early on, but Mr. Sutherland was too far gone to understand. The tension in the room was electrifying, not a single student making a sound through the back-and-forth between the captain and the substitute.

Normally, detentions were handed out as a one-day punishment. It was clear that Mr. Sutherland was being unreasonable, letting his anger fuel his actions. Kaleb realized this a little too late, and was now sitting quietly in his chair, looking to the substitute for permission to speak. Receiving none, he went ahead and gave his name anyway.

"Kaleb Evans."

"Now was that so hard?" Mr. Sutherland growled, writing down Kaleb's name on the pink slip. He ripped it out once he was done, handing it to Kaleb, along with a yellow copy. "Take this to the office," he ordered. "And if I find out that you didn't, I'll have you suspended, you hear?"

"Yessir," Kaleb grumbled, keeping determined eye contact as he accepted the papers and stood to leave. He gathered his crutches and flimsy, temporary backpack, then left the class without another word. The silence was deafening, and all that could be heard in the class was the echoing of Kaleb's crutches clicking down the hall as he did as he was told.

"Let's find this as an example, shall we?" Mr. Sutherland spoke to the class. "Don't be a smart ass like that guy."

Many students wanted to rebuttal his argument, telling him that Kaleb was, in fact, *not* a smart ass, and that no decent teacher would use that word in front a bunch of minors. Nor would they lose their temper so quickly over such simplistic gestures. However, no one wanted to suffer the same fate as Kaleb, no matter how convincing they thought they could make it.

"And you," Mr. Sutherland looked straight at Taylor, then pointed to him, making him freeze. "You should know better."

"But I do," thought Taylor. He could feel the burning eyes of Kaleb's friends bearing into him. No doubt they would blame him for getting their captain in trouble, and he would unfortunately suffer the consequences for it later. He couldn't tell that to Mr. Sutherland, though. He couldn't tell anybody. Nobody cared. He was the son of an abandoner, an outcast to all, even his own blood. Instead, he nodded to the substitute, and turned back to his desk, ready for the lesson to continue.

"Three weeks detention?" Mrs. Hilton was aghast at the enormous punishment that had been given to Kaleb, who merely shrugged. "I was having a bit of fun with him, and he completely took it the wrong way."

"What kind of fun?" Mrs. Hilton asked, suddenly suspicious, but Kaleb shook his head.

"He caught me in an experiment, then when he asked for my name, I gave him an alias." Kaleb shrugged his shoulders again. "I guess he didn't like it, because he just went completely crazy, he raised it up a week every time I said something."

"How ridiculous." Mrs. Hilton took the pink slip and ripped it into small pieces before throwing it in the trash. When Kaleb gave her a look of confusion, she explained herself. "I know Mr. Sutherland's temper," she said. "Besides, between you and me, I don't really like him anyways." She threw him a grin. "Don't worry, Kaleb. I'll take care of it." Kaleb smiled at her.

"Thanks, Mrs. Hilton."

The final bell rang out, signaling an end to the day. "Looks like you're free, kid." Mrs. Hilton smiled, waving off her student. "See you tomorrow." Kaleb returned her gesture.

"Bye, Mrs. Hilton." Kaleb left the multitasking woman on her own to finish her duties as the school's principal, and headed to his locker so that he could leave for home.

Like every other student, he had a locker in the hallway, lined up with the other metal boxes. He used this one only to hold his books in between classes, and even then, it was rarely used. The locker that he lived out of was in the boy's locker room. He needed to switch out some things in there already, but a visit with the guys wouldn't hurt. Plus, he could walk there with Gerrit.

"There he is!" Gerrit chided, walking up along-side Kaleb. "Oh, captain, dear captain."

"What's up, man?" Kaleb asked, still clicking along to his locker.

"Not much," Gerrit replied. "Just wanted to see you off before practice." Kaleb gave a half-hearted smile, happy that Gerrit had thought of him, yet disappointed that he could not join him, even if only in spirit.

"Thanks," he said.

Gerrit only shrugged, then asked, "Hey, did that Tommy kid get you in trouble today?"

Kaleb nodded. "Yeah, kind of. I got caught trying to see something with him and the sub was a real monster. I got out of it, though. How'd you know?"

"Jacob told me," he said curtly. "You walking home?" Gerrit was full of questions today.

Kaleb nodded again. "I've got nothing else to do, might as well."

Gerrit shrugged. "Too bad. It's no fun without you around." This brought a little chuckle out of Kaleb.

"I think you'll survive," he told his smaller friend.

"Just a few more weeks, right, man?" Gerrit threw his friend his usual grin, receiving one from Kaleb as well.

"Right."

Kaleb glanced over at his friend from the corner of his eye, then swiped Gerrit's hat from his back pocket.

"Hey!" Gerrit complained when Kaleb slipped it over his head. "Dude- mine." He jumped up to try and take it back, barely missing the brim as Kaleb dodged his advances.

"Oh, so close!" Kaleb snickered. "Just a few more feet and you could have made it!" Gerrit didn't find the humor.

"Dude, seriously, gimme back my hat." He jumped up again and snatched it from the giant's head.

Kaleb chuckled at his friend's grumpiness. "Dude, you gotta learn how to share."

The smaller boy huffed at him, shoving his hat back into his back pocket. "I don't like other people touching my stuff, you know that," he grumbled.

Kaleb chuckled at him again. "Whatever you say, Highness."

Gerrit gave him a queer look. "'Highness?'" he asked.

Kaleb looked down to him. "Of course," he explained. "You're a royal pain in the ass." Gerrit shoved the laughing giant, countering his attack with a bit of name calling as well.

"Alright, man, I'm late." Gerrit slapped Kaleb's shoulder in farewell. "See you later."

Kaleb watched him go as he left. "See you later," he murmured. Kaleb had reached the boys locker room a few minutes later, and after dodging a few strewn shoes and clothes on the floor, managed to make it to his own locker. A few of the guys had lingered behind while changing to say hello to their captain, but shouts from their coach stole them away just as quickly.

Kaleb was alone again, left in the humid, rank room to empty the contents of his bag and switch it out with other trinkets from his locker. With no real reason to stay, he sluggishly went through the process, hoping someone might be late, or have someone come back for something that had been forgotten. Still, no one came. He hated being alone. He needed companionship in order to feel comfortable. The silence he could deal with, and even enjoy; but the emptiness…

With no sign of anyone coming through to keep him company, Kaleb threw on his backpack, and left the locker room. The hallway was equally empty, leaving goosebumps up and down his arms as he quietly clicked down the length of the hall to the exit. Once he had made it outside, the chills went away, and the unease began to dissipate.

There was life in the outdoor world. The chirping of birds, chittering of squirrels, the rustling of the leaves on wind; even the sun had a heartbeat that Kaleb could enjoy. The very grass beneath his feet sprang to life as he left it with each step, and even the sound of the distant rivers raging on brought something to the world. Even when void of people, the outside world was never empty. Never devoid of life.

Kaleb clicked on, slow and steady, hobbling down the road towards home, taking a shortcut through the park. He had gone a good distance before catching a glimpse of something from the corner of his eye. When he turned to look, he saw that it was Taylor walking home, just across the park from him. He had his head hanging low, as usual, with his hood over his head. If it hadn't been for his signature hoodie, Kaleb probably wouldn't have known it was him. Kaleb was about to call out to him when he saw Taylor's headphones strapped tightly to his ears beneath the hood. What really caught Kaleb's attention, though, was that Taylor was limping.

As far as Kaleb knew, Taylor hadn't been having trouble walking that day, so the only plausible conclusion would be that he was faking it for attention. Kaleb frowned at the thought, but then realized- Taylor didn't know Kaleb was watching him. The light haired boy had his head down low, watching his feet move as he walked, and with that hood blocking anything else, he couldn't have noticed Kaleb from across the park. Not only that, but with no one else around to see, there really was no point in acting as though he had been hurt.

"Maybe he tripped after class," Kaleb thought.

Now Taylor had his back to Kaleb, he had gone off the sidewalk and was heading towards the trees at the edge of the creekbed surrounding the park. *"What are you doing?"* Kaleb wondered. He saw Taylor lower his hood to look around when he drew closer to the treeline, walking backwards as he scanned the park. Kaleb, being curious, ducked down low, hoping to be hidden behind a slide not to far from him, and to his surprise, it worked.

"Unbelievable," Kaleb thought.

Taylor turned back around to face the trees, and started to push away some foliage. Kaleb watched in curious wonder as Taylor disappeared from view, and dissolved into the trees. Without a second thought, Kaleb rushed forward on his crutches as fast as he could towards the bridge. If there was a chance, he wanted to see exactly where it was that Taylor was going.

"A short cut? A girl? A secret base? Who knows!"

Without even realizing it, Kaleb found himself rather curious of Taylor's actions and wanted to know precisely what was going on behind the curtain of green. In such a small town, there was precious few chances for mystery and adventure, and with a bum knee, those chances dwindled into practically nothing.

Kaleb made it to the bridge breathless and somewhat sweaty, but he forced himself to quiet down in order to spy on Taylor without him knowing. Kaleb dropped his crutches from his shoulders into his hands to hover just over his ankles and crept down low past the trees, following the bridge railing as close as possible. Then, careful as he dared, he raised himself up to see over the railing. What he saw was nothing but rocks, plants and the trickling of a stream running the length of the creek.

"Aw, man," Kaleb groaned, then picked up his crutches and replaced them under his arms. He was genuinely disappointed in not seeing Taylor running off to his 'secret base.' *"Bored yet again,"* Kaleb grumbled. *"Thought I might actually get something cool to watch."* Without another thought, Kaleb resumed his trek towards home.

It didn't take him long to make it up his front steps and through his front door. As usual, Skitters was there to greet him, but soon lost interest and retreated to soak up a bit of sunlight on the floor before a window. Both parents were working again, so Kaleb was on his own until dinner at sunset. Once again alone. Once again quiet.

"Last day of class, last day of class."

Taylor kept repeating the same sentence over and over again in his head, not really listening to the lecture. The alchemy teacher, Mr. Finnigan, flailed about the front room, going on about a biochemical reaction of some sort forming a new protein for plants- or something of that nature that was equally tiresome. His voice, though enthusiastic, droned on in the ears of his students who had no desire to learn it. The classroom had been darkened for Mr. Finnigan's on-screen presentation, which didn't help to ease the class's sleepiness in the slightest, and certainly not Taylor's. None of that mattered, though; at least, not at the moment.

Once again, it was the end of the week, and Taylor's favorite day: game day. No troublesome classmates, more free time with Bubbie, and hopefully, a new letter waiting for him with Hector. He was zoning out at his desk, transfixed on the idea of getting out of class and getting on with his day, not really bothering with paying attention. His body was relaxed, slouching comfortably in his seat, completely lost in thought. It wasn't until he saw from the corner of his eye that his pencil was shivering from the motion of his tapping heal beneath his desk.

He quickly straightened himself, looking around him as he sat up to see if he had been spotted in his daze. He ran a hand through his hair, silently sighing, now trying to at least attempt to hear what his teacher had to say. Time was against his efforts, however, as the bell rang out over Mr. Finnigan's voice, ending class until they could resume at the beginning of the week. Chairs scraped and students chattered as they gathered their belongings and exited the room. Taylor was all too glad to do the same- when Mr. Finnigan called to him.

"Taylor," Mr. Finnigan asked, waving him over. "May I have a word, please?"

"Great," Taylor thought, trying to come up with an excuse or apology for his sudden dose of disinterest during class. He was about to open his mouth to exert said

apology, when his teacher stopped him.

"I have some bad news, son."

"That's something every person wants to hear," Taylor stated.

"Right." Mr. Finnigan lost a grin to that remark, but it was soon tucked away behind his worried beard. "It's just that, well, I'm afraid you're failing my class."

Taylor's sarcasm melted away instantly to show his serious side. "Failing?" he asked. "What do you mean I'm failing?"

"Exactly what I said. Failing," Mr. Finnigan reiterated.

Taylor shook his head, confused. "But, Mr. Finnigan, all of my homework has passing grades on them, and I study for every test-"

"Your homework is just barely passing and your quizzes- well, I'm not going to go into that right now." Mr. Finnigan crossed his arms, looking down at his feet as he spoke. "I understand that you're a tutor, yes?" Taylor nodded, and the teacher heaved a disappointed sigh. "That's what I thought."

"Is that bad?" Taylor asked, receiving a look from the older man.

"Well, son, yes. Unfortunately, if you fail my class, then that means you're not eligible to be a tutor anymore."

Taylor's eyes went wide in disbelief. "What, why? I don't even tutor alchemy."

Mr. Finnigan shook his head. "Doesn't matter," he said. "You have to be passing your basics in order to tutor, and alchemy tops the list."

Taylor sat down onto a nearby desk, completely distraught. Without his tutoring jobs, it would be even harder for him to save his money. Not to mention, what college would want some stupid kid who couldn't even figure out one of the 'basics?' Then another thought occurred to him: there was no way he could graduate without this class. Meaning no scholarships. Meaning no college. Meaning another year in this shit hole called River Hill.

Taylor ran his hands over his forehead and through his hair, exhaling slowly so as not to hyperventilate or panic. "What are my options?" he asked, not looking away from his focal point on the floor.

"Well, I have a few extra credit papers that you could do for me," Mr. Finnigan listed. "Extra assignments, reports, all that fun stuff, but the biggest problem will be the final exam during spring harvest. The way you're headed, though, even with all of that extra work, not to mention keeping your homework up as well, it won't be enough if you fail the exam."

Taylor closed his eyes, trying to breathe properly again.

"I don't have time for this."

"Might I suggest something?" Mr. Finnigan asked, seeing the discomfort in his student and waiting to continue until Taylor looked back at him in confirmation. "Get a tutor to help you with all of this," he said. "They might be very helpful to you, and they can even help you with your homework once they've finished helping you with the extra credit. They might even help you study for the test, if you're willing."

Taylor nodded. Although he disliked the idea of spending money on a tutor, the thought of staying in River Hill an extra year due to his own stupidity burned him even more. "Here." Mr. Finnigan walked around to his desk, retrieving and writing on a small square of yellow paper, then handed it to Taylor. "Mr. Goodson is head of the Alchemy department," he said. "If anyone could give you a good tutor recommendation, it'd be him."

Taylor accepted the note from his teacher, swallowing down hard on this new information, then turned to leave for his final class of the day.

"I hope you make it, son," Mr. Finnigan called after him. "You're one of the few who actually pay attention in my class."

Kaleb's excitement grew larger with each passing second. Today was game day, and for once, Kaleb could observe his teammates playing from afar, see what couldn't be seen at eye level, and possibly, find new ways to use their strengths and weaknesses to their advantage in any upcoming games. Truthfully, while he was disappointed that he couldn't play alongside his friends, he was even more eager to watch and learn.

As usual, everyone had had their pre-game warm-up and practice over and done with, and were now given the option to leave and do as they please while they waited for the bus. Kaleb eagerly clicked over to Gerrit coming out of the locker room.

"Burger?" He nudged Gerrit, who shook his head.

"Money."

Kaleb rolled his eyes and swatted Gerrit on his butt with one of his crutches.

"C'mon."

A few other boys had accompanied them to the diner, enjoying a meal before the game as well. There was laughter and all around merriment through the evening while the athletes riled themselves up. Stories and playful teasing went about the diner with ease, and in the middle of their fun, Dylan, caught up in the moment, made a toast to Kaleb, promising him that their victory would be in his name. Every boy cheered at this, raising their glass with a shout and slamming it back down on the table so hard, some spilt their drink all over their hand.

After a good thrashing from Tammy, and emptying a few napkin holders, the boys went back to being playful and happy as ever. The mood was light, and every toothy grin could be seen; for their giddiness was contagious, and spreading to the other residents of the diner as well. Finishing their meals, they paid Tammy her dues and left for the bus back at the school.

Along the way, the laughter continued. The jokes, the playfulness, the sarcasm; at one point, someone had started singing the team's battle song, sending the rest of the group into torturous shouts of the lyrics in an attempt to sing as loudly as they could. Their song carried them the rest of the way back, though their voices reached the field before they did.

"Alright, alright, enough!" Coach Abernathy shouted over them, jerking a thumb towards the steaming engine. "Get on the bus."

One by one, the boys lined up and boarded the bus, still giddy from their adventure. Kaleb handed his crutches to Gerrit inside the bus, grabbing onto the inner hand railings to hoist himself up.

"Evans!" Coach shouted. "What do you think you're doing?"

Kaleb looked to his coach over his shoulder, now using the rails to keep his balance. "Going to the game, sir?" he answered.

"Not with us, you're not." Coach came to stand next to Kaleb, reaching for his crutches from Gerrit. Gerrit, not knowing what to do, obediently handed over the crutches to his coach, all the while looking to Kaleb for answers. Coach Abernathy then presented the crutches to Kaleb once again, staring him down and not moving until they were firmly placed under each arm. "No deadweight," Coach said to him.

"Yeah, but, coach-" Kaleb stumbled. "You said that I could-"

"You can come to the games, just not with us," the older man interrupted. "Now get going, we're late." Each team member had been alerted of the skirmish at the front of the bus and were now all watching in despair. Kaleb backed away from the bus, letting his coach enter and slam the door shut. Kaleb could see the coach saying something to the driver through the glass, but heard nothing over the power of the steam engine roaring to life. Each and every team member watched Kaleb watch them leave, and suddenly, the giddiness could no longer be found.

"Kaleb," a voice called from the distance. He turned to see that it was Mr. Phillips, the maintenance man. "Need a ride?" Kaleb gave a small smile to the man, thanking him as he hobbled over and entered the cabin of his truck. "Don't worry," Mr. Phillips told him. "I'll get you there on time." Kaleb thanked the man again as steam escaped the confines of the truck's engine.

He rode in silence, letting Mr. Phillips do all of the talking, which he was certainly no novice at. Kaleb responded when he needed to, but mostly kept quiet with his thoughts. Mr. Phillips didn't mind one bit, rather enjoying a chance to speak with someone new for once.

When they arrived, Kaleb thanked the man once more before leaving to find his own seat in the stands, and while he was grateful, he was also intimately hurt at the harshness of his coach, and cruelty of his friends.

"I know you're doing your best, and I'm trying to work just as hard as you are everyday. I'll keep working until you and I can be together again. I love you, Bubbie. I hope to hear from you soon.

Love, Mom."

Taylor was sitting against the cave wall, repeatedly re-reading his mother's final words from his latest letter in his head while Bubbie ate his food. It had been so long since he had heard her voice that it was hard to recall the sound of it, but he remembered her sincerity, and it burned a hole of guilt into the deep confines of his stomach with every word.

"I know you're doing your best"

Taylor dropped his head between his upright knees, drawing them closer as his hands found their way into his hair. He couldn't bring himself to respond to her letter this time; not with the news of his latest failure. Regardless of her being his mother and an understanding woman, he didn't want to face her disappointment, even from afar. It wasn't just *his* dreams that were crushed today.

Bubbie had finished his meal, and seeing Taylor in the state he was in, padded over to try and nuzzle his friend's arms away from his face. When this was successful, he gently placed his head on Taylor's knee, sweeping his tail across the floor and peering up into Taylor's eyes with a soft look of his own. Taylor rubbed Bubbie's ears, but it wasn't enough. He leaned into Taylor, whining slightly, pawing and pushing his way up Taylor's chest, all the while wagging his tail furiously. His furry companion nuzzled his scarred cheek, sniffing his face for any sign of tears and finding none. Taylor smirked, giving in to the dog's commands by scrubbing his neck with a newfound gusto.

"Alright, happy now?" he asked, rubbing the dog's now uprighted belly. Bubbie snorted, flipping over to madly sniff Taylor's face. Taylor pushed the dog's nose aside, wrapping his arms around his neck and leaning his head against Bubbie's neck and shoulder in a loving embrace; which Bubbie gladly endured. Taylor stroked his hand down the length Bubbie's furry body while still holding him in the crook of his arm, though little effort was needed to hold the dog in place. Bubbie sat still, save for his tail, allowing his friend to hang onto him and pet him.

"Thanks, bud," Taylor murmured into Bubbie's fur.

Bubbie's tail continued to wag as Taylor opened his eyes and pulled away from him, giving him another scratch behind the ears. Then, Taylor took his mother's letter and placed it with the others inside his box. Once this was done, he reached over to Bubbie's ball next to the letter box, gaining Bubbie's attention and excitement all over again.

"Let's play."

Chapter 5

Kaleb slouched glumly in his seat at Gerrit's kitchen table, fiddling with a paper football between his fingers. He had all day to play with Gerrit, in hopes of finding something to keep themselves busy while they waited for his parents to come home from work. These hopes crashed miserably as soon as they entered the smaller boy's house and heard word of some of their friends playing base-tag; a game Kaleb had invented as a child.

"Man, this is boring," Gerrit grumbled ten minutes in. "Let's go play some real ball with the guys." Kaleb said nothing, but merely looked at his friend from under his cocked brow. "Oh, right," said Gerrit when he glimpsed Kaleb's cast from under the table. "Well, you could watch? Be the ref, maybe?" He was trying desperately to get them out and about and away from that table, because if there was one thing that was known about Gerrit Ford, it was that he could *never* sit still.

"Go on," Kaleb groaned, releasing his partner from his friendly duty to entertain him.

"Thanks, man," Gerrit replied, practically running out the door to play ball with the other boys. Kaleb sat at his table, flicking the paper football with his thumb before trying to flick it into the garbage bin across from him, landing just short of its target. He sighed to himself, thinking back to his series of failed attempts to be normal with his leg bound in that accursed cast.

He couldn't play sports anymore, that was a given. No running was allowed, and even if he could, he would be undoubtedly slower than the rest of the boys. There was his pride as well. Worse than losing to them because of his leg would be winning because they held back their efforts to beat him. He couldn't go hiking, or explore the woods with his crutches beneath his arms, he couldn't race his friends to class, he couldn't even catch a ball with his hands preoccupied with his crutches. He couldn't do anything that the majority wanted to do.

No, Kaleb wouldn't be able to join his friends in their adventures for another month at least, and even then, that was iffy. Once he had healed completely, and the cast came off for good, there was still physical therapy, and taking it easy for a while so as not to injure his knee again. Kaleb was, as his father liked to put it, 'out of order' until then.

Kaleb stretched in his seat, enjoying the sensation of his muscles straining then relaxing as he lowered his arms, then rose from his chair to head home across the street. He didn't need to lock the door behind him; not in this neighborhood. Everyone knew everyone, and everyone knew everything. There was no chance of a burglary attempt, not with all the eyes the neighborhood had.

Kaleb slowly trecked across the street to his own house, seeing his father working in the open garage on his latest project. "I'm home!" he called out over the whirring of tools being used in his father's work room.

"So soon?" his father responded, turning around to face Kaleb. "I thought you'd at least be out until dusk." His father was wiping away spare oil from his fingers, taking a break from his work to speak to his son.

"Gerrit had something else to do," Kaleb said. "So I came back."

"Oh, that's a shame," said Mr. Evans, receiving a shrug from his son.

Vance Evans was, first and foremost, a doctor in a small hospital in the next town over, both parents working in their major fields as husband and wife. In his spare time, however, he was a brilliant engineer, especially skilled in the arts of prosthetic limbs that he himself had christened mecha-limbs. He worked day and night to perfect his work, hoping to one day make arms and legs that would be perfectly compatible with the wearer, as though they had been born with them all along. He had made incredible progress already, with mechanics that wriggled toes at will, and almost perfectly matched skin, but Vance knew he could go further in his research, and toiled away almost every waking hour he could towards his progression.

Many a time, the Evans family would receive complaints from their neighbors about the noise of his work late at night, or even more often and disturbing, the sight of hanging limbs from their garage. Once, their next door neighbors, Mr. and Mrs. Copperfield, had approached Vance while he was working on a hand in his garage. Mr. Copperfield had caught sight of the twitching hand and stiffened, while his wife went pale. Vance, being a trickster himself, held up the hand to his neighbors, touching wires together to make the fingers wave, and effectively scaring off the two intruders. It had taken them a while to warm up to the Evans' again after that.

Still, even with the importance of his work, Mr. Evans made it a point to spend time with his family, and with the sudden appearance of his son, his afternoon of work on flexible kneecaps would have to be put on hold for a while.

"Well, what are your plans now?" Mr. Evans asked. "Want to toss the ball around with your old man?"

"Nah," Kaleb smiled. "I think I'll go watch some t.v."

"You sure?" Vance asked again. "I may be an old fart, but I've still got some moves."

Kaleb's smile broadened. "No," he replied. "You can keep working." Now Vance shrugged.

"Aright. I'm here if you need me."

Kaleb nodded, turning to leave. "Thanks, dad." Once again, Skitters greeted Kaleb as he entered from the garage door, meowing to him as he clicked down the hall. "I know, I know," he said. "I'm coming." Skitters rubbed herself against Kaleb as he settled his crutches up against the wall, welcoming him home as she wound herself around his legs. "You only love me because I feed you." Kaleb snorted, earning a mew from his beloved pet.

He bent over to carry her to the kitchen, rubbing her ears and earning a series of ferocious purrs from his affections. When he finally hobbled to the cabinets, Kaleb released Skitters and filled her dishes with fresh food and water. Now concerned with emptying the newly filled bowls, Skitters left Kaleb to begin his own desires.

Kaleb was banned from his bedroom by order of his mother, and had taken refuge on the livingroom couch until he could manage cleaning again. With his room in the cluttered state that it was in, she feared her son would slip on any trinket on the floor and hurt himself even further. It was his duty to keep his own messes clean, and therefore, no one else was allowed to touch his room, regardless of his injury. In Mrs. Evans' own words, she described it as "his own fault for screwing it up," and considered his banishment as punishment for being so messy. Aside from this, and more importantly to his mother, Kaleb would be across from the master bedroom. If he needed anything, all he had to do was call out to her, and Mrs. Evans would come.

Now Kaleb lay on his bedded portion of the L-shaped couch, clicking through the channels until something of interest could catch his eye, and finally settling on a nature documentary. He sat listening to the narrator drone on about the beaver's habitat when he heard his mother come in through the front door loaded with groceries.

"Hi, honey," she said, beginning to unload in the kitchen. "What are you doing home so early?"

"Nothing else to do." Kaleb sighed. Mrs. Evans cocked a brow.

"Poppycock," she said. "There's plenty to do. You just need the motivation to do it."

"Well, I have none," he replied, sounding very bored.

Trish Evans placed her hands on her hips. "Then you're not trying hard enough."

Kaleb rolled his eyes, smirking at his mother's spunk. He heard her mumble something about needing a snack before dinner, then bustling around the kitchen in preparation.

"Did you finish your homework?" His mother bent down out of sight to grab something.

Kaleb would have given her a queer look if the kitchen bar were not in the way. "Do you really have to ask?"

Mrs. Evans chuckled, popping back up from whatever she had been storing."Why don't you work on your bike?"

"I'm stuck," said Kaleb. "I can't figure out how to connect the dots just yet, and it's too frustrating. I'd end up breaking the whole thing."

"Too bad." Trish came around the bar and plopped down onto the couch next to her son's head with a sandwich in hand. "I'm looking forward to seeing the finished project." She pinched off a corner of her snack and held it above Kaleb's head, waiting for him to open his mouth and accept it. When he did, she began eating as well.

"What about your books?" she asked. "I'm sure your personal library could use some more material." She tore off more of her sandwich, offering it to Kaleb's lips again.

"The book store here sucks, I've pretty much cleared it out. The one in Carter city is way better," he managed before taking the food in his mouth. "But, you don't want me going too far, remember?"

"Now don't blame me for that," Trish scorned lightly. "I just don't want you tiring yourself out too quickly and not have anyone else there to help you."

"I'm not a baby, mom," Kaleb grouched with a hint too much irritation.

"You're *my* baby," Trish spat back. "Doesn't matter how old you are." She offered him another bite of her sandwich, pulling her fingers away quickly when his teeth scraped her skin. "Whoo, almost got me that time!" She smiled. "Maybe you're a beast instead of a baby."

Kaleb grinned. "Oh, mom. I *am* a beast. A mighty beast indeed. See? Roar."

"Better hide my bunny slippers then," Trish muttered through a bite. "They scare easy." Kaleb grinned again, accepting the last bite of sandwich from his mother. Like his father, his mother also worked in the medical field, at the same hospital as her husband. Her expertise, however, was herbal alchemy. Trish Evans had her garden in the back, and a second bedroom connected to a greenhouse fully devoted to herbology and chemical reactions. She devoted her skills to remedies that didn't require a prescription, and was also extremely accomplished in her work.

As far back as Kaleb could remember, he had never once taken a factory-created drug to cure him of his ails. His mother had always given him her own recipes of healing, and through that, had taught him many different ways of healing the sick or injured. Even in the hospital, after receiving his cast and coming out of a dreadfully loopy drug-high, he would refuse the hospital drugs in favor of his mother's alchemy instead.

"I'm going to make some tea. Would you like some?" Trish rose from the couch to head for the kitchen.

"Sure. Do we have any blueberry left?" Kaleb heard his mother move about the cabinets, searching for ingredients.

"Uumm… About a cup and a half," she said finally. "We'll have to plant more."

"That's fine." Kaleb clicked off the television, stretching again. "The greenhouse could use a bit more blue anyways." Trish went to work creating their beverages as Kaleb worked his way off the couch and into the kitchen.

"Can I help with dinner?" he asked, once he reached the kitchen doorway. Trish smiled at her son.

"Sure, honey. I was thinking mahshi tonight." She pulled out four freshly-picked bell peppers from the fridge and handed them to Kaleb, who immediately rinsed them and began gutting the vegetables for stuffing, while his mother began working on the rice.

"See?" Trish smiled. "Something to do."

Taylor gave a sigh of satisfaction as he leaned back in his chair. He rewarded himself with a long stretch after having earned himself another job in the city of Carter, just East of River Hill. Although it would be another day before he could leave, it was still a success in his opinion. Sinking into his chair, he closed his eyes, thinking of his encounter with the head of the Alchemy department earlier that morning.

"If you need a tutor, this is my best guy," Mr. G said. "He's got the best grades in any of my classes. He even leads study group for me from time to time." Taylor nodded, waiting for the man to continue. "Here," The teacher scribbled on a slip of paper, then handed it to Taylor. "That's his school e-mail contact. Tell him I sent you." Taylor stared down at the paper in his hands, memorizing the name as best he could before slipping it safely into his pocket.

"Thank you, sir."

Slowly, Taylor opened his eyes, the memory still lingering in his mind. He snuck his fingers into his pocket, fishing out the slip of paper he had been given that morning to hold it before his face. The name "Alchemyst_32" read back to him in sloppy handwriting, ringing in his ears as he re-read it over and over again in his head.

After a while, Taylor pushed himself upright in his chair, leaning into his computer to come up with a request for this stranger's help. His fingers hovered over the keyboard, flexing and curling in place as he decided how to word his plea. He was never any good at social contact in the first place, but this- not even knowing his face- made it even harder.

Taylor bit his lip, still unsure of how to interact with this stranger for the first time. Suddenly, the delightful ringing on his computer alerted him of Bekah calling to him for a chat. He quickly accepted his saviour's request and soon saw her usual figure; orange kitty hat and all.

"Hey, Tay," she joked. "What's up?"

Taylor gave a fleeting grin to his friend before speaking. "I need your help."

"Shoot." She sat up straight in her chair to re-adjust herself properly.

"I need to ask this guy to be my tutor, but I don't know how," Taylor responded.

Bekah flicked her hair from her shoulder, crossing her arms upon her desk to lean in to her computer. "Well, what's his name?"

Taylor touched the paper slip on the desk, not really needing it. "Alchemyst," he said. "Alchemyst_32."

Bekah smirked, tightening her shoulders as she did so. "You don't know his real name?"

"It's a safety thing," Taylor replied, shaking his head. "I won't know who he is unless he wants me to. Same rule goes for me; he won't know who I am until we meet in person."

Bekah's face scrunched up in confusion. "What name do you use, then?"

"Same as usual." He leaned back in his chair.

"So, Dallas_Lori," she said, more of a statement than a question. The confused look reformed on her face. "Where did you come up with that anyway? I mean, I get Lori, the country, but what about Dallas? It sounds like one of your character's nicknames."

Taylor shrugged. "I actually thought about making a character with that name," he admitted. "but really, it just sounded cool, so I took it for myself."

"Hmm." Bekah nodded, placing her chin on her fist, and looking to the ceiling in thought. "Well, I guess you just get to the point."

Taylor blinked. "Excuse me?"

Bekah smirked again at her friend. "Don't give me that," she scolded. "There's no need to get into detail with a stranger, right? So just say, 'hey, I need your help on this one thing, think you can help me out?' And that's that. If he says no, no big. If he says yes, score. You can start the small talk once you get to know him better. You know, 'nice weather' and junk."

Taylor shook his head, furrowing his brow at his friend. "You make it sound so easy."

Bekah cocked a brow at his reaction. "Well, I'm not the social butterfly that you are, but I can get by in a pinch."

Taylor rolled his eyes, brushing off her sarcasm, then leaned into his keyboard to try and type again. "'Kay, how's this?"

"I was told that you were the best in alchemy. I'd like to see for myself. I need this done A.S.A.P. Let's meet up sometime to work on some assignments of mine-"

"Okay, stop," Bekah interrupted, even going so far as to hold up a hand in case he didn't hear her. "You really are bad at this."

Taylor blinked, glancing at his friend from his screen. "What?"

Bekah pinched the bridge of her nose. "How can you be such a moron at this when you're so good at writing?"

"Actual social contact is not my forte," Taylor grumbled. He leaned back into his chair, crossing his arms as he did so. "Pretending on paper is much easier."

Bekah's head snapped up from her massaging fingers. "Seriously? This is exactly the same thing!"

Taylor's face went flat. "No. It's not."

"Alright, whatever." She dismissed his annoyance and pondered another solution, pushing her glasses back over the bridge of her nose.

"What would 'Little Miss Halfling' say? Wait, scratch that," she changed her mind when she remembered that Taylor had created this character with social awkwardness as well. "Miss Editor, then. She's a bad ass, and she gets to the point." Taylor tasted the idea for a moment, considering what his character would say in this circumstance.

"Probably the same thing," he said finally, throwing Bekah his flat face again. She, in turn, smothered her face in her hand. Then, realizing he was right, agreed with him.

"Fine," she sighed. "Send this then."

"Hey there, I'm Dallas. I'm having some trouble understanding alchemy and was wondering if you could help me. I have some extra assignments that I need to get done quickly, and when I asked for a tutor, you were recommended to me. Please get back to me whenever you can, I'd really appreciate it if you did. Thank you for your time."

Taylor frowned at the words typed in his message box and pulled away from his computer. "I sound like a sissy," he grumbled again. Bekah shook her head at her stubborn friend.

"It's called professionalism," she said. "And being mannerly." Taylor looked at his friend from beneath his brow.

"A mannerly professional without a backbone and some other vital muscle."

Bekah feigned a dull, fake laugh, but was cut short when the sound of Taylor's computer rang out a message alert.

"That was fast." Taylor clicked open the response and read aloud for Becka to hear.

"Hey, Dallas. Sorry, I happened to be on when I got this. (I'm not a creeper, I swear.) I've recently come across more spare time than usual, so I'm free anytime after school if you're up for it. We can meet up in Riviera's alchemy lab; I've been given permission to use it whenever I want, so we won't really be bothered. Oh, and I charge about five papers an hour.
I look forward to working with you. (If you still want to.)

-Alchemyst"

"He's certainly used to this," Taylor commented, but Bekah crumpled her face in disagreement. "Pretty cheap, too," he commented. "I wonder why."

She shrugged. "Maybe he doesn't need the money?"

Taylor sighed, touching his fingertips to his forehead. "What should I send back?" he asked, looking to his friend.

"'Sounds cool,'and then set up the meet and greet for tomorrow," she replied, but Taylor shook his head, simply stating;

"Work."

Bekah rolled her eyes. "The next day, then."

Taylor did as he was told, instantly being rewarded with confirmation on the other end of the conversation. "Looks like that's all set," he droned.

"You sound so very excited," Bekah sassed, earning a glare from her friend. "Down, boy," she said. "Just think of it as a social experiment."

Taylor threw her a pouty glare. "I hate experiments."

This earned him a glare from her in return.

"Which is why you're failing alchemy."

"You alright, hun?" Trish asked, looking back at the young man over her shoulder. Kaleb gave his mother a half-hearted nod, mostly ignoring her due to the book in his hands capturing his attention. He flipped through the pages, feeling the texture of the paper, and smelling the aroma of a fresh book as it wafted up to his nose.The fibers and ink that lived within the flexible cover tantalized the reader, any reader, to come inside it's pages to enjoy the adventures and wonders woven through words.

Kaleb stopped flipping the pages of the book to read the details inside the cover, using this information to determine his final decision. Once his mind had been sated with the first few sentences, he closed the book with a resounding *thunk* that was pleasing to his ear, and went to tuck it beneath his arm; only to remember that it was possessed by his crutch. Instead, he grasped the spine with whatever fingers he could spare from beneath the handle of his titanium leg, then clicked towards the front of the store to buy his newfound treasures with his mother.

"Is that all you're getting?" Trish asked when he placed the newest book in her handbasket.

"For now," he replied. Then with a little more hope in his voice, "I might find something to do later." Trish smiled at her son, pleased with his outlook, then turned to pay for the basket's load. Kaleb lazily clicked over to the front of the store as their items were being scanned and processed, eyeing the reversed words painted in the window that read '*Carter City's Bookshelf*,' and watching the people who happened to pass by. It was a common thing for him to do, to notice things as time passed. Often times, he would sit and observe people, just to see how they lived through everyday trials. Out of habit, Kaleb tilted his head as he spied the people beyond the glass, losing himself in the view.

In the street, steam-powered vehicles sped away to their destinations, but along the sidewalk, he could see more of a story. He saw a mother and her toddler walking along the sidewalk, holding hands and bracing their skirts against the sudden breeze. As this was happening, he watched a man in a hat and dapper suit holding a briefcase hurry past them, not bothering to pay them any attention. Across the street from the bookstore, he spotted a homeless man begging for coins around the corner of the building, out of sight from the windows and store manager who would regularly shoo the man away.

With nothing else to see, Kaleb turned away from the angle straight across from him to see the occupants on the street to the right of him. There, at the bus stop tucked inside under the glass weather shelter, he had the chance to spy on more people.

An older woman, plump in every way, sat on one end of the bench provided for the riders, fanning herself with her hand. Beside her, an elderly man in a tie holding flowers, staring down at the ground lost in his thoughts, and ending the bench, a young man in a hoodie, possibly college age, reading a book in his lap. Not one single being interacted with the other, nor were they prompted to do so, despite sitting so intimately close to one another.

Kaleb was about to turn away,when he noticed another person appearing around the corner of the building to the right of him. This young man was also wearing a hoodie; hands in his pocket and hood pulled over his head in his usual glum way, not really hiding his bright white headphones.

"*Tommy?*"

Kaleb squinted, trying to disprove his eyes. Sure enough, it was his brooding rival, trudging in gloomy steps towards the bus stop, only to lean against the outer wall of the weather shelter. Taylor glanced around the street in search of the bus coming for him, seeing not a thing, and settling back into one of the weather shelter's poles. He reached up to his headphones, fiddling with knobs to most likely change the song or the volume being played, then tucked his hand back inside the safety of his pocket.

"Why do I keep on running into him?" Kaleb wondered. He thought back to all the years he had been in school with him, shared classes with him and taunted him with his friends, only to realize that he had only been given the chance to see him in between football practices. Now, with sports out of the way, Kaleb had more time to see the rest of the world around him; which included Taylor.

Taylor glanced up from his shoes, shifting away from the pole as his bus pulled up to its stop. He went to the end of the line while the other occupants boarded, slowly inching forward as each person stepped aboard the steaming vessel. He stopped, however, when he noticed something over his shoulder, in Kaleb's direction. Kaleb stiffened, straightening up from off his crutches. He looked away, rubbing the back of his head and trying to think of a way to explain himself through the glass. He looked back up to Taylor, who was now turned towards Kaleb, and offered the gloomy teen a sheepish wave. Taylor ignored this, and instead, began walking towards the street.

Kaleb panicked, not really sure what to do. In all his years of people watching, he had never had someone catch him in the act; let alone confront him about it. He scrambled to think of an excuse as to why he was watching the young blond, when he was stopped, again, by the actions of Taylor. The strange boy had stopped in the middle of the street, holding up a hand to a very annoyed driver in a blue car, halted in the middle of the road. Kaleb blinked, entirely confused, until he saw what Taylor had noticed before him.

Huddled together at the edge of the sidewalk were two children, a boy and a girl, that could not have been older than six years old. Taylor jerked his head to the children, allowing them safe passage across the street before stepping away from the angry man in the little blue car- which sped off in a cloud of steam- and all the other cars that followed behind it. The two little ones clambered aboard the bus under the watchful eye of the music-bound Taylor, then he, himself, climbed up behind them, and sat himself down in a window seat in the middle of the bus.

"Kaleb, honey," Trish called, catching his attention. "Ready?"

"Uh, yeah." Kaleb turned back in time to catch the last glimpse of Taylor and his bus pull away from the stop, leaving nothing but a cloud of steam in its wake. To say he was confused would have been an insufficient deduction, though not entirely wrong. He turned to leave with his mother, conflicted by his negative feeling towards Taylor, and what he had just witnessed before him.

"What's wrong, hun?" Trish asked, noticing her son's sudden change in attitude. "You're quiet."

"Nothing, mom," he replied. "Just thinking."

"About what, dear?" she questioned, waiting patiently while her son searched for the right answer to give her. After a long, silent pause, he finally answered.

"Who's really the bad guy anymore."

__Chapter 6__

The final bell had rung for the day, and as usual, Taylor held back to wait out the rush-hour effect of students slamming into each other to leave the cursed building that was known as Riviera High. He yawned, rubbing away a bit of sleep in his eye and resting his hand across his scarred cheek when he finished. The ticking of the overhead clock tocked by each second, reminding him of his upcoming appointment with his new tutor, Alchemyst, waiting for him in the school's Laboratory.

"Guess I better get going, then." Taylor sighed. He was still irritated at the idea of failing a class and needing a tutor, but he knew that if he dwelt on it, rather than acted, he could never move forward. He sluggishly hung his backpack over his shoulder after pushing himself off of his seat, then made his way towards the Alchemy Hall. His footfalls echoed along the metal lockers lining the hallways, bringing some peace to him as he walked.

Taylor enjoyed the silence of it all. The lack of people gave him room to walk freely, without the worry of running into someone unpleasant. It wasn't hectic, it wasn't crowded, it was just Taylor. Taylor who didn't have to think about escape routes or avoidance techniques, who didn't have to actively practice being invisible in order to keep away from another embarrassment, or even a bruising. Yes, Taylor did, indeed, find peace in the quiet of the hallway, but more so in the solidarity of it.

Taylor slowed his pace slightly, if only to enjoy the silence even further, and to find an excuse to evade his lesson. He hated the idea of close contact with another student, let alone a stranger. As he told Nekko before, social contact was not one of his strengths in the slightest. Just imagining himself sitting side-by-side with some strange being sent shivers down his spine. In the end, though, he pushed forward to the Alchemy hall.

Taylor groaned, irritated with himself, then resumed his earlier, quicker pace. Trying to find a reason to avoid his inevitable meeting was useless. He would never forgive himself if he failed at anything, especially if he had been given the chance to keep it from happening in the first place. He needed to finish what was started. He needed to succeed. More than anything, Taylor longed to be with his mother again, safe in the confines of his home, and in her loving embrace. He would endure it if it meant he could get home any sooner.

When he finally reached the doorway to the laboratory, he stopped, giving himself a moment to breathe and prepare himself for what was to come. Then, taking in a deep breath, he turned the handle and pushed open the door. There, sitting front and center, was the one and only Kaleb Evans. Taylor's face dropped instantly.

"Why is he here?"

Taylor's scowl melted into his hoodie as he shrunk into his shoulders for a moment, looking for a seat far enough away from the jock, but in clear view for Alchemyst when he came. Once spotted, he quietly made his way to his determined seat and sat down, crossing his arms as he leaned back into his chair. Kaleb tried not to be obvious when he watched Taylor enter and sit, but Taylor's keen senses could feel his glances weighing him down.

"Hey," Kaleb offered. Taylor blinked, sneaking a glimpse of his own from the corner of his eyes.

"Hey," he replied, never turning his head. Kaleb fidgeted in his seat, actually twiddling his thumbs.

"What are you doing here?" he finally asked, more curious than demanding. Taylor kept his gaze forward.

"I'm meeting someone," he said curtly.

"Oh." Kaleb looked around the room, looking for another way to speak. "For whom?"

Now Taylor was truly annoyed. He turned to Kaleb, irritation plastered on his face and ingrained in his body language. *"'Whom?' Seriously?"* Taylor's thoughts were raging in his mind. *"Why is he trying to act smart now? And why is he talking to me? WHY IS HE HERE?"*

"Why are you here?" Taylor grumbled, trying to quiet his mind by answering at least one question.

Kaleb shrugged. "I'm waiting for someone too."

"Oh, no," Taylor groaned inwardly. *"He's being tutored too."*

"He never said we'd be in a group," Taylor mumbled, rubbing his face.

"He?" Kaleb inquired. Taylor shook his head, dropping his hand.

"Look, I'm sure you and Alchemyst had an agreement to meet up today, but if you could just stay out of my way, we can both get out of here a whole lot quicker." Kaleb rose his eyebrows.

"Alchemyst?" he said, more of a statement than a question. "I'm not here for Alchemyst," he said, a grin slowly creeping onto his face. "I'm here for someone else."

"Thank my lucky soul." Taylor sighed in quiet relief. "Then we don't have a problem." He returned his stare to the front of the room, but Kaleb wasn't done talking.

"So you're here for Alchemyst?" he asked, rubbing his chin.

Taylor rolled his eyes behind the safety of his hoodie. "What's it to you?"

"Nothing. 'Cept, he's pretty good," Kaleb went on. "Your grades must really suck if you're going to him, Tommy." Taylor stayed quiet, trying not to let Kaleb see him seething at the mention of his loathed nickname. "This the first time you're meeting him? You're in for a surprise."

"Why?" Taylor's curiosity betrayed him, but his annoyance pulled strongly through to his voice. Kaleb merely ignored this.

"He's not what you'd expect… Dallas."

Taylor's scowl melted as his eyes widened slowly, the realization sinking into him like poison as he turned to the jock. *"You're* Alchemyst?" He spoke softly, but incredulously. Kaleb wiggled his fingers at him.

"Hi."

Taylor shook his head. "No." He stood up. "No. I don't know how you did it, but you're not going to fool me." He angrily threw his backpack onto his back and began marching towards the exit.

"Wait, *'fool'* you?" Kaleb tried to stand and follow, but his bulky cast caught in between the legs of the desk and his chair, trapping him momentarily. "What are you talking about?"

"I'm not going to just sit here and take this!" Taylor shouted, slamming the door shut behind him. Taylor stormed down the hallway, headed for home. He was absolutely furious with himself, the situation, and most of all, Kaleb. How he had managed to pose as his tutor, Taylor would never know. Maybe he had intercepted Alchemyst, or maybe they were friends and they thought they could get a good laugh out of it; perhaps they had Mr. Goodson play a role in his prank and give him Kaleb's account- whatever the reason, however he did it, he wouldn't trap Taylor in one of his schemes. Taylor simply wouldn't allow it.

The blonde stormed through the exitting doors that lead to the outside world, marching along the sidewalk in a fury. He detested the situation, re-thinking everything he had done, and would now have to do in order to fix everything. His mind was a whirlwind, thoughts crashing into each other as he planned his next move, each one completely clouded over with frustration.

"What a waste of time."

Kaleb peered over his menu, not really needing it for the meal suggestions as he knew every serving at Tammy's diner. Now it was being put to use as his disguise instead. There was Taylor, sitting at his usual table in the far, back corner, writing a reply to his latest letter. It had been a few days since the tutoring fiasco, and Kaleb wanted to know what the angry teen would be doing instead. He had come to Tammy's directly after school had ended in order to beat Taylor to his destination, and just as Tammy had predicted, Taylor soon followed after from Hector's, more focused on the letter in his hands than anything else.

Again, Kaleb went unnoticed as Taylor ordered his drink and read his letter, making it easy for the lame jock to spy on the moody blond. He watched Taylor's expressions while he read, studying his face and figure, hoping to see a lighter side of the Taylor than the one he was used to. There was a definite change in his behavior, though not for the better.

He seemed tense, unpleased with something, whether it was in the letter or not. As he read, he grew more exasperated, running his hand through his hair when he finished. Taylor rubbed his eyes, holding his head for a moment before giving in and reaching for his notebook to reply. He still seemed hesitant to write, but continued on regardless.

Kaleb took on a look of quiet confusion, pondering the possibilities as to why the young man across the room from him was so distraught. When Taylor had finished writing, he folded his papers and tucked them neatly into a fresh envelope, licking the seam when they were safely stowed away inside. He smudged the stamp on and scribbled down the return address, then, when it was finally ready to be sent away, he gingerly held it in his hands, staring at it carefully. Kaleb's confusion thickened from this, but his attention was replaced when Taylor set the letter to the side and brought out his smaller notebook.

The menu in Kaleb's hands was slipping down further and further as he strained to see what might be inside Taylor's notebook, until he finally noticed that his face was no longer concealed, and righted it back into place.

It was worn down from use, practically falling apart in his hands, and nearly full. Kaleb realized that he had seen this notebook many times before. Taylor carried it with him everywhere, and though he tried to hide it, Kaleb realized that he couldn't remember a time seeing the blond without it.

"You look like you're hiding from an old girlfriend."

"Tammy!" Kaleb jumped, quickly looking to Taylor to see if he had been discovered from his sudden outburst. He breathed a sigh of relief when he saw the blonde still wrapped up inside his notebook, then turned back to the waitress. "Hi," he mumbled.

"Good grief," she said. "Didn't mean to scare you, kid. What in the world are you doing, anyway?"

Kaleb rubbed the back of his head in thought. "I don't... Really know..." he admitted. "I just... Well, I don't have anything better to do, so, I guess I'm spying."

Tammy's face took on a humorous, but skeptical look. "Spying?" she asked. "What for? There's nothing to hide in this town; *especially* not in my diner."

He shook his head, smiling. "Then I guess you could call it people watching."

Tammy crossed her arms, her raspy voice cracking in amusement. "And who exactly is it that you are people-spying on, mister?"

Kaleb looked away, offering a sheepish shrug. "No one especially," he lied. "Just whoever catches my eye." That part, at least, was truthful.

"Mmmhmm," Tammy humored, turning to leave. "I'll bet she's a pretty one, too." Tammy chuckled, leaving Kaleb to continue his 'people-spying' on his own. He looked to Taylor's seat again, finding it empty, and when he searched the diner, caught the last glimpse of him leaving through the front door towards the post office. Kaleb gathered his things to follow suit, but just as he stood to leave, Gerrit and a few other players barged into the diner for their pre-game burger.

"Hey! Captain!" the boys sang, pushing forward to meet him and sit at his booth.

"Hey, guys," Kaleb mumbled, trying to casually glance back at Taylor leaving the post office, and walking out of sight.

"How's it going?"

"I think this one will work," Taylor said. "He goes to the high school across town from us. He wants twelve papers, though, so I'd have to keep it short." Bekah popped a piece of chewy candy into her mouth.

"That's not too bad," she said through gummy squishes. "How much for travel again?"

"Fifty coin for the trolley, five papers for the bus."

"Okay, so eleven papers a day, for five days is-"

"More than I'm willing to spend." Taylor sighed. "Nevermind."

"Now hold on, grumpy," she smacked. "Is he your best option?"

"Rebekah-"

She shuddered at the mention of her full name. "Dude, we've talked about this," she said. "I feel like I'm in trouble; just call me Beck, like you usually do." Taylor rolled his eyes.

"You only feel that way because your real name is usually used when you're in trouble with someone."

"Yeah, like my mother," she grumbled. "Back to the point; you need a tutor, yes?"

"Yes," he droned.

"Then you shouldn't be too picky," she piped. "Who else?"

Taylor scanned through the list of advertising tutors, clicking his teeth and he did so. "There's SugarSugarHoneyHoney," he chided sarcastically. "I'm sure she could help me in no time. Oh wait- sorry, *he* could help me." He plastered on a smile so fake, it hurt to look at.

Bekah smirked. "Get serious."

"Here's one." Taylor clicked open a new profile. "Edgar_Crow, from Carter. That's a city just north of here, I just went there for a job."

"How much?" She started chewing on another piece of gummy candy.

"Bus fare is cheaper there," he told her. "Plus, he only wants eight papers an hour. I think we've got him."

"Great," Bekah smacked. "Send him an e-mail too." Taylor cocked a brow at her.

"You're eager to get this done," he droned. "Am I boring you?"

"No," she replied with a smile. "I just want your next chapter up."

Kaleb was enjoying the shade of the trees when he spotted Taylor leaving school much later than anyone else. The grounds were quiet now, without a soul in sight, save for Taylor's. Like Taylor, Kaleb had stayed behind not only to avoid the crowds, but he had agreed to work on a project with Kara that afternoon. When he had finished with her, he dawdled behind to enjoy the outdoors, and now, he was given the chance to spy on the blonde again.

Kaleb armed himself with his crutches and clicked after him, keeping well behind him so as not to be noticed. Thankfully, as usual, Taylor had his headphones on, so he couldn't hear Kaleb clicking along far behind him, and again, his hood was up, blocking his peripheral vision should he decide to glance about him.

"Why am I doing this?" Kaleb wondered. He thought about all the possible reasons as to why he was following the boy who hated him as much as he hated Taylor; something to do for exercise, to kill his boredom, or simply to satisfy his curiosity. Any of these were a factor, of that there was no doubt, but he felt in his heart that they weren't the real reason. Still, he clicked along, following Taylor as he walked towards the town.

He was about to turn around the edge of a corner building when he saw Taylor lean against the weather station for the trolley. Kaleb stopped, pulling himself back behind the building to lean around it in order to see Taylor. It didn't take long for the trolley to show up and take Taylor away, and when it did, Kaleb couldn't help but feel some disappointment. He sighed to himself, wondering why it bothered him so much that he had missed out yet again on where Taylor was going.

"Guess my curiosity is getting to be a problem with nothing else to do," Kaleb thought to himself. He shrugged, then quietly turned to leave and head for home.

Taylor's forehead was beginning to bruise from all the times he had slapped himself, or simply banged his head on his school desk from frustration. Already, he had gone through three different tutors from three different schools and not one of them could teach him anything. The first was too advanced, the second, too dimwitted, and the third, the latest contestant, was too fast.

"How, by the mighty soul's power, did I end up with a bunch of rejects?" Taylor groaned to himself. The classroom was quiet with the absence of students, leaving Taylor to brood over his thoughts on his own. He laid his head on his desk, thankful for the silence, but irritated all the same. He had been searching for a suitable tutor for a little over a week, and he was even farther from his goal now than when he had started. He huffed, frustrated with this fact, turning his head on it's side to stare aimlessly at the door. He stayed this way for a few minutes longer before sitting up to leave.

Taylor slowly trudged through the Alchemy hall, considering his options for a better tutor since his lesson from the day before had gone south. Truly, he was tired of it all. He was tired of trying to communicate with strange, new people, tired of traveling to different towns on multiple forms of transportation, tired of being disappointed when his efforts were wasted, but most of all, he was tired of wasting his time. He wanted a quick and easy answer, and when he thought about it, he figured that was what everybody wanted. It was a normal, human thing to want, and he couldn't be partial to this feeling, no matter how hard he tried.

"In the end, I'm really no different," Taylor sighed to himself. He stopped abruptly, sliding his pack off his shoulders to dig out his headphones. When the bright white plastic could be seen, Taylor stopped again. He had heard something popping somewhere in a room close by. He looked around the hall, but not a person was in sight. This bothered Taylor; with this being the Alchemy hall, and he being the only person there, if someone had been dumb enough to leave a burner on, or something equally stupid that might hurt the school, he was certain that he would get the blame for it.

He listened again, trying to pinpoint the sound coming from a room two doors down from him, and when he looked closely, he could see that the door in question was cracked slightly ajar. Taylor shoved his music piece back into his backpack, then quietly approached the open doorway to clean up whatever mess that had been left behind. When his hand reached for the handle, however, he stopped.

Through the partially opened door, he saw something he wasn't expecting to see. More over, *someone.* There was Kaleb, dressed in a lab apron, gloves and goggles, measuring a purple liquid in a test tube. He held it high to the light to inspect it before pouring its contents into a flask filled with a green fluid bubbling from the fire beneath it. When the two substances combined, the popping sound resounded around the room yet again. The source of this sound came from the solidified foam balls that popped up and out of the flask, spilling over onto the table.

Kaleb grinned, picking up a ball to inspect it as well, pinching it a few times only to have it fluff back into its original shape. He set it down to write his findings on a clipboard placed not too far from the workstation, then gathered the balls up into a beaker. Once all the foam balls were packed tightly inside, he reached around to the fridge behind him and pulled out a jug of distilled water. He filled a second beaker halfway with the water, then poured it into the first beaker with the foam balls. The balls instantly fizzled and deflated when touched by the water, turning into a pinkish-brown froth that eventually melted into liquid form.

"Cool," Kaleb grinned, completely lost in his experiment. He took a moment to admire his handiwork, then returned to the clipboard again to record what he had just discovered, his smile still prominent upon his face. Unbeknownst to both Kaleb and

95

Taylor, the first concoction of purple and green was still sitting above the open flame; boiling.

Taylor jumped back a step when suddenly, the bubbling liquid shot out of the beaker like a geyser. Kaleb had taken quick action to avoid any drops that tried to touch him, diving over a chair to slide under an overhanging counter, only to watch in awe as the fiery lava slam against the ceiling, and splatter down across his work station.

"Woah!" Kaleb laughed. Taylor composed himself, stepping up to the door again to watch. Slowly, Kaleb crawled out from beneath the counter, careful to avoid any puddles near him, then stood to gawk at the damage. "Well that was unexpected," he mumbled. He looked about the room, looking for something in particular. He surprised Taylor when he picked up the clipboard that had gone flying when Kaleb dove for cover, and wrote down, most likely, the events of what had just happened.

Taylor was completely dumbfounded by this, proven by his open mouth. When Kaleb finished with the clipboard and began cleaning up the mess, Taylor couldn't keep his jaw off the floor. He watched as Kaleb carefully disposed of the chemical waste, even going so far as to take a mop to the ceiling. Taylor backed away from the door, still watching whatever could be seen, then shook his head to make sense of things. He turned to leave, still shaking his head, but walked away nonetheless.

Silently, Taylor left the school, playing the same scene over and over again in his mind as he walked home. Nothing could pry his attention from his thoughts; not the warmth of the sun on his skin, nor the rustling of the wind through his hair, not even the children riding their bikes through the streets could keep him away from his thoughts. He had even forgotten that his music was buried deep inside his pack instead of wrapped around his ears. He was more focused on disproving what he had just seen. He intensely scoured over every detail, making sure not to miss a single moment that might prove untrustworthy, and when he finished, he restarted the process all over again.

Nothing he went over could prove to him that Kaleb was a fake. Kaleb had shown himself to be, without a doubt, an *intelligent* being. At least in alchemy, that is. For as long as he could remember, Taylor had always imagined Kaleb to be just as dull in the skull as the rest of his cronies, simply because not one of them could even spell their teacher's name properly. They were lazy, and stupid, and with Kaleb being their ring leader, it only made sense that he be just as imbecilic. He certainly acted that way.

Kaleb was constantly joking around, never taking anything seriously, and from what Taylor saw of him in class, never considered it important to pay attention. It was always about Taylor; embarrassing him at every chance, bugging him to make him squirm, picking at him to watch him break- if he could make him. None of it really mattered. It was all a game to Kaleb.

From the experiment, though, Taylor didn't see that. He saw Kaleb be serious for once, and more importantly, responsible. He watched Kaleb respect the academic side of him rather than the foolish jock he usually was. Never, in a million lifetimes, would Taylor ever consider Kaleb the scientific type, though with the explosion and further pondering as evidence, it was simply too difficult for him to deny it as a fact.

Not once had Taylor ever seen Kaleb fear his homework papers when he passed them to him. Instead, he laughed it off as he passed the assignments along to the person behind him. Before Taylor could turn back around in his seat, he would always catch Kaleb as he hunched over his work to scribble down the answers. Taylor had always assumed that he was just fooling around, as usual, but now that he thought about it, it was possible that Kaleb was writing down the correct answers.

Aside from that, when called upon in class, he would always produce the correct answer. Kaleb would even ask insightful questions from time to time- which, at the time of asking, sounded to Taylor as though he were wasting time to avoid more dreadful lectures or just showing off to the rest of the class. The teachers never seemed to mind him, and-

Taylor stopped abruptly in the middle of the sidewalk with a sudden epiphany; one that he almost slapped himself for. Kaleb couldn't play football with failing grades.

It was so simple, so obvious now that Taylor had to physically resist the urge to hit his head repeatedly for missing such a huge truth in the first place. Instead, he ran his hands through his hair, sighing long and slow as he curled into his chest to hold his head. He didn't know what bothered him more: the fact that he had wasted so much time because of this, or the fact that Kaleb would be teaching him now.

"Ahhg!" he growled aloud, completely frustrated. "This is so messed up," he mumbled. Taylor dropped his elbows, locking his fingers behind his neck as he leaned his head back to look at the sky. He sighed again, closing his eyes and continuing forward. Eventually, he let his arms fall to his side and nestled his hands in his pockets as he strode up his walkway to his front steps.

Taylor paused a moment to listen to the front door. Hearing nothing, he entered his home, quietly closing the door behind him. His father was asleep in his chair again, bottles strewn about him from various stores. Taylor stepped closer to him to remove a haphazardly dangling bottle from his father's hands and gently set it on the side table next to him for when he awoke. Taylor took a moment to stare at his father, seeing his tired face and worn body up close. He rose a hand to move some hair from his face, but stopped in fear of waking him.

Taylor pulled back from his father, shifted his pack, then headed for the stairs to his room. Just as he was about to reach the first step, a whistling bottle came flying at him from behind, exploding on the wall too close to his head for his liking. Taylor whipped around to see his father awakened, and prepared for battle with another bottle.

"Sand scum!" Mr. Thompson slurred under his breath.

"Dad, no!" Taylor tried. "It's just me!" Wasted breath. Friedreich raised the bottle to fire at the boy again, missing just as the teen dodged away from it. He threw his pack off for better agility moments before Friedreich charged after him, ramming him into the beer stained wall with his shoulder. The smaller male was crushed beneath him, the air whooshing out of his lungs from this blow.

"Dad…" the boy wheezed, "Dad, listen-"

But Friedreich wouldn't listen. He grabbed the teen by the collar, lifting him off the ground with the support of the wall behind him, then rammed his knee right into his gut. A resounding cough escaped the young man, gasping for air as Friedreich dropped him to the floor to kick him against the wall.

"Sneak up on me!" he screamed. "Not on your life, peice of shit!"

Kick after kick, insult after insult, the younger man crumpled further into submission as much as he could, knowing that there was no escape if he tried. Slowly, the kicks started to fade as Mr. Thompson began to awaken completely, seeing the room he was in. He stopped mid-kick, his foot hovering over the battered body which slowly revealed to him that it was his son, Taylor, as he peeked out through the gaps of his arms that were protecting his head. Mr.Thompson sighed, lowering his foot to the ground, still staring at his son.

"Clean this shit up," he murmured, motioning to the broken glass and stained wall, then turning to leave the room entirely. Taylor stayed frozen in his protective huddle, shivering from pain and frustration. He curled tighter, breathing heavily to return the air to his lungs and to calm his nerves all at once. He clutched the back of his head, grabbing handfuls of his hair, and hiding his face from the reality that he was in a terrible situation.

"I don't care anymore," he thought. *"Just get me out."*

Chapter 7

Taylor never approached anyone, and he never let anyone approach him. He stayed invisible, stuck to the shadows, never did anything to stand out. He did whatever he could to avoid people at all costs, always ducking his head at any sign of human contact. So when he walked up to Kaleb in the hallway before school that morning, needless to say, things were a bit awkward.

Kaleb blinked in surprise when Taylor stepped up to him, shoulders scrunched and his usual, foul grimace morphed into what he assumed was discomfort. He stopped within an arm's length of him, gripping his backpack and shifting on his feet. He had his head low, though it looked to Kaleb as though he had to actively remind himself that eye contact was proper in a conversation. He said nothing, but his mouth worked to keep moving in effort to find the words he wished to use.

"Good morning?" Kaleb offered with a smile. Taylor stiffened.

"Morning," he returned, then coughed to loosen his muscles a little before speaking again. "I uh," he started, running a hand over the side of his head, tangling his fingers in his hair. "I was wondering if… I mean, I just…" Kaleb waited silently while Taylor struggled to speak to him, listening expectantly to his words, jumbled as they were. Finally, Taylor sighed, slightly drooping in defeat and straightening up again to face Kaleb head on. "Look, can you tutor me… Again...?"

Kaleb's grin broadened into a humored smile. "*That's* what was so hard to ask?" he chuckled. Taylor grimaced to the side, sliding out of eye contact once again.

"Are you gonna do it or not?" he asked.

"Sure," Kaleb grinned. "If you think you can handle it."

Taylor cringed, turning his eyes back to glare at Kaleb but keeping his head locked in place. "Don't get cocky, *you son of a bitch*."

Kaleb's smile dropped with his crutches when he lunged for Taylor, grabbing him by the shirt and slamming his back against the lockers beside him. The students walking about the hallway stopped to see the commotion, silencing only enough to let the whispers and shocked glances take throne. Taylor's backpack had slipped off his shoulder when Kaleb grabbed him, and now lay on the floor with Kaleb's crutches, giving Taylor little room to escape the cold metal behind him, and the angered Kaleb before him.

"*Don't you* ever *say that again*," Kaleb threatened, mere inches from Taylor's face. He was so disgusted with himself and with Taylor, letting his thoughts slip into verbal form if only to let him know.

"I can't believe I thought for one second that you were-"

"I'm what?" Taylor hissed back. "Say it!"

"You're despicable!" Kaleb growled.

"What tipped you off?" Taylor scoffed.

Taylor glared back into Kaleb's steely gaze, saying nothing. Kaleb glared right back at Taylor, mirroring the hatred he saw in the blonde's eyes. He vaguely felt the smaller boy gripping his wrists in return, but it barely registered in comparison to the fiery burn of their intense stare off. Finally, Kaleb roughly shoved Taylor to release him, gaining no further ground as he was already pressed tight against the lockers. Their eyes were still locked on one anothers, but it wasn't until Kaleb had let go of Taylor that he realized Taylor had been on his toes when he was holding him in his death grip.

"You alright Kaleb?"

Gerrit had appeared, holding up the crutches behind Kaleb, but neither Kaleb nor Taylor would break eye contact. Finally, Kaleb grabbed the crutches from Gerrit to storm off, saying not a word. He was too furious to speak, and his fury emanated off of him like death, making the students step aside as he clicked past. By now, teachers were wandering the hall, looking for the problem, or even a witness, but finding none. Either by loyalty or fear, no one spoke of the events that had unfolded in the hallway.

All day long, Kaleb sat in his foul mood. He did not speak. He did not listen. His friends didn't even bother talking to him, as dealing with the dreadful form he took on was too much to bare, even in a group. In each class, he sat quietly, replaying the events in his head, and growing ever more disgusted with each re-run. Even the sky was dreary, showering the school with heavy sheets of rain and broody thunder all morning long.

Finally, gym class had rolled around and, due to the rain, it would be held indoors for the day, playing dodgeball. Kaleb, of course, was not allowed to play, which didn't help his sour mood in the slightest. He didn't even bother changing in the locker room with the other students. Instead, he climbed up to the highest bleacher in the gym room to watch the game from afar.

Kaleb watched his classmates enter the gym, chatting and laughing amongst themselves as they gathered in the large, echoey room. It didn't take coach Abernathy long to rally the chittering high schoolers in order for a game of dodgeball, and soon, the game commenced. Rubber balls were sent flying across the court in search of a target to hit, and once its duty was done, a brand new player would grab and throw it all over again. Those who were hit, either left the arena glumly, or retreated quickly.

Kaleb saw Gerrit draw himself closer to some of his other friends who happened to be on his team, and they to him. In total, Gerrit, Daniel, Jason, and Max had gathered into a somewhat spacey huddle, each with a ball in one hand, and their target in sight. One by one, each boy threw his ball in a rapid fire attack at one offending player in particular: Taylor.

The young blonde was pelted by ricocheting rubber, having to physically step back from the force of the balls that hit his upper body and torso. The four perpetrators who hit him rejoiced their victory with fist pumps and high fives. Taylor, on the other hand, glared back at the boys, shaking his head as he walked to the bleachers.

Kaleb couldn't help but grin, albeit it be a short one. He watched Taylor take a seat on the sidelines, far away from anyone else who had been tagged out already. He ran a hand through his hair, sighing, but stopping short to wince and touch his ribs. He let his hand drop as he shook his head again, mumbling something he couldn't hear.

"Might have gone a little too far with that," Kaleb guessed. Still, he couldn't help but feel that Taylor deserved it. The game soon ended, followed by two more with similar endings for Taylor. Even some of the members on Taylor's team would pitch in, blocking his view from the opposing boys by standing in front of him just long enough before jumping out of the way to avoid getting hit themselves. Some would even 'accidentally' hit Taylor in the sidelines, pretending to be aiming for another player standing in front of him, who would then step aside to let the flying ball take it's course.

Kaleb frowned, debating whether or not he liked this method of punishment. At last, coach Abernathy blew his final whistle, ending the class for time to change before the bell rang, but not before one last fly-ball could miss Daniel and hit Taylor instead. Rather than following the other classmates to the locker rooms, though, Taylor stayed behind to gather the balls and place them in their bin.

"Thanks, Thompson," Coach Abernathy barked, receiving a nod from the teen. He dragged along, taking his time as he picked up the rubber balls and tossed them carelessly into the large bin, all the while being watched by Kaleb, high in the bleachers.

"You could've at least *tried* to fight back," he called, startling the boy below. Taylor looked up to see Kaleb hidden in the high corner, and instantly threw on a scowl. He gathered the last handful of balls and dumped them into the bin just as the bell rang out for the end of class, giving Taylor signal to leave the gym to go get changed.

"Whatever," Kaleb mumbled, then he gathered himself over his crutches, and left as well. For the rest of the day, it was quiet. No excitement to follow after gym class, and no contact with Taylor. Kaleb wouldn't even look at him... Not with him knowing, at least.

At lunch, he would throw glances at the gloomy boy only to quickly return to his food. In the halls, he stared straight ahead as Taylor passed by, and grimaced after he had passed. During class, Kaleb couldn't help but glare at the back of Taylor's head- mostly because he sat in front of him, but the rest was out of frustration. By the time the final bell had rung, Kaleb was ready to snap.

By now, the storm had passed, and students were eager to leave- except for Kaleb. He clicked down the hallway, passing student after student as he strode towards the Art department in search of Kara. He knew he would find her in her usual place, setting up her work station in preparation for a new masterpiece, yet when he entered the painter's studios, it was empty. He clicked over to her designated work station and sat down on one of her stools, waiting for her. He didn't have to wait long, and when she entered, her usual sarcastic charm radiated in her greeting.

"Oh, dear," she said, placing her hands on her hips. "It's back." Kaleb didn't feel like playing along, glaring at her from under his brows yet keeping his mouth shut to stay out of trouble. "That bad, huh?" she asked, leaving the doorway and heading towards her cubby. "I figured I'd see you today. What with this morning and all." She dragged out her tools from her cubby, bringing them to her workstation with a heavy *thunk* before turning to her friend. "Talk."

"He's a jerk," blurted Kaleb. "All he ever does is mope around, bring the mood down and act like he's better than everyone- I can't stand it!"

"So what did he do this morning?" She began tying her wrap around her waist as she spoke. Kaleb was fuming.

"He came up to me asking for help, then he went and insulted my mother right after I agreed to it."

Kara stopped, hands still tightening the knot behind her. "Wait, what?"

Kaleb huffed, looking to the ceiling before smothering his face with his hand. "He called me a 'son of a bitch.'" He sighed, knowing he was being given a dirty look from Kara.

"We've talked about this," she scolded flatly. "He was talking about *you*, not your mother. That's the problem with insults," she went on. "People don't take the time to listen to words and understand their meaning. Ignorant idiots. All of them. And you're no better for falling for it."

Kaleb's annoyed eyes popped open at her through his fingers. He knew she was right, yet he didn't want to give in so easily. He had been brooding all day long; he didn't want it to go to waste. Still, as much as he tried thinking of a rebuttal, he couldn't find anything suitable enough to back his argument up. Kara gave him an annoyed look of her own.

"You know I'm right," she said, placing her fists on her hips. "Besides, you probably deserved it."

That triggered it. Kaleb shot up from his seat, slamming his hands down on the high work table so hard, he rattled the contents resting atop it. Kara cocked a brow at him, challenging him where he stood.

"I didn't do anything." His growl slowly rose into an enraged shout. "He was the one who *started it*!"

Kara's defiance turned to skeptical boredom. "Seriously?" she droned. "How *old* are you?"

Kaleb was ready to break someone in half, but he knew better than to get her started on a rampage. He was already giving her enough material to work with, so a lecture was no doubt coming his way, but he simply didn't have the energy to deal with her in full-battle mode.

"Quit whining for a minute and consider the possibilities, here." Thus, the beginning of her lecture. "Ever think about *why* he's so moody? Why he doesn't like you?" She leaned over the table, supporting herself on her long, lean arms. "I swear, every time I see you two, you're pushing his buttons one way or another."

"What are you talking about?" Kaleb interjected, truly unknowing, but still irritated.

"It would take a complete idiot not to notice!" she shouted. "I don't think I've ever seen you be serious around him- you're *always* picking at him, and your buddies don't help much either."

"What?!" Kaleb was getting angry again. "What 'buddies?' They've got nothing to do with-"

"You truly are blind."

"I am not!"

"Then prove it!" Kara stared down her friend, just waiting for him to fight back. When he didn't, she lifted herself up from the table to rest one fist on her hip, and the other pointing to the door. "Go find him," she ordered. "You might still be able to make it if you hurry."

Kaleb glared right back at her. "And what am I supposed to do if I do?"

Her stare intensified. "You have plenty of time to figure that one out when you get there."

Kaleb looked away, stewing in his own rage. After a moment, he finally calmed down enough to speak again.

"Why are you doing this, Kar?" he asked quietly. Kara dropped her pointing arm to fold it over her chest.

"Somebody's got to."

Kaleb lazily clicked down the sidewalk, trying to avoid any puddles and still simmering over the little spat he had with Kara back in the Art Department. As much as he loved her, he could really hate her guts sometimes. *"That woman is the only one I know who pushes buttons,"* he thought. He started looking back at what had happened, dissecting her words and trying to find meaning- or fault- in what it was that she had said. He let his mind wander, finding nothing of interest.

"Your buddies don't help much either."

"Tch," Kaleb scoffed under his breath. "They help me just fine." He thought back to the fight he had that morning with Taylor, how Gerrit had been there to hand him his crutches, or to back him up if he needed it. He even considered the people who had witnessed him lose his temper, and how they hadn't ratted him out to any teachers- *especially* with Mr. Sutherland on the prowl.

He didn't know what she meant about being a jerk to him either. Taylor had never said anything to Kaleb about being bothered. He never said anything at all. If Taylor had half a mind- which Kaleb knew he had plenty of- he would have said something by now. Kaleb simply could not understand why Taylor hated him so much. He didn't understand why he hated people. Not once had he ever seen Taylor interact with another human being since the day they had met.

Kaleb slowed even further. Taylor never interacted with people in a fun way. He always, *always* chose to be alone. The more he thought about it, the more he realized how Taylor would always push back, how he would never say anything to people, how he always *tried* to be alone. Why anyone would choose that way of life was beyond Kaleb.

"Maybe it's got something to do with his mother," Kaleb thought.

Up ahead, he saw two small children quivering at the end of the curb. They looked way too young to be alone, no more than four at the very least. The smaller one was a boy wearing a white and blue striped shirt, picking at his hands, trying to figure out a solution to their problem. The bigger one was a girl with golden curls and a dress that matched the boy's, who turned to Kaleb when she saw him and began waving him down.

"'Scuze me! Can you please help us, mis-ter?" she asked, her chubby baby cheeks getting in the way of her words.

"I don't see why not," Kaleb smiled, raising his voice to a pleasing tone. "What can I do for you?" T

he little girl turned back around and pointed to the other end of the street. "We're not 'loud to cross the street without a grown-up," she said, absentmindedly looking across the street and twirling a curl in between her fingers. "And Glenn's gotta-he hasta go, go potty."

"Oh, I see," Kaleb said, looking at the barren road. "How did you cross the street last time?" The girl frowned.

"We were playing with Jason, but he was too fast."

Kaleb nodded. "That is a problem, huh?"

The girl nodded in return. "Yeahp. So, can you stop the cars if they come? We're too little."

Kaleb smiled. "Well I am nice and big. How about we go together? I need to cross the street too." The girl blinked at Kaleb, completely baffled.

"Do you hafta go potty too?" she asked. Kaleb couldn't help but chuckle.

"I guess I do." He bent down on his good knee, stretching his cast out in front of him after removing his crutches from his underarms. "My name's Kaleb. What's yours?"

"Noel," she sang bashfully, twirling her dress side to side. "And his name is, that's, that's Glenn." She pointed to the boy at the end of the curb, who waved back when he heard mention of his name and offered a quiet "Hi." Kaleb waved back to Glenn, his smile still stuck to his face.

"How about we make it a race?" Kaleb asked, receiving an excited gasp from Noel."Well, are you ready?"

Noel bounced in giddy delight as Kaleb stood up to meet the two children at the edge of the curb. "Okay, first thing's first," Kaleb said, looking to the children.

"Look out for cars, right?" Noel piped, looking up to Kaleb's grinning face excitedly.

"That's right," he said. "So, left?"

All three looked to the left in an exaggerated manner, with even Kaleb holding a hand up to his forehead in efforts to see farther down the empty road.

"Now right! Right!" Noel joyously bounced. Again, all three looked to the right of the street, this time, Noel nearly bent in half trying to see over the deserted street.

"All clear," Kaleb said. "Ready?" The children crouched in anticipation. "Set... G-oh, would you look at the time?" Both Noel and Glenn jumped onto the street, but came scrambling back when they realized they had been fooled.

"Kay-leeeb!" Noel whined, but Kaleb could only chuckle.

"Alright, alright, GO!" All three left the curb this time, all laughing, all racing to the other end as fast as they could.

"Hurry! Hurry! Hurry!" Kaleb yelled, slowing behind the two squealing children to chase after them. "Better hurry, I'm catching up!" Kaleb laughed. "I'm gonna getch'ya!"

Noel was the first to reach the other end of the street, screaming with delight, with Glenn following soon after. "Aw, man!" Kaleb shouted, touching the curb with a crutch in last place. "I lost!"

"I didn't! I won, I won!" Noel smiled brightly.

Kaleb smiled back. "Oh well. At least it was fun, right?"

Noel nodded vigorously. "Yeahp!"

Glenn wasn't too upset about winning second, he was more focused on tugging at Noel's dress. "Nell," he whined. "Gotsta go."

Noel looked to the smaller boy. "Go where?" she asked. Then, seeing his dance, "OH! Oh, we hasta go so he can go potty!" She turned to Kaleb for her final goodbyes. "Bye-bye, Kay-leb!" They waved, then turned to run down the sidewalk to the first house at the edge of the block. Kaleb watched them go, making sure they went inside the house before continuing on with a smile.

"That was fun," Kaleb thought, passing the house with his ever-growing smile. *"Why Taylor can't see that I'll never-"* Kaleb stopped, turning to look back at the house.

"Oh." Kaleb breathed, thinking back to the night at the bookstore in Carter. It hadn't been Noel and Glenn that Taylor helped to cross the street, and it wasn't in the same way, but he had helped a couple of kids get home safely, the same as Kaleb had not even seconds before. Kaleb's face crumpled in on itself into a bizarre frown.

"Crap," he muttered, thinking of how Kara would smear this all over his face. She was right again. Maybe Taylor wasn't all that bad. Kaleb sighed, continuing his quest towards home.

"Maybe I can catch him at the bridge again," he wondered. *"If not, then I guess I'll find him tomorrow."* Kaleb clicked forward with a new steadfast pace, hoping to find the moody teen while he still felt this moment of clarity. He soon left the South Neighborhood and made his way through its bridge to Midway Park towards the bridge leading home- the same bridge Taylor used. As he got closer, Kaleb could see that it was vacant of any soul, let alone Taylor's.

At last, Kaleb reached the bridge, panting from his efforts. He searched the bridge, the park, the surrounding neighborhoods, but still, no sight of Taylor. Kaleb couldn't help but feel a bit disappointed, though he knew how futile his efforts were in the first place. He puffed out a long stretch of breath, leaning against the railings when he remembered seeing Taylor popping into the creek the last time he saw him here.

"Better than nothing."

Kaleb shrugged, then settled in comfortably to the stone railing behind him to wait for Taylor. A chill in the wind caught Kaleb by surprise, sending shivers down his whole body.

"About time to get my jacket."

Kaleb smiled, rubbing his arms for warmth. His team jacket was one of his most prized possessions, having earned it for his loyalty. No other member on the team had one, as it was law for the team members to have stayed in football for four full seasons in a row. Kaleb was the only one who fit the bill.

For four seasons in a row, he had been given the title of captain, a combined total by both middle and high school. Every year, whether in season or not, he had sat with the coaches as they reviewed their plans for action. He had gone to every practice with enough vigor to set the school ablaze. He had worked every game, every member to their fullest potential, earning win after win, whether the game counted towards their record or not. Indeed, there was no other member more devoted to the team than Kaleb Evans, and his jacket was proof of that.

When it was presented to him at the end of his first high school year, he was so proud of himself, he wore it for the first Summer month. He would have worn it year round if he hadn't made himself sick with heat stroke. After that, his mother locked it away in the attic with the rest of the winter clothes. Now, with the autumn breeze coming through, he would be allowed to reunite with his jacket, and again, wear it proudly down the halls of Riviera High for his fifth season as captain.

Kaleb smiled to himself. With this year, and the next, he would be given an even higher honor. Completing six years of service would not only give him six patches to sew onto his sleeve, but also give him the chance to earn his name in the school District's hall of fame. Six years of playing was a piece of cake; six years of being captain was the cherry on top. One more year, and he would be the very first player to have the most consecutive runs as captain in the District's history.

He would be given a plaque, a trophy, and the head seamstress would even be designing a brand new patch to sew onto his jacket. Most of all, he would be the town legend. No one could accuse him of being unpatriotic if he had the status to back him up. In such a small town, he wouldn't have to defend himself against anyone; his neighbors would do it for him.

Kaleb yawned, noticing the golden glow of the setting sun. *"A little bit longer,"* he decided. *"Then I'll head home."*

He settled against the railing again, relaxing into a slouch as he watched the clouds roll by. He closed his eyes after a while, listening to the sounds of the lively park. The birds tweeted their lovesong to one another, the squirrels chattered as they searched for food, and an extra bit of water from the earlier rain tumbled over river stones in the creek bed below. Amidst all of this, however, there was another sound.

Kaleb couldn't turn around completely to see the source, but he knew it wasn't natural all the same. Pebbles tapping together as pressure was quickly applied and removed, dirt slipping down the miniature cliff's edge, then finally, the rustling of branches being pushed aside to let a bigger beast through.

Just as Kaleb had expected, out popped Taylor from the shrubbery, shaking leaves from his hair. When he looked up to find Kaleb sitting nonchalantly against the railing waiting for him, naturally, his face fell into it's usual frown.

"Hey," Kaleb offered, holding a hand up from his arm resting against the railing in greeting. Taylor shrugged his backpack higher onto his shoulders, saying nothing, only staring at the jock in his way.

"How're your ribs?" Kaleb asked, remembering gym that day. Taylor's frown deepened.

"Come to gloat?" he asked. Kaleb shook his head, turning it to watch the creek over the other side of the railing.

"Nah, that's not it," he muttered. "Just got some sense knocked into me, is all." Taylor's glare became quizzical, if only just. "Look, just do me a favor?" Kaleb asked. "If we're gonna do this, then don't call me the son of a bitch, alright?"

"'*The* son of a bitch?'" Taylor asked, cocking a brow. Kaleb whipped his head back to the blonde, realizing what he had said, then dropped his gaze to the flooring beneath him, rubbing the back of his head. He shifted his feet, then turned back to Taylor.

"I'm sorry, alright?" he said, not wanting to explain himself. Though, from Taylor's response, he didn't have to.

"Guess I'll have to call you something else, then," he said, earning a smirk from Kaleb.

"What's wrong with Kaleb?"

"Don't set yourself up again."

"Right." Kaleb couldn't help but snicker a little. As annoying as he was, he couldn't deny Taylor of his quick wit when he needed it. "Tomorrow then?"

"Tomorrow."

"He apologised?!" Bekah couldn't believe what had just been said to her, but Taylor was anything but a liar.

"Yeah," he said passively, not really focussing on anything as he sprawled out in his chair. "I don't know what to make of it either."

"Are you going to go?" she asked, actually breathless from wonder.

"Yeah," Taylor repeated, still unattentive and loopy. "I meet him tomorrow after school." Bekah's eyes went wide.

"WHY?" The exasperation in her voice caught Taylor's otherwise spacey gaze. He looked at her, then sat up in his chair, rubbing his jaw as he leaned in to fill the computer screen, his elbows supporting his frame.

"I'll tell you why," he muttered. "In the past week and a half alone, I have spent well over a hundred and eighty papers traveling to and from all these so-called tutors, and having to pay each of them for their 'services.' That's why," he emphasized.

Bekah leaned back in surprise. "Oh," was all she could muster. "Geez," she went on when she regained herself, pushing her glasses up her nose. "How much do you have left?"

"Around four hundred," he replied. "Just barely enough to get me to the coast." He stopped for a small shadow of a smile. "I'll be getting my border's pass this weekend, though," he said. "After that, I can cross the border anytime I want."

Bekah piped up with a smile of her own. "That's great!" she nearly yelled. "Does your mom know?"

Taylor shook his head. "I just sent my letter a couple days ago; I don't think it's reached her yet."

Bekah slouched slightly, a small frown tugging at her lips. "I wish there was a way for you to talk with your mom," she admitted. "It's not right that you talk to me more than your own blood."

Taylor's eyes fluttered to his desk, agreeing with her silently. If it were possible, he would have bought his mother a computer and talked with her every day, but with the dangers of bringing even her name home, that wouldn't be possible- not unless he wanted to send his father deeper into his depression. That, as well as the fact that communicational technology couldn't stretch that far across the Great Waters.

Although Bekah and Taylor were separated by mountains, meadows and other stretches of landscapes, they were allowed to communicate to one another through underground wires stretched all throughout Alteria. Cross-country communication simply was not possible with an ocean in the way, and there wasn't a suitable form of connecting the wires safely in any constructed contraption imaginable, though many were tried. Boats, buoys, underwater construction; you name it, they've tried it. Until someone could figure out another solution, the fastest way of multi-country communication was by paper letters across a boat.

Taylor longed to hear his mother's voice again, to see her smiling face- even if only through a screen and speaker. For now, though, he would have to settle for hand-written letters, once a week, every week, until they could once again be reunited with one another. He would do anything it took to get to her any faster; even if it meant studying with his nemesis.

"It's better this way," Taylor said, bringing the subject back to Kaleb. "Less travel means more time and more money. I can save more papers, spend more time with Bubbie afterwards, and hopefully, get my grades up before it's too late. Maybe even some more work. It'll keep the old man off my back, at least."

Bekah smirked halfheartedly, also gazing into space from atop her fist.

"If you say so."

"So," Kaleb said, plopping his backpack onto the ground beside him. "Where do we start first?"

Taylor was quiet, still apprehensive of Kaleb, no matter the intention. Kaleb slipped off his leather jacket as well, carefully placing it across the back of his chair, then motioned to the one next to him.

"Well, go on," he said. Taylor stiffly stepped up to the seat next to Kaleb, pulling it out to sit, but also making sure to slightly pull it away from the jock to put more space between them.

"You said you have some papers that need to be worked on, right?" Kaleb asked. "Why don't we start there?" Taylor stayed quiet, bending over in his seat to pull out a small, but thick stack of papers given to him by Mr. Finnigan for any extra help at all.

"Ooh…" Kaleb bit his lip. "That's a lot."

"Are you sure you can help?" Taylor asked, still unconvinced. Kaleb dropped his shoulders and leaned in to the desk before speaking.

"Look," he started. "I may not be what you thought I was, but that doesn't mean I'm a superhero." He paused for a moment, thinking. "I can help you, but only if you let me. So can you do that?" He looked Taylor dead in the eye. "Can you trust me?"

Taylor couldn't escape Kaleb's questioning stare, but then he realized that he needed to take this moment to study him; a task that wasn't at all difficult. He noticed that Kaleb's eyes held no sarcasm, or trickery. For once, there wasn't a glimmer hiding away the jester's foolishness, nor was there any playfulness asking for some fun at Taylor's expense. His eyes were truly honest, just waiting on him to answer.

Taylor broke eye contact, taking a deep, silent breath, then nodded his reply. "Yeah," he mumbled, digging out a pencil from his pack.

"Alright, then," Kaleb said. "Let's start with your homework."

"Knock, knock," Miss Hart chimed. "Got a second?" Kaleb had just helped Taylor finish his second homework assignment and an extra credit paper when Miss Hart had poked her curly head into the laboratory where they were studying.

"What are you still doing here?" Taylor asked.

Miss Hart shrugged, casually gliding into the doorway. "Had some extra papers to grade," she remarked, crossing her arms. "A lot of my students are *dumb*, did you know that?"

Taylor rolled his eyes to the sky with a huff. "You're not supposed to say that," he reminded her.

"Yeah, but it's true." She sat on the edge of a table not far from them. "It's kinda hard *not* to say it." She thumbed her nose and pointed in thought when a memory crossed her mind. "I was talking to Jim about it too, and when we got to talking about this one kid, we were both like, 'man, he *dumb*.' Horrible grammar included."

Taylor shook his head, but Kaleb couldn't hide his snickering. "What are you doing here?" Taylor was always one to get to the point.

"Ah." Miss Hart straightened. "Just wanted to let you know that I signed you up for president, and that you were accepted." Taylor's eyes went wide.

"You *WHAT?*"

She stood from the table, holding her arms out in a questioning manner. "Well, you never got back with me, so I just decided for you." She turned to leave, giving the boys a farewell wave over her shoulder. "Congrats, kid." Taylor wasn't about to let her leave just yet.

"Hold on a min- Miss Hart!" He got up from the table to chase after her, but she was already strutting down the hallway back to her own classroom.

"See you tomorrow, Taylor!" She gave him another back-handed wave as she powered on back to her room.

"Miss Har-! Aruhg!" Taylor growled in frustration, retreating from the doorway back to the laboratory table where Kaleb sat. Kaleb couldn't keep the grin off his face.

"Well that was fun," he snarked. Taylor glared back at the bigger boy, saying nothing out of habit. "What?" Kaleb asked. "I'm just saying." Taylor shook his head, turning his attention back to his assignments and muttering to himself that he didn't 'have time for this,' but Kaleb wasn't done with the matter at hand. "Why not just tell her no?" he asked. Taylor slapped a paper down atop another, reading through them to see what was needed next.

"Miss Hart is not a woman you can just say 'no' to," he replied, irritated. "She's stubborn, and always gets what she wants."

Kaleb looked to the ceiling, processing this thought. "Hm," he agreed. "I can see that." Taylor sighed, dropping the papers to run a hand through his hair.

"She's always deciding stuff like that. I should've known from the start that there was no way she'd let me out once she brought it up." Kaleb crumpled his face.

"Wouldn't this be a good thing?" he asked, receiving a questioning glance from Taylor. "I mean, just seems to me that it would be right up your alley, you being so smart and all." Kaleb admitted. "Plus, it boosts your profile for college. They're always on the lookout for successful kids, doesn't matter what it's in." Kaleb paused. "What's it for, anyway?"

"I think that's it for today," Taylor said, growing tired of the conversation. "We'll meet up again tomorrow." Kaleb smirked again.

"Come on," he said. "Would it be so bad if you told me? It's not something embarrassing, right?" Taylor began packing his things, shoving his papers in his pack just as quickly as he could zip it closed.

"Does it really matter?" he asked, shouldering his backpack. "Besides, what other club does she run?"

"Oh!" Kaleb belted, leaning back in his chair. "Seriously? You're turning down technology stuff." Kaleb's confusion couldn't be contained. "What is *wrong* with you?" Taylor was already two steps away from the door, but he couldn't stop his mouth from responding.

"According to you? Lots."

"You're kidding me, right?" Bekah was utterly astounded.

"I know," Taylor agreed. "We've met up three times now, and I can actually say that I'm not entirely lost in class anymore. Can you believe it?" Bekah shook her head.

"No," she said flatly.

"Yeah, me neither." Taylor ran a hand through his hair. "He's the real deal, Beck," he admitted. "I'm actually *learning* from him."

Bekah shook her head again, trying to make sense of it. "That's nuts," she muttered, though mostly to herself.

"I know," Taylor agreed again. "What a world we live in."

"What about your grades?" Bekah suddenly piped, but was turned down by a wave from Taylor.

"It hasn't even been a week yet, nothing's been graded," he told her. "Besides, according to Mr. Finnigan, even if I ace every paper he shoves at me, I'd just barely pass for average."

"Well at least that's something," Bekah replied. "He's helping you study for the finals too, isn't he?"

Taylor nodded. "Through the work we're doing already."

Bekah squinted in thought, still blown away. "This is just too weird, man."

"I know." Taylor huffed. "We're meeting again tomorrow, maybe even through the weekend."

She perked up, interested. "A bit of rapid fire learning, huh?" Taylor frowned.

"No other way," he admitted. "I gotta get this done."

Bekah threw her hands up, backing into her chair. "Alright," she said. "Go team."

Taylor rolled his eyes. "Yeah. Whoo." Needless to say, he was less than enthusiastic.

"Head's up," Taylor warned. Behind Bekah, he could see the slight crack of her opening door, and the sudden arrival of her furry companion as he jumped onto her desk.

"Hey, Thunder," she cooed, scooping up the black cat. "How's my boy?" She began simultaneously scratching his ears and rubbing his belly, earning a thunderous pur from him, congruent with his name.

"Yeah, how's my boy?" she asked again, sneaking a kiss onto his neck before releasing him. Taylor smirked, shaking his head. "Oh, come on," Bekah scorned. "I'd bet money that you do the exact same thing with Bubbie."

"Yeah," Taylor admitted. "but Bubbie's a dog. And I don't use that baby voice, either."

Bekah scoffed at her friend. "It's the same thing!" she argued.

"No it's not," he snickered.

"Whatever," she huffed, raising her nose at him. "If it's wrong to love my animals, then you'd better lock me up now." He raised a hand in defense.

"Alright, alright," he retreated, then, "I'll see you later, 'kay?" Bekah popped up.

"So soon?" she asked.

"Gotta make dinner," he told her, earning a shrug.

"Alright," she receded. "See you later."

He closed off his communication line with her, then quickly shut down and packed away his computer in his pack. Although he wasn't lying when he had said that he needed to make dinner, the real reason he had stopped their conversation short was that he had heard the slightest bit of scuffling from his front door. If his father had returned, and in a horrid mood, no less, Taylor didn't want a repeat of the last tantrum caught in between their conversation.

Taylor cautiously unlocked and opened his bedroom door, peeking out from the frame to check the stairs for any sign of life. With his senses satisfied, he quietly left his room, and made his way towards the stairs. Step after silent step, he carefully made his way down to the living room, seeing no one. He scanned the room for danger, but no harm seemed to be searching for him in return.

Keeping alert, Taylor made his way to the kitchen to prepare dinner. Usually, when seen with food in his hands, his father seemed to calm down in the tiniest bit. He opened the fridge, checking it's contents for ideas, and when none came, checked the freezer. Nothing popped out to him there either, so he retreated from the fridge all together to check the pantry closet. He stood in the doorway, listing off items that needed to be eaten before their own expiration. Suddenly, Taylor heard the shriek of rubber against tile, and was instantly shoved into the pantry, the door slammed closed and blocked behind him.

"Shit!"

Taylor's mind raced. He was crammed in between the pantry door, and the shelves meant to hold their food.

"Dad!" Taylor called. "Dad! It's me, Taylor! Open up!"

No answer. He attempted to maneuver himself to face the door, but the tight space wouldn't allow it. When he tried the handle, it turned, but something from the outside was stopping the door from opening.

"Dad!" he tried again. "You're not gonna get any dinner if I can't cook!"

Still no reply. When he quieted his struggles, he could hear the television speaking in the distance; no doubt with Friedreich sitting comfortably in his chair it front of it. Taylor sighed in defeat, resting his forehead against the edge of a shelf.

"Great."

With no possible way to escape, Taylor stood trapped inside the pantry all night long. When his hunger took hold, he managed to pull out unseen bits of dried goods that could fit between the door and shelves up to his face, scoring a box of cereal from one of the lower shelves. Occasionally, he would call out to his father to let him out of his prison, hearing nothing but the television in reply.

By the time his father did remove him, Taylor was exhausted from standing for hours, and ordered to go to his room. Taylor caught a glimpse of a clock on his way to his bed reading six-forty in the morning, but by then, he was too tired to care about changing into pajamas, or worrying about school in a few hours. He simply fell into bed, flopping his head around in search of his pillow, and soon, fell fast asleep.

Chapter 8

Taylor's night did not go unnoticed. All day long, Kaleb had seen Taylor in a worse mood than ever, barely comprehending whatever was placed in front of him, and even watching through another class's window as he left for his locker to replace his books for the correct ones.

Now, in class, he had his head buried in his arms on his desk, *sleeping.* Kaleb wouldn't allow it. It was his own fault for not sleeping the night before, so he shouldn't punish Miss Hart by missing her class. He snuck over towards the snoozing boy, careful not to make a sound; quite the difficult task with a heavily booted leg. Soon, he was standing in front of Taylor's desk, hovering over him, deciding what it was that he wanted to do.

Then, out of nowhere, Kaleb slammed his hands down on Taylor's desk with extra help from the movement of his entire body. The blonde in question shot up from his slumber, spooked by the sudden, noiseful force brought on by Kaleb. Kaleb's plan, however, backfired.

Because of his brute strength, Kaleb ended up leaning over the desk, while Taylor, who had sat straight up, landed within a hair's breadth away from the bigger teen's nose. The two boys caught each other's shocked eyes, then immediately reacted, howling in disgust and pulling away from each other as quickly as they could.

"What th-what-*why*?!" Taylor shouted, too misplaced to form a complete sentence.

"You were asleep!" Kaleb answered, rubbing his nose to rid himself of the sensation of Taylor's. "Somebody had to."

Taylor shook his head, glaring at the jock. "Just sit the fuck down, asshole."

"I'm not an asshole," Kaleb griped.

Taylor couldn't care less.

"Well, you could'a fooled me."

The rest of the day was quiet. Kaleb didn't want to replicate another incident between them, and mostly kept to himself. Even Kaleb's friends took notice of Taylor's disposition, and didn't want to bother with it, if it meant they wouldn't get the usual rise out of him. Aside from this, it was game day, meaning their minds were busied by something more important than their favorite geek. When the final bell rang, Kaleb left his classroom for the laboratory to meet up with his pupil, but one look at Taylor's bleary eyes forced his decision for him.

"Go home," he ordered.

"What?" Taylor asked, confused. Kaleb merely shook his head.

"You're half dead, Tommy," he told him. "You're no good to me." Taylor mumbled something under his breath, but Kaleb was already packed and ready to go.

"Go home," he repeated. "Get some sleep. I'll see you tomorrow."

Irritated as he was, Taylor was thankful to Kaleb for sending him off early. After the night he had had, he realized that he in fact *did* need to go and rest up. Kaleb was right, he wasn't in any shape to be learning anything, and quite frankly, he was surprised that he had managed to make the day without nodding off- save for Miss Hart's room…

Taylor yawned a great big, breathy yawn as he drug his feet over the river stones. He had passed up his usual visit with Hector and Tammy in order to head straight for dreamland. As much as he wanted to sleep in his own bed, though, he didn't want to risk being caught off guard by his father again, and in the shape he was in, it wouldn't be too difficult. Instead, he trecked to his second home in the chutes with Bubbie.

Bubbie was delighted to see Taylor, hearing him before seeing him, and happily running up to him in greeting. Taylor pushed up a smile, trying to calm the dog, but too exhausted to really do anything about it. He made his way to the chute, lighting his lantern as he entered. Once his eyes set on his rolled up sleepsack against the wall, nothing could get in his way.

He paused a moment after unfurling his bed when Bubbie pawed at him for food, and made a quick detour to fill the pleading dog's bowl. The flannel blanket his mother had sent him was folded so that part of it was tucked inside his sleeping bag while the rest was curled up into a makeshift pillow, and when he took off his shoes and nestled inside, the warmth of the blanket from underneath helped to keep away the biting chill of the concrete below him.

Bubbie soon finished his meal, then turned his attention to Taylor, seeing him bunker down for bed. The dog padded up to Taylor, sniffing his face and wagging his tail.

"Uhg," Taylor huffed, pushing the furry face out of his own. "Fish-breath," he muttered. Bubbie didn't mind the name, instead he took his usual role curling up beside Taylor in his sleeping bag, lying lengthwise of him to share warmth and space. Taylor, in turn, wrapped his arms around the pooch's neck and chest, bringing him in close for a quick nuzzle before finally relaxing his tired body, and settling in for a long, hard rest.

With the school being closed for the weekend, Taylor dreaded the idea of visiting Kaleb's home for tutoring- or even worse, staying at his own house with his father to finish his work. Kaleb, however, had quelled his worrisome mind moments after meeting. After months of keeping the teachers locked inside with him, Kaleb had been given a key to the Alchemy hall in secret, so as to conduct his experiments whenever he so desired, and today, he so desired.

They set up shop at their usual table, going over paper after paper of both homework and extra assignments, all the while teaching Taylor studying tricks to remember what he had learned from Kaleb during their session. They paused only to eat whatever food they had brought, but even then, Taylor bombarded Kaleb with questions that were soon answered.

"How about an experiment?" Kaleb asked suddenly. Taylor's sandwich hovered halfway between the table and his lips.

"What?" he asked.

"An experiment," Kaleb reinforced. "We are studying alchemy, aren't we? Let's go beyond the paperwork." Taylor scowled at the idea.

"That's not something that needs to be done," he said, leaning in for a bite of his food. "We don't have the time."

"Sure we do," Kaleb said. "It's not a matter of needing, but of wanting." Taylor looked to the golden skinned boy, not bothering to swallow his food before speaking.

"Then I don't want to," he said, swallowing. "I need to learn this." Kaleb scoffed.

"You can't learn everything from a book." He grasped his fists before himself and Taylor, closing the gap between the two of them. "Sometimes you gotta dive right in."

"Dive yourself," Taylor mumbled. "I'll be finishing my homework."

Kaleb gave Taylor a condescending look. "Alright, fine," he said. "But you're on your own." Taylor whipped back to Kaleb.

"What? But we had a d-"

"You're on your own until we get at least one lab out of the way today," Kaleb snarked, crossing his arms. "Since it *is* a part of your criteria." Taylor heaved a heavy breath through his nose, staring down the contented jock sitting across from him. He could see it in his eyes, Taylor wasn't getting out of this one.

"Fine," he grumbled. "What do you want to do?"

Kaleb's grin grew."For starters," he said. "Gimme your sandwich bag." Taylor became confused.

"My *what*?"

However, Kaleb waved off the idea. "No, you're right, no explosions," he said. "We'll do something else instead." His eye caught sight of a small canister sitting on the professor's desk, returning his grin to his face. "Got it."

Kaleb stood, leaving his crutches at the table to use his hands freely for gathering supplies. Snagging the canister, he hobbled over to a nearby sink to let the hot water run while he rustled up the rest of his supplies from the desk.

"Open that." He pointed to a locked cabinet behind Taylor, tossing him a key he had retrieved from the professor's desk.

"What am I getting?" Taylor asked, working the lock.

"Potentially nothing," Kaleb said, rummaging through the desk more. "Unless I can't find any antacid tablets." Kaleb shut the drawer with a huff. "Which I can't. Try vinegar and baking soda then."

Taylor looked back to the bigger boy. "Are we seriously making a volcano?" he droned, but Kaleb merely scoffed.

"Give me some credit."

Taylor turned back to the opened cabinet, retrieving the requested items before closing the doors and joining Kaleb at the sink. The jock quickly measured out what was needed, separating the vinegar into the canister and the baking soda into a tissue. By now, the still running water was steaming from the spout, which Kaleb also measured out and poured into the canister with the vinegar.

"Okay," he muttered, closing the canister and rushing towards the windows. "Let's go."

"Go?" Taylor speculated.

"Yeah, come on." Kaleb had slid open a window by now, and was sitting in the pane putting his jacket on, waiting for his partner to follow. "Hurry, before it gets cold." He jiggled the canister before tucking it away safely inside the lining of his leather jacket.

Taylor sighed heavily. "I never agreed to this," he mumbled but followed anyway, throwing his hood over his head on the way out.

A stiff breeze hit him as soon as his foot touched the grass on the other side of the window, forcing him to tighten his grip on his hoodie. Kaleb looked to him, surprised.

"Don't you have something warmer?" he asked.

"Can we just get this over with?" Taylor snipped. Kaleb shrugged.

"Alright, here." He held out the canister and folded tissue to Taylor. "Take these about a hundred steps out."

124

"Then what?" Taylor asked, taking the items.

"Then, put the tissue inside the canister, close it tight, and put it on the ground; lid side down," Kaleb ordered.

"And then?" Taylor shivered with another gust of wind.

"Run."

Taylor cocked a brow at the larger boy, but did as he was told. Once he had counted out his hundred steps, he pulled out the items and crouched down low to the ground. He was careful to pop open the canister so as not to spill any of it's contents, but the heat of the water rose out from it in a light steam.

"Do it quick!" Kaleb shouted.

"'Do it quick'," Taylor mimicked irritably. He then dropped the tissue into the canister, snapped it shut, and placed it cap side down on the ground. When he stood to leave, Kaleb waved him down.

"Run, Tommy, run!"

Too late. The canister hissed like a beast before exploding straight up into the clouds, causing Taylor to duck and cover as it rocketed above him. Kaleb hooted with victory, while Taylor picked himself off the ground.

"What was that?" he asked, truly shocked. Kaleb grinned at him as he drew closer.

"That, my friend, was a rocket." He clapped Taylor on the back when he came near enough to do so.

"A rocket?" Taylor studied the experiment sight, looking for answers that were easily explained by Kaleb.

"It was made from carbon dioxide." He laughed lightly. "The tissue gave you about a second to get away safely, but you weren't fast enough for it." Taylor turned his attention to Kaleb.

"Isn't carbon dioxide poisonous?" he asked. Kaleb held up a finger. "Close. You're thinking of carbon *mon*-oxide. That stuff will kill you." Taylor nodded, returning his attention to the launch site. Kaleb smiled.

"Wanna do it again?" he asked, catching Taylor off guard with his question.

"Well, I…" he started. "I guess it wouldn't hurt to try."

For the rest of the afternoon, the two boys worked together to launch the rocket perfectly straight into the air, modifying paper around the canister to make it more aerodynamic; of course it didn't hurt to make it more fun and pleasing to the eye. They managed to make it fly higher with different measurements of ingredients, and more than once, it had flown over the school. They finally had to end their fun when the canister flew out of sight, forcing the boys to search for it. After a little more than half an hour, they finally found it trapped between branches in a bush, and Taylor, not wanting to lose it, had decided that it would be a good idea to stop for the day.

"Whew, it's cold," Kaleb wheezed, rubbing his hands together as he stepped into the class from the window. Taylor nodded in agreement as he blew onto his own hands to try and bring life back into them.

"I could go for some of Tammy's coco right now," Kaleb admitted quietly, clasping the window shut. "You?"

Taylor stopped, his back to Kaleb, not knowing how to answer. Never in his life had Kaleb ever offered his companionship to him unless he was to be paid, so to be asked for a warm drink so suddenly like this had caught him completely off guard.

"Uh, no," he mumbled. "I should get going." After all this time, he still didn't trust Kaleb not to fool him.

"C'mon." Kaleb motioned to Taylor's hands. "Your fingers are blue, you should warm them up." Taylor shied away from Kaleb's advances, tending to his backpack instead.

"No, I should get back," he said, tidying up his papers and slinging his backpack onto his back.

"Okay," Kaleb gave in, turning away. "Guess I'll go home too, then."

"Your choice," Taylor said, shouldering his way out the door. "See you tomorrow."

"See you tom..." Kaleb held up a hand in farewell, but slowly dropped it as Taylor stepped out the door, not bothering to hear him. Taylor didn't care. He made his way down the hall and out the door, quick to the step. The chill in the air was fast to greet him as he left the school, forcing him to hug his arms tightly to his body. He trudged along the sidewalk, considering what might have happened if Kaleb had gotten his wish and shared a drink with Taylor.

The experiment had loosened him up a bit, freeing him from his usual, controlled self, but the more he thought about it, the more he realized he had given Kaleb enough material to tease him with. His slightly smiling face when the rocket shot high into the sky, the way he ran away from it as quick as he could before it launched, even the way he had asked questions about how to make it, and the science behind it; all of it was a new, more excited version of himself, and this was more than enough to use against him if need be. Seeing more of that would only fuel the fire.

Aside from wanting to avoid any more teasing, Taylor had another reason for leaving when he did. Today, he would be traveling to Carter city to get his Border pass. Without it, there was no chance of him crossing the Alterian border, meaning no chance to live with his mother. Today, he would make sure that didn't happen. He had been looking forward to it for a while, and now was his chance. He had even been carrying a comb in his back pocket all the day long just so he could ready his hair when they took his picture, knowing that his mother would want to see how he looked in it when he showed her.

Another gust of wind blew at Taylor, taking his hood with it. He fumbled against the wind, trying to replace his hood over his head and keep it there, when he remembered his letter. With his unexpected nap, he had missed his mother's letter the day before, and was no doubt still sitting in the post office with Hector, just waiting for him. The thought of Kaleb, however, put a pause to his steps. Running into him after all his efforts of avoiding the jock would be quite awkward indeed.

"He did say he was going home," Taylor considered, then decided on retrieving his letter from Hector and made his move towards the post office. As usual, the walk didn't take very long, and he arrived shortly thereafter, and as usual, Hector was more than happy to see Taylor when he came.

"Missed you yesterday," he said to the teen.

"Sorry, Hector," Taylor apologized, leaning into the counter. Hector only smiled.

"That's all right, son,"he said. "Figured you had something more important to do anyway." He excused himself to bring back another package for Taylor, this box smaller than the last, but still as enticing.

"Now remember," Hector said. "If it's food, you gotta share." Taylor smiled genuinely at the man.

"I remember."

Kaleb had locked up the school and was walking home already, wondering why Taylor's mood had changed so suddenly. They had been having a good time, as far as Kaleb had considered, then all of a sudden, Taylor went and ran away. Kaleb had meant it when he told Taylor that he had decided to go home, but a strong, icy wind paired with the thought of being home alone changed his mind. Tammy's coco was calling his name, and he wasn't going to refuse it.

Kaleb was slow with his second set of legs weighing him down, and the chill in the air didn't speed things up for him either. What should have been a quick walk to the diner ended up being a hard trek with a much needed rest at the end. By the time he had finally reached Tammy's Diner, he was exhausted, and downright frozen to the bone. Just a few more steps to cross the street, and Kaleb would be rewarded with a warm drink, and a fine place to rest before he began his treacherous journey home. His footfalls stopped, however, when his eye caught sight of Taylor through the large front windows, settling down in the far corner, as usual.

Tammy had just left for his order, leaving Taylor to his own accord with a small box sitting on the table before him. He was quick to use the knife provided to open his mystery box, and once he did, confusion settled on his face once he had taken a proper look at the contents inside. He reached in to pull out a long, beautiful silver scarf, about the length of his outstretched arms.

Taylor inspected the scarf, rubbing a part of it between his fingers as he fished for the letter that accompanied it. After a few moments, the words sank in, and a small smile crept to his lips. He further explored the scarf, wrapping it around his neck and over his chin. He took a moment to let the knitted fabric hold him tightly, breathing it in with a long, deep breath. Taylor's smile stayed in his eyes as he finished the rest of the letter, still rubbing bits of it between his fingers as he read.

Tammy came by again with a mug in her hands, the top overflowing with whipped cream. She pointed to the scarf as though she were complimenting it. Taylor's smile fell from bliss to politeness as she spoke, and when she asked, Taylor unwrapped the scarf from his neck for her to inspect it herself. Tammy's smile was genuine, however, as she discovered it's softness and fine craftsmanship. She finally returned the scarf to Taylor, giving more praise to it as she did so, then left him to service the rest of her customers. Meanwhile, Taylor had carefully wrapped the scarf around his neck again, and drawn out paper from his pack to write a reply.

"It's his mom," Kaleb realized.

Kaleb gathered his thoughts, realizing that this was the only reasonable explanation as to why Taylor reacted the way he did with every letter he received. With no other way of communication, it was only logical that it be Mrs. Thompson. It couldn't be a girl; Taylor was far too anti-social for something as brash as a female companion. Knowing anyone outside of Alteria would be difficult without knowing them firsthand, and as far as Kaleb was concerned, every resident of River Hill was a true-blood Alterian, so any other relatives wouldn't possibly bother writing every week when there was the alternative of video-chatting.

Every week.

That's what Tammy had said, and that's what Kaleb had seen. Once a week. Meaning Taylor waited for six days before hearing a reply from whoever it was that he was writing to. Every week. Who else would one have more devotion to than their own blood? Who else would one be so happy to hear from- especially with Taylor's foul demeanor? Kaleb's heart sank when he thought of this, thinking of what he would have done if his own mother were so far away for so very long.

It was then and there that he chose to leave without staying in the diner. Should Taylor interrupt Kaleb's moment of peace with his mother, he wouldn't be too pleased with the blonde. He decided it best to leave Taylor with whatever precious bits of his mother he had. That's what he intended, at least, but another harsh wind blew right through his leather jacket, reminding him of how cold his body was.

"To-go cup," Kaleb decided, then turned back to the diner to warm his insides. As he entered through the front door, the jingling of the bells alerted everyone of his arrival, including Taylor.

"Kaleb!" Tammy smiled, walking up to the larger boy for a hug. "Oh, you're freezing!" she exclaimed, ushering him to a booth. "Sit down, I'll get you something to warm you up."

"That's alright, Tammy," Kaleb declined. "I was actually on my way home. I figured I'd just get it on the run." He caught Taylor watching him from the corner of his eye and became extremely uncomfortable.

"Nonsense!" Tammy hushed the jock. "Have you felt your hands? Of course not, they're frozen solid, I'm surprised you can still use them."

"Really, Tammy, I-"

"How are you going to hold it, then?" Tammy asked.

"... What?" Kaleb stared at her, dumbfounded. Tammy gestured towards Kaleb's crutches.

"You certainly can't expect me to believe that you can hold anything while you've got your hands full with those."

"Damn it," Kaleb thought. "Didn't think of that, actually," he admitted.

Tammy nodded in satisfaction. "Then have a seat, hun."

Kaleb glanced at Taylor as he sat, seeing the blonde gather his things to leave, and cursing himself for ruining whatever moment he had been having with his mother's letter. Kaleb rubbed the back of his head as Taylor neared the door, but was completely surprised when Taylor sat down across from him, rather than leave.

"So you're following me now?" he asked. Kaleb blinked, still perplexed at his sudden appearance.

"You said you were going home," Kaleb answered quietly.

"So did you," Taylor shot back just as quiet. Kaleb raised his brows at Taylor, leaning back into his booth while speaking.

"Then I guess we're both wrong."

"Here you go," Tammy returned to Kaleb with a steaming mug, overflowing with whipped cream. "Enjoy." She placed the mug down in front of Kaleb with a smile before turning to Taylor. "Get lonely?" she asked him.

"No ma'am." Taylor shook his head as he pulled away from the table, putting more space between him and Kaleb.

"Well, would you like another cup of coco?" She took a napkin from her apron and placed it next to Kaleb's mug. "It's pretty cold out there, I'll go get you a refill."

Before Taylor could refuse, Tammy was gone to make him another cup of warm, chocolatey goodness to heat him up from the inside out. Taylor sighed, running a hand through his hair as he watched the waitress leave him and Kaleb alone together. Kaleb felt equally uncomfortable, staring down into his mug and dunking the white, fluffy cream into the dark beverage beneath it with his spoon.

"Cool scarf," he muttered, taking a moment to point it out. Taylor looked back to Kaleb before studying the floor and table, touching the scarf around his neck carefully. Kaleb was about to speak more, but Tammy interrupted him with the renewal of Taylor's coco. When she left, and the proper thank yous had been made, they were thrown back into uncomfortable silence.

"This is ridiculous." Kaleb sighed, dropping his spoon into his mug for good. "Why don't we finish your homework?" he offered, then to himself. *"It's better than this."*

However, Taylor shook his head. "No, I have an appointment." With that, he shouldered his backpack and made a quick escape around the booth and out the door.

"Tommy, wait-" Kaleb couldn't reach him even if he tried. Taylor was gone, leaving behind a leather-bound booklet behind him. It hadn't fallen out, it was merely forgotten when he set it down beside himself in the booth. Kaleb stretched over the table, trying to reach the booklet and failing. With a huff, he raised himself from his seat to reach what he finally recognized as Taylor's journal.

Kaleb was careful to inspect the outer detail of the journal, seeing the worn leather along its spine and little scratches scattered across its cover. No doubt it was used on a daily basis, the nearly empty pen residing along the edge of it was simply more proof of that. He flipped through the pages, absentmindedly reviewing the booklet as though it were a book he were interested in buying, and was late in catching himself as the smell of ink and worn pages rose to his nose. He closed the journal with a soft thud, having to remind himself that it wasn't another book for his pleasure.

Kaleb carefully set the journal aside to finish his cup, then, not wanting to waste it, drank Taylor's untouched mug as well. He paid and left with a polite smile that didn't last long. The walk home, although rough, passed by quickly, and he was soon home again, being welcomed by Skitters and her hungry belly. A few hours later, his parents returned home from working overtime, and soon they were having dinner, and talking about their day; his parents about their peculiar patients, and Kaleb about his lesson with Taylor. Though, he left out the after bit of running into him at the diner.

The evening flew by; dessert, dishes, and family time passed on as quickly as it came; and by the time Kaleb had showered and lay on the couch prepared for bed, he had forgotten all about the leather-bound journal. His father, however, noticed it firsthand when he stumbled over Kaleb's backpack trying to lock the front door.

"What's this?" he asked, holding up the journal for Kaleb to see.

"Oh," Kaleb remarked. "That belongs to that Tommy kid," he answered, reaching for the booklet. "He forgot it today."

Vance examined the journal before handing it over to his son. "It's pretty worn down, isn't it?" he asked. "Let's you know how much he uses it."

"Yeah," Kaleb agreed. "I don't think I've ever seen him without it."

Vance cringed a bit, making a strange frown. "Hope he's not freaking out, then," he said. "I know I would."

Kaleb turned his attention to the leather journal in his hands, pondering what his father had just said. If Taylor really did value this book as much as his father valued his own notes, then no doubt, he would be furious if he found out that Kaleb had had it all along. He might even accuse Kaleb of reading it.

"I'll slip it in his bag tomorrow," he decided. "Maybe he won't even notice."

"Let's hope so," Mr. Evans replied, flicking off the light switch. "Night, kid." Kaleb set the journal aside to settle in for the night.

"Night, dad."

Taylor flipped out his pass again, spying carefully into every detail. In the dark of the night, he felt secure in knowing his father was asleep, and that chancing a peek at his handy work while he lay in bed would be safe enough. His picture had turned out alright enough for his standards, but he wasn't so sure about his mother's. He was sure to drape his new scarf around his shoulders for the camera, but his dingy hoodie and lack of smile were sure to cause a fuss when his mother caught sight of it.

Worse of all, it revealed his scar beneath his eye. Taylor touched the N shaped engraving of his cheek in his picture, trying to think of how he would explain it to his mother, and wondering what she would say about it when she saw it. As small as it was, it was still visible due to its depth, and he hoped to his very soul that she wouldn't cry. Taylor closed his Border pass and tucked it away safely inside his backpack. In doing so, his scarf, still wrapped around his neck, gently reached over his chin.

"I learned how to knit for your special day! I hope you like it, Bubbie."

Even without her voice, Taylor could still hear the joy in her words. He tugged at the soft wool taking refuge around his neck, breathing in what was left of his mother's scent. He closed his eyes, imagining her warm embrace in place of the scarf she had made for him. He took in another long whiff, remembering the smell of her hair in his face when she hugged him. His heart ached at the memories, but his steadfast determination kept him at bay.

"Just a little while longer," he whispered to himself, opening his eyes to the moonlight glowing against his bare wall. His fingers wrapped themselves up in the folds of his scarf, taking care to remember every fiber that was carefully woven together to create this wonderful gift.

"Just a little while longer." Taylor rolled onto his side, still cradling the scarf close to his face as his eyes drooped. Finally, they started to flutter closed as the weight of the day caught up with him, and his exhaustion took hold.

The next morning, Kaleb met with Taylor at the school, just as planned. He opened the Alchemy hall as usual, and set up for another day to study in peace, alone in the laboratory. Again, Kaleb helped Taylor to finish a few extra credit assignments, and by the third one, he was looking for any excuse for Taylor to leave the room to replace the journal. He didn't need to work hard at it, however, because Taylor excused himself.

"I'll be right back," he said. "Forgot my chemistry book."

"'Kay," Kaleb replied, relieved. As soon as Taylor was out of sight, Kaleb dug out the journal from his own backpack to bury it deep inside Taylor's. In his haste, the journal slipped from his hands and fell to the ground, sprawled flat on its pages. Kaleb cursed his clumsiness, and picked up the journal to inspect any damages that may have befallen it. One of the pages had folded over onto itself, causing Kaleb to carefully rub the crease flat again.

As he did this, his eyes, out of habit, stole the words from the page, and he began reading. Kaleb was captivated by the way the words made their way from the page to his imagination, flowing gracefully like a dove into his mind's eye. Inadvertently, he turned the page to discover how the stories continued on the next section.

Kaleb instantly fell into the story, relating to the heroine as though she were his kinship, and wanted more. More battles against her foes, more tender conversations with her friends, more lessons to be taught by her teachers. He laughed at her wit, and craved her cooking more and more with each descriptive word. He was so lost in Taylor's created world, he had forgotten that he was still kneeling on the floor, his encased leg spread out to the side of him. He was reminded, however, when a voice made him jump, and bump his head against the table.

"What are you *doing*?" Taylor suddenly appeared in the doorway, reminding Kaleb of where he was, and what he was doing.

"I- uh-" Kaleb stumbled, trying to stand back up but falling onto his butt like a klutzy child learning to walk. "You left this, and I-" Taylor wouldn't have it. He snatched the journal from Kaleb, shoving it and the rest of his papers into his backpack.

"That's private," he growled, shouldering his pack and turning to leave. Kaleb was pulling himself up on a crutch as he reached out to try and stop him.

"Tommy, wai-"

"MY NAME IS TAYLOR!"

The angry teen whipped around to scream this at Kaleb, scaring his outstretched hand back to his chest. Taylor whirled back around to escape out the laboratory door, but

Kaleb had regained himself, and was chasing after him.

"To- Taylor- hey!"

Finally Kaleb had had enough. He took his only crutch from under his arm to catch one of Taylor's feet, causing him to fall face first onto the tile flooring. Kaleb cringed at the sound of Taylor's contact with the floor and offered his apologies, but the blonde yanked his still ensnared foot to drag down the jock with him. Kaleb picked himself off the floor to find Taylor struggling to free his foot from the titanium trap.

"Alright, stop it." Kaleb held up his hand before reaching over to rest it over the irritated blonde. "Stop struggling, stop running away from your problems- just stop it, stop everything." Kaleb managed to look Taylor in the eye when he said this, earning him first views to the hatred re-growing in his eyes.

"'Running away from my problems'?" Taylor mocked. "If only I could!"

"Well, you're doing a pretty damn good job of it now," Kaleb shot back. "And yesterday, too!" Taylor pushed Kaleb's hands off of him.

"What are you talking about?" Taylor hissed.

"When you lied about going to Tammy's," Kaleb answered. "And then your 'appointment' too." Taylor finally managed to untangle himself from Kaleb's crutch.

"I *did* have an appointment," he replied, kicking the crutch a fair distance away. "The rest of it was none of your fucking business." He tried to stand, but Kaleb grabbed his arm to yank him down and hold him in place.

"Even if you didn't have an excuse, you still wouldn't stick around," Kaleb growled. "Too good for anyone, is that it?" Taylor ripped his arm out of Kaleb's grasp.

"Shows what you know," he uttered.

"Then tell me!" Kaleb challenged. "When was the last time you spent time with someone, huh? When was the last time you actually sat down and had a conversation with someone here? Me? Miss Hart? That's bull shit!"

"*You're* the one who's full of it!" Taylor shouted, but Kaleb wasn't done.

"You only talk to people when you're forced to; if you weren't so fucking stupid in alchemy, I don't think we'd even be talking right now!" Taylor pushed away from Kaleb, but he grabbed hold of the blonde's wrist.

"Face it, you wouldn't dare step out into the real world unless you were forced to."

"Get off me!"

"What are you so scared of?"

"I said let go!"

"Not until I get a straight answer out of you!"

"Why should I?!" Taylor spat. "Why should I do anything at all?"

"Because it's good for y-"

"Bull shit!" Taylor interrupted. "I've gotten along just fine on my own, and it's not like you ever cared before now anyways!" Taylor glared Kaleb down as he spoke. "Why the sudden change? Why are you *suddenly* so interested in me and my affairs?"

Kaleb struggled for an answer, but found none. He raced through his mind, trying to answer it himself, but still, no answer came. Then, he found the tail end of an excuse, and went for it.

"I think you can help me," Kaleb tried.

Taylor scoffed. "Oh, really?" he mused. Kaleb nodded, his face still stern.

"I've got this project," he started. "It's something I've been working on for a while now."

Taylor's face darkened. "I'm not doing it for you," he said in a low, irritated voice.

Kaleb furrowed his brow. "I haven't even told you what it is yet."

"Don't have to; I'm not doing it." Taylor successfully stood this time, brushing himself off before reaching for his fallen backpack.

"Then you've already proven my point," Kaleb stated. Taylor stopped to glare at the jock on the floor.

"Proven what?" he asked exasperated. Kaleb crossed his arms as he spoke.

"That you run away from everything."

Taylor's face hardened. "Forgive me for not actually beating you senseless after reading through my private property like I wanted to," he said flatly.

"Nope," Kaleb denied. "We're past that. Now it's about you not stepping out of your bubble and helping me."

"I'll help, I just won't do it," Taylor replied. Kaleb crumpled his face.

"That makes no sense at all." He shook his head. "Whatever, how about a bet then?" he asked. Taylor's shoulders sank.

"A bet?" He was less than amused. Kaleb fished out a coin from his pocket.

"If I win, you come and help."

"What makes you think I would-" But Kaleb had already flicked the coin into the air, causing both boys to keep a close eye on it as it flew.

"Heads I win, tails you lose- call it!"

Chapter 9

"I can't believe I fell for that stupid trick," Taylor grumbled, hiking his pack higher onto his shoulders.

"I can't believe you called it," Kaleb chuckled, clicking ahead of Taylor to lead the way home.

"It was a reaction, you would have done it too," Taylor snipped, bringing more muffled laughter from the jock before him.

Taylor had called out while the coin was still in the air, but lost all the same due to Kaleb's trickery. When Taylor tried to deny him of his win, Kaleb reasoned that by participating in the bet, he henceforth committed to the deal, and would therefore have to comply with the rules. To make sure he followed, though, Kaleb also told Taylor that if he did not, he would double his tutoring rates.

"This is so stupid," Taylor griped, still irritated with himself for falling for it more than anything.

"Quit your belly-aching," Kaleb called. "A bet's a bet. Besides, we're almost there." Kaleb held up a crutch to point to a lovely white house with a large porch and grassy lawn just two houses down from them. "That's the one," he said, replacing his crutch to the ground. "That's where we're going."

Taylor stared at the house as he drew closer to it, admiring it from afar, and secretly curious of every nook and cranny it may hold. Kaleb cut through the shared strip of grass between his house and his neighbor's, clicking along it to the side of his house.

"C'mon," Kaleb motioned. "It's in the back."

"Oh- okay," Taylor mumbled, jumping back into reality to follow Kaleb along the side of his house. Kaleb reached the fence door and was about to open it when he stopped, and turned to look at Taylor questioningly.

"You're not allergic to anything, are you?" Kaleb asked, earning a confused blink.

"No," Taylor responded. "Not unless you have any kiwi back there." Kaleb's smile returned to his face.

"Good," he said, then pushed through to his backyard.

When Taylor walked through, he thought he had been transported to another world entirely. Flowers he had never seen before grew vibrantly in every shade and breed all around him. Herbs grew plentiful in the company of the wild plant life, and Winter barren fruit trees lined the fence's border. From the grass on the ground, to the trees hanging above him, there was life surrounding his every move.

"Maybe I *should* keep an eye out for kiwi," Taylor mumbled, bringing a chuckle out of Kaleb. Vines climbed the side of the house in efforts to spread as far as they could reach, and from the steps off the back porch, a gravel walkway led its way to three different locations. The first being a greenhouse that looked to be connected to the side of the house, the second wrapping around to the exit, where he and Kaleb stood now, and the third to a shed tucked away in the far back.

Kaleb ventured towards the path leading to the shed, speaking warnings over his shoulder to Taylor. "Try to stay on the path," he said, then with a chuckle. "And try not to get too distracted."

Taylor looked in silent awe at the beautiful arrangement of brilliant life displayed all around him. "Whose is this?" he breathed, thinking aloud.

"We all pitched in," Kaleb answered for him. "The greenhouse belongs to the family, but the backyard's mostly mine." Taylor looked to Kaleb, astounded.

"*You* did this?" he questioned.

Kaleb smiled proudly. "Yep," he said.

Taylor's amazement grew as he searched. "*How?*"

Kaleb sucked in his lips, rubbing the back of his head. "It's kind of a long story," he said, finally. Taylor accepted the answer, not really wanting to stay in a long conversation with Kaleb unless it was about his studies. Instead, he crept along the gravel, taking in every sight, sound and color as he walked, but stopped when something slithered by that caught his eye.

"There's a snake in your grass," Taylor alerted, slightly startled himself.

"Yeah, that's Pete," Kaleb said nonchalantly. "He's harmless. Mom hates him, but I think every garden needs a good garden snake. Keeps the balance."

"Oh," Taylor said, watching Pete slide underneath a bush full of winter-ready flowers. "Is that why you wanted me on the gravel?" he asked, catching up to Kaleb at the shed's door. Kaleb looked to Taylor plainly.

"Wouldn't you be upset if someone stepped on your tail?" Kaleb asked, then grinned at his own joke as he removed the lock from the door and swung it open. "C'mon."

Taylor followed Kaleb inside, but the light was dim, and it was hard to see anything unless he came close to it. Taylor held his hands out by his waist and kept his steps low to the ground in efforts to keep him from bumping into anything. Kaleb, however, marched into the darkness. Having set his crutches up against the outer wall of the shed upon entry, his steps clumped in the inky blackness, shuffling a bit when he paused for a moment.

"Where is that…" Kaleb muttered, then, "Ah!" Light swarmed the room, revealing Kaleb in the center of it, still holding the chain to the light above him. "That's better."

Along the walls were three long shelves that stretched along the interior of the shed, overflowing with parts and tools and cables of every kind. Behind Kaleb, in the center of it all, was a motorbike, standing alone, gutted and rebuilt halfway, in a style that Taylor had never seen before.

"This is it," Kaleb smiled. "My project."

Taylor cocked a brow, staring at the bike questionably. "You want me to help you build a bike?" Taylor stated.

Kaleb nodded. "Yep," he smiled.

"That's what I'm here for?" Taylor speculated. "I'm not a mechanic, what made you think I could help you?" Kaleb held up a finger.

"Ah, good question." He clumped around behind the bike. "See, this isn't a normal bike," he said. "It's different."

"How?" Taylor asked flatly, but Kaleb's grin grew.

"This bike's not steam powered like the rest of them."

Taylor's brow furrowed. "Come again?"

Kaleb knelt down to sit next to where the engine was normally stored. "Here, have a look for yourself."

Taylor dropped his bag from his shoulders, placing it down next to Kaleb's crutches, then stepped over next to Kaleb to inspect what it was he was doing.

"Here, see?" Kaleb pointed as he spoke. "Here's where they usually put the heater, and over here is where you would put your water." Taylor squinted, taking in what he was being shown. "Every car, every truck, every transportation device ever created runs off the power of steam. We're so dependant on it, we use it everywhere. We drink it, we bathe with it, we use it to fuel our cars, we just use so much of it every year." Kaleb continued. "And what happens every year?"

"A drought," Taylor realized quietly.

"Exactly!" Kaleb's excitement grew. "Every summer, there's a drought. It makes it hard on everybody, even us- the river town *surrounded* by water. So what would happen if we ran out of water?"

"Everything would stop completely," Taylor answered, starting to consider Kaleb's theories for himself.

"But," Kaleb grinned. "What if there was an alternative to steam power?" Taylor looked to Kaleb, waiting for him to answer. "Electricity," said Kaleb calmly, yet enlightened.

Taylor's eyes squinted at the thought. "Electricity... " he pondered, exploring the insides of the bike.

"Why not?" Kaleb went on. "I mean, they use it in toys, right? Why not boost it up a notch and try it in real life?" Taylor traced a finger along the outer edge of where the water tank used to be, considering Kaleb's words. "Think of what it could do for the economy. And the water resources!" Kaleb's excitement was rising by the second. Taylor had other thoughts.

"And I suppose the money from this idea wouldn't hurt either?" he stated. Kaleb paused a moment, processing Taylor's words.

"You know, I hadn't thought of that," he answered truthfully. Taylor returned his attention to studying the interior of the bike. After a long stretch of silence, he voiced his thoughts.

"I can't help you," he said. "I don't have the time." Kaleb was about to protest, but Taylor stopped him with more reasoning. "School, work, tutoring, and now, thanks to Miss Hart," his voice dropped distastefully at the mention of her name, "I also have to run her stupid technology club. Not to mention all the other things I have to do at home."

Kaleb's gaze dropped to the floor. "Oh," he muttered, tracing an invisible pattern on the floor with his eyes. Then, he popped up with a sudden thought. "What if I joined the club?" he asked. Taylor turned to him, weary at his sudden outburst.

"Huh?"

Kaleb rearranged himself to sit on his good foot. "If I joined the club, this could be our project," he said. "I mean it *is* technology. We could at least try." Taylor considered the idea, though he was shocked that Kaleb would come up with such a clever, yet simple solution.

"Maybe." He sucked in his lips, thinking of how it would work.

"It'll work," Kaleb confirmed. "Miss Hart can teach like she's supposed to. All you have to do is work on something technological, and *this is it*." Taylor took in a breath before finally answering.

"Alright," he sighed. "Let's give it a shot."

It was the start of a new day, at the start of a new week; starting with good news, and a gruesome school-issued breakfast. Taylor fiddled with his new key, considering the power he had been given. He had proposed Kaleb's idea to Miss Hart, to which she wholeheartedly agreed, and in doing so, had given him a key to the technology center. This power, equivalent to Kaleb's in the Alchemy hall, now granted him access to the school after everyone else had left.

Taylor took a sip of his drink, still feeling the structure of the metal key in his hand. Out of nowhere, Kaleb plopped down in the seat across from Taylor, setting his crutches against the edge of the table. Taylor watched him carefully, hiding the key in his pocket while eyeing him from beneath his brow with a condescending look.

"What are you doing?" he asked.

Kaleb ignored the question entirely to speak of his own. "Did you ask her yet?"

Taylor huffed at the boy. "She said it would be alright," he replied irritably. "Though it would have been better if we both went to her during class."

Kaleb shrugged. "Couldn't wait."

Taylor dropped his fork onto his plate. "What are you doing here?" he griped.

Kaleb shrugged again, a queer look to his face. "Can't a guy sit to eat?"

"You've never done it before," Taylor quipped.

"Sure I have."

"Not with me."

Kaleb's face dropped. "Is that a bad thing?" he asked. "I mean, jeez, it's like you're allergic to people or something."

Taylor's condescending brow became bored. "Something like that."

Kaleb peered at Taylor. "You don't like people?"

"More like hate." Taylor popped a forkful of food into his mouth. Kaleb scrunched his face in shock and confusion.

"How can you hate people?"

Taylor shrugged, finishing his bite before speaking. "It's easy when you think about it." He toyed with his food, deciding what to eat next. "The way I see it, there are two types of people in the world: shepherds, and sheep."

Now Kaleb was truly confused.

"I'm not a sheep."

"No," Taylor moved some food in his mouth to speak clearly. "You're a shepherd. Everybody else here is a sheep."

Kaleb crossed his arms on the table. "You're going to have to explain that a little more to me," he said in a low voice.

Taylor waved his fork at the other students around them. "People who lead, and people who follow. If you told them to do something, they'd do it. No questions asked. Especially if it came from you."

Kaleb furrowed his brow. "That's not true."

Taylor looked Kaleb right in the eye, his fork still in hand as it supported his chin. Then, suddenly, and very loudly, Taylor opened his mouth in reply.

"MOO!" he shouted, his face still bored, even as he belted out the animal's cry. Kaleb flinched at the sudden sound, ducking in embarrassment.

"What are you-"

"MOO!"

"MOOOO!"

"MOO!"

"MOOOOOOOOO!"

All around the cafeteria, students were mooing as loud as they could, trying to 'out-moo' each other. Even some of the boys from the football team were screaming it at one another, standing over the other as they grew louder and louder with each shout.

144

Taylor kept his gaze on Kaleb throughout the ordeal, listening quietly to the madness. When Kaleb looked back to Taylor, the blonde merely waved out his fork wielding hand, presenting the insanity to him. Kaleb sat quietly, turning to sit properly in his seat again before speaking.

"... That's not what sheep sound like," he said quietly.

Taylor dropped his fork to his plate. "I'm not gonna do it again after I've proven my point," he griped. "Look, all I'm saying is that I would rather hang out with people who have a mind of their own."

"Like shepherds?"

"Exactly."

"Okay," Kaleb said smugly. Taylor tensed, realizing what had just been said.

"Wait, that's not what I meant-"

"No, no," Kaleb chuckled. "I know what I heard." Taylor sighed in frustration, irritated that the jock had once again tricked him into doing what Kaleb wanted. "So, if I heard you right," Kaleb started. "According to you, there's nobody here but sheep; is that right?"

Taylor picked up his fork to play with his food again, anything to keep away from eye contact. "Yeah," he mumbled to his food.

Kaleb looked to the table. "Doesn't leave much room for any fun, does it?"

Taylor cocked a brow. "What do you mean?" he asked. "I have fun."

Now it was Kaleb with the condescending brow. "I'm not even going to touch that one," he muttered. Taylor glared at Kaleb, his irritation growing. "You never answered my question yesterday," Kaleb said. "About being around anybody other than me and Miss Hart."

Taylor lowered his glare to his plate, avoiding eye contact. "So what?" he said. "I already told you, I prefer to be alone."

"That's no way to live." Kaleb leaned in closer to the table. "How about a deal?"

Taylor looked to him from beneath his brow. "You've got a gambling problem, you know that?"

Kaleb grinned. "It's not gambling if I win." Taylor rolled his eyes, but Kaleb interjected before Taylor could come back with a snarky remark. "How about this," he leaned in closer, lowering his voice. "For every fun thing you do, that's another paid tutoring session right there." Taylor looked to Kaleb, now searching his eyes for mistrust.

"Seriously?" Taylor muttered. Kaleb nodded.

"You need proof, though," he said. "Otherwise it doesn't count."

Taylor blinked, thinking of all the better outcomes from this proposition all at once. Free tutoring, but only if he had proof of activities. The idea was too enticing to handle. He swallowed to try and calm his busy mind.

Overhead, the bell rang, signaling the students to leave for their classes. Taylor licked his lips, gathering his tray to leave, but staying in his seat.

"Alright," he said finally.

Kaleb grinned, leaning back to grab hold of his crutches. "Alright," he copied, then started towards the exit. Taylor trashed his tray and made his way out as well, trying to avoid Kaleb and the crowd, some of whom were still "mooing," making the crowded departure more herd-like than it already was. Taylor pocketed his hands, moving through the crowd as invisible as possible.

"Free lessons. All right."

Kaleb made his way through the crowd, clicking along the halls with his usual, cheerful smile. The morning was still fresh on many a student, each of them bleary-eyed and yawning, wishing for more sleep. Kaleb, however, was elated. With any luck, this new bet would change Taylor into a happier person, someone that people would like to be around, and not the sour grump he already was.

He caught sight of Taylor, hidden in the crowd, trying to reach his locker. Kaleb smiled at the thought of Taylor hanging out with his teammates and making new friends with each new activity that he came across. The idea that he could help change Taylor into a better person made him light on his feet, regardless of the crutches and cast that weighed him down.

Taylor had reached his locker now, slipping off his pack to set it on the floor beside him. He was just about to unlock it when it burst open, revealing a horrid little monster. A screaming Gerrit popped out of Taylor's locker, forcing Taylor to stumble back and fall in surprise, but not before slamming his fist into Gerrit's face. The surrounding students roared with laughter at the scene that had just been displayed, including Kaleb himself. Gerrit, however, was less than pleased.

"You hit me!" he howled, rubbing his cheek.

"Of course he did!" Kaleb laughed. "Wouldn't you?"

Taylor looked from Kaleb to Gerrit, not making a sound. He looked like a wounded animal, highly irritated and ready to strike if necessary, but Kaleb was too tickled to care. His laughter almost overthrew his words.

"How did you get in there, anyways?"

"It's not my fault Tommy here left it open," said Gerrit. Taylor rose up to quickly empty his pack and replace his book, his irritation growing with every breath. He slammed his locker shut, only to have it ricochet back open. Upon closer inspection, he saw some tape strapped over the lock. He ripped it off, holding it up for Gerrit to see. Kaleb cocked a brow.

"Really now?"

"We may have kept it open," Gerrit shrugged holding up his hands. "Quarter." Taylor crumpled the tape and dropped it on the floor.

"This doesn't count as a fun thing," Kaleb giggled. Taylor glared at the lame jock.

"You think this is *fun*?" he growled, then slammed his locker shut, making sure it closed and locked this time around.

"See you around, Tommy," said Gerrit with a menacing smile, but Kaleb's giggles had left him as soon as Taylor did. He caught up with the blonde surprisingly well, considering.

"Taylor, wait." Kaleb grabbed hold of his sleeve, tugging slightly to stop him. "It was just a bit of fun, what's wrong?"

Taylor rolled Kaleb's hand away. "You have a strange idea of fun," he grumbled.

Kaleb's brow furrowed. "You're not reneging on our deal already, are you?"

"No," Taylor griped. "But that doesn't mean I have to get all buddy-buddy with you or your friends either." Kaleb recoiled, scorned by the moody teen's words.

"Tayl-"

"Just leave me alone and go to class, asshole," Taylor interrupted. "We're not gonna get anywhere like this." With that, Taylor ended the conversation, and was gone. Off to his first class, leaving Kaleb to stand in the hallway on his own.

For the rest of the day, Kaleb moped on his thoughts, replaying what had happened from beginning to end. He was sincerely hurt by what Taylor had said, not only because of how he said it, but also because it ruined his visions of the future he had had of Taylor hanging out with Kaleb and his friends. He was certain that being around people that enjoyed a good laugh would help to brighten the young teen's darkened spirits, and that he would eventually become a nicer person to be around. Alas, these theories were dashed.

Whenever he saw Taylor, either in the halls or in class, the wounds he had inflicted on Kaleb reopened, making him wonder where things went wrong. New ones were made as well, as the young man did everything in his power to avoid Kaleb at all costs. Once, in between classes, he noticed Taylor coming out of the mens room, clutching his ribs and not standing entirely straight. When Kaleb tried to ask him if he was alright, the blonde merely brushed him off, ignoring him for his journey to class instead. By the final bell, Kaleb was not only miserable, but irritated and confused as well.

He had decided a meeting with Kara was needed before his session with Taylor in order to keep from wringing the little shit's neck. Kara was already preparing her station and her clothes as he entered the studio, pausing a moment for a greeting when she saw him.

"Uh-oh," she snarked.

"Hello to you too." He plopped down onto one of her stools.

"Haven't seen you in a while," she said, propping up a blank canvas. "I was starting to think you were cheating on me." Kaleb gave a dry, humorless laugh, pulling a chuckle from his friend.

"How are the tutoring lessons going?" she asked, receiving an exasperated groan in reply. "I see." Kara began tying her shawl around her waist. "What's on your mind, Kay?" Once Kaleb had explained the situation and expressed his views on the whole ordeal, Kara waited a moment, soaking in what she had just heard. Then,

"You really are stupid."

"Huh?" Kaleb belted.

"You can't change someone that easily," she explained. "Especially someone really set in their ways like him." Kaleb thought about this, eventually nodding his agreement. "He'll come around," she told him. "You just need to be patient with him. Give him some space, and let him know what you mean *clearly*. Oh," she pointed to him to emphasize her words. "And try to be understanding. Your fun and his fun are two completely different things."

"I guess you're right." Kaleb shrugged, sighing.

"Of course I'm right," Kara quipped. "That's why you come to me for advice." Kaleb smirked at his old friend, receiving a grin and a wink in return. "Go on," she told him. "If he sees you're not there, he might think you ran out on him."

Kaleb straightened. "You think so?"

"Go!" She shooed him out with a painters rag. "And bring him over here sometime," she called after him. "I'd like to check him out for myself."

Kaleb clicked out the door, but stopped to turn back to her. "Hey, Kara?"

She turned back to look at him as well. "Yes?"

"Are people sheep?"

"Definitely."

Taylor stuck his head into the laboratory room, only to find it empty. He sighed quietly, looking to the floor in disappointment. He stood in the doorway, hiked his pack higher onto his shoulders and debated whether or not to stay or go, cursing himself for quarrelling with Kaleb earlier that morning.

"If I had known he'd be this sensitive about it, I'd have kept my mouth shut."

Taylor stepped into the empty room, loafing around as he waited. Now that the school was emptied, the Alchemy hall was theirs for the taking. There had been plenty of time for Kaleb to get there before him, and he usually did. Now, having to wait on him made Taylor nervous. He shuffled his feet, hoping the lame jock would appear. When he didn't, Taylor sighed again, and turned to leave.

He berated himself for arguing with Kaleb that morning with every step he took, wishing he had kept his mouth shut and wondering why he had spoken out in the first place. Taylor made it to the double doors leading home and was about to pass through them when he heard the familiar clicking of Kaleb's extra footsteps echoing in the far distance.

The blonde's heart raced, trying to decide what it was he wanted to do, and finally decided on scrambling back to the classroom as quickly and as quietly as he could before Kaleb could see him trying to leave. Just as he skidded to a stop at the door;

"Oh good, you're still here." Kaleb popped around the corner. Taylor nodded his greeting.

"Hey," he said nonchalantly, though secretly he was trying to catch up on his breathing.

"I didn't think you'd come," Kaleb told him. "You know, after this morning."

"Yeah." Taylor ran a hand through his hair. "Sorry."

Kaleb's smile gleamed in his eye. "No prob," he replied.

Taylor coughed to distract his tension, then scuffled his way through the door. "I've got something for you," he said, slipping off and rummaging through his pack.

"Aw, for me?" Kaleb snarked. "You shouldn't have." Taylor threw him another one of his signature glares from beneath his brow before pulling out a sheet of paper.

"Here."

"What's this?" Kaleb asked, taking the paper.

"My proof," Taylor replied. Kaleb began reading, only to stop short when he realized what it was.

"This is a book report," he said flatly.

Taylor shrugged. "How else was I supposed to prove it?" Kaleb dropped the paper to the table beside him and smothered his face with his hand. "What?" Taylor defended. "I like to read."

"That's not what I had in mind," muffled Kaleb through his fingers, then a thought occurred to him. "You like to read?" he asked, dropping his hands and looking to Taylor.

"Yeah, so?" Taylor puffed. Kaleb smiled.

"I have an idea."

No matter how many times Taylor grouched at him for "playing fifth grader," Kaleb denied Taylor any knowledge what-so-ever of his plotting until they had finished with the day's lesson. Now with a four page essay out of the way, they could embark on the journey that Kaleb had had in mind. Starting with the trolley.

"Are you gonna tell me *now*?" Taylor grumbled as he sat down in a vacant window seat.

"We're off to Carter," Kaleb said plainly. "After that, who knows?"

"You do," said Taylor flatly.

Kaleb shrugged, unable to deny him of that truth. They soon arrived at the end of the trolley's stops, and made their way to the bus stop. The ride was quiet, though Kaleb tried to fill the silence with conversation. He mostly succeeded with Taylor, earning a few remarks here and there, but Taylor was never one to talk much in the first place.

Every time the bus stopped to pick up or drop off passengers, the cold air seeped in through the open door, making Kaleb button his coat more, and Taylor tighten his scarf around his neck. When they finally reached their stop, Kaleb hopped off the steps to the pavement one-legged, holding his booted leg up in the air and his crutches in each hand for balance. "Here we go," Kaleb said, smiling at the building across the street. "The Bookshelf."

Taylor dug his hands deep into his hoodie pocket. "Yay," he droned.

"Come on," Kaleb chastised, leading the way across the street. Taylor followed suit. As much as he loved reading, spending money on things that weren't a necessity wasn't in his nature. Pleasantries like books were meant for celebrations alone, so although he adored The Bookshelf, going in with nothing and coming out with nothing seemed like such a bore to him. Still, Kaleb considered it to be a 'fun thing,' which meant he could endure browsing for a little while to pay off his lesson.

As Kaleb neared the door to the bookshop, he stopped to hold it open for a young woman walking behind the two boys. As she walked through, he gave her his charming smile, earning a smile and thanks from her in return. Once she was safe inside, he motioned for Taylor to go in before him and followed right after.

"Alright," he said. "Let's check it out."

"Meet you back here," Taylor mumbled, moving before Kaleb could agree. They separated in search of what pleased them, but ended up together in the fiction section despite Taylor's efforts. Kaleb caught sight of Taylor and shrugged before diving back into the rows upon rows of books. Taylor, on the other hand, decided to search elsewhere.

He browsed throughout the store, teetering through different sections from front to back. Historical, language, how-to, and eventually, back to mythical fiction books with dragons and flying ships. Kaleb was still in this section, only an aisle away, holding a book before him. Taylor watched as he closed his eyes and traced his fingers along the outer covers of the book. He flipped the pages, breathing in as they flew by in his hands, and finally, opened his eyes to read the inner cover of the book, his smile hiding in the crook of his mouth and in the light of his eyes.

Taylor turned away from his spying, and found himself in the art section. He strolled along the aisle, taking his time as he admired the display of crafts, games and books. At the end of the aisle, however, there was a bookstand filled with titleless books. Taylor's curiosity took hold of him, and he gave in to look through the mysterious books. As he drew closer, he realized that the nameless books were not books at all, but journals.

Taylor thought of his own journal, and how he would be needing a new one soon. His beloved booklet was worn, and nearing its end of usable paper. It held every dream, every story, every wonder that came from Taylor's mind, and though the outer leather had cracked and stained over use, his journal still remained one of his most treasured belongings.

Taylor picked up one of the displayed books closest to him and flipped through it, enjoying the view of crisp, virgin pages that had never been touched by the ink of a pen. He replaced the journal and looked through a second- a green one- feeling the scaley exterior before stopping abruptly.

He replaced the green journal with a remarkable navy blue one in its stead, bound in both soft leather and suede. He traced the stitchwork along the spine and unhinged the magnetic flap that slid in from the back and through the front as a makeshift lock. The paper inside was just as pleasing, with dark blue numbers printed finely in the bottom right corner. Taylor flipped through to the back of the journal to see a dark "500" printed on the last corner.

A deep blue ribbon page-holder snaked in between pages 23 and 24, and to top off the whole thing with a bright red cherry; inside the spine, between the cover and its pages, was a little nook hiding a shiny, silver pen. Taylor removed the pen to test it on his knuckle, showing a brilliant blue ink that matched the journal's cover and page-holder. Taylor closed the journal and returned the pen carefully, sliding the flap back into place and gently replacing the notebook back to its original home on the bookshelf. He looked to the floor, disappointed in himself for even looking at such a wonderful journal. Then, from out of nowhere,

"Moo."

Taylor tensed, gripping his pack's shoulder straps.

"Mooo," the voice repeated.

Taylor whipped around to find Kaleb, still in the fiction section with an open book up to his face.

"Moooo," he called again, shoulders shaking.

Around the shop, people searched for the elusive cow, confused as to why anyone would want to imitate such a creature in the first place.

"I should have never taught him that." Taylor hiked his pack, then quietly made his way over to the idiotic cow.

"Moo."

"What are you doing?" Taylor asked quietly, casually inspecting a nearby book to avoid any chance of looking at him, as he did not want to be associated with the cow.

"This room is full of shepherds," Kaleb whispered despairingly.

"You think?" Taylor replied. "Sheep don't flock here."

"Moo!"

The boys froze at the sudden interjection, looking straight ahead at nothing.

"Moo!"

It called again. Both Kaleb and Taylor tensed, one trying to hold back a laugh, the other sucking in his lips, disbelieving what was really happening. It wasn't the mooing that humored them, but the sound of it. It was a child's voice that replied, squeaking as it changed pitches.

"Moooo!"

"Moo!" Kaleb finally replied, shaking behind his book.

"Stop it," Taylor hissed. "You're gonna get us kicked out."

"Don't care, MOO."

"Moo!"

"You're abusing your power."

"Totally worth it, MOO!"

By now, Kaleb was shaking terribly, trying to suppress his laughter. Taylor held the back of his knuckles to his mouth, walking away to leave Kaleb to fend for himself, but the child continued responding to Kaleb's calls, causing Taylor to break down in embarrassment at the end of the aisle. He curled down low, hiding behind the bookshelf so as not to be seen, occasionally smothering a tiny snicker with his fist when the child squeaked particularly high.

Kaleb was near his breaking point as well, and gathered his things to ready himself at the check out. Taylor waited for him behind the safety of the shelf, still trying to hide his face; all the while, the child grew louder, squeaking as he called for the other cow. Kaleb finally leaned over Taylor's shelf and wheezed:

"Okay, let's go!"

Taylor bolted out the door with Kaleb, where the jock collapsed into a fit of hopelessly contagious giggles as they crossed the street.

"Looks like we found ourselves a little lamb," Kaleb remarked, sending both of them into hysterics while they waited for the bus.

Their laughter subsided as the behemoth of a bus rolled to their stop, and they boarded into the belly of the steaming beast. "What were you even doing?" Taylor asked as they sat, taking the window seat again.

"I had to do something to get you away." Kaleb pulled out an item from his shopping bag and tossed it into Taylor's hands. The very same blue journal Taylor had been fawning over now lay in his lap, waiting to be used. Taylor looked to Kaleb for an answer.

"This-"

"*That's* proof," he said, tucking the shopping bag under their seat. "What fun is it to leave a bookshop empty handed?" Taylor blinked back to the journal in his hands, his mouth agape. "It's also my way of apologizing for reading your notebook," Kaleb remarked, rubbing the back of his head.

"Yeah," Taylor managed. "Thanks."

He ran his thumb over the magnetic lock, still dumbstruck at the idea that it was now his to be used. He shook his head, bringing himself back to reality, and began to reach for his pack. He stopped however, when he realized that he didn't want to pack away his new journal just yet, and sat back, holding it tightly in his lap until they had to switch stops.

That night, after the boys had said their goodbyes, Bubbie had been fed and played with, and Taylor had prepped for the day ahead, he drew out the journal again to admire it as he lay in bed. He held it high above him, rubbing the soft exterior with his thumbs. He noticed the ink stain on his knuckle that matched the book in his hands, and a small smile gripped at the corners of his mouth. He thought of his adventures in receiving both momentos; then of his scarf that his mother sent him, letting his smile take hold as a thought connected the two.

"Happy birthday."

Chapter 10

Bubbie was ecstatic to see Taylor so early in the morning, and Taylor couldn't help feeling just as happy as the excited shepherd bounced around his feet in greeting. Now that Taylor had a new schedule with Kaleb, pre-dawn morning was the best time for him to tend to his furry friend. Originally, Taylor had believed his afternoons would be free after his tutoring sessions, but the lessons weren't the real issue. It was having to fit in the tutoring sessions, then leaving to work on Kaleb's bike, or leaving to work out of town, and now doing something fun for Kaleb; all before making it home in time to make his father dinner. Once he was home, Taylor had zero chance of leaving the house without the risk of his father finding out.

As he lit his lantern and entered the chute, Taylor set forth to the essentials before anything else. He filled Bubbie's food bowl a little more than usual, giving him extra to help last throughout the day. He also set aside a raw-hide for Bubbie to gnaw on once he left. Water was plentiful from the creek beneath them, though it gave Bubbie a horrible mouthful of what Taylor tended to call "fish breath." With these responsibilities out of the way, Taylor picked up Bubbie's ball, waving it in front of the dog's snout to excite him before throwing it.

The shepherd rushed after it in a black and white blur, jumping out of the chute with careful precision to not land on unstable ground or water. They played together until the rising sun began to peek through the trees, signalling Taylor that his time was nearing its end. He drew in the dog, scrubbing him up and down with furious affection, then parted ways to leave for school. As usual, Bubbie complained of his absence, but obeyed Taylor's wishes nonetheless.

Once Taylor was on the bridge, making his way towards school, he dug out his headphones to enjoy some music during his commute. The morning chill bit through his hoodie, but the sun helped to warm him through the dark fabric as he walked along the path.

"I wonder how Bubbie keeps warm," Taylor thought, suddenly more worried about his friend than usual. He sank his hands into his pockets to warm his fingers, but felt something cold and hard instead. Out came the key Miss Hart had given him when he pulled out the mysterious object. Taylor's face dropped. *"That was way too easy."*

Taylor considered the idea, wondering if he could pull off such a maneuver in the first place. His thoughts instantly turned to the empty creekbed a little ways behind the school, wondering if it was in any way connected to his creek at all, and began plotting.

"This is way too easy!"

The simplicity of it frightened him, assuring himself of being caught, but the more he thought about it, the more he considered it as a good option; albeit it a risky one.

Taylor was so caught in his thoughts and planning, he hadn't noticed a certain person gaining up behind him. He tripped over a well maneuvered kick, paired with a shove from behind in a painful one-two hit combination. He landed hard, making Taylor's headphones slip from his ears to his neck, hanging onto his scarred cheek and temple. He hissed in pain, his scraped palms and knee already glistening from clotting blood trying to heal his open wound. A familiar laugh roared in Taylor's ears from behind, though he didn't need to look to know it was Gerrit.

"Thanks for yesterday, Tommy," Gerrit sneered, stepping over Taylor as he charged towards his friends ahead of them, already laughing and congratulating Gerrit for his deeds. Taylor shook his head, watching him join his friends.

He thought he was safe from any other attacks since the beating from the day before, but apparently, Gerrit was still sore about being punched in the face. Taylor let out a snicker as he stood. He had to admit, it felt good hitting him for once. Even if it was a reflex, Gerrit's momentary look of shock and terror before contact was enough to satisfy Taylor's amusement for hours.

Still, the fear that followed the encounter did quiet him for the rest of the day. He kept on his toes, hoping to fly under the radar so as not to get into trouble with the school. After his previous affairs with the smaller boy, Taylor's record wasn't entirely clean. One word from Gerrit, and Taylor's entire future could be destroyed.

Taylor brushed off his pants, knowing his skin was torn beneath them, even if his jeans weren't. Later he would visit the nurse's office for bandaging if there was a need for it, but for now, as far as disinfecting his wounds, the sink would have to do.

Kaleb wiped his brow, frustrated with the stubborn bolt staying true to its duty inside the bike. The boys had gathered in Kaleb's shed to work on the bike after their lesson, and were now at a standstill because of one finicky bolt stuck in place.

"Here, let me try." Taylor held his hand out for the wrench, trading places with Kaleb. He inspected the bolt, drawing close to it. "Hand me the oil can?" he asked, still staring it down.

Kaleb complied, sitting back to watch as Taylor thoroughly greased the bolt, then rubbed the outer edges clean. Once he was satisfied, Taylor tried his luck, earning a successful squeak from the rubbing metal.

"Here. You do it," Taylor puffed. The bolt truly was stuck to its position, even greased, and although Taylor had quite a bit of muscle himself, Kaleb had more. The boys switched places again, and it was now Taylor watching Kaleb struggle with the troublesome bolt. After a few more pushes, Kaleb was successful in removing the blasted piece of metal, holding it up for the two boys to glare triumphantly at it.

"Good idea," Kaleb offered, tossing the bolt into a marked can for later replacement.

"Just friction," Taylor said, never seeing the grin from Kaleb as he remembered teaching the science to the blonde. A knock from outside brought their attention to the door.

"Hey, boys." Mr. Evans held a hand up in greeting as he entered the shed. "Any luck?" Kaleb began wiping his fingers on a dirty oil rag.

"Just missed our little victory party, actually." He grinned. "Sorry, Pop. Snooze, you lose."

The man sorrowfully gripped his chest. "Whatever will I do?" he whined.

Taylor took the rag from Kaleb when offered and began cleaning his hands as well, wincing when the oil entered his scrapes. Vance was a tall man indeed, with trimmed brown hair and blue eyes, looking almost too young to be a father.

"I don't believe we've met." Vance came further inside. "I'm Kaleb's old man." He held out a hand for a shake, not minding the grease.

"Hello, Mr. Evans." Taylor was about to take the handshake, but jumped back when Vance came rushing at him, holding his hands up to stop the older man.

"Sh-No!" Vance hissed, checking behind him before turning back to Taylor. "Don't let my wife hear you say stuff like that."

Taylor cocked a brow, hands still up. "Mister?" he asked.

"Yeah," Vance nodded. "It's just Vance."

Kaleb rubbed the back of his head as best he could without the use of his filthy hands, looking away in thought. "Yeah, she'll rip your spine out," he agreed.

"You think he's kidding," said Vance, finally relaxing and backing away from Taylor.

"Okay," Taylor said, watching the two men carefully. The father and son shared a chuckle at Taylor's expression.

"Just don't call her Mrs. Evans if she comes by," Kaleb told him. "If you say stuff like ma'am or Misses like any polite person, she'll go on a rampage."

"It's not pretty," Vance puffed.

"Duly noted," said Taylor, giving up on finding any sanity between the two men. Another knock on the door startled the men, each turning to the door.

"Hello!" Trish sang. Her hazel eyes shone bright, and her wavy auburn hair curled around her face, making her look much younger than a traditional mother of a teenager. "May I come in?"

Vance crossed his arms. "I don't know, dear," he said. "This is a man cave; females such as yourself may swoon at it's manliness."

Trish smiled. "If you can handle it, honey, I think I can manage," she replied, earning a snicker from the boys behind Vance, and it was then that she noticed Taylor.

"Hi there," she stepped forward. "I'm Trish, Kaleb's mom."

Taylor nodded in greeting, hiding his dirty hands in the folds of the oil rag.

160

"Hello, M-" Vance began waving frantically behind his wife. "M-iss Trish," Taylor switched. "I'm Taylor."

Trish cocked a brow at the mention of 'miss,' but said nothing. Both Kaleb and Vance looked to each other, surprised. "Now that's a new one," she said. "I like it."

Vance threw his hands high to the sky, turning away from the group completely flabbergasted. "All this time," he muttered.

"Will you be joining us for dinner, Taylor?" Trish asked expectantly.

"Uh, actually," Taylor ran a hand through his hair. "I need to get back soon."

Trish and Vance chuckled. "Not like that, you're not," said Vance, pointing. Trish stepped forward to Taylor, touching his shoulder gently when he retracted, and tried to rub out the dark oil that Taylor had inadvertently scrubbed through his light hair.

"Yep, that's not coming out," Trish mumbled. "Come inside. You can get cleaned up."

"It's fine, I can-"

Kaleb clapped a hand on Taylor's shoulder. "No use changing her mind, dude," he told him, ushering the dirty blonde along. Even Vance coincided, shouldering Taylor's backpack as they exited the shed.

"Come along, dear." Trish wrapped an arm around Taylor's shoulders. "You sure you can't stay for dinner?" Trish asked again. "We're having goulash."

Taylor glanced at her. "Goo-losh?" he repeated, confused.

"It's really good," piped Kaleb from behind, locking the shed door. "You should try it." Before Taylor could deny again, Kaleb held up a greasy finger. "It counts," he said, changing Taylor's mind.

"… Okay," Taylor muttered, still unsure.

"Oh, don't act so scared." Trish gave Taylor's arm a squeeze.

"Yeah," Vance joined in. "I mean, it's not like *I'm* cooking."

"That *would* be terrifying," Kaleb joked, catching up with the others along the gravel path in time for Vance to swat the back of his son's head. Trish could only laugh at the two, still holding Taylor as they walked up the back porch and inside.

"If you two kill each other before dessert, that's fine. More for me and Taylor."

"Hey!" the two men complained, following close behind.

"What kind of vegetables do you like, Taylor?" Trish asked suddenly.

"Uh, any kind, I guess," he replied.

"You're not a broccoli fan, are you?" she asked, looking expectantly in his eyes.

"Um," Taylor shook his head. "No, not really."

Trish smiled a smile that could challenge Kaleb's. "Good."

"You're so weird!" Kaleb called.

"Are not," Trish called back. "It's gross, and prickly, and sticks in your teeth. If anything, you're the weird one. What child likes broccoli?"

Kaleb puffed up his muscles. "I'm a man!" he said, displaying said muscles. Vance reached around to poke Kaleb in the ribs, trying to get around him but caused a surprised yelp to escape his son.

"Very manly," he droned in a deep voice, finally passing his son. Taylor's grin crept at the corners of his mouth. If nothing else, the Evans family was humorous.

"Kaleb, go show him where to wash up," Trish ordered. "And clean up yourself, too."

"'Kay." Kaleb obeyed, ditching his crutches and clunking down the hall with Taylor following slowly behind. The interior of the house was just as nice as the exterior, but it wasn't by any means perfect. It wasn't spotless, it wasn't all white polish and marble flooring; it was merely well kept.

The walls were lined with desks and bookshelves filled with organized clutter,

162

and above them, framed pictures of the family throughout time hung proudly in various patterns. The carpet had old wear and tear near the back and front doors, and became flattened in every doorframe from years of use. If Taylor could describe it in a single term, the house was lived in. In a word, it was home.

Kaleb led Taylor to a small bathroom near the master bedroom, flicking on the light switch as he entered. "Here." Kaleb crouched down to gather some fresh soap. "You can use this for your hair." Taylor accepted it, finally catching a glimpse of himself in the mirror.

"They weren't kidding," Taylor murmured, touching the now dried, black oil that slicked back his hair from his forehead to the back of his head.

"Rough, man." Kaleb chuckled. Taylor stiffened.

"If you tell anyone about th-"

"Chill," Kaleb held up a hand. "My lips are sealed." In the distance, they could hear Trish calling to the boys to hurry up from the kitchen.

"I better get in there," said Kaleb, quickly scrubbing the grease from his fingers. "Take your time, man." Kaleb told him, drying his hands. "If you have to, you can always use the shower." Taylor nodded his thanks, taking a look at himself in the mirror again as Kaleb left.

He set to work, washing his hands free of oil before leaning his head into the sink to rid his hair of the greasy intruder. He managed to remove most of it, but his hair was so fair, even the slightest hint of oil could be seen in the mirror. Eventually, Taylor decided to fill the sink and dunk his head under the water, finally clearing him of any remaining residue. He took hold of the towel Kaleb had left behind and furiously scrubbed his head with it, trying to dry his hair in one go. His hair fell limply over his eyes to graze his cheeks, and with the towel already dampened through, declined a second attempt. He hung the towel over the rack to let it dry, then set out to find Kaleb in the kitchen.

"Over here, Taylor." Trish waved when she saw him wandering through the living room. Kaleb had his back turned, chopping something beside the sink, while Trish disappeared behind a cabinet. Taylor leaned up against the bar separating the kitchen and living room to peek inside, when something soft and furry rubbed against his legs. He looked down to see a silver cat, looking up at him.

"*Maow*."

Taylor knelt down to pet the kitty, who greedily accepted. "Out of garlic," Trish muttered, closing the cabinet. "Where'd you go?" she called, jumping when Taylor popped up. "Oh!" she startled. "There you are." She smiled, laughing at herself for being surprised. "Waiting to surprise me, were you?"

"No," Taylor backed away, suddenly fearful. "The cat-"

"Oh, Skitters." Trish waved him off. "Figures, she likes new people." Kaleb chuckled behind her, still chopping by the sink.

"It's because she thinks you'll feed her," he said. "Here." He held up a sliver of white. "See if she'll eat this."

Taylor took the spongy sliver, taking a look at it before kneeling down to present it to Skitters. She was already sniffing for it on her hind legs, meowing for him to give it to her faster. When they settled on the floor together, she sniffed at the spongy food for a moment longer before quickly sinking her teeth into it and running away to eat the rest of it on her own.

"She loves her mushrooms," sighed Kaleb, smiling.

"Why don't you come in and help us, Taylor?" Trish asked. "Do you cook?"

"Some," Taylor said quietly.

"All right," Trish said, brushing a stray hair out of her face. "Have you ever picked your own vegetables before?" Taylor shook his head. "Then why don't we give it a shot?" She smiled, holding her hand open to allow entrance to the kitchen. Taylor looped around the bar, following Trish to the back wall as he neared.

"Come along." She grabbed a small, weaved bowl and took his hand, holding him behind her as she opened a glass door and walked through.

"Pick what you like," she told him, ushering him inside.

"Woah," Taylor breathed. Behind the glass door was the greenhouse, connected to the main house by custom home construction. From top to bottom, greenery flourished

164

along the walls of the greenhouse, and rows of herbs, fruits and vegetables and other goodies grew perfectly in line.

"The vegetables are over here." Trish guided him down the steps towards a very healthy tomato plant. "Go ahead," Trish urged, picking a ripe tomato. "Go on."

"So, this is all yours?" Taylor asked, kneeling down to inspect his options.

"Yes," Trish replied, placing a garlic bulb in her bowl. "We had to build it ourselves, but I think it was worth it. Hard work makes it all the more sweeter."

Taylor gently explored a green bell pepper with his fingers, careful not to hurt it. Taylor looked to Trish, who nodded her consent, then tried to pull it off the vine.

"Twist it," Trish advised. He did as he was told, and the pepper came off in his hands. She smiled, holding out the bowl for him to place the pepper inside. "What else?"

Taylor carefully strode around the garden, searching for more to put in, choosing a sweet, red bell pepper, a small eggplant, and eyeing some zucchini as well.

"Pick it," Trish told him. "If anything, we can bake some zucchini bread." Suddenly, Kaleb shouted from inside the kitchen.

"I heard zucchini bread!" he called. "You have to make it now!"

Trish chuckled at her son, rolling her eyes. "Fine!" she called back, pointing to the plants for Taylor to bring them to her. Taylor complied, picking a few more zucchini when Trish ordered, then returned to go back inside.

"Oh, Taylor, dear." Trish stopped and upturned his palms when she caught sight of his scabbed hands. "What happened?" Taylor shrugged, pulling away.

"I fell," he said, pocketing his hands. "It's no big deal." Trish frowned.

"Next time, let Kaleb have a look at them," she ordered. "We have stuff to make it heal quicker." Taylor nodded.

"Yes, Miss Trish."

Trish had Taylor wash the vegetables and herbs before handing them to Kaleb to chop, while she browned some meat and readied the pasta.

"Smells good!" Vance suddenly appeared at the bar. "You should invite him over more often," he joked, nodding to Taylor. Kaleb and Trish gave a chuckle, while Taylor merely shrugged, returning to his work washing the produce.

"Kaleb, you and Taylor are on dinner duty," Trish ordered. "I'll get started on that bread." The boys agreed, stepping aside for her to ready dessert.

Kaleb took care in teaching Taylor how to make their dinner, surprising Taylor with his knowledge of the kitchen. "When you think about it, it's just like chemistry." Kaleb shrugged, stirring pasta sauce into the concoction. When dinner was prepared, and dessert in the oven, Trish shooed the boys out of the kitchen, handing Vance the dishes to set the table. Once this was done, he set the pot filled with their dinner in the center of the table, opening the lid to smell its delicious contents.

"Oooh." He smiled. "Nice work."

"Pretty simple, right?" Trish asked, sitting down as Vance pushed her chair in for her.

"Meat, veggies, pasta," Kaleb interjected. Trish smiled at Taylor.

"It's just whatever you can find and stick it in a pot," she told him. Vance sat down as well, beginning to serve the plates, ladies first.

"I don't know how they do it," he said. "If it were me, I'd burn down the kitchen."

"Again," both Kaleb and his mother replied, snickering. Vance became defensive.

"How was I supposed to know that water evaporates when it boils?"

Trish shook her head. "Oh, my darling Vance," she said. "How in goodness name did you ever become a doctor?" Vance plated Taylor, then Kaleb, and finally himself.

"The nurse is the one who disinfects things with hot water," he replied, mocking superiority. "I just pop limbs back on."

The family shared a laugh, and even Taylor let a grin slip from behind his glass. The night went on with stories from work and school alike, with Trish prompting many a topic from Taylor throughout the evening. When the timer on the oven signaled the zucchini bread's completement, Vance quickly retrieved their dessert and brought it to the table along with the butter dish, replacing the dinner pot entirely. Kaleb cut an extra two slices from the loaf after everyone had had their fill and wrapped them up in a napkin, placing it in front of Taylor.

"Proof," said Taylor simply. Kaleb grinned.

"Try it cold for breakfast," he advised. "Even better."

When dessert was finished, Vance set towards his duties as dish washer, clearing the table and kitchen with ease. "We do the work, he does the clean up," Trish explained. Taylor was all packed and ready to leave, bidding farewell to the Evans' who had taken him in.

"Where's your hat?" Trish asked. Taylor tried to explain that he didn't have one, nor did he have a need for one, but she wouldn't accept it. "You're not leaving this house with wet hair." She scolded, even though his hair had mostly dried.

She dug out an old, dark grey beanie from the coat closet and secured it safely over Taylor's ears. "There," she said. "Much better." She told him to keep it as a gift, then surprised Taylor as she drew him in for a hug, patting his shoulder as she pulled away. "Come back anytime, you hear?" she told him, holding his face in her hands to look him in the eye.

"Yeah, kid," Vance agreed. "You can cook whenever you like." Trish swatted her giggling husband as he came over to hold her from behind. "It was good having you, Taylor." He laughed. Taylor nodded, offering a polite smile.

"Taylor," Kaleb piped, holding up a hand in farewell from the dining room table. "See you tomorrow." Taylor returned the gesture, then turned to leave. He tightened his scarf around his neck as a harsh wind pulled at his hood, exposing his head as it dropped, making Taylor thankful for the hat Trish had given him. He ignored the wind though, and hiked his pack higher onto his shoulders to start along the sidewalk.

"I wonder if dad would like goulash."

Kaleb stretched in his seat, already bored with class. He was browsing the internet whenever the teacher wasn't looking, trying to find something that would satisfy his hunger for entertainment. The games he normally played were blocked by the school, denying him access no matter how hard he tried. Now, he was looking for something new, tapping his finger as he thought.

Kaleb recollected the book he had bought at The Bookshelf with Taylor, wishing he had paced himself instead of burning through it in a single night. He stretched his fingers over the keyboard, entering "*good reads*" into the search bar. Up popped various websites, all lined up for his approval. Some were blocked by the school, while others were sale sites offering bargain books, narrowing his search further.

He scrolled through his remaining choices, clicking a few links to read what they had to offer. Most were written by teens who could hardly spell their own names, turning him away from the story all together. A handful were properly written, with a good story and correct grammar, but they ended too soon. He exited from a sweet love story between a shy girl and outgoing boy, clicking on to the story lined up beneath it.

Suddenly, Kaleb's eyes lit up. As he read, he recognized the characters, the story, even the writing style. The similarities were too in sync to be a coincidence, but he wanted, he *needed* to make sure his hypothesis was true. He scrolled to the top of the page in search of the writer's name, gasping quietly when he saw it.

Dallas_Lori.

Kaleb clicked on the name, searching through the profile connected to it. The stories he had read in Taylor's journal were all prominently posted in a row, each properly titled and in order, with many more accompanying them.

He clicked the biography, wanting to know what was written there as well, but was stopped by a warning sign from the website. He silently cursed the website, warning him that in order for him to become a reader with them, he had to first make a profile for himself.

Though it bothered him, Kaleb agreed to the terms and began typing his username. He froze his fingers before they could type "Alchemyst," figuring that if he did so, Taylor would find him as easily as Kaleb had found Taylor. From his last encounter with Taylor's stories, he had a feeling that the moody blonde would be a little less than pleased if he learned that Kaleb was reading his work. He curled his fingers, biting his lip as he thought of an alias. Finally, he began typing, deciding on "TheBookWorm." He entered his username and password, creating his profile for good. Kaleb nodded affirmatively, glad to get that out of the way, then dove head first into Taylor's profile, starting with chapter one.

"C'mon." Kaleb waved. "We're ending a little early today." Taylor looked to Kaleb, a mixture of confusion and irritation on his face.

"Seriously?" Taylor said. "Why?"

Kaleb armed himself with his crutches and stood to leave. "Got somewhere to be," he said simply. Taylor sighed, but obeyed nonetheless, figuring it was probably another one of Kaleb's 'fun' projects.

Taylor shouldered his pack and chased after Kaleb who had already left the lab. He stopped short on his way towards the exit when he didn't see Kaleb down the hall, only to turn around to find him clicking in the other direction towards the belly of the school. Taylor paused for a moment as he watched Kaleb entering the school. His confusion turning to curiosity, wondering what the jock could be doing, and hurried after him to find out.

They walked in silence towards their goal, their footsteps and clicking echoing off the walls and lockers. After a while, when the walls began to display the creations the students had made, Taylor noticed that they were walking in the direction of the Art department. Paintings, charcoal sketches, even models and clay pots were pleasantly placed one after the other in glass cases buried deep within the walls.

Taylor took this opportunity to take a longer look at these creations, as he hardly ever wandered down the Art department. Even when he did, he kept to being invisible, which meant maneuvering through the halls as quickly and as quietly as possible, with no time to admire the decorations.

Taylor took his eyes away from the display cases when Kaleb clicked through an open door, leaving the blonde behind just long enough for Taylor to catch up with him. When he entered, he saw a young woman completely covered with paint standing before a canvas that was taller than her own body. She absentmindedly rubbed her hands together, smothering them with caked layers of creamy paint, and her smock was stained with fresh oils from her latest creation, littering her face, neck and feet with sprinkles of colors as well. She was inspecting her work, dipping her hands into bowls of paint before

169

wiping them onto the abstract canvas. Taylor stuck close to the entrance to watch her work, while Kaleb, on the other hand, clicked right on in.

"Hey, Kar," Kaleb tried, but the woman was lost in her paints.

"Kar?"

She squiggled a red hand over the painting, using her fingers to add lines. Kaleb huffed, not liking being ignored.

"Hey, Beep-Beep!" he shouted, causing the woman to stop mid-wipe. She turned to Kaleb with death in her eyes.

"What have I told you about that?" she growled, referring to her abhorred nickname. Kaleb merely shrugged.

"Sorry," he grinned. "It was the only way to get your attention."

"How about tapping me on the shoulder?" she said, wiping her hands clean on a dirty rag, but Kaleb refused.

"And risk getting painted myself?" he said. "No thanks." The woman caught a glimpse of Taylor standing in the doorway.

"This the guy?" she asked, motioning to Taylor. Kaleb stepped aside to let her see him better.

"Taylor," he nodded him in. "This is Kara. Kara- Taylor."

Kara charged forward, dropping the rag when she had finally finished wiping her hands, and drew in close to inspect the boy Kaleb had stressed so much over. The blonde took a step back as she neared, making her slow to stop as well. She eyed him up and down, a small smirk finally growing on her face when she finished.

"He'll do," was all she said, then turned back to properly clean her hands in the sink. Taylor caught Kaleb's eye, questioning the strange artist, only to receive a pat on the shoulder.

"Yeah," he chuckled, guiding him further in. "You get used to it." Kara was drying her hands as they approached her work station, this time with a cleaner towel.

"So," she announced. "I've got a project for you." Her eyes bore into the two boys as she leaned against the table, once again using her long arms as support.

"Not another modeling job, is it?" Kaleb complained, causing a brow to raise from the other two.

"No," Kara said grumpily. "It's an art project. Only this kind needs more hands than my own." She began untying her smock. "It doesn't even have to look good."

Now Kaleb cocked a brow. "You never like your work," he said.

"That's because I'm picky," she replied, snapping down the smock onto the table. "You see what I did there?" she asked, jerking her thumb over her shoulder to the large canvas leaning against the wall that she was working on before. "That's it."

"Scribbles," Kaleb stated, then, shrugging. "All right."

Taylor kept quiet, silently cursing Kaleb for getting him mixed up in these affairs. "Here you go." Kara brought up two empty, styrofoam bowls and two bottles of paint. She slammed the bottles on their lids against the table before opening them; pouring a baby blue into one bowl, and a bright yellow in the other. She handed the yellow one to Taylor, leaving the blue for Kaleb.

"Hang on to these," she ordered. "I'll see if we have any spare smocks." With that, she left the boys on their own in search of the elusive smocks.

Taylor sighed, tapping his finger against the bowl. Kaleb threw him a smile, to which Taylor merely replied with annoyed eyes from beneath his brow.

"I hate you."

Kaleb's smile dropped. "Thanks?" he replied, confused. "What's wrong?" Taylor stood to wander.

"Painting?" he said. "Is this another one of your ideas of fun?"

Kaleb frowned. "What's wrong with painting?"

Taylor looked to Kaleb, jerking a thumb at the mess Kara had left on the

171

canvass. "*That's* considered art," he replied. "I could make that blindfolded and some idiot would come groveling at my feet to buy it for way more than it's worth."

Kaleb's frown deepened. Then, instead of replying verbally, he stood up to show him Kara's other pieces, leaving his crutches and coat behind, but bringing his bowl.

"Come here," he said, finding the garden painting Kara had shown him a few weeks before. "Hold this." Kaleb handed Taylor his bowl so that he could properly display Kara's painting on a nearby easel.

"Can you do *this* blindfolded?" Kaleb challenged. Taylor looked away, grumbling his denial. "Kara works on her paints just as hard as you do with your studies," Kaleb told him. "Don't belittle her talent so easily."

Taylor looked to the floor, begrudgingly agreeing with him, but not wanting to give him the satisfaction of a nod. He held out Kaleb's bowl, returning it to him as Kaleb raised his hand to retrieve it, resulting in Kaleb's hand being doused in blue, and the bowl splattered on the floor.

"Oops." Kaleb snickered, biting his lip. Taylor stared at the bowl, closing his eyes in frustration with a heavy sigh.

"Hey," Kaleb said, opening Taylor's eyes. "You've got something on your face." Taylor rose a hand to his scarred cheek.

"Where?"

Kaleb wiped his blue hand down the entirety of the left side of his face. "There," he said with an impish grin. Taylor opened his unpainted eye to glare flatly at the snickering jock.

"Really?" he droned. "Shouldn't you be cleaning this up?"

Kaleb looked to the bowl on the floor, realizing the blue boy was right, and bent down to pick it up. As he did this, Taylor dumped his bowl of yellow paint over Kaleb's head, smearing it over the right side of his face. Kaleb froze in place while the paint dripped from his ears and chin, his eyes completely covered by the color.

"Now *that* was fun," Taylor snarked.

Kaleb couldn't help but chuckle, giving a playful, blind shove to the boy before him. Taylor shoved back, though with a little more force than intended, causing the jock to stumble over his braced leg. He had no idea where to fall, nor where he actually *was* falling, but as he rose from his crumpled heap off the floor, he could hear by Taylor's swearing that it definitely was not a good place to land. Kaleb wiped at his eyes as best he could, but the paint was refusing to come off cleanly, when he heard Kara enter the room.

"What's going on?" she asked, seeing Kaleb on the floor, and both boys covered in paint.

"Shit," Taylor hissed. Kaleb was still trying to rub paint out of his eyes.

"Whatever it is, it was an accident," he said. "And for soul's sake, could someone *please* hand me a towel or something?" Kara tossed him a smock, retrieving her painting from off the floor as he cleared his vision. When he finally opened his eyes;

"Shit."

Kara's painting was indeed destroyed with the yellow imprint of the side of Kaleb's face now gleaming in the middle of it. His bone structure made a clean outline of his jaw, nose and parted lips, looking slightly down to the empty space in the lower left corner, and dripping down whatever was too heavy to stay in place. Kara kept a steely eye on it, observing the intruding face on her creation.

"Kara, I'm so sorry," Kaleb started. Taylor began joining in as well.

"We shouldn't have been messing around, I'm so-"

Kara had taken Taylor's head and shoved it, paint-side onto her painting, leaving a blue face in it's wake staring up into the yellow face dripping paint and parted lips included. Now, with the addition of the faces staring at each other on the blazing background and the flowers growing around them, Kara took a step back, leaning her head to her shoulder as she interpreted the new creation.

"Huh," she muttered. "I'll be damn." She turned to the boys, looking at Kaleb in particular. "That's it." She grinned. "That's what was missing." The two boys stared back at her in shock, looking between her, and to one another.

"You're kidding me," Kaleb mumbled, a laugh bubbling up from deep down inside his chest. "You have *got* to be kidding me." His laughter grew, spreading to Kara, and then finally Taylor, quiet as it was.

"I guess there's no use for these anymore." Kara chuckled, dropping the remaining smock on Kaleb's unpainted shoulder. "You're covered."

Kaleb looked down to his clothes, finally realizing that half of his black shirt was now bright yellow. He shrugged, smiling to himself, still too giggly to care.

"Proof," he chuckled, causing Taylor to shake his head into his hand.

"Idiot," he muttered, though when he pulled his blue hand away, he realized that he himself was marked as well, and began frantically searching his clothes for any mess.

"You're good," Kara told him, ending his search for him. "But there's no use wiping it off now," she told him. "We've got work to do."

For the next hour, the three smothered an empty canvas with handfuls of paint. At one point, Kara flopped the board to the floor so she could leave her footprints in a wild, pointless path around the piece. This made it easier for them to reach the top edges of the canvas as well, though Kara had other plans in mind as she dipped her toes into a second shade of red. By the time the plain, white canvas had turned into a wild, multi-colored mess, Kara was satisfied with it enough to permit Taylor to leave for work.

"This is no good."

Kaleb had stayed behind with Kara as Taylor trudged through the hallway, his hands and face still tinted with the remains of paint. In the condition he was in, he could never go to work and look like a professional. There wasn't any time for him to walk home, shower, then walk back to town for the trolley; especially when it was so difficult to leave the house while his father was home. Canceling wasn't an option, as he had no way of communicating with his client on such short notice. Not only that, there was no way Taylor would walk away from money.

Taylor hiked his pack up, determining his course towards the locker room. After barely paying off all of the bills with his father's Soldier's Compensation checks, Taylor had already decided that things would have to be cut back- including the water. He had already used the locker room many times before with no one being any the wiser, and hopefully, this would help to put a dent in their water bill. This way, he didn't need to use his own money to support them as much.

The vacant room echoed his footsteps, confirming his presence as being the only one there. He walked over to his locker and shirked off his backpack, digging out his headphones after seeing the speakers hanging from the coach's office. Even with his booming voice, coach Abernathy had a loudspeaker connected to his office for announcements in the morning, though he rarely used it. Taylor smirked, entering the office with his headphones. Once he had chosen a song, he hooked his headphones up through wires to the speaker system, and pressed play.

Kaleb waved his goodbyes to Kara, clicking down the hall towards home. The empty halls echoed his lonely footfalls, reminding him of how big the school was. Three combined towns entered their children into Riviera High, rather than just the folk of River Hill. Should that be the case, the grand, two story school would go to waste, as only a handful were natives to the little town on the hill. The school acted as a center point for the towns, making it easy for each teen to commute every morning without the use of steam-powered engines, though busses were offered as a courtesy.

Kaleb paused to stretched his arms in the hallway, rolling his sore shoulders in hopes of relaxing them a bit before returning them to the torture that was titanium crutches. He rubbed the back of his head, counting the weeks left with his fingers only to realize that this was his final few days with the wretched brace and crutches. A smile curled his lips high over his cheekbones as he thought of this, hoping to his soul that the day would come sooner than later.

Kaleb resumed his trek towards home with a new skip to his limp, thinking of all the things he would be able to do again once the acursed hindrances had left him for good. His steps slowed, however, when he heard the sound of music sneaking out of the men's locker room. He turned, closing in on the sound, confirming that it was, indeed, coming from behind the door to the locker room. Curiosity took hold of Kaleb as he pushed through the swinging door, entering to find the source of the music. He rounded the block wall that kept peering people away from seeing inside, deciding to leave his crutches leaned against it.

Steam filled the room from an ongoing shower that slowed to a stop, quieting to allow Kaleb to clearly hear a voice singing along with the music. A towel hanging over a separating wall disappeared as the singing person yanked it down to dry himself. The now toweled man came around the wall, revealing himself to be Taylor, quietly singing along with the words and slightly dancing towards his locker, strumming along with the

175

beat on an invisible guitar.

Kaleb kept quiet, watching this rare form of play for as long as he could before he was noticed by the blonde. The lyrics had ended, allowing the instruments to finish the song, and Taylor to follow along as he dressed himself from under the towel. Kaleb wanted to wait, wanting to see the finished song, until he realized he was watching a naked man getting dressed. A moody, socially awkward man.

"I didn't peg you for a classic rock lover," Kaleb called over the music, surprising Taylor, who instantly quieted.

"What are you doing here?" Taylor's hair had whipped over his face when he whirled around to see Kaleb, mostly covering his eyes, but not the aggravation. Kaleb rubbed the back of his head, regretting ever alerting Taylor of his presence and wishing he had simply walked out unnoticed instead.

"Well," he started. "I heard music," he admitted, looking to Taylor for forgiveness, but finding ugly, painful looking bruises covering his skin.

"What are those?" Kaleb asked, stepping closer to look, but Taylor retreated away from his advances.

"What's it to you?" Taylor snipped. "I fell, remember?" Taylor quickly turned away from Kaleb to grab his shirts and layer them on one at a time, but Kaleb stopped him.

"Wait," Kaleb held out a hand, receiving a glare from the blonde. "I just…" He stumbled, realizing how awkward his request was. "... Can I… Can I have a look at your crest?" Taylor's glare intensified.

"No," he said, matter-of-factly. "Why would you even want to?"

Kaleb rubbed the back of his head again, looking to the floor. "Everyone has a different one- I've always found them fascinating," he admitted. "And, I know what everyone else's looks like from the showers. I know all of my friend's crests." He looked to Taylor. "Except for you." He returned his gaze to the floor, realizing that Taylor had always been missing during gym as well, never giving him a chance to even catch a glimpse, especially with all his layers.

"That still doesn't answer my question," Taylor said, bringing Kaleb's attention to him.

"I want to know because you're my friend," he replied. A queer look flickered over Taylor's expression.

"I'm your what?" he asked. Kaleb shrugged.

"Well aren't we?" Kaleb asked expectantly. Taylor said nothing, eyeing the jock before him. He reached for his shirts again, trying to cover his exposed torso that was littered with blue and brown splotches.

Kaleb huffed, stopping the blonde as he rid himself of his jacket and dropped it on the bench beside him. Then, he yanked his stained shirt right over his head, revealing his well carved muscles and golden skin. He dropped his shirt next to his jacket on the bench, clapping his hands on his thighs before letting them dangle about his waist as he turned his back to Taylor.

There, centered between his shoulderblades, was an outline of a carefully printed tree. Its roots curled into intricate loops beneath it, and newly growing branches peeked out from the trunk. Four small circles boxed in the top half of the tree, with a fifth one in the center of the trunk just below the leaves from the top half.

Taylor froze where he stood, not daring to near Kaleb, but unable to take his eyes off of the inked in crest on Kaleb's back. Taylor clenched one of his shirts tightly in his fist, holding it close to his body.

"There," Kaleb said, turning back to Taylor. "No biggie." Taylor kept away from Kaleb, fearful of moving at all. Kaleb sighed, picking up his shirt to cover himself again.

"What's it feel like?" Taylor couldn't stop the words from leaving his lips, cursing himself for letting his thoughts wander to his voice. Kaleb shrugged, thinking of the different reactions connected to each person.

"Tickles, mostly," he answered, staying his shirt. "With Gerrit, it's like when a beetle clings to your finger. But, with my mom, it's like when you touch a feather to your skin, and dad's like when you barely touch your arm with your fingernails." He looked to Taylor. "You try."

Taylor didn't move, merely watched the jock as he came close enough to sit on the bench and turn his back to the blonde. For a few moments, Taylor held his hands tightly in his shirt, staring at the tree tattooed on Kaleb's skin. Kaleb waited patiently, not expecting Taylor to explore his soul crest right away. He sat quietly, looking straight ahead to give Taylor enough time to gather his courage. When he did, his tentative fingers took a few tries to actually make contact with Kaleb's skin.

Taylor frowned, mentally calling himself a sissy for taking such a long time, and finally reached out to touch Kaleb's soul crest. Upon contact, Kaleb shivered, and Taylor was overcome with a wave of tingles from his fingers rippling to the rest of his body. He ripped his hand back, desperately flopping his hand to rid himself of the tingling sensation still chilling his fingers.

"That was weird," Kaleb muttered, rubbing the chills out of his shoulders as well. "Your hands must be cold." He turned to look at Taylor, who had turned away from Kaleb, still hiding his fingers away from the jock. Not thinking, Kaleb caught sight of Taylor's crest as well, and reached out to touch it. An icy blast slammed into him through his fingers, sending his hand back flying, and Taylor into a shivering state crouched over his knees.

"Woah!" Now Kaleb was flinging his hand around, trying to shake the feeling back into his fingers. His smile dropped when he saw Taylor quivering over his knees.

"Are you alri-"

"Don't touch me!"

Taylor held an arm out to separate them, but his body and face were still shaking, curled over his knees hidden from sight. Kaleb stared down at the quaking blonde, regretting touching the crest without permission first. With this invasion of privacy, Kaleb worried that he had gone too far, and pushed Taylor away for good this time.

"I'm so-"

"Don't touch me."

Taylor repeated, still curled over his knees, trying to breathe properly. Kaleb recoiled, taking a few steps away from Taylor to give him some space. He returned his shirt over his chest, slipping on his jacket to try and send the chills away. He turned back, seeing Taylor's back perfectly displayed as he hovered over his knees, but Kaleb was too worried about the blonde trying to recover from the golden boy's invasion than to actually notice his design.

"What are you still doing here?" Taylor wheezed. "Get out!"

Kaleb obeyed, rushing out of the locker room as quickly as he could. He grabbed his crutches by the door, not even bothering to shoulder them as he left. He clumped down the hall until he reached the double doors, leaning against them as he caught his breath.

"Idiot!" Kaleb scolded, banging his head on the door. He unclenched his hand, looking down at it with a mixture of fear and shame.

Kaleb fisted his fingers and pushed out the doors to leave for home, shouldering his crutches as he left, and choosing to believe that it was the autumn air that left the chill still tingling in his fingertips.

Chapter 11

"You saw him *naked*?!"

"NO," Taylor huffed, changing Bekah's approach with a cocked brow.

"He saw *you* naked?"

"Rebekah," Taylor growled, causing his friend to wince and retreat behind her hands.

"Sorry," she said. "Just trying to lighten the mood."

Taylor glared at her from beneath his brow. "It's not working," he said flatly. Taylor smothered his face with a hand, still shivering every once in a while. "I've never felt that before," he told her. "It was like I couldn't breathe."

Bekah folded her arms over on the desk. "I've heard that it's different for everybody," she said. "But I've never heard of something like that before."

Taylor sighed despairingly. "Has anyone ever felt like their skin was on fire but freezing at the same time?"

Bekah's face folded into a strange frown. "I don't know," she said, looking away.

Taylor shook his head. "I swear my heart stopped," he said. "I seriously think it stopped." He started rubbing his eyes. "I thought I was gonna be sick right there."

Bekah cocked her head. "What do you mean?" she asked. Taylor left his forehead in his hand, letting his eyes rest for a while.

"My stomach fell, I went weak in the knees, my head was spinning- it was like I was falling off a cliff," he listed. "And just as terrifying."

Bekah looked to her friend, suddenly concerned by how tired he looked. "How are you now?" she asked quietly.

"Tired," he confirmed. "Still dizzy, and my stomach is fluttering, but, it's better than it was at work." He slid his hand over his forehead to glide it through his hair. "I think I'm gonna call it a night and sleep it off."

"Okay," Bekah looked to her friend, wishing she could comfort him better. "Night," she offered.

"Night," Taylor returned, then shut down his computer with shaky fingers. He fell right into bed, not even bothering to change into his pajamas. He grabbed his pillow, too dizzy to use it for his head just yet, and held it tight against his chest, curling around it to fall into a deep sleep.

As the morning sun rose, Taylor curled tighter around his pillow, having not moved at all since first falling asleep. Even with the night to restore him, he still felt less than his best. Aside from this, he didn't want to face Kaleb again. Taylor would risk seeing his father before seeing Kaleb again. He could sneak out later to play with Bubbie, and maybe even follow the creek to see if it led behind the school like he hoped. So, with his mind made up, Taylor rolled over in his bed, drawing the covers over his head to fall back to bed, drifting back into a dreamless sleep.

Kaleb moped around school the entire day. Taylor hadn't shown up for school, and after his little fiasco with the soul crests, Kaleb was terrified at the idea of him never returning. Lunch rolled around, and the students gathered to eat with their friends, but Kaleb had worried himself sick. He wanted to be alone, not in a loud, crowded room full of people asking him what was wrong every five seconds. He gathered his lunch from his locker and left for the courtyard outside of the Alchemy hall.

Kaleb propped his crutches on the floor to hold open the door as he made his way towards the shade of a the tree. The wind had settled for the day, allowing the sun to warm his golden skin. He looked across the field, remembering the day Kaleb had first introduced the carbon rocket to Taylor and all the fun they had had that afternoon. He looked to his sandwich, remembering how he had also argued with Taylor that day, and the day after as well.

Kaleb gripped his lunch, wondering if he was really doing any good by being Taylor's friend if all they ever did was argue. He thought of every instance when he had annoyed the blonde, disagreed with him, or used his power over him to make him do what Kaleb wanted, exaggerating each memory and growing more discouraged with each one.

Being allowed into someone's soul took a great deal of trust, something Taylor simply didn't have for anyone. The more Kaleb thought about it, the more he realized that he hadn't really given Taylor a reason to trust him- or anyone else for that matter.

Kaleb had abandoned his lunch altogether, too sickened to eat. He sipped at his tea as best he could, but the thermos sat mostly forgotten in the grass beside him. He kept his hands holding the back of his head for a while, leaning over his lunch, trying to bribe himself to eat every once in a while, but not really getting anywhere.

Kaleb sighed, removing his hands to lean against the tree, only to stop short. In the distance, behind the fence, a grey head bobbed up and down in the empty creek. Kaleb sat up straight, almost lifting himself off the ground, trying to see who it was that occupied the beanie, remembering the old hat his mother had given Taylor. He jumped up, using the tree for support, then bolted towards the fence as fast as his booted leg would allow him. As he reached the fence, the grey beanie had disappeared curving into the woods, the empty creek now more barren than ever.

Kaleb hoisted himself onto the fence, determined to catch up, but his brace wouldn't allow it. He huffed, growling in frustration and ripped off the buckles and straps to free himself. He left his removable cast at the edge of the fence, then carefully made his way down the creek and into the woods. As much as he wanted to race after grey-beanie, Kaleb wasn't used to walking without his brace just yet, let alone walking over unstable, stony terrain. Not only this, but he was a few days early in taking it off, making the threat of straining something else all the more promising.

As carefully and as quickly as he could, Kaleb followed the creek in hopes of catching up to grey-beanie, hoping against all doubt that it was Taylor. After about an hour of hiking downstream, water began to trickle down the sides of the creek, rolling to the center of it to make it grow into a proper creek, forcing him to begin walking farther inland to avoid stepping through water. Along the way, there were many different paths and smaller creeks that connected to it, but Kaleb stayed his course in following the main creek as the time passed.

Soon the scenery began to look familiar, and it didn't take Kaleb long to pinpoint where he was. The bridge that he and Taylor used to go home over came into sight, reminding him of Taylor's secret adventures in the creek and becoming hopeful. He hiked up the last bit of creek, then carefully climbed up to the park above, clearing himself of any bit of nature that had attached to him during his journey.

Now above ground, Kaleb searched the area, seeing not a soul. He sighed, disappointed, but not ready to give up. He trekked forward, going further into the park's playground. As he drew closer, he kept his eyes open, sweeping across the trees that lined the park. In his search, he happened across a tennis ball abandoned by the swings, but no Taylor. Kaleb pocketed the ball and leaned against a pole supporting the swing set, rubbing his face in disappointment. He dropped his hands to his thighs, lasting only a second before reaching one up to rub the back of his head.

There was a shuffling sound that made him whip around behind him, hoping to see Taylor. Instead, there was a black and white dog staring at him, ears perked. Kaleb stared back, watching the shepherd's every move, and trying to slowly back away. His attempts were in vain, as the dog padded closer to him, barking loudly.

Kaleb panicked, running away from the dog before it could attack. In his haste to get away, he climbed to the top of the 'monkey-mountain,' a domed, metal climbing net for children to play on. The dog's bark became more and more frustrated with every failed attempt at reaching Kaleb, leaving the shepherd on the ground to wait for him.

"Go away!" Kaleb shouted. "Go home!" His attempts were useless. The dog was out for blood. Kaleb was going to die.

"What are you doing?"

Kaleb looked up to see Taylor, grey beanie and all, leaning against a shade post. Watching.

"Taylor!" Kaleb's attention went straight to the dog. "Look out, he'll bite!" Taylor cocked a brow at Kaleb, leaving his place at the shade post to nonchalantly stride forward.

"You mean him?" Taylor asked, stopping behind the shepherd. The dog was still glued to Kaleb, watching for any sign of him coming down, and hadn't noticed Taylor behind him yet.

"Caref-"

Taylor whistled, gaining the dog's attention. He looked to Kaleb from beneath his brow when the dog instantly turned and sat at his feet. Kaleb sat open-mouthed, bewildered at the control he had over the beast.

"Where's the ball?" Taylor asked.

Kaleb blinked, surprised that Taylor knew about the little trinket he had found. He pulled it out of his pocket, the dog's ears perking upon the sight of it. Taylor jerked his head towards the creek when Kaleb looked to him for answers, then watched as the dog chased after the ball thrown towards the creek. The dog shortly returned with it in his jowls, running up to Taylor and dropping it at his feet, tail whipping back and forth, begging the blonde to throw it for him. Kaleb frowned, suddenly realizing that the wild beast wasn't so wild.

"You could have told me he was yours," Kaleb grumbled.

"This was far more entertaining," Taylor replied. "I thought you wanted me to do fun things."

Kaleb gave an unamused smile. "Ha, ha," he droned, taking a tentative step down the mountain, only to withdraw back up as the dog turned his attention to Kaleb.

"You're scared of dogs?" Taylor said. Kaleb upped his nose.

"Not 'scared,' per say, but, more aware of them," he replied, readjusting to sit more comfortably on the metal bar.

"You're scared of dogs," Taylor repeated bluntly. The dog pawed at Taylor, asking him to throw the ball again, then chased after it when he did.

"Look," Kaleb said. "Can you just... Send him away, maybe?" He looked to the metal bars he sat on. "This is kind of uncomfortable."

"Oh," Taylor said quietly, eyeing the mountain. "I see." He took the ball from the dog again, this time rolling it under the monkey mountain. Kaleb pulled his legs up from out of the bars, keeping away from the dog as much as he could.

"That's not 'away'," Kaleb stressed.

"Who said I wanted him away?" Taylor said. "He's good jerk repellant."

Kaleb looked up from the dog to Taylor, feeling guilty all over again. He lowered his head, trying to think of what to say.

184

"Look," he started. "I'm sorry about yesterday." Taylor stood still, waiting for Kaleb to finish. "I shouldn't have... I shouldn't have done a lot of things,..." Kaleb continued. "Most of all, I shouldn't have broken your trust like that." He looked up to Taylor. "I'm sorry. I know it's not enough, but I am."

Taylor remained still, ignoring the dog pawing at his legs to stare Kaleb down. Then, after a few lengthy minutes, he reached down to pick up the ball, and threw it towards the creek.

"Go play," he grunted, turning to stare down Kaleb as he climbed down one bar at a time. Once on the ground, Kaleb started towards Taylor, stopping short when the blonde took a step back.

"Back to square one."

Kaleb sighed, though pleased he could appease Taylor enough to escape the terrors of the dog. The shepherd, however, returned to Taylor, but dropped the ball to investigate Kaleb. The jock stumbled back as the dog padded forward, sniffing his trousers and shoes thoroughly.

"He won't hurt you," said Taylor, quietly. "Let him get a whiff." Kaleb froze, closing his eyes to the sky and clenching his fists close to his chest as the dog took what seemed like ages to smell Kaleb.

"Why is he still sniffing me?" Kaleb groaned, chancing a peek.

"Probably your cat," Taylor pointed out.

"Shit." Kaleb squeezed his eyes back shut, hoping the dog wasn't hungry. Taylor let out a disbelieving chuckle.

"I can't believe you're afraid of dogs," he puffed. "No wonder you're a cat person."

"Cats can't rip your throat out in a single bite," Kaleb defended himself.

Taylor merely cocked a brow. "Ever hear of mountain lions?"

"That's different." Kaleb stiffened as the dog sniffed higher along his jeans.

185

After a few more sniffs from his jacket, the dog was finally satisfied with Kaleb's scent, and left him for Taylor, tail wagging as he plopped down at the blonde's feet for a scratch behind the ears.

"You've got him wrapped around your finger," Kaleb noted, slightly relaxing his tense muscles.

"Keep that in mind," Taylor told him. Kaleb coughed, trying to hide his nervousness. Taking a deep breath, Kaleb took a chance at bravery, and kneeled down, allowing the dog to return to him. He stroked lightly down the length of the dog's back, careful not to touch the swinging tail. Taylor shook his head, taking his hands out of his pocket as he started towards the two.

"You're hopeless."

The blonde knelt down with them, scrubbing the dogs ears as he lowered himself, then easily guided the dog onto it's back for a belly rub.

"'Atta boy," Taylor mumbled, pulling back for Kaleb to pet the dog on his own. The mutt seemed happy, accepting the rub down from Kaleb until a sneeze rolled him back over, and Kaleb ripped his hand away. Taylor chuckled at Kaleb, shaking his head as the dog walked away to play on his own.

"Shouldn't you be at school?" Taylor asked.

Kaleb shrugged. "Shouldn't you?" He watched in silence as Taylor looked to the ground, remaining quiet. " … Was it that bad?" Kaleb asked. Taylor stood to leave, not putting up a fuss when Kaleb followed. He walked slowly, watching the field to keep out of eye contact.

"Where are your crutches?" he asked quietly.

Kaleb looked to his now freed leg before answering. "I left them at school," he admitted. "They slowed me down." Taylor looked to his feet.

"How much longer do you have?"

Kaleb pocketed his hands. "Not long," he answered. "I don't think it'll hurt anything as long as I'm careful." They walked along the sidewalk circling the park, speaking only when Taylor would ask a question. The dog would walk up to them occasionally to check up on them, but grew bored with them quickly when they didn't bother to pay attention to him.

They stayed like this for a while, conversing quietly. They were walking along the path that led to the bridge when Taylor permitted a personal story from Kaleb, stepping aside as a truck came up behind them to pass through. Once it did, Taylor stopped- as well as the truck.

"Shit," he whispered, turning pale. Kaleb looked between Taylor and the truck.

"What's wrong?" he asked as the driver door opened.

"Run," Taylor ordered.

"Wha-"

"Just go!" Taylor hissed, stepping away from Kaleb as a man charged forward, eyes burning through the blonde.

"Taylor!" the man shouted. "What the fuck are you doing out of school?" Taylor stepped up to the man rushing towards him.

"Dad, I-"

"Don't give me excuses, boy, tell me!"

"School was let out early!" Kaleb interjected, causing both Taylor and his father to look to him.

"Who the fuck are you?" the man griped.

"Kaleb Evans, sir," he answered, stepping up to him. "Taylor and I have class together." He held out a hand to shake, but Taylor's father merely stared at his hand with disgust. He returned his attention to Taylor.

"Why aren't you in school?" he asked again. Taylor kept his gaze strong on his father's face.

"Like he said," he told him. "School was let out early."

"Oh, really?" the man challenged. "Why?"

Kaleb pocketed his hands, trying to act calmly. "A pipe burst," he answered. "It flooded the school, so they let us out early."

Taylor nodded, agreeing with the jock. Taylor's father leered at the boys, the wheels in his mind turning. Just then, the dog came running up around the truck to the boys.

"What the fuck is this?"

The dog ignored Taylor's father and came panting up to Taylor, tail wagging. Taylor began shaking his head.

"He's not-"

"You have a dog?!" he shouted, coming closer to bear down over Taylor.

"He's mine!" Kaleb butted in before the man could rip apart his son. "That's my dog." Again, both Thompsons were staring at Kaleb. The jock began patting his legs. "Here boy," he tried, the dog cocking his head. "Come here." The dog obeyed, tail wagging. He feigned his interest in Kaleb as the boy knelt down to hold his neck, turning his head to his real master when Kaleb tried petting him.

"What's his name?"

Kaleb swallowed. Taylor never told him the dog's name, and judging by the way he looked now, there wasn't a chance of him interjecting for Kaleb now.

"His name is Napkin," the jock said, looking to the men, who returned his glance with a look of disbelief of their own. "He cleans up my crumbs," Kaleb explained. Taylor threw a hand to his forehead behind his father, who seemed fed up with this useless conversation.

"Get in the truck," the man ordered, and Taylor obeyed, walking towards the red vehicle quietly with barely a look to Kaleb.

The dog tried to follow, but Kaleb kept his arms around it's neck, hushing the dog before it could whine. Kaleb stood to walk away, taking the dog with him in his arms so as not to blow Taylor's cover, but the dog kept his eyes glued to the blonde over

Kaleb's shoulder, whining slightly for his friend. Suddenly, the dog became intensely upset, barking and growling and struggling to free himself from Kaleb, succeeding in tossing the jock to the ground as he made his escape.

"Shit!" Kaleb hissed, picking himself up to see the dog charging toward an angry man gripping the blonde's shoulder.

"Bubbie, no!" Taylor shouted, but he had already clamped his teeth around the man's ankle. The man screamed in rage, kicking the dog off of his leg, and ripping his pants in doing so.

"Bubbie stop!" Taylor held up his hands, ordering the dog with visual triggers as well. Bubbie growled menacingly at Taylor's father, but stayed put, obeying Taylor's wishes. The blonde swallowed hard, staring up at his father who turned to him with fury in his eyes.

"'Bubbie'?" the man growled. Taylor was instantly pounced on, his hoodie being stretched when the man grabbed his son's collar and started shaking him, screaming in his face. "'*Bubbie*'?!"

Kaleb lept to his feet, racing towards the two with Bubbie as back up. The dog sank his teeth into the man's leg this time, causing an enraged, painful scream, but still, his fists clamped around Taylor's hoodie.

"Get off me!" he ordered, though Taylor was already shouting at the dog to stop. He wasn't given the chance to obey, however, because Kaleb shot up to tear the two apart, shoving the man away and Taylor to the ground. The man took a swing at Kaleb, missing him as he ducked. Kaleb swung back out of reaction, hitting the man square in the face to stumble over the dog, still chewing on his ankle.

"BUBBIE!" Kaleb shouted, finally scaring the dog into submission away from the man. Taylor's father stood watching the three, panting with frustration, then turned to leave. The boys watched in silence until Taylor looked up to Kaleb from the ground.

"What did you do?" he whispered. Kaleb's heart was still pounding, he didn't quite know himself. The door slammed shut against the truck, then reversed quickly, causing Taylor to pale even more.

"Run," he breathed. The truck stopped to switch gears, facing the boys. "Run!" Taylor scrambled to his feet, racing towards the treeline with Kaleb and Bubbie following close after. "Go! Go! Go!"

The truck rumbled behind them, gaining ground quickly. The boys didn't bother climbing down the creekbank safely, there wasn't time. Instead, they jumped through the trees, sliding and tumbling down the bank just as the truck slammed into the treeline. The boys picked themselves up, continuing their retreat upstream. They didn't stop until the truck was out of sight, and they could no longer hear Taylor's father shouting from the window.

"So much for being careful," Kaleb panted, rubbing his knee. Taylor sat on a large stone, bringing Bubbie close to him for a squeeze and a rub down.

"How's your leg?" he asked, keeping his eyes on the dog.

"Too early to tell," Kaleb replied, sitting as well. "My adrenaline's pumping." He leaned back, closing his eyes to the sky and taking a deep breath to calm his nerves. He kept them closed for a moment longer, then turned to the blonde.

"So," he started quietly. "That was your father?" Taylor kept his eyes on Bubbie, refusing to look at Kaleb, whose expression darkened. "Those bruises I saw-"

Taylor stood up, turning away from Kaleb. "It's none of your business," he muttered.

Kaleb popped up. "But, Taylor-"

"I said it's none of your business!" Taylor scolded. "Just leave it, okay?" He looked to his hands, picking at something Kaleb couldn't see from behind. He dropped his hands, sighing.

"I've gotta go," he muttered, trying to pass Kaleb, but the bigger boy took hold of his wrist as he passed, holding on to him with their backs to each other.

"Don't go back there," Kaleb warned, keeping his eyes forward.

Taylor carefully twisted his wrist free of Kaleb's grasp. "Get your leg on ice," he said quietly, keeping his back to Kaleb. Then, he clicked his teeth for Bubbie to follow, and made his way down the creek.

Kaleb turned to watch him leave, frustrated that he couldn't stop him. He watched until the blonde was out of sight around the curve of the creek, then turned to head back upstream to return to school. By the time he had returned, school was coming to an end. His things were right where he left them, untouched by human hands, so he gathered them up, and made his way towards home- this time over the sidewalk.

As he entered his home, Skitters greeted him in her usual way, but he was too frustrated to be happy about it. He fed his cat, then marched to his room for his laptop to chat with Mrs. Evans. He pulled up the hospital's registry, being polite enough to deal with the secretary without snipping at them while they found his mother. When she finally popped up on his screen, one look at his face told her something was wrong.

He spent the next ten minutes ranting about Taylor and his father, about the mishap between their soul crests and seeing his bruises, and everything else that was on his mind. By the time he was finished, Trish was holding her head in her hands, equally frustrated, and trying not to cry from it.

She lifted her head, sniffing and clenching her hair against her head. "Kaleb, I don't know what to tell you," she said quietly. "Unfortunately, honey, unless he files a complaint himself, there's nothing we can do about it." Kaleb's anger rekindled anew.

"That's bull shit!"

"Language, sweetie." Trish closed her eyes. "Though, you're right."

Kaleb licked his lips. "But he's a minor, right?" he said. "Can't we do it for him?"

Trish opened her eyes. "How much of a minor?"

Kaleb thought for a moment, realizing he didn't know his age. "Well, we're in the same grade, so he can't be far off from sixteen or seventeen. I doubt he's older than me." Trish dropped her hands.

"Well find out!" she ordered. "If he's sixteen, we can help him. If not, the higher-ups won't care." Kaleb's face darkened.

"That's sick," he muttered, earning a nod from his mother. "All right, fine," Kaleb said, calming down. "I'll ask him tomorrow at school."

Trish nodded, a relieved smile pulling at her lips. "The sooner the better." She rubbed the worry from her face. "I need to get back to work, dear," she told him. "I love you."

"I love you too," Kaleb replied, signing off. Then, after a thought, clicked onto the internet in hopes of finding Taylor's information through his profiles. Neither school nor the writing site could answer him, but he wouldn't give up. For the rest of the night, he poured through Taylor's posts, asked his readers about him, did anything he could to find out; all in vain. Kaleb sighed, rubbing his tired eyes. A knock on his door turned him around to see his father in pajamas.

"It's two in the morning, kid," Vance told him, alerting Kaleb of how long he had been at it. "You'll have better luck tomorrow." Kaleb's stomach answered before he could, reminding him of his two missed meals. Vance chuckled.

"Come on." He patted Kaleb on the shoulder. "We saved your dinner for you. We had to fight off the cat, though. Nearly lost my hand." Kaleb smiled, glad that his father was trying to make him feel better.

"It'll be alright, kid," Vance said, wrapping an arm around his neck. "I promise."

Kaleb wanted nothing more than to run up to Taylor and ask him his age, but the elusive blonde veered away from Kaleb all throughout the school day. He was more than relieved to find that the blonde had returned to school, but the separation between them grated against his nerves like a cheese grater. Even at lunch and breakfast, as hard as he tried, Kaleb couldn't find Taylor long enough to talk to him. He finally gave up, choosing to wait until their tutoring session after school that day.

As the final bell rang, Kaleb bolted out of his chair, weighed down by his boot. His mother nearly tore off his head when she found out he had taken it off, and forced him to wear it no matter how "fine" he felt. He refused his crutches, however, and left them at home to rust for all he cared. He marched forward, clumsily bumping through people as he passed, only to be stopped by Gerrit holding a big, heavy looking box.

"Gimme a hand?" the smaller boy asked. Kaleb wavered for a moment, but rushed after the box when it slipped from Gerrit's grasp. "Thanks," Gerrit sighed, flinging his arms to renew the blood flow.

"What is this?" Kaleb asked. Gerrit shrugged.

"Coach wanted us to bring in the new supplies before the game started, so here we are." He opened the locker room door for Kaleb to walk through, following close behind.

"Hey, Cap'n!" Jason smiled.

"Long time no see!" Daniel and Max came forward to greet Kaleb as well, each laying down a box. Kaleb placed his box down next to theirs, nodding his greetings politely.

"Hey guys," he muttered. Gerrit took on a sly demeanor.

"Kaleb had a good question," he said. "Let's find out what's in here."

Daniel looked around. "What about coach?"

Gerrit only waved him off. "He's gotta open it sooner or later. C'mon." Kaleb began backing away.

"I've gotta get going, actually-"

"Hold up," Gerrit said. "Lemme borrow your pocket knife."

Kaleb sighed, digging out his knife from his back pocket. "We're not supposed to use these at school," he muttered, handing it to his friend.

"We're not supposed to use *weapons* at school," Gerrit told him, grinning. "This- as you constantly shove down my throat- is a *tool*."

Kaleb shook his head, but let Gerrit use his knife to cut the tape off the seam and open a box. The boys peered inside, finding large packets of powder to line the football field.

"Open another one," Max ordered, taking the knife. In the second one were several six packs of duct tape at least two feet thick wrapped around each roll.

"Woah!" said Daniel.

"Jackpot." Gerrit grinned darkly. "We should totally string someone up on the goal post."

Kaleb snatched his knife back, closing it to return it safely to his pocket. "This is for the team," he said. "Nothing else."

Gerrit shrugged, grinning. "We *are* the team," he said slyly.

"Pack it up," Kaleb told him. "I've gotta go." With that, he left the locker room for the Alchemy hall, hoping with all his heart that Taylor would meet him there. Once inside the classroom, he waited impatiently, watching the clock as the seconds ticked by.

Kaleb paced in the laboratory, rubbing his head as he walked back and forth. Taylor was late, and Kaleb was starting to worry that he wouldn't show up at all. He sighed, frustrated with the blonde for running away again, and set out to search for him. He marched down the halls, searching down each empty hallway as he passed them. As he neared the gym, he noticed something lying on the floor. It was a backpack, abandoned in front of the men's locker room.

"Gerrit," Kaleb growled, growing suspicious. His thoughts proved true as he entered the locker room to find Gerrit, Daniel, Jason and Max all struggling with a boy on the floor. They were trying to undress him, mostly succeeding in getting his shirt trapped over his arms and head, and working on his pants.

Kaleb became suddenly enraged. Taping someone to the goal post was one thing. Taping them to the post naked, battered and beaten on the verge of Winter was another. He bolted forward, grabbing a football from a nearby bin and hurling it at any one of the four boy's heads.

"GET OFF, NOW!"

Taylor sighed, picking at a paper on his desk with his thumb. He was debating whether or not to meet with Kaleb for tutoring. True, he desperately needed help with the rest of his homework, but he wasn't quite ready to face him again after the day before. He huffed, thinking of the argument they had had on the floor in the middle of the hall.

"Stop running away from your problems."

With Kaleb's voice ringing in his ears, Taylor leaned forward in his desk, running a hand through his hair with a heavy sigh. Then, he stood up to shoulder his pack, and left the room for tutoring. He took his time, walking slowly towards the Alchemy hall, thinking of how he could convince Kaleb to leave his affairs alone. He watched his feet, barely noticing Daniel standing against the wall ahead of him. Daniel said nothing, just grinned and slid through the locker room door.

Taylor cocked a brow, weary of the jock being out of practice on game day, but continued walking. He knew this to be a mistake when a pair of hands grabbed him, yanking him so hard his backpack fell to the floor. He tried to yell, but another soul covered his mouth with duct tape, wrapping the strip around his head a few times before stopping and letting the heavy roll fall to the floor.

More hands grabbed hold of him as he struggled, picking him up to hold him horizontally in the air. Taylor kicked and wriggled, but the jocks were too strong for him, and the more he struggled, the more they hit him to make him stop. There were four of them, each holding onto a limb as they carried him further into the locker room.

"Get his pants!"

It was Gerrit speaking, clinging to his leg to hold him still. Taylor bucked, trying to deter the advancing hands, but they pushed forward to unbuckle his belt. Taylor's muffled shouting went unnoticed as they struggled to tug down his pants while he was still in the air. Meanwhile, the two bigger boys at his arms and shoulders pulled at Taylor's shirts, trying to rip them over his head. They ended up stuck at his shoulders, tangling Taylor's arms and head between his layers, his arms stuck in a defensive position between his hoodie and three of his shirts.

The struggling and beating made their hands slip from his torso, dropping Taylor to the floor with his legs still in Gerrit and Max's arms. Taylor grunted in pain on contact, but used the momentum from the floor to blindly kick free of Gerrit and Max's grip, kicking one boy somewhere soft- most likely a stomach- and earning a resounding cough from the boy. Taylor managed to wedge himself between two of the benches, accidentally trapping himself.

"Hold him down!" Gerrit's voice ordered, followed by several hands scrambling over Taylor's flailing body. There wasn't much he could do tangled in his shirts, and fighting blindfolded didn't help matters either, so they easily took control of the situation.

More hands gripped the waist of his pants, pulling at them to rid his lower half, only to readjust when his boxers didn't follow down his legs with them. Taylor kicked and wriggled and struggled and fought back with all his might, losing to the four boys

195

pounding on him, holding him down to their will. Still, Taylor was relentless with his struggles, dreading what they would do to him once he was naked. He had given up hope of getting out of this situation with his pants on when suddenly, a voice boomed over all the commotion.

"GET OFF, NOW!"

The voice shouted angrily at the attackers, followed by a cry of pain from one of the boys as something hard hit him. The hands stopped touching him just as Taylor's pants were barely covering him.

"We were just having a bit of fu-"

"GO!" the voice demanded. Feet scrambled away as Taylor's savior charged forward. Taylor lay still, panting hard through his uncovered nose on the floor.

"Are you alright?" the voice asked, kneeling down to see his bruises. "Jeez, they really did a number on you."

Taylor knew this voice, and he wanted nothing to do with it. He didn't want Kaleb to see him like this; not after yesterday. A warm hand reached over to tug on his pants, sending Taylor into a frenzy of kicking and bucking as he scrambled back against the lockers.

"Easy-eas- stop!" Kaleb stumbled, trying to calm Taylor. "I'm just trying to put you back together." He waited for Taylor to respond, only to hear his heavy breathing. "Hold still," he said, gripping onto Taylor's belt loops to bring his pants and underwear back up to their proper resting place around the smaller boy's waist. Kaleb tried to maneuver himself between the benches to help with his shirts next, but with his leg in its case, he couldn't find a good spot.

"Alright," he started. "This is gonna be weird, but don't panic." Without any sign of the boy refusing, Kaleb stretched his braced leg over the fallen torso, kneeling over his stomach with his good knee. Taylor could feel the warmth of Kaleb's body hovering over him, and then the fingers working to remove his undershirt from his tangled mess. Taylor jumped, unsuccessfully backing away from Kaleb due to him being pinned between the benches, the lockers, and Kaleb himself.

"Hold it! Hold it!" Kaleb tried. "It's alright!"

It was no use. Kaleb would see him, no matter how much Taylor didn't want him to. Slowly, Kaleb managed to bring down Taylor's undershirt, his long sleeved shirt, then his short sleeved shirt before working on his hoodie. Taylor's elbows were peeking out from under it above his forehead, making it difficult to tug it down onto his body. The strip of duct tape stuck to it as well, slipping out the bottom of his hoodie and snaking out onto the floor, but sticking to the entangled boy all the same.

"I'm just gonna take this one off, alright?"

Taylor clenched his eyes shut, begging whatever soul that powered the universe to hide his face when it popped out of his hoodie.

"Taylor?" Kaleb's eyes widened at the revealing of the beaten blonde, pulling back in shock. Taylor stared back at Kaleb, still panting slightly and ashamed of the position he was in. His nose had bled over the duct tape covering his mouth, surely making him look even more pathetic in Taylor's eyes, and he reached for it below his chin, barely picking at the edges.

"Here." Kaleb pulled a switchblade from his back pocket, freezing Taylor on the spot. "Oh, don't be worried," he said sheepishly. "Dad and I usually go camping, and it comes in handy so-" He stopped himself short, clearing his throat to move forward with his plan. "Hold still," he said quietly, slowly working the dull end against the blonde's cheek under the tape.

He was careful, never taking his eyes off the blade as he inched it slowly beneath the tape. Taylor could feel the cold steel against his skin, not daring to breathe as it climbed up his face because having a scar on each cheek was less than desirable.

The tape was meant to hold together industrial things such as the football training equipment, so a simple little thing like skin was all too easy to cling to. This made it all the more difficult to remove it, but Kaleb took his time to slowly wiggle the knife, cutting along as it rose up Taylor's cheek. The last bit of tape was finally cut off, letting Taylor reach up to remove it himself when the knife had been pulled away for good.

He was struggling to get the last of his hair unstuck when Kaleb finally found the guts to speak."What happened?" Kaleb asked, receiving an odd glance from Taylor. Kaleb looked down at himself, noticing that he was still straddling the blonde with his awkward legs.

"Oh!" Kaleb shot up, hopping away on his good leg. Taylor picked himself up with the help of the benches and lockers, but wasn't quite ready to stand just yet, and settled on a bench, wiping the last of the blood off his nose and face. Kaleb had his back turned to Taylor, rubbing his head as Taylor reached for his hoodie to put it back on, pulling it off of the tape.

"Are you alright?" he asked, still turned away from Taylor, who didn't even bother answering. The blonde had regained himself, and stood to brush past Kaleb, trying to leave the locker room. Kaleb stopped him, whipping him around when he grabbed onto an arm, suddenly furious.

"How long has this been going on?" he ordered.

"Stop it." Taylor turned away, but Kaleb pulled him back.

"Why didn't you tell me?" Kaleb glared into the blonde's eyes, who tried to escape.

"It's none of you-"

"Don't give me that crap!" Kaleb shouted, gripping tighter to Taylor's elbow. "You're my friend! They're my team! Don't *tell* me it's none of my business!" Kaleb's voice became more feral. "Don't you *dare* try and tell me that I'm not involved." He growled into Taylor's face, barely a breath away. Kaleb glared into Taylor's eyes, entirely furious with the blonde, until he took a good look.

Hidden behind the anger, there was fear in Taylor's eyes, and when Kaleb realized what he was doing, he couldn't blame him. He became fearful himself, letting go of Taylor and backing away. The blonde held his arm close to him as he turned and rushed out of the locker room, leaving Kaleb alone with his fears.

Chapter 12

Taylor clenched his hair from behind his head as he curled over his knees against the chute wall. No matter Bubbie's attempts, he couldn't clear Taylor of his protective cage behind his arms, and lay quietly beside him, looking up to him with sad, worried eyes. Taylor had cradled his head like this ever since he had entered the chutes, not even bothering to light his lantern when he arrived. His pack lay abandoned at his side, still holding his hat and scarf, but not even the chill of the chute could bring him out of his huddle.

Taylor's mind was swirling with memories, each one more horrid than the last. Voices screamed at him, telling him he was worthless, a waste of breath, that no one would ever love him- the son of an abandoner. The voices raged on, each one whispering harsher words than the last, degrading him further and further into the hole he wished he could hide in. Taylor curled himself tighter, every muscle in his body too tense for his own good. Finally, he had had enough.

Taylor slowly rose to his feet, and began walking deeper into the chute. The darkness enveloped him as the voices raged on. With each step, they grew louder, angrier; more wretched than the last as they put him down. Taylor stopped, completely covered in darkness with only a hint of the light from the opening at the end of the tunnel.

He tangled his fingers in his hair growling in frustration as the voices swirled around him, telling him he could never amount to anything, that he should just give up because none of it would ever matter, screaming every insult, name, injury or any other slander that had been thrown at him over the years until finally, Taylor ripped his hands away to his sides and let out a vicious roar, scaring Bubbie as it ricocheted off the concrete walls. His scream lasted until his lungs were cleared of air, then he took another breath and shouted again.

"LIES! ALL LIES, ALL OF IT! I CAN DO IT! JUST YOU WATCH, I CAN DO IT!"

He took another breath, ready to scream again, but his body refused. "I can do it!" His voice faltered as he held back dry sobs, refusing to cry. "Just you watch." He whimpered, taking a moment to find his strength again. Bubbie padded up to Taylor cautiously, wagging his tail to see if he was allowed to come near. Taylor sighed, reaching down to scrub the dog's ears.

"Just you watch."

Kaleb couldn't sleep. He tried, goodness knows he tried, but he couldn't get the fear from Taylor's eyes out of his mind. What's worse, he had learned from Miss Hart that Taylor was, in fact, seventeen years old, leaving no hope for rescue when he was already legally considered an adult. Kaleb sighed, rolling over to try a different position, but still failing to fall asleep. He quietly rose from the couch to make himself a cup of tea, with Skitters close behind in hopes of being fed.

The light from the kitchen momentarily blinded him, but after years of use, Kaleb continued on, knowing where to step. His vision returned once he had made it to the oven for the kettle, placing it in the sink to be filled with water. He dug out some chamomile from his choices of flavors, and picked some mint from the windowsill to add to it. As he dropped the ingredients into the infuser, Kaleb heard the shuffle of footsteps coming up behind him.

"Sweetie?" It was Trish, bleary-eyed from the light. "What are you doing up so late?"

Kaleb shook his head, facing the sink. "I've done wrong, Abi," he said quietly, keeping his back to his mother. "There's no denying it."

Trish came up behind him, placing her hands on him before leaning her head on his shoulder. "What did you do, dear?" she asked quietly.

"Taylor," he said simply. He looked to the sink, gripping the edges of it as he shook his head. "I've made it so much harder on him," he admitted, watching out the kitchen window. "I don't think my friends have been helping things either."

"Your buddies don't help much either."

Kaleb closed his eyes at the memory, finally realizing what Kara had meant when she yelled at him so long ago. It wasn't that his friends were a problem to Kaleb, it was that they were a problem to *Taylor*. He thought of all the times he had picked on the blonde, all the times his friends ganged up on him with Kaleb, and he wondered how many times they had messed with him without Kaleb's knowledge.

He remembered all the times he had heard some of the adults whispering about him too, because of his mother. With their consent, it was all too easy to make him a target. The kettle sang out to Kaleb, pulling him from his thoughts. He sighed, looking to his mother who had removed the kettle for him.

"What do I do, Abi?" he asked, turning to his mother. Trish poured the steaming water into Kaleb's mug before answering.

"Well," she started, dipping the infuser into his tea as she spoke. "What would you want?" She looked to her son. "What if it was you?" Kaleb looked to the floor, playing with his lip. Then, he looked up to his mother to give his answer.

"I don't think an apology is enough, mom," he said quietly. Trish clicked her teeth, leaning against the counter as she dipped the infuser.

"Then you're going to have to think of something else."

After spending the morning listening through the grapevine at Tammy's, Kaleb learned of Taylor's address and set out to find him. He pulled out the napkin with his scribbly handwriting, making certain that he searched for the correct house. As he matched the address, he noticed that the house didn't look anything like he had imagined.

It was a two storied, light-yellow house, much bigger than Kaleb's, with a fine lawn and wrap around porch. The grass was kept, and behind the windows were delicate sheen curtains. There was nothing out of the ordinary with this house. In fact, it looked just as nice as the others next to it. Kaleb paused a moment, taking a second look at it, when he remembered having seen this house before. He had been here, sitting on the curb when the man chased out whoever it was that knocked Kaleb over the head, realizing now that it must have been Taylor.

Kaleb sighed, shoving the napkin into his pocket as he strode forward. From the look of the sky, a storm was on its way, and his newfound ache in his knee confirmed it. If he wanted to get home before it poured, he would have to make this quick. He stepped up the front steps and took off his hat before opening the screen door to knock on the main door and waited for an answer. A few seconds later, the handle turned, and there stood Taylor in the doorway, looking surprised to see him.

"Kaleb," his said, eyes wide when he saw the jock. "What are you doing here?"

"You know, you say that a lot," Kaleb told him with a sheepish grin. "Can I come in?"

Taylor paused a moment, looking to the empty driveway as he thought cautiously. "For a minute," he said finally, stepping aside to let Kaleb through.

"Thanks."

Taylor closed the door behind Kaleb and motioned towards the stairs. "Up here," he said, leading the way. The inside of the house was just as normal as the outside, though the walls were completely barren. As they climbed the stairs, Kaleb noticed that the walls were still empty, not a picture in sight. Taylor led him to his room and had Kaleb sit down on his bed, leaving the door open after giving it a second thought. When Kaleb took a closer look, he noticed a slide lock mounted on the door frame, but looked away as Taylor turned to sit down at his desk.

"What's up?" Taylor asked. Kaleb rubbed the back of his head.

"Well," he started, not knowing where to go with his words. He sighed, frustrated with his cowardice. "How are you?" Kaleb wanted to strangle himself.

Taylor looked to the floor, turning the chair back and forth slowly. "I'm fine," he muttered. "Is that all you wanted?"

Kaleb shook his head. "No, no." He looked to the floor as well.

"Your brace is gone again," Taylor noted.

"Yeah," Kaleb looked to his leg. "Yesterday was my last day." He cleared his throat. "I start physical therapy next." Taylor nodded, keeping his eyes out of reach. Kaleb sighed again, growing frustrated with both of their dancing around.

"Look, Tayl-"

"Shh!" Taylor perked up, hearing something Kaleb did not. Then, Kaleb heard the slamming of a truck door in the distance, followed by the scrape of keys against the front door's lock, and the jiggling of the handle being clumsily turned. Taylor jumped up, closing his door as quickly and quietly as he could before sliding the lock over the other end on the door frame.

"C'mon!" Taylor whispered harshly, leaning over his desk to open his window.

"What are we doing?" Kaleb asked, ready for action.

"There's a tree at the end of the roof," Taylor explained, stepping over the sill. "You're gonna climb down and run around the front before he ever even knows."

"Got it." Kaleb nodded, climbing over the desk and onto the roof just as quickly. He started making his way down towards the tree when Taylor hopped back into his room and shut his window. He caught Kaleb's glance through the glass, giving a look that warned him not to follow before turning away to unlock his door and leave down the stairs.

Kaleb cursed his foolishness, but made his way towards the tree nonetheless. Chasing after him now would only lead to more trouble. Kaleb carefully climbed down the tree one step at a time, making sure to keep the majority of his weight off his bad leg. He maneuvered himself to land on the ground behind the trunk of the tree, out of sight to anyone inside the house, but that couldn't stop him from peeking around it to see in through the sliding glass doors.

Taylor had made it down the stairs and was searching cautiously for his father, who was hidden out of sight from his son, but not to Kaleb. He tried desperately to get Taylor's attention without alerting Mr. Thompson, but was unsuccessful. Taylor turned away to search the kitchen, giving his father the perfect chance to pounce.

He hit Taylor on the back of his head, stunning the blonde, then wrapped his fingers around Taylor's neck to shake him relentlessly. Kaleb bolted from behind the tree to the glass door, ripping it open and charging forward with a ferocious scream.

Taylor's father flung the blonde aside and took Kaleb's tackle head on, sending both of them to the ground, but Friedreich's military training kicked in against Kaleb, sending the jock flying over the dining room table with the tackle's momentum. He crashed into the chairs, tangling himself between the wooden legs in a vulnerable position for Friedreich to strike. His eyes lit up a fire when he saw Kaleb stuck on his floor.

"Sand scum!" he shouted, racing to his feet to attack, but he stopped suddenly, when Taylor jumped onto his back, gripping him to the point of breaking skin.

"GO!" the blonde screamed, being thrown over Friedreich's head. Kaleb scrambled to free himself from the chairs as Taylor was swung over his father's shoulders and thrown against the wall, falling limply to the floor. Friedreich grabbed a nearby marker, turned his unconscious son over to lie on his back, and began trying to stab him repeatedly.

"Fucking sand scum!" he screamed, hitting harder with each strike. "Scum! Scum! Scum!"

Kaleb charged after Taylor's father again, this time with a chair. He swung it over Friedreich's head, sending the man toppling over himself and left him struggling with the seat as he took an arm and leg from Taylor, rolling him over his shoulders, and bolting out the open back door. Friedreich tried running after them, chasing them as far as the woods behind his house before giving up, but Kaleb kept going.

He raced through the trees, keeping a tight grip on Taylor's arm and legs as he hid deeper in the woods. Once all was quiet, Kaleb slowed, looking around to see where he was, and finding himself lost. He panted hard, hiking Taylor higher over his neck before he could slip off, then decided to lay him on the ground. He carefully set the blonde over a bed of fallen leaves, taking care to catch his head as he rolled him off his shoulders.

The boy was still unconscious from his father's latest attack, and bruises were already starting to form around his neck beneath his headphones where he had been strangled. Kaleb lifted the blonde's shirts to see if Friedreich's dull marker had succeeded in penetrating his skin, finding more bruises, old and new. He replaced Taylor's shirts over his battered skin when a heavy wind rolled by, moving the storm clouds in the sky and chilling the boys on the ground.

Kaleb took his hat from his back pocket to cover Taylor's head, realizing that the hoodie was all he had to keep warm. As he pulled his hands away, he noticed the scar under his right eye, and couldn't keep himself from wondering. He stared at the boy, not knowing how to process everything that had happened between them from day one to right then.

He held his hands to his forehead, sliding them back to hold the back of his head before deciding to gather the local plantlife. He had already seen at least three different breeds that helped with open wounds and bruised skin in the area that he grew in his own garden, but turning them into a makeshift salve was another thing entirely. Without the proper tools, he wasn't sure if any of them would work. He decided to chance it though, feeling the need to do something other than sit there and wait for the blonde to wake up.

If he woke up.

Darkness. That was all he could see. No light, no warmth. Just a sea of black that he was in the middle of. He could vaguely feel the wind tossing his hair around over his forehead bringing the chill along with it, but he was too tired to care. He just wanted to lie there, not to be bothered until he chose to rise on his own, which didn't seem like any time soon. He was forced to move, however, when something cold and slimy spread itself over his stomach.

Taylor tried opening his eyes, trying to pull himself out of the darkness, but he had a rough time with the task. He managed to see a black blob reaching towards him, kicking his instincts into gear, and reached out to snatch it before it could touch him. He blinked a few times, trying to clear the black from his vision and noticing the blob he was holding was a hand covered in pulposus. He connected the hand to Kaleb, who seemed to be talking to him but couldn't quite understand his words just yet.

"... lor? ... ey, ... aylor?"

Taylor's ears woke up with the rest of his body, reminding him of the aches in his muscles and throbbing head.

"Stop talking," he groaned, blinking still.

"So you can hear me?" Kaleb asked.

"Apparently you can't," Taylor snipped. A sigh of relief escaped from the jock, knowing that a snarky remark meant the blonde wasn't completely brain dead. Taylor released Kaleb's hand to cover his tired, blue eyes, wishing for the darkness to return and take his pain away, but the cold, slimy feeling returned over his chest, causing him to jump, seeing that Kaleb had lifted his shirts and was smearing mashed up plants over his skin.

"I know it's weird," he started. "But it'll help."

Taylor cocked a brow at the jock. "Get off me, asshole," he said, matter-of-factly. Still, Kaleb pulled away, wincing at Taylor's sassy remark. He wiped his hand free of the plant-guts, keeping his eyes away from Taylor's. He looked at Kaleb curiously, not knowing if it was his head playing games with him, or if there was something wrong with the older boy.

"What's gotten into you?" Taylor asked. Kaleb looked away, rubbing the back of his head before speaking.

"It's just that…" He looked to the woods. "You've had to go through this all by yourself at… At home, in… In the town and… At school…" Kaleb finally turned to Taylor, tears threatening to fall from his eyes, surprising Taylor. "I'm sorry," he said quietly, keeping his voice under control. "I'm sorry for everything. I never meant-" He stopped, wiping his eyes with a brush of his palm before turning away to the woods again. "Please forgive me," he barely whispered, not expecting a reply.

None came. No sound at all. Not even a sarcastic jab. Kaleb slowly turned back to the blonde, who was staring in amazement at him. For once, his mouth wasn't stuck in a frown, but slightly parted from shock. There was no hatred in his eyes, nor fear, nor irritation. His eyes were filled with wonder and confusion, hiding the working thoughts in his mind as he searched for words. Kaleb's watery eyes had dried, but he still rubbed away at his face with a swipe of his hand.

"What?" he asked. Taylor blinked, still dumbfounded, but took a breath to speak.

"I didn't… I didn't think there was anyone left," he said quietly.

Kaleb became confused. "Left for what?"

"… Who cared," Taylor replied, still staring up at Kaleb, who sighed into his hand.

"That's what I've been trying to tell you from the start."

Taylor looked away to the woods, not wanting to tell him that he had never believed Kaleb before now. "Guess I'm just stubborn," he muttered instead. This brought a chuckle out of the jock.

"You think?" His chuckle grew into a laugh that shook his whole body. A roaring thunder cut Kaleb's laughter short, reminding him of the oncoming storm. He kneeled to stand, only to remember that they were lost. Kaleb looked around the woods, trying to find something close to familiar, biting his lip as his search continued.

"That way," Taylor pointed, straining up to sit. Kaleb reached his hands out to hover around Taylor, which were pushed away as he managed to sit up on his own.

"You sure?" Kaleb asked, receiving a nod.

"I know these woods," Taylor told him. "The park's that way. You can make it home from there." Kaleb frowned a little as he looked to the blonde.

"What about you?"

"I've got a place," Taylor admitted. "I'll be fine." Kaleb shook his head, unsatisfied with Taylor's answer, but the blonde waved him off. "We'd better get going if you don't want to get wet." This time, Kaleb insisted on helping Taylor to his feet, and waited uncomfortably close as he gathered his balance. Taylor held a hand to his pounding head, noticing that he was wearing a beanie. "Did you-?"

"Come on," Kaleb said, walking away.

"Kaleb," Taylor called, waiting for the jock to turn to him so that he could point him in the right direction. Kaleb coughed, rubbing the back of his head as he righted his direction in his proper place: following behind Taylor. They hurried through the trees to try and outrun the rain, but mother nature was too quick for them, and started sprinkling over the boys as they reached the creek.

"We've got to stay away from the creek!" Kaleb's voice sounded on the verge of panic, and his face confirmed it. Taylor bit his lip, not wanting to share his secret with Kaleb, but not seeing any other option.

"Come on," he led the way to a smaller path hidden beneath years of overgrowth and fallen leaves, following it to the edge of the creek to reveal the hidden chute. Taylor hoisted himself inside, turning to make sure Kaleb had made it as well. Bubbie shot out of the dark to greet the boys, happy to have company during the loud, scary storm.

Thunder shook the very air as the storm heavied and poured over the land, slowly filling the creek beneath them. The thunder frightened Bubbie, as well as Kaleb.

"Don't tell me you're afraid of thunder too!" Taylor shouted over the rain, but Kaleb was too far gone.

"We have to get away from the creek!" he shouted, near hysterics.

"Kaleb-"

"It's gonna fill up-"

"That's never hap-"

"No, listen to me-"

"Kaleb, stop-"

"We have to move!"

"Kaleb!"

"You're not listen-"

"No, *you* listen!" Taylor took hold of Kaleb's head with his headphones, cranking maximum volume to drown out the sound of the storm. Kaleb gripped Taylor's hands over the headphones, trying to remove them, but Taylor refused, yanking the jock's head into submission. He looked him right in the eye, assuring him that everything would be alright, and slowly calming Kaleb's breathing from hyperventilation to heavy panting. Taylor could feel Kaleb quivering beneath his hands, regardless of his efforts to calm him.

"You really are scared," the blonde marveled. After a thought, Taylor carefully slid his headphones off of Kaleb's ears to speak to him, keeping their eyes locked.

"Kaleb," he said calmly. "Listen to me." Kaleb waited for him to speak, swallowing hard. "We're safe here," Taylor continued, keeping his eyes on to Kaleb's. "I promise." Kaleb kept his frightened eyes on Taylor.

"You're sure?" he asked, receiving a slow nod that never broke contact with him. Kaleb nodded in return, still shaking, but at least breathing.

Taylor replaced his headphones over Kaleb's ears and led him to the wall while he lit the lantern, showing Kaleb his second home. Kaleb looked over the chute, seeing Taylor's rolled up sleeping bag and blanket, a cooler next to Bubbie's bowl, and a box protecting some spare clothes from the outdoors. He turned to Taylor, who wouldn't meet his gaze as he walked further in to sit against the wall with Bubbie.

Kaleb went to join him, sitting next to the dog to give Taylor his space. "Looks like we're stuck here for a while," he mumbled, not hearing a response from Taylor if he had one, thanks to the headphones. Kaleb closed his eyes, clamping his hands over the headphones as he buried his head in his knees. He must have fallen asleep that way, because when he rose his head up again, there was a blanket draped over his head and shoulders.

The storm had passed, and the night sang with the chirping of crickets and frogs from the creek while the moon shimmered in the sky with a fresh halo around it. Taylor's headphones were gone from around Kaleb's head, and the lantern had been turned off, but placed beside him in case he had woken in the middle of the night- which was exactly what happened.

Kaleb switched on the light, finding Taylor curled up inside the sleeping bag not too far from him. Bubbie was out of sight, no matter where Kaleb searched, but what bothered him more was the fact that Taylor wasn't moving. He drew closer to the blonde, leaning over him to see if he was still alive. His body was unnervingly still and silent, as though he weren't even breathing at all. Suddenly, Taylor bolted up, turning to face whoever it was that hovered over him. In this case, literally.

"Sorry!" Kaleb whispered, backing away to rub his grazed nose. "I thought you were dead." Taylor threw a disbelieving glare at him.

"What?" His tired voice cracked. Kaleb rubbed the back of his head.

"You're a silent sleeper, I take it," he mumbled. Taylor shook his head.

"Asshole," he muttered, raising up on his elbows. "What time is it?"

"The sun's not out yet," Kaleb said. "It can't be too early." Bubbie's head popped out of the sleeping bag from Taylor's waist, widening Kaleb's eyes. "That was unexpected," he muttered, looking away. "Think we should get going?" Taylor looked to Kaleb quizzically.

"'We?'" he asked.

Kaleb quirked his face. "You don't want to be left here, do you?"

"That was the plan, actually, yeah," Taylor told him. Kaleb suddenly became serious.

"You are not going back to that house," he stated quietly, though the sternness was clear.

Taylor sighed to the ceiling, running a hand through his hair. "Fine," he groaned. "Let's go."

Kaleb nodded to Bubbie. "What about him?"

Taylor rubbed the dog's head, scratching his ears as he spoke. "He'll be fine," he told him. "He always stays behind."

Kaleb shrugged, letting the issue drop, then stood to fold the blanket while Taylor rolled up his sleeping bag. Bubbie whined the whole way through, but sat obediently at the edge of the chute as he watched them leave, his sad face following them even if he couldn't. The moon was bright now that the clouds were clear of the sky, but Taylor took the lantern to light the way as they hiked over the freshly polished river stones.

They made it to the bridge in a timely manner, easily finishing their journey to Kaleb's house in no time. As they approached his porch, Kaleb fumbled around his pockets for his key and fit it to the door. He hadn't even begun to turn it before the door swung open, revealing a terrified Trish in her pajamas. She instantly threw her arms around her son's neck, clinging to him as she tried to control her distress.

"Are you alright?" she asked, eyes glistening. "Are you okay? What happened?" Vance came up behind her from inside the house, sighing with relief at the sight of the two boys. Trish released Kaleb to grab Taylor, checking his face and shoulders for any visible disfigurements before squeezing him tightly to her as well.

"Patricia," Vance mumbled, quietly ushering everyone inside. Trish held Taylor close as they regrouped inside the house, still asking if they were alright and wanting an explanation.

"Taylor can't go back, mom," Kaleb said, interrupting her questions. He looked to his father, shaking his head. "He can't."

Vance shrugged, looking perplexed. "Did you think we'd let him?"

Trish smiled quietly at her husband's response, squeezing Taylor's shoulder before rubbing his arm. "We'll get your things tomorrow," she said. "Tonight, let's just get some sleep, okay?"

Vance rubbed the back of his head. "Looks like it's official," he sighed, looking to Taylor. "You're kidnapped."

Taylor kept quiet, not sure how to react to the Evans' acceptance. He had come along for the night to appease the jock so that he could get some sleep and return home in the morning, but he never expected to be taken in to *live* with him. He went along with it, though, as Trish guided him further into the house and set him up with some of Kaleb's shorts from the dryer to sleep in, giggling at the fact that they would fall off unless being rolled over a few times, then sent him off to sleep in Kaleb's room.

Kaleb had a strange bunk bed, bought especially for when his friends came to visit. It was nice, but strange nonetheless, as the top bunk was at least a third of the size of the bottom bunk. Taylor was too tired to care though, and climbed up top to slide right under the covers, his head not even touching the pillow before falling asleep.

Chapter 13

Kaleb yawned, stretching in his bed as he sat up to the sun on his face. He stood up to see Taylor still lying in his top bunk facing the wall, sound asleep- dreadfully so. Kaleb left him to rest, mussing his dark hair as he left his room. Trish and Vance had already awakened and were having tea and coffee at the dining room table when he arrived.

"Morning, sweetie," Trish said, placing Vance's coffee in front of him.

"How's the kid?" Vance asked.

"Still sleeping," Kaleb replied, making a face. "It's kinda creepy."

Trish cocked her head. "How so?" she asked, replacing the coffee pot back in the kitchen and sitting down to her own cup of tea.

"He's just so quiet," Kaleb explained. "Like he's dead or something."

"Maybe he does die," Vance joked. "He dies in his sleep to come back from the dead each morning as a zombie at school." He pointed to his son. "Now that's a book." Trish threw a balled up napkin at her husband, bouncing it off his head.

"There's still some blueberry left if you want it, dear," Trish told Kaleb, taking a sip of her tea.

"I think I will," he said. "We're in for a long story."

As the family sipped at their morning drinks, Kaleb went on to tell his parents about the horrible lifestyle Taylor had lived through from what Kaleb had seen since first meeting his father. He told them of his thoughts and explanations to Taylor's mannerisms and skittishness, and of what he had seen from Friedreich since the day he chased Taylor out of the house- including how the blonde had given him a goose egg from his escape.

Friedreich hadn't cared who watched him tear apart his own son from the experience at the park, and he didn't seem to know where he was from time to time, judging by how he continually screamed "sand scum" when he went on the rampage in the house, earning a shared look between Trish and Vance.

"Sand shock," Trish mumbled, fingering her mug.

Vance shook his head, looking to the floor. "Not everyone can escape it," he agreed. Kaleb leaned against the table, drawing himself closer.

"What about Bubbie?" he asked, receiving a confused look from his mother.

"Bubbie?"

"The dog," Vance answered, tapping a finger over his jaw in thought. He stretched his face from a thoughtful smile. "I've always wanted a dog."

"I thought you didn't like dogs," Trish said, looking to her son, but Kaleb shook his head.

"Taylor's got him real trained. He's nice. If you let him give you a sniff."

Trish rubbed her temple. "I don't know," she muttered.

Vance gave his wife a reassuring smile. "C'mon, Trish," he started. "It'll be fun."

"What about the cat?" she looked to her husband who shrugged.

"She's quick. She can run away. If not, she'll make a good chew toy." Trish glared at Vance, not finding his humor. "We can separate them," he said with a smile. "She's an indoor cat anyway."

"He can sleep in the shed if he needs to," Kaleb piped in. Trish pursed her lips, looking between the two men.

"Looks like I'm outvoted," she mumbled, taking her mug to the sink. Vance fisted the air, high fiving his son as he walked away from his chair.

"I've *always* wanted a dog!" he grinned victoriously. Kaleb leaned back in his chair, smiling at his father's giddiness when his mother called for his help in the kitchen.

"What do you think Taylor would like for breakfast?" Trish asked, rinsing out her infuser.

Kaleb shrugged. "I don't know, why don't you ask him?"

Trish scrunched her nose at him. "You said he was asleep."

"He can wake up for a few seconds," Kaleb replied, earning a whack over the head with a dish towel as she passed by him. A few minutes later, she returned from the bedroom, looking uncomfortable.

"You were right, he does sleep like the dead."

"Thank you!" Kaleb threw his arms to the air, receiving another towel slap to his side as Trish re-entered the kitchen. "So what are we having for breakfast?" he asked, leaning against the counter. Trish pulled out a pan from a lower cabinet.

"He said he didn't care, and that it was whatever I wanted," Trish grinned at him, drumming her fingers on the pan. "So you know what that means."

Kaleb nodded, stepping forward.

"Pancakes."

It took a moment for Taylor to realize he was in Kaleb's house, sleeping in his bed. When Trish had poked her head up onto his mattress to see what he wanted for breakfast, he frightened her by quickly popping his eyes open, surprised by her sudden presence. He lay in bed for a few more minutes after she left, trying to wake up properly and trying to remember everything that had happened in the last twenty-four hours.

Taylor groggily climbed down from the bunk and shirked on his jeans, rubbing the sleep out of his eyes to awaken completely. He stumbled into the hallway bathroom and splashed water on his face from the sink, taking a good look at himself in the mirror.

His father's handprints were marked around his neck in a dark bruise, reminding him of the fear of not getting out of that fight alive. His hoodie would help to cover them once he put it on, but that wouldn't make them go away. He looked to the sink, ashamed of the situation he was in.

Battered, beaten and half dead, now living with the one person who had always made his life more difficult. Taylor scoffed at the irony, finding sanctuary in his arch rival's house. Still, after the time he had spent with Kaleb, Taylor had to admit that he wasn't as terrible as the blonde had originally thought him to be. He was annoying, and pushy, and aggravatingly happy at the weirdest moments, but he wasn't a bad guy.

His parents were pleasant people, almost to a fault. He didn't know what to make of Trish's kindness, and had the fleeting thought that her blood was made of sugar, being as sweet as she was. Vance joked around like one of the guys, but from what Taylor had seen, Kaleb looked up to him; respected him even. Taylor blinked away the wish that he still had that with his own father, wiping the rest of the water off of his face before leaving the bathroom.

Kaleb was busy helping his mother make breakfast in the kitchen, while Vance was packing up to leave.

"Hey, kid," he greeted when he saw Taylor. "How's it going?" Taylor nodded to him, still finding silence to be his most comfortable form of conversation. Vance grinned at him. "Hey, you got a key for me?" Taylor gave a confused look.

"Key?" he asked.

Vance picked up his own keys, tossing them in the air before catching them and walking over to Taylor. "I need your house key," he said. Taylor took a step back, shaking his head.

"Why do you need my key?" he asked.

"So I can go get your stuff," Vance told him. Taylor was about to protest when Trish came out of the kitchen to better explain things.

"Vance is going to go to your house for you," she said, taking Taylor to look him in the eyes. "I don't want you going back there," she said softly. "Not even with somebody else with you."

Taylor stepped away from her grasp, shoving his hands in his hoodie pocket. "I don't have my keys," he said, swiping his nose and looking to the floor. "We sort of ran out before things could get crazy."

Trish shut her mouth as though she wanted to say something, taking a breath before telling him it was alright and returning to the kitchen. Vance saluted his farewell, then made his way out the door.

Taylor was given free roam while breakfast was cooking, save for one locked door in the hallway. His curiosity nipped at him to find out what lie behind the mystery door, but he smothered it in search of other things, allowing him to browse the books in their many bookshelves. One caught his eye, and he sat cross-legged on the floor to read it in front of the bookshelf.

Hidden behind the couch, he was given privacy to admire the book's contents while the cooking was finished. He had just started chapter three when Kaleb popped his head from around the corner, having to take a few tries to get the blonde's attention before alerting him of breakfast ready for them on the table.

Just as the trio sat down to eat, Vance walked through the front door with Taylor's backpack in hand. He set the blonde's belongings down by the door and joined the group at the table.

"I just grabbed what I saw," he told Taylor. "If there's anything missing, just tell me."

Trish took her husbands hand. "How did you get in, dear?" she asked, but Vance shook his head.

"Doesn't matter," he smiled at the spread on the table. "Let's eat."

"Well," Kaleb started, entering his room. "I guess I can make room in my dresser."

Taylor stepped up behind him to stand in the doorway, now able to see the jock's room clearly without the hindrance of night or lack of sleep. The walls were painted a dull, light blue with white trimmings along the ceiling, floors and window panes. There was a black area rug with thick, shaggy fibers splaying about over the cream carpet. The strange bunk bed was to the far right wall, the top bunk covered in a blue striped comforter while Kaleb's was all black. His desk and swivel chair sat next to it, leaning against a large window in the middle of the room.

Every other space in between was lined with bookshelves, filled to the brim with books. There were so many different books, there were even stacks piling high on the floor next to the shelves, and several stacks lined Kaleb's bed and desk. Above the books, on some of the walls, were posters with chemical grids and atomic mass charts. Taylor scoffed, humored by this.

"What?" Kaleb asked, peering over his shoulder from his dresser hidden in his closet.

"You're a nerd," Taylor realized.

Kaleb scrunched up his face. "No, I'm not."

Taylor spread his arms to the mass of books surrounding his room. "If I were to find you playing a game in here, I bet your mother would be truly surprised," he said. "That is, if you're not alphabetizing your books first."

Kaleb frowned. "I like to read," he excused. Taylor rose his brow.

"I can see that," he replied. "But I'm not done." He then pointed to the posters. "You're a big, famous football player who, instead of sport posters and bikini models, has the periodic key on his wall to look at every night." He leaned against the door frame, still tickled.

"Well, what do you have on your walls?" Kaleb snarked, dropping Taylor's smirk. As personalized as Kaleb's room was, Taylor's was depressingly simple. With only the clothes that fit and didn't have holes in them, the only things that really belonged to Taylor were his journals and laptop.

"Nothing," he realized, looking away.

Taylor stuck his head out the door, looking down the hall for a reason to change the subject, and found the locked door. "Hey," Taylor mumbled. "What's in there?"

Kaleb looked over his shoulder. "Where?" he asked, not seeing what Taylor was talking about.

Taylor nodded to the door. "That room. With the lock on it."

"Oh," Kaleb turned back to his work. "Just a storage room, I guess. Nothing important." Kaleb finished with the dresser, standing up to let Taylor use it. "This'll have to do for now." Kaleb told him. "We'll figure something else out later." Taylor nodded his thanks as Kaleb left to give him his privacy. "Oh." He pulled himself back into the door frame. "Wanna work on homework later?"

Taylor shrugged. "Why not?"

Now with Kaleb gone, Taylor set to work emptying his pack into the bottom drawer. His few shirts, jeans and other essentials fit in nicely, though packed to the top once he placed in the hat Trish had given him and his mother's scarf on top. How Vance had managed to get all of his clothes was impressive, even if there was only a handful. Taylor's laptop and journals stayed inside his backpack, along with his school work. He pulled out his computer, readying it for a chat with Bekah, when something else fell out with it.

Taylor picked up a broken chained, dog-tag necklace from the floor, recognizing it instantly. He had thrown this trinket away after the chain had snapped in half, not paying much mind to it as he had hardly ever worn it anyway. The charm was more powerful now, sinking his stomach the longer he stared at the metal tag in his hand. The simplicity of Vance's answer at breakfast became suddenly clear to Taylor, as the only way he could have gotten the necklace was if he pulled it out of the trash with the rest of Taylor's things.

Taylor sat quietly alone on the floor, letting the reality of the situation sink in as he stared at the tag in his hand. Friedreich was done with his son; tossing him out with the rest of the trash. Taylor was stuck here, now. There was no going back to that house, even if he wanted to. He had been tossed out for good this time.

Taylor gripped the tag in his fist. After a while, he decided on keeping it, even if it was broken; as a reminder that he could now only go forward. He tossed the charm into his pack, returning to his duties with his laptop and closing the bedroom door. As soon as he was up and running online, Bekah was already ringing for him to answer.

"There you are!" she exasperated. "You had me worried!"

"Sorry, Beck," he waved, but she was too preoccupied with his surroundings.

"Where are you?" she asked. Taylor looked her right in the eye.

"You're not gonna believe this."

Bekah sat in astounded silence, her eyes wide with disbelief. She tried speaking a few times, stopping when the words wouldn't come out and she was left with her mouth open. Finally, she was able to speak again long enough to ask;

"So, you're there now?"

Taylor nodded, sucking in his lips. Bekah held a hand to her forehead, mouth still open from shock. "Woah," she muttered, receiving another nod from Taylor. He had the volume turned down low, so as not to alert anyone of Bekah's presence, and he was speaking to her just as quietly to keep their conversation private. Bekah was used to the quiet, but this latest update had shaken her to be even quieter.

"And your dad...?"

Taylor looked to the desk before turning his eyes away. "He's done with me," he told her quietly. "So that's that."

Bekah's face softened, and she too looked to her desk. "Don't hate me for saying this," she started. "But I'm glad." Taylor looked to her for answers. "You're in a safe place now," she explained. "I don't have to worry about you anymore." She shrugged. "Even if it *is* with Kaleb... I'm glad to know that you're safe."

"Yeah," Taylor said, resting his forehead in his hand, sighing. "I guess you're right."

Bekah cocked a brow. "I know I'm right." She grinned. "Always."

Taylor smirked at this. "Right," he mused. "Because adding strawberry jam to a grilled cheese sandwich was just *so* brilliant."

Bekah pointed a finger. "I was right when I said that the two don't mix."

"After the fact that you tried it," Taylor remarked.

Bekah raised her nose to the sky. "I don't have to take this. I can take my brilliance somewhere else, thank you." Taylor wiggled his fingers at her.

"Toodles."

Bekah frowned at him. "Rude." A knock on the door, followed by a head peeking through it caused Taylor to slam his laptop nearly shut and whip around to face whoever it was that intruded on his conversation.

"Hey," It was Vance. "Ready to go?" Taylor kept his eyes on him.

"Go where?"

"To get the dog," Vance answered, causing Taylor to become surprised.

"Dog?"

Vance smirked. "Bubbie," he explained. "Why does everyone forget the dog?" he muttered, then back to Taylor. "We're leaving in a few, c'mon." With that, he left to ready the truck. Taylor turned back to his laptop, lifting the screen to find Bekah with a strange face.

"What?" Taylor asked. "It was a reaction." Bekah sighed.

"They seem like nice people to me so far," she explained. "You're gonna have to learn to be around them without jumping out of your skin." Then more quietly, "They're not your father." Taylor quieted, taking in Bekah's words. "Go on," she told him. "Go bring Bubbie home." A smile crossed her face when she said this, making Taylor realize that he would finally be able to live with Bubbie under a real roof. A small smile tugged at his lips as well while he made his goodbyes with his friend, then packed away his computer to go fetch his pet.

Kaleb was already there waiting for him in the truck, but he slid out to let Taylor sit in the middle. The drive was filled with Vance's questions about Bubbie, and for once, Taylor didn't mind the conversation. Taylor's responses were still short, but after having to hide him for so long, Taylor felt relieved to finally be able to talk about the one thing he loved most: his dog. As they reached the bridge, Vance pulled over into the grass, clearing the path for any oncoming traffic.

"You two go on," Vance ordered, readying the truck for another ride. "I'll be back later to pick you up here." With Vance out of the way, the trek to the chutes continued with Kaleb, who had questions of his own.

"So, he just walked up to you one day?" Kaleb asked.

Taylor shook his head. "I found him hiding in the bushes. It took a while to get him out, but once he knew I wasn't a threat, he started to open up." Taylor looked to the treeline above them. "Didn't take me long to figure out he only plays with the ball; everything else scares him away."

Kaleb nodded, taking in the information. "What about 'Bubbie?'" he asked, receiving a curious look from the blonde.

"What about him?"

Kaleb pocketed his hands. "Where'd you come up with it?" He shrugged. "I dunno, it just sounds kinda girly for you."

Taylor kept a close eye on his feet when his toes slipped off some polished rock. "It's sort of a family name, I guess," he replied, earning a pointed look from Kaleb.

"Is that why your dad freaked when he heard it?" This question momentarily paused the blonde before confirming the answer with a nod. As they approached the chutes, Bubbie had gotten a whiff of them from the oncoming breeze and came charging out to greet them with a happy tail.

"Hey, buddy." Taylor gave the dog a good scrub between the ears, just as happy to see his friend. Bubbie bounced over to Kaleb, who tensed for a moment before giving in to his affections.

"Think we can grab everything in one go?" Kaleb asked, smiling at a happy Bubbie. Taylor furrowed his brow.

"Everything of what?" he asked, confused. Kaleb caught Taylor's gaze and stood to answer him.

"You don't need to hide here, Taylor. Not anymore."

Taylor looked to his second home, shuffling over his feet uncomfortably. Kaleb patted him on the shoulder as he passed by. "Come on."

Taylor stayed a moment longer, not wanting to abandon this home as well, but realizing that Kaleb wouldn't take no for an answer. Aside from this, if Taylor did need to run away again, this cover was blown. So, with a heavy sigh, Taylor climbed into his chute for the last time.

Kaleb took his flashlight from his pocket while Taylor unhooked the lantern from his belt loop, lighting it as they walked deeper into the darkness. They soon caught sight of Taylor's things and set to work. Kaleb reached for Taylor's box of spare clothes thinking he could use it to carry more of the smaller things, but time had gotten to the tape holding it, and the bottom fell through, dropping everything inside to the floor.

"Oops." Kaleb gave Taylor an apologetic shrug. "Sorry." He knelt to fold the bottom flaps over each other and refill it with Taylor's things while the blonde set to work on his sleeping bag and cooler. A smaller box had fallen out of the broken box, and when Kaleb reached for it, noticed it to be full of open letters addressed to 'Bubbie.' After seeing Sarah Thompson's name written tidily in the top corner, Kaleb held the box out to Taylor.

"Why is your mother writing to your dog?" Kaleb asked, grinning when Taylor snatched the letter box.

"I told you," he grumbled. "It's a family name."

Kaleb chuckled. "Okay, you have to tell me how that happened."

Taylor ran a hand through his hair after tucking his box inside the cooler, looking to the floor and away from Kaleb.

"It's stupid," he mumbled.

"So?" Kaleb shrugged. "Who am I gonna tell?" This brought a particularly annoyed, dark glare from Taylor, causing Kaleb to shirk away. "Okay, I promise I won't tell." Taylor shook his head, tending to his blanket.

"Not gonna happen."

Kaleb grinned in an impish nature. "I'll count off two lessons if you tell me."

Taylor stopped, eyeing the jock.

Kaleb's grin broadened. "Three?" he said. "Final offer."

Taylor turned away, tucking his blanket over his sleeping bag. "It's just something I came up with as a kid," he brushed off, but Kaleb wouldn't let up.

"I need more details than that," he told him. "The whole story, or no deal."

Taylor straightened, glowering at Kaleb. He sighed, turning to the wall. "When I was little, I thought baby puppies were called 'bubbies' because I couldn't say my P's yet." He leaned down to pick up his stacked bedding and cooler. "My mom thought it was cute, and ever since, she's used it for things she likes."

Kaleb grinned. "That wasn't too hard, now was it?"

Taylor glared at Kaleb, shouldering past him to the exit. "Hurry up," Taylor grumbled. Kaleb grabbed Bubbie's bowl and the last handful of Taylor's things and shoved them into the cardboard box, chasing after the blonde so as not to be left alone in the dark chutes.

Bubbie complained at the two for taking his home apart, following close to Taylor in fear of being left behind, no matter how much Taylor tried to console him. Even as they hiked downstream, Bubbie's discomfort followed with them. As they struggled up the bank with Taylor's things, Taylor dug out Bubbie's ball to help calm him while they waited for Vance to return. Their playtime was cut short, however, when Vance pulled into the grass, smiling as he held up a new red collar for the dog to wear. He had gone to buy other essentials, including a leash and food and other goodies for Bubbie, and upon meeting the dog, Vance spoiled him with a handful of treats.

"He really wanted a dog," Kaleb muttered, shoving Taylor's things into the bed of the truck alongside him. With no room in the cabin for Bubbie, Taylor opted to sit in the bed of the truck with his dog, and silently enjoyed the view as they rode back to the house.

Trish wouldn't admit it, but she loved Bubbie on sight. As the men pulled into the driveway, Trish had come out to the front yard to meet them- and to remind them not to let the dog inside the house with the cat. However, upon seeing the shepherd, Trish dropped to her knees to rub his ears and began cooing over his "cute little face;" all the while, Bubbie panted happily, letting Trish lavish him with affection.

Kaleb shook his head at his mother, helping to unload the trinkets from the bed of the truck while his mother loved on Bubbie. He stopped, though, when he caught sight of Taylor slinking into the house, running away from something he noticed across the street.

Trish's admiration grabbed the attention of Gerrit in his front yard, and he was now running over to greet Kaleb's new dog. Bubbie's ears perked at the sudden intrusion, and was sent into a ferocious barking spree, guarding the house from Gerrit and scaring everyone out of their skin. Gerrit skidded to a halt, backing away from the angry dog before he could attack, but Vance was already nearing the dog to latch on his leash and drag him around to the back of the house.

"I don't think he likes you," Kaleb snickered as his mother huffed inside the house.

"Whatever," Gerrit grumbled. "That dog's dumb anyway." Kaleb smacked the back of Gerrit's head. "Why'd you get a dog anyways? Won't he eat the cat?" Gerrit leaned against the truck, waiting for an answer.

"Not my dog," Kaleb said, hoisting the cooler and bedding into his arms.

"Whose is he?" Gerrit asked. Kaleb nodded to Gerrit to take the sleeping bag, but the shorter boy waved him off.

"If you must know, I'm getting a roommate," he told him. "And that's all you're getting out of me."

Gerrit frowned at his friend. "You're lame," he whined. Then, "Hey, I'm bored. You wanna hang out today?"

Kaleb furrowed his brow at the smaller boy. "No," he grumbled. "I still haven't forgiven you for your last stunt." Gerrit became confused.

"What stunt?"

Kaleb frowned. "The locker room?"

Gerrit clicked his teeth, following Kaleb to the front door. "C'mon, Kaleb!" he tried. "You're not still sore about that, are ya?"

"Yes," Kaleb exasperated, dropping the items inside by the front door. "You could have seriously hurt him- maybe even killed him if the weather had gone bad." He shouldered past the smaller boy. "You shouldn't have tried it in the first place; especially after I told you not to."

Gerrit rolled his eyes. "Alright!" he caved. "Quarter already. I won't do it again." Kaleb still wasn't happy, but he knew that would be the best answer he could pull out of his friend no matter how hard he tried to drill it into his head that he had done wrong.

"So, are we gonna hang out or what?"

Kaleb shook his head. "You're hopeless," he sighed, but shrugged agreement. "Gimme a sec."

Gerrit slapped his shoulder in approval, then trotted back to his house across the street while Kaleb entered his own home. He found Taylor in the backyard with Bubbie, hidden out of sight behind the house.

"Hey, Taylor?" Kaleb asked, jerking a thumb. "Gerrit and I are gonna go hang out, you wanna come?"

Taylor cocked a brow at him. "No," he said matter-of-factly.

Kaleb shrugged. "Okay," he retreated. "Never hurts to ask." He turned to step through the back door. "I'll see you later then."

Chapter 14

Taylor spent the rest of the night playing with Bubbie, helping the dog get adjusted to his new life in Kaleb's shed. Trish was a little more apprehensive of Bubbie after his little stunt with Gerrit, but when she saw Taylor's eyes light up when he played with the shepherd, she let the issue drop. The thought of being able to see Bubbie whenever he wanted put a smile in Taylor's eyes as he played with his friend, and he was relieved that he wouldn't have to resort to hiding the dog in the school after hours. Bubbie was safe for the Winter, and that was the most important thing to be happy about.

Dinner came all too quickly, ending the Evans' weekend together as the adults had work through the week, and the boys had school. When the sun rose and the house was emptied, Taylor raced ahead of Kaleb, not wanting to be seen with him in public just yet. He sat down in the cafeteria out of habit, used to buying his breakfast each morning, but not now having a reason thanks to Trish shoving granola bars and raisin toast at him earlier that morning. He sighed, letting the air passed through slowly as he closed his eyes. His stories had been itching to escape him for days now, and his fingers agreed to the challenge, drumming along at the table. What set him over the edge, however, was the fact that he had finished writing through the last page of his old journal, and now needed to spread his imagination over the virgin pages of his new one.

With his mind made up, Taylor bent over to his pack and dug out his headphones before grabbing his new notebook, wanting to listen to the sound of his tunes rather than the chatter of the other students. He looked through his selection, picking which song he wanted to hear first, then slipped on the headphones over his ears, only to have them suddenly ripped off his head.

"Hey!" Taylor griped, turning to find Jason, Dylan, and then Daniel dangling his headphones off of a finger.

"Whoops," Daniel chittered, waving the headpiece in his face. "Lose something?" Daniel tossed Taylor's headphones to Jason, who examined the headphones with a wicked grin before tossing them to Dylan.

"Give'em back," Taylor ordered darkly. Dylan took his inspecting eyes off the headphones to look at Taylor.

"Why should I?" he asked. "You're not one to help people out." He twirled the headphones around from his fingers. "I should know."

Taylor grimaced, remembering how he had previously turned Dylan down for 'tutoring.' He and his friends had already pounded on Taylor because he refused Dylan's requirements to do the work for Dylan, rather than help him, but apparently, he still held a grudge over Taylor for it. Dylan's grin reeked of wicked intent as he swung the headphones around in his hands.

"Catch."

He tossed the headphones over Taylor's head, out of reach from his grasp as they were snatched by Jason. The boys had circled around Taylor, starting their own game of monkey-in-the-middle, with Taylor being their own personal monkey. The blonde tried not to look ridiculous as he chased after his headphones, but jumping after them from boy to boy made it quite impossible. The athletes got a good laugh at his efforts, poking fun at him when Jason caught sight of Kaleb walking into the cafeteria.

"Heads up!" he shouted, throwing the headphones to his captain as he joined the group. Taylor turned and stopped just in time to see Kaleb catch them, and stood staring up at him awkwardly as he was yet again caught in the middle of trouble. Kaleb cocked a brow at him, then to his friends as he returned the headphones to their rightful owner. Taylor took them quietly, not making eye contact and furiously looking to the floor.

"What'd you do that for?" Daniel complained, accompanied by the others.

"Leave Taylor alone, you guys," Kaleb said plainly. "Three against one isn't a fair fight." There was a shared, confused look between the three boys.

"Taylor?" Dylan asked, not used to his real name. By now, Taylor had started back over to his pack, and the athletes were dispersing. Kaleb walked over to Taylor, noticing a change in his behavior.

"Are you-"

"I don't need your help," Taylor snipped. Kaleb shrugged.

"Looked like it to me."

Taylor zipped up his backpack and shirked it over his back to shoulder past the jock. "Just keep to your own kind, asshole. I see enough of you as it is."

Kaleb sighed, rolling his eyes to the ceiling and shaking his head. "You're welcome," he muttered to himself. As usual, Taylor spent the rest of the day avoiding Kaleb as much as he could, and by the time the end of school had rolled around, he had rethought his actions towards the jock, and was hesitant in greeting him at the laboratory.

"Where do you wanna do this?" Taylor asked, looking away. Kaleb smirked, accepting that this was how the blonde was going to apologize and walked into the classroom.

"We might as well do it where we're used to," he said. "Fewer distractions in here, too." They set to work catching up on all their missing days, and even managed to get some extra credit done as well. They were working on a three-hundred word essay when the boys got a little too close to one another, and when Taylor turned to ask Kaleb a question, brushed his nose against the jock's.

"We have *got* to stop doing that," Taylor griped, scooting away from Kaleb, but the jock had remained silent, looking for the courage to ask a question.

"Can I ask you something?" he started, not looking directly at Taylor as he spoke. " … Where did you get your scar?"

Taylor's face fell, and his eyes began to wander around, looking for a purpose. Kaleb finally turned his eyes to him as the blonde started rummaging through his paperwork, stacking them into neat little piles.

"What's done is done," Taylor told him. "Leave it in the past."

Kaleb looked to the table, disappointed with the answer Taylor had given him, but let the issue drop. Asking about embarrassing childhood stories and family names was one thing, but digging around in- what Kaleb was assured was Friedreich's handy work- was another. There was no bribing Taylor this time, and there wouldn't be any attempts. Instead, Kaleb silently sighed, then turned to his own paper to ready himself and Taylor for another round of chemical symbols and equations.

"You sure you don't wanna come?"

"N-"

"It counts."

"I'm sure," Taylor said flatly.

Kaleb was off with Gerrit again, and again, Taylor turned down his offer of joining them. He trudged down the sidewalk towards home, when he stopped, and turned around, remembering that he no longer lived with his father. As he walked through the Evans' front door, the eerie silence crept under his skin. He set forth feeding Skitters, then made his way to Bubbie in the backyard. His friend was more than happy to see him, and for the next hour, Taylor tossed Bubbie's ball around the yard for him to fetch and be thrown again.

It wasn't the cold that brought him in, but the arrival of Mr. and Mrs. Evans. Trish had poked her head out from the back door, calling Taylor in to warm up with a cup of coco. While he sipped from his mug, he took notice of the pictures around the house. In every one, there was a smiling Evans, be it Trish, Vance or Kaleb. One picture in particular caught his eye, though.

Atop the fireplace, there was a picture of Vance and Trish in a dusty, sandy place. She had her arms wrapped around his neck, kissing him while he held her around her waist. They were covered in dust to the point of no recognition, but they didn't seem to mind. Hidden behind Vance's head, there was a cloth armband safety pinned to Trish's right shoulder, barely broadcasting the symbol of a military medic beneath the caked-on dust, and if Taylor had a guess, Vance had one on his sleeve as well, hidden behind Trish's body.

"That was our first night." Vance came up behind Taylor, startling him into almost spilling his mug. "Careful!" Vance chuckled. "Don't wanna waste it."

Taylor righted his mug, checking for any stains. "Sorry," he mumbled, receiving a pat on the back.

"It's alright, kid," Vance told him. "No worries."

Taylor turned back to the picture, gesturing to it before speaking. "Do you mean first night in the deserts?"

Vance picked up the picture, taking a good look at it. "No foolin' you," he muttered, then louder. "Trish and I were medics, back in the day." He thumbed at the frame, recalling when the picture was taken. "We had just spent the last twenty-two hours patching up soldiers on both ends. I was exhausted; pretty much dead on my feet, and to make it worse, there was a giant sand storm that lasted for a good four hours near the end there. When we finally got a break, Trish was the one who picked me back up."

Taylor kept his eyes on Vance. "How so?"

Vance smiled, replacing the photo back to the fireplace. "She told me, 'Vance, my darling, we've saved the day today. Let's do it again tomorrow.' Then she kissed me to seal the deal. The nerve." Vance chuckled a bit. "Didn't even notice the photographer until after he had taken the picture. So Trish bargained with him that he could keep the picture if he let us have a copy." Vance tapped the frame's glass. "It ended up in the papers with an article on how the medic's are making a difference in the war. We were known as the 'healing couple' for a while after that."

"Sounds nice," Taylor said, fingering his mug.

"It wasn't all fame and glory, kid." Vance chuckled, leaning an arm along the fireplace. "There was always work to be done. We didn't have time to enjoy being fame monsters." Vance's grin slowly faded. "War was the only monster that lasted."

Taylor looked to the picture, his questions bubbling up in his stomach. Vance noticed his hesitation and prodded him to ask away.

" … How did you get over the nightmares?" Taylor asked quietly.

Vance's grin faded away to nothing as he looked to the photo. He took his time before answering, and when he did, he kept his voice quiet and steady. "I didn't," he answered. "I just learned to live with them." Taylor looked to Vance, silenced by his truthfulness. Vance dipped his head to Taylor and added;

"And so did Trish."

"So, he's living with you now?" Mr. G asked. Kaleb nodded, leaning against the edge of a student's desk.

"Is that gonna be a problem?" the boy asked. "I mean, is there a rule against tutoring someone in the same household?"

Mr. G furrowed his brow, trying to find any such law in his memory. "I think you'll be alright," he said finally, leaning comfortably against his desk. A grin pulled at the corner of Kaleb's mouth, relieved by this news. Mr. G crossed his arms in thought. "Is he the kid I sent to you before?" he asked. "The blonde one?"

"Yeah, Taylor." Kaleb nodded. "I remember him saying something like that before."

Mr. G ticked his head. "Now that you mention it, I think I've heard of him before," he said. "Amy's been raving about this one kid in her class. Says he could outsmart anyone in tech."

Kaleb snickered. "You mean Miss Hart?" he asked, receiving a nod. "Sounds about right."

"So why is he living with *you*?"

Kaleb bit his lip, looking away. "I'm not sure if I should go into that," he muttered. Mr. G nodded.

"I understand." he said, holding up a hand. "But you should probably tell the school. Let them know he's had a change of address." Kaleb looked to his teacher, confused. "In case they need to send home something." The teacher explained. "Or call someone in case of emergency. You know;" he rose his brow in mock importance. "*Serious* stuff."

Kaleb chuckled at his teacher's attempt at silliness, agreeing with him. "Well, are you at least happy about the new situation?" Mr. G asked, crossing his arms back over his chest.

Kaleb gave his teacher a curious look. "I guess so," he muttered in thought. "I mean it's better than where he was before…" He stopped himself before he went any further, rubbing the back of his neck. "I'll have to learn how to be a little cleaner, though." He gave a sheepish chuckle. "Don't want him tripping over my stuff when he tries to cross the room."

"That would definitely be a problem." Mr G smiled. "Look at it this way, you get to room with your friend." Kaleb paused at this, letting the words sink in.

"I'm not so sure."

Mr. G cocked his head, curious for an explanation. "We're not really that close," Kaleb admitted. "And I'm not sure he even likes me." He rubbed the back of his head. "I mean, all we ever do is bicker and fight." He huffed. "I don't think we even agree on anything."

The teacher sucked in his lips in thought. "I think you two are closer than you think," he said. "People who agree on everything will never be able to grow together. If you can argue, grind against each other, even, then you know you are your own person. You're not stuck in one mindset because you're afraid of what might set the other off." He scratched his temple. "Do you understand?"

Kaleb grimaced, trying to comprehend what was said, but shook his head. "Let me put it this way," Mr. G tried. "You care about each other whether you realize it or not. I'm sure of it."

Kaleb looked to his teacher. "How do you know that?"

The older man shrugged, offering a simple smile. "Otherwise, you wouldn't have invited him, and he wouldn't have stayed."

"I need your help." Taylor had surprised Kaleb with this while they were walking home from school, but he played it off.

"Shoot," he said, not making a big deal of it. Taylor frowned a bit, trying to think of how to say his next sentence.

"Your dad missed something when he grabbed my stuff," he said finally. "I need to get it." Kaleb's face hardened.

"You're not sup-"

"That's why I'm telling you first," Taylor interrupted. "So you can either come with me, or I can go alone."

Taylor quickened his step towards his house, leaving Kaleb behind. Kaleb furrowed his brow, speeding up to match pace with the blonde.

"This is a bad idea," he told him. "Can't my dad go get it for you like last time?" Taylor looked straight ahead.

"Not where I'm looking," he said flatly. Kaleb sighed.

"Fine. But you better make it quick." Kaleb begrudgingly followed the determined blonde down the sidewalk, looking at him curiously as he did.

"I don't get you," Kaleb blurted.

"I'm easy to get," Taylor replied, still looking ahead. "I just want to get through my studies long enough to get out of here." Now the blonde turned to look at him. "It's *you* I don't get." Kaleb gave a queer look.

"What do you mean?"

Taylor turned back to stare ahead of him. "You've got the whole world at the tip of your fingers with football, and yet, you prefer science. Take your bike, for example." Taylor grimaced when the sun glared in his face. "What football player in their right mind would waste time pulling apart a perfectly usable bike and try to turn it into something else without any certainty of it even working?" Taylor hiked his pack higher onto his shoulders. "Your room is full of scholastic advancement rather than super models and sports posters, and you have to actively dumb yourself down in order to talk with your friends." He glared back at Kaleb. "Why do you even hang out with them, anyways?" He turned back to look ahead. "They're nothing but a bunch of sheep."

Kaleb frowned at this, not liking how easily Taylor put down his friends. "They're not as bad as you make them out to be," he defended. "If you sat down and actually got to know them, you'd see that."

"I can see just fine from afar, thanks," Taylor brushed off.

"And what exactly *do* you see?" Kaleb argued, growing irritated with the blonde.

"Single-minded folk who care more about their own advancement than anything or any*one* else." The blonde turned around to Kaleb, stopping this time. "I guarantee it that if you asked them to describe you in one word, they wouldn't be able to tell you anything useful."

Kaleb looked to the blonde, his irritation swept away by the sudden seriousness in Taylor's eyes. "What about you?" he asked. "What can you tell me?"

The younger teen turned around, resuming his journey. "You're not like the others," he said. "You're happier with science. You just don't want to admit it to anyone for some reason. I'm not even sure most of your friends even know about that."

Kaleb shrugged, hugging his pockets close to him when a stiff breeze blew through them. "As far as football goes," he said, taking control of the conversation. "I don't know, I guess it's expected of me. I'm so good at it, why not, right? If I'm gonna do something, it might as well be excellent." Taylor frowned.

"What's so hard about throwing a ball?" he muttered. "I'm pretty sure you could walk it to the goal post if you wanted." Kaleb chuckled.

"It's not that simple," he said. "But if I did, I'd have to make it one impressive walk. I mean, look at my parents."

Taylor turned his head to Kaleb's direction. "What do you mean?"

"You've seen them," he explained. "They're accomplished medical scientists." Kaleb smiled. "They've saved lives, they've given people a reason to live again. Dad's given people their legs- their *freedom* back, and mom; she's saved so many people from their deathbed with her herbs, you could probably fill a whole town with the survivors. They've changed so many lives." He shrugged. "They help people. That's all I want to do, too."

"You've already got a head start there," Taylor mumbled.

"What?" Kaleb leaned forward to hear him, but Taylor stopped.

"We're here."

Kaleb looked to Taylor's house, unease spreading over him the longer he stared. "Do we *have* to go in there?" Kaleb asked, not taking his eyes off the house.

"You don't have to do anything," Taylor said, hiking his pack higher onto his shoulders and stepping forward alone. Kaleb groaned in frustration, speeding up to catch up with the blonde.

The truck was gone, but Taylor was cautious when he entered nonetheless. Kaleb scanned his eyes along the road, keeping watch for Friedreich's red truck should it come, finding nothing but kids playing in a nearby yard. Taylor kept his head in the door frame for a moment longer until he was satisfied that it was safe to enter, then quietly stepped forward, keeping his senses on high alert as Kaleb followed. Once the door was shut, Taylor hiked his pack higher onto his shoulders again, keeping his attention locked on to his room.

"Let's go."

The two carefully climbed the stairs to Taylor's room, finding it to be ransacked upon entry.

"Dad went wild in here," Kaleb mumbled, not seeing the glimmer on Taylor's face. Instead, the blonde stepped further in, pausing when a thought occurred to him.

"Guard the door," he said, not wanting Kaleb to see what he was doing. Kaleb did as he was told, keeping watch on the ground below for any signs of danger. Taylor set to laying on the floor, crawling deep beneath his bed to find his lock box in the far off corner. Once he was out from under the bed, Taylor shoved the metal case into his pack. Just as he zipped it shut, glass shattered in the living room, sending both boys into a panic.

Kaleb instantly turned back to grab Taylor by the hood and yank him out of the room as fast as he could, stumbling the blonde backwards towards the stairs. Taylor couldn't find his feet beneath him with Kaleb continually pulling him and ended up falling into Kaleb's legs, knocking the jock off his feet to give himself more room on the floor. Kaleb tried to fight it, he really did, but gravity won in their game of will, and sent Kaleb tumbling down the entire flight of stairs, lying flat on his back at ground level.

"Kaleb!"

Taylor bolted to his feet and flew down the stairs, jumping over the jock to avoid stepping on him and kneeling to frantically shake his shoulders.

"Kaleb! Kaleb, can you hear me?"

Kaleb was dazed, blinking away the darkness that tried to take hold and tried to roll over with the blonde to run away. Taylor threw one of the jock's arms over his shoulders, practically dragging him to the front door until Kaleb could find his feet again. Taylor swung open the door for a quick escape, only to jump back from the person standing in the doorway, blocking Kaleb from exiting as well.

A frightened boy with wide, watery eyes was shaking on Taylor's doorstep, looking about to melt down in front of him. "I'm sorry!" he whimpered. "We were playing and Willie said it would be fun and I thought so too and so we did and we shouldn't have but we did and it went through and it broke and then Willie ran away but mom always told me to say you're sorry and so I am and now I have to give you all of my money and- and-" The boy faltered, stumbling over his gasping and sobbing. "But I don't wanna pay for a new window, I wanted to buy a bike!" The boy broke down in tears before the two terrified teens, confusing them to no end.

"What?" Taylor wheezed, completely out of breath from trying to escape.

"It wasn't me!" the boy cried, pointing to his hiding friend. "Willie did it!"

Kaleb had regained his footing when Taylor flung himself between Kaleb and the sobbing child, and was now standing over the two.

"Willie did what?" he asked. The boy pointed to Taylor's front window, showing a great big hole in the middle. Taylor leaned back to see a rock lying in his kitchen floor, then turned back to the boy, mouth agape.

"You broke the glass," he realized, sending the boy into hysterics.

"Not me! Willie!"

Kaleb's knees gave out on him as he laughed himself to the floor along the door frame. "Kid, you scared the crap out of me!" he laughed, confusing the boy. Taylor pressed his head to the door frame, a nervous laugh leaking out of him as well.

"It was just you," he breathed.

The teens took a few more moments to compose themselves before getting up to fix the situation. Taylor set to cleaning up the kitchen while Kaleb followed the boy home to tell his mother what a good job he did in taking responsibility, and to not worry about the window- but keep an eye out for that Willie kid. The whole mess took less than five minutes, and their nervous laughter covered their fear of being there, but once Taylor had patched up the window and locked up to leave, the two boys bolted down the sidewalk, trying to get away as quick as they could.

"How's your leg?" Taylor asked after things had gotten quiet.

"Now that the adrenaline's gone?" Kaleb gingerly took a step. "Probably gonna have to stay in and read tonight." Taylor dropped his gaze to the sidewalk, gripping his shoulder straps.

"Sorry," he muttered. Kaleb shrugged.

"Hey, just don't tell my mom." The two grimaced. "If she finds out, we're done for."

Taylor reached a hand up to run it through his hair, bumping into his grey beanie Trish had given him. "I think I'd rather face my father." Taylor shivered. Kaleb quieted.

"Speaking of," he started. "What was so important that you would risk it?"

Taylor looked away from the jock. He didn't want to tell Kaleb, but after all the trouble he had gone through to protect Taylor in that house, all the help he had given him to get it out of there, and getting hurt in the process, Taylor figured Kaleb had earned a little honesty from him. He rearranged his pack on his shoulders, still looking away, not making eye contact.

"I left my life savings in there. Plus my border pass," he muttered. "My dad wouldn't have let go of them if he found out."

Kaleb sighed, looking to the ground before speaking again. "Well," he began. "I guess I can understand that." He looked to the blonde. "But next time, bring some more back up."

Taylor huddled closer inside his pockets as he walked up the last steps to the house. Kaleb was off with Gerrit again, and Trish and Vance were still off at work, leaving Taylor alone with the house to himself. Things were going smoothly for once. The cold, however, was another problem.

There was no heating in the shed, and Bubbie's blanket did little to no good at all to help warm the poor beast. As Taylor came in that evening, Bubbie was too cold to get out of bed, and lay there shivering, the tip of his tail wagging at the sight of his friend. Taylor rubbed the dog down, trying to warm him with contact, but his hands couldn't bring any warmth to the shepherd.

Taylor kneeled down into Bubbie's bed, sitting in it while he lay the dog in his lap and chest to hold him close, wrapping the dog's blanket around the both of them. Bubbie gave a little lick to Taylor's earlobe, shivering in his arms as the blonde swept his arms up and down the length of the furry little body. Taylor stayed this way with Bubbie until Trish and Vance had come home from work, then he carefully placed the dog back in his bed to go speak with them.

"Miss Trish?" Taylor asked.

"Taylor, honey, your face is bright red," Trish noted. "Don't tell me you were out in the cold this whole time?"

Taylor pocketed his blue fingers. "That's actually what I wanted to talk with you about," he said. Trish hung her coat and scarf over the pegs along the front wall, ushering Taylor to sit at the dining room table.

"What's wrong, dear?" she asked, nodding to Vance when he held the kettle up. Taylor picked at his fingers at the table.

"It's Bubbie," he started. "It's getting cold out, and the shed doesn't block it out much." He sighed, looking to Trish. "He can't handle the cold."

Trish sucked in her lips, thinking of an answer. "Well that is a problem, isn't it?" she muttered, sighing.

"What if we try a test run?" Vance interjected, placing a steaming mug before his wife. "We can introduce Skitters and Bubbie and see where it goes, and if it goes South, we'll just keep them in separate rooms." At this, Taylor had a thought.

"How about the storage room?"

Trish became perplexed. "The 'what' room?" she asked. Taylor threw his thumb over his shoulder.

"The locked room," he explained. "Kaleb said it was a storage room."

A light came on in Trish's mind. "Oh, that," she sighed. "Well, it's worth a shot." She nodded to Taylor to grab Bubbie's leash and fetch his dog, while Vance set forth to nab the cat.

When Taylor returned with Bubbie in the living room, he found Vance cuddling Skitters close to his face, comforting the cat before settling down on the ground with her to hold her in place. Vance nodded to Taylor, allowing him to come closer with Bubbie, who was sniffing profusely in Skitters' direction. Taylor brought him up to the end of Vance's outstretched leg and had the dog sit down, still sniffing in the cat's direction. Skitters pulled back her ears, not pleased with the dog's sudden appearance. She whipped her tail around, turning her head away from Bubbie.

Bubbie cocked his head to the side, watching Skitters carefully. He lifted a paw, placing it gently onto her shoulder to push her over, his tail wagging. Skitters didn't appreciate this, and hissed at him loudly, scaring Trish off on the sidelines. Bubbie's ear pricked, cocking his head again at this, and dropped down to lay on the floor in front of the cat, wagging his tail and pushing her over again, as gentle as ever. Skitters bat at Bubbie's nose, claws sheathed as a warning, but this only enticed the dog. His tail quickened, and when Skitters bat at him again, he tried licking her paws. Skitters retreated from the slobbery tongue just as Bubbie raised another paw to her, surprising her into a nervous yelp as she tripped over her own tail. Bubbie's ears pricked and he removed his paw immediately, sniffing her to see if she was alright. Vance smiled, watching the two animals.

"I don't think we have anything to worry about, Trish."

Taylor awoke to the sight of a wagging tail on the floor and smirked. He inched closer to the edge of the bed, peeking over the railing to find Bubbie staring up at him. His ears perked when he caught sight of the blonde, and his tail swept across the floor even faster. Taylor wiggled his eyebrows at the dog, making him become more excited.

"Boo," Taylor whispered, popping his mouth over and under the covers quickly to speak and hide in one swift movement. Bubbie rose to his feet, ears and tail ready to play.

"Boo." Taylor popped again, just as quiet as before. "B-"

Bubbie jumped up onto the bed to reach Taylor, but landed on Kaleb. The jock sat straight up, yelping from the surprised dog, then swearing when he slammed his head on the top bunk.

"Damn," Taylor said, peering over the mattress. "I felt that." Kaleb groaned, rubbing the pain away in his skull. Bubbie had lost interest in Taylor, and was now doting on Kaleb to see if he was alright, and trying to apologize with little licks to his cheek and chin.

"Stop i- stop!" Kaleb muttered, pushing the dog away. Once Bubbie was off his lap, Kaleb peeked up above him to Taylor's dangling head.

"Morning," Taylor smirked. Kaleb growled a reply, sweeping the blanket back to leave the bed. Taylor hopped down from his bunk, scrubbing his dog's ears for a morning greeting while Kaleb stretched out the kinks in his back.

"C'mon," Kaleb mumbled. "He probably needs to go out."

Taylor admitted Kaleb's idea to be right, and lightly called for Bubbie to follow him as the boys made their way to the living room. Kaleb parted from the group towards the kitchen, allowing Taylor to care for his pet while the jock cared for himself. He gathered the ingredients for a morning brew, and waited leaning against the counter, his sore head hanging from his shoulders.

"How can you drink that stuff?" Taylor asked, crossing his arms on the bar. Kaleb looked up to him, still waking up.

"What?" he asked, bleary eyed. Taylor nodded to the infuser waiting in Kaleb's mug.

"It's just boiled grass, really," Taylor said. "I don't see how it can be good." Kaleb hung his head again, too tired to lift it just yet.

"Leaves," he murmured. "It's leaves, not grass." He rubbed his tired eyes. "And it's pretty good, once you find the kind you like." The kettle sang out, calling to Kaleb for rescue, and was soon poured into the mug, sending wonderful aromas to his nose that properly woke him up. Taylor shook his head, scrutinizing the slowly purpling water.

"Just don't get it," he muttered.

"Well, here." Kaleb lifted the mug to Taylor, almost catching him on the nose with it. "Try it."

Taylor squinted into the cup. "Isn't it still cooking?"

"Steeping," Kaleb corrected. "But, you're right." He pulled back the mug, fiddling with the infuser a bit before leaving it to cool. Taylor came around the bar to inspect the fridge's contents, finding his stomach to still be asleep and retreated to lean an arm against the sink. Kaleb turned to face him, leaning against the opposite counter.

"It's still early." Kaleb yawned. "Sun's barely out."

Taylor glanced at the kitchen window, shrugging indifference. "You're too awake this early," Kaleb said. "You must be in a good mood." Taylor shrugged again.

"No more than usual," he muttered, but Kaleb shook his head.

"You're hyper. I can tell."

Taylor frowned. "No I'm not."

Kaleb crossed his arms, unconvinced. "You really love that dog," he said quietly. Taylor's face crumpled into confusion. "He stayed inside last night," Kaleb explained. "And he was the first one you saw this morning, was he not?" Taylor looked away, picking at the lining between the sink and counter. "I think it's good," Kaleb said. "You know, having someone you care about."

Taylor rubbed a finger over his eye, rubbing some sleep away, but saying nothing. He pointed to the mug behind Kaleb, wanting the focus on that instead of himself. "That done yet?"

Kaleb turned to retrieve his mug, dipping his infuser a few more times as he shuffled to lean against the sink like the blonde.

"Here." Kaleb held the mug out to Taylor, who took it tentatively. He swirled it around a few times, sniffing the liquid before pressing his lips to the mug for a sip.

Taylor's face distorted into displeasure, tasting the bitter drink and wanting nothing more than to get it out of his mouth.

"Nope." He gagged, turning to dump the cup in the sink only to be stopped by Kaleb.

"Don't waste it." Kaleb cradled the mug back into his hands. "It's the last cup of blueberry." He began walking to the dining room table to drink it, taking a swig along the way, and missing Taylor raise a hand to stop it, but brought back his hand to bite a knuckle, deciding not to tell Kaleb that he had spat the drink back into the mug.

Taylor was helping Vance with the dishes, drying them as Vance handed each dripping plate to him, and then stacking them atop one another to be replaced in the cabinets later. It had been a little over a month since Taylor first began living with the Evans', and he had fallen into the rhythm of things quite easily. Wake up, go to school, study with Kaleb, come home and play with Bubbie, dinner, then off to bed to start all over again. Jobs came along every now and then, and with Kaleb's deal with Taylor, it was easier to save up. Weekends were spent doing family things, and when Trish needed to shop for essentials, Taylor didn't mind going along with her to help carry things.

Now, Trish was with Kaleb at another one of his physical therapy sessions while Taylor stayed behind with Vance, who didn't mind one bit of the young blonde's help with his chores. The two men finished with the dishes relatively quickly, giving them plenty of time to play with Bubbie. They bundled up to take the shepherd out for a walk around the neighborhood.

Afterwards, they came back to the house to play inside where it was warm. Vance had gotten the dog a braided rope toy that looped into a figure-eight, and after a few trials of uninterested sniffing, Bubbie had learned to love it. Both Taylor and Vance tossed the rope toy around, letting the dog chase it around the house and wrestle with it between the two of them when he had caught it.

Taylor had gotten used to enjoying this time each evening, and it didn't bother him as much as it used to when Vance came to join in with him. In fact, Taylor had started to become more comfortable in the Evans' home. He didn't flinch as much anymore when someone came near him, or walked up behind him, and his avoidance of contact became almost minimal at best. He spoke up more during dinner conversations, and every now and then, his small smile was genuine.

Even his lessons with Kaleb were easier to handle; filled considerably less with dread and more, dare he admit it, leaning more towards anticipation. Each afternoon, Taylor waited for the crowds to leave as usual, but rather than dragging his feet to the Alchemy hall, Taylor put a skip to his step, quickening his pace to the laboratory. As they worked through the paperwork, Taylor learned more from Kaleb than from his teacher in class, and he didn't mind working through the extra work- especially when Kaleb would switch from extra credit work to chemistry experiments.

As the weeks passed, Taylor's skin had almost cleared of the awful bruises that tattooed his body. Without any new ones each day to cover the old, his darkened, spotty skin once again became smooth and porcelain. His skinny body was no longer malnourished thanks to the stocked kitchen and full meals, and his muscles peeked out more with the extra protein Trish would sneak into his diet.

Taylor's appetite had grown considerably as well. Having a full plate was a requirement in the Evans house, no exceptions, and after dinner had settled in their stomachs, dessert would be given freely. It was a pleasure that Taylor had never been accustomed to before, and rather enjoyed it now that it was a regular occurrence.

Taylor's conversations with Bekah were lighter as well. With Kaleb off with Gerrit, and the Evans' out until sundown, he was given plenty of time to talk with his friend in complete privacy, without the use of a lock on the door, and without fear of being caught by unfriendly hands. Without the threat of danger, Taylor became a whole new person. Living life with the Evans' was becoming a simple pleasure to Taylor, and it showed through him prominently.

Taylor couldn't control his smiling when Bubbie barked at Vance, demanding the rope toy from above the man's head. Vance started waving the toy over Bubbie's head, pulling away as he jumped up to try and snag it. After the third try, Bubbie's teeth latched onto the rope, snatching it out of Vances hands. Vance hooted his surprise, chasing after the dog around the couch, and eventually dropping to all fours to pull at the toy in Bubbie's mouth.

The dog's tail went wild as he wrestled for the toy, whipping his head back and forth to try and shake off Vance. The man was victorious, however, and pulled the toy high over his head again. Bubbie's ears perked and chased after the rope, tackling Vance off of his knees. Just as Vance had been tackled by Bubbie, and was rolling around on the floor begging for mercy, Trish and Kaleb came in through the door.

"Hey, honey," Vance called from under Bubbie's chest. "Nice day?"

Trish shook her head at her husband. "What am I going to do with you?" she breathed, getting a quiet chuckle from Taylor. Kaleb finished hanging his jacket and other essentials and dropped to his knees to receive a warm welcome from Bubbie.

"You look happy," Vance noted, sitting back up on his knees.

Kaleb smiled at his father. "That obvious, is it?"

Taylor got up for the kitchen to ready the kettle for Trish while she spoke with her husband. "He got some good news from the therapist today," Trish said, sitting down at the dining room table.

"Oh, really?" Vance mused, grinning at his son and shrugging. "Care to share?"

Kaleb stood up to let Bubbie out in the backyard. "Today was my last session," he told him, freezing Taylor at the sink. "Doc said I could go back to football as soon as tomorrow."

"Hey, that's great, kid!" Vance beamed. Taylor stopped the faucet and turned to set the kettle on the stove while Kaleb was being congratulated. He quietly turned on the the heat on then left it to boil.

"Where are you going, dear?" Trish asked when she caught sight of him leaving for the hallway.

"Bathroom," he mumbled over his shoulder. "Great news, Kaleb." Once locked in the bathroom, Taylor looked at himself in the mirror. It was great that Kaleb was fully recovered and healthy, but going back to football meant going back to football practice; which meant no extra time for anything else.

"Great."

Chapter 15

Taylor kicked a fallen branch out of his path, hugging his pocket tightly to him as a harsh wind beat down on him. Kaleb had skipped yet another one of their sessions thanks to football, and Taylor was less than happy about it. The jock had been back on the team for four days now, and each day, Kaleb pulled farther and farther away. He had promised Taylor that his practice wouldn't get in the way of his teachings, but when the tired jock came home each night, he barely had any energy left to eat his own dinner before passing out.

Broken promises were one thing, but dropping Taylor out of his life completely was another. They barely spoke to one another, and when they did, it was in the audience of Kaleb's teammates. Taylor huddled closer to himself, disgusted with the thought that Kaleb was reverting back to his old self. Even at home, he would leave little tricks for Taylor to find, and would get a hearty chuckle out of the end result. He told Taylor they were his way of 'thinking of him' during the day, but the blonde didn't find the sentiment.

The bike had been put on hold, both due to the cold, as well as Kaleb not having any time. It wouldn't be right without the owner of the bike, and Taylor had no idea what he would be doing anyway. He spent his wasted afternoons checking in on Miss Hart, and making excuses to go home early to get out of his presidential duties, wanting nothing more than to go home and grouch.

As Taylor entered the house, and Skitters and Bubbie had greeted him appropriately, he shirked off his things, fed the animals and grumbled to his bed, irritated with the jock. Taylor plopped down on his bunk, only to hiss at the impact. For the past few days, his back had been tender to the touch. He had tried to find a bruise or cut in the mirror, but nothing out of place could be seen. Taylor rolled to his side, glaring at the wall and huffing his irritation through his nose.

"This is so stupid."

Taylor griped about Kaleb and his stupid hobbies and his stupid friends and every other stupid thing in between, and why even bother with that stupid game if he doesn't even care about it- but most of all, he irritated himself with how he was allowing

245

the jock to ruin his mood. Kaleb was a football player, Taylor knew that from the start. Thinking that things would be the same between the two of them after he healed would be naive and immature, and that simply wasn't Taylor's style. Still, it took a while for his brooding to stop, and even after he left his bed, his irritation lingered onto his shadow.

He decided to take his pet for a walk to let the cold air clear his mind. Bubbie was still getting used to his new leash after being able to walk freely with Taylor for so long now, but the dog knew the leash meant some time outside of the house with his friend. He sat still just long enough to hear the clasp click around his collar, then let his excitement take over as they prepared to leave. After a few blocks, it was imminent for a bathroom break, and left for Taylor to care for his responsibilities. Taylor wasn't used to cleaning up after his dog, but considering the fact that he now lived with the little furball, and didn't have to work so hard to hide him, the blonde didn't consider it to be too much of a hassle.

Still, Taylor's irritation stubbornly stayed with him as they walked around the neighborhood, picking away at him with each step. No matter how hard he tried, he simply could not get Kaleb's irritating face out of his head. Taylor sighed, reaching to his headphones to crank up the volume for a particularly quiet song, when Bubbie stopped, ears perked and alert by a pair of boys walking towards the blonde and the shepherd. Taylor grimaced, trying to pull Bubbie away to avoid the oncoming athletes even after they had seen and acknowledged him; however, the dog refused to move, and insisted on barking at Kaleb and Gerrit instead.

"Shh- Bubbie!" Taylor hissed, but the dog was too angry to be stopped. Gerrit stopped, taking a step behind Kaleb, who looked to the shepherd with concern.

"What's wrong, Bubbie?" Kaleb asked, stopping short when the dog snapped at the air between them.

"'Bubbie?'" Gerrit scoffed. "What a stupid name." Kaleb frowned at his friend hiding behind him, turning back to Taylor.

"What's wrong with him?" Kaleb asked. Taylor shook his head, struggling to keep the dog a few inches away from the athletes.

"I have no idea," he grunted.

Kaleb took a closer look at Bubbie's line of vision, looking between Gerrit standing behind him and the dog in front of him, and stepping between the two. Bubbie's glare veered left, trying to peek through Kaleb's legs and growling angrily at the small boy behind him. Kaleb and Taylor looked to each other, finding the problem together.

"You really are good jerk repellent," Taylor muttered. Gerrit's eyes widened as he recognized the dog, connecting him to Taylor.

"This is your dog?" he pointed at Bubbie. Taylor wearily looked to the smaller boy, not saying anything.

"C'mon, bud," Taylor offered, pulling the angry dog away from the other two boys.

"See you later, Taylor," Kaleb called, confirming Gerrit's suspicions.

"Yeah, 'bud,'" Gerrit grinned a sinister grin. "See you later."

Taylor never walked with Kaleb to school. He prefered to be alone, and with the silence of the morning, he was free to imagine the next chapter of his story without the interference of anyone else. Taylor's other world helped to get him out of bad moods, and lately, he'd had plenty of time to think himself into better moods. As he entered the school, he settled himself in the cafeteria to write down his latest thoughts until the first bell rang. Once school had begun, he packed his things and left for his first class, only to have Gerrit swing an arm around his shoulders and drag him to the nearest bathroom for a little talking to.

"Tommy, Tommy, Tommy," Gerrit sighed. "Guess what I just found out."

Taylor hiked his pack onto his shoulders, saying nothing. Gerrit brushed off the blonde's glare with a wide eyed look of his own.

"Someone's been living with my best friend," he told him. "And he's been messing with him ever since."

Taylor's glare intensified. "What are you talking about?"

Gerrit laced his fingers against his lips. "I'm talking about you bringing Kaleb down everyday," he said, giving Taylor an intense look of his own. "His A-game hasn't been the same since you've come around, so the only logical explanation is *you*. Although, I'm not really surprised, to tell you the truth."

"You realize I've been living with him for almost two months now?" Taylor snarked. Gerrit gripped Taylor's shoulders, clenching down far too hard over his skin as he locked eyes with the blonde.

"Stay away from him," Gerrit warned. "Or we'll have to have another talk later." He glared at Taylor for a few moments longer before melting into a twisted grin. He patted Taylor's retreating cheek, scoffing at the blonde's irritation.

"You think you're clear because of him," Gerrit chuckled lightly. "That's cute." Taylor roughly shrugged off Gerrit's hand, still glaring at the snickering athlete. "You can't hide behind him forever," Gerrit told him. "Keep pissing us off, and you'll end up in trouble again, whether Kaleb says to leave you alone or not." Gerrit slapped Taylor's shoulder as he passed by, leaving the blonde for his first class.

"Remember that."

Kaleb was furious. He marched down through the lunch aisles in search of Taylor for an explanation, and once he found the blonde, he ran over and slammed his fists down on the table.

"You killed her!" Kaleb shouted, surprising the blonde.

"What?" Taylor asked. Kaleb leaned in close to growl in his face.

"You *killed* her!" he repeated. "How could you do that?!"

Taylor was still confused. "What are you talking about?" he asked, pulling away from the jock.

"Kiddo!" Kaleb cried. "You killed off Kiddo!" Gerrit and some of the other boys were off staring at the two from another table, watching the scene play out. Taylor grimaced.

"You mean the *character*?" he said, then glared at Kaleb. "How did-"

"Don't turn this around on me!" Kaleb hissed. "How *dare* you? Murderer!" Taylor reclined from him, still sitting in his chair.

"She's a fictional character, asshole," he told him. "You can't call me that. Besides," Taylor's glare darkened. "I want to know how *you* know."

Kaleb's angry stare flickered, but he stayed put. "You can't get mad at me for reading your stuff," he said, earning a cocked brow from Taylor.

"Oh, really?" he challenged, watching Kaleb nod his head. "Even when it's from *my* private journal?"

Kaleb huffed. "It wasn't in your journal, it was on your website." Kaleb stopped short, realizing what he had just done. Taylor leaned back, eyes wide in horror.

"You found my profile?" Taylor asked quietly. Kaleb looked away, still irritated, but now uncomfortable.

"It's a public site," he excused. "You can't get mad at me for that."

Taylor's eyes flicked to the snickering table across from him. "How many others know?" he demanded quietly.

"What?"

"How many of your friends know about this?" Taylor's face grew angrier by the second, but Kaleb scoffed him off.

"They don't read," Kaleb told him. "You really thought they did?" Taylor kept his steely gaze on him, watching his every move. "I'm the only one, Taylor," Kaleb said, more seriously this time.

Taylor stared at him still. "Who are you?" he asked, but Kaleb shook his head.

"Huh-uh," he denied. "If I tell you, you'll block me."

"That's exactly what I'll do," Taylor said, eyes still locked on Kaleb, who frowned at the blonde.

"Give me a break, man," he said. "I like your stuff, don't send me off like that because you're embarrassed." Taylor remained silent for a moment.

"You what?"

"What?" Kaleb questioned. Taylor looked Kaleb up and down.

"You said you…"

"What? That I like your stuff?" Kaleb finished for him. "Yeah, why?" Taylor looked over Kaleb one last time before turning away.

"Nothing," he said. "Nevermind." The overhead bell rang, signaling the end of lunch period and on to the next class. Taylor shouldered his pack, then shoved past Kaleb, trashing his tray on the way out. Kaleb watched him leave, still standing at the table, and cursing himself for not getting any answers.

"What about Kiddo?"

Students were whispering all down the halls and in class, and everywhere Taylor went, he could feel the burning of several pairs of eyes on him at once. The hushed chatter in his classroom quieted the moment he entered, and for a second, Taylor glanced around the room, looking for answers as he sat down at his desk. Eyes watched his every move, making Taylor extremely uncomfortable.

He reached into his pack in search of something, bringing out a gasp from a nearby girl. Taylor eyed her for a moment, then brought his book out onto his desk to flip it open. One boy standing off in the corner with his friends, carefully made his way over to Taylor, making sure the desk in front of him was between he and Taylor.

"Who was she?" he asked. Taylor looked to the boy, confused.

"Who?"

The boy's eyes widened. "You didn't even know her name?" he asked, completely shocked. Taylor frowned.

"What are you talking about?"

"The girl," said the boy. "The one you-" He stopped, fearfully looking at Taylor when he moved in his seat. Taylor gave him a queer look, noticing the entire room had their eyes locked onto him.

"What's going on?" Taylor asked, looking to the boy, who swallowed nervously.

"It was Gerrit," he said. "He's the one who ratted you out." Taylor cocked a brow.

"Gerrit?" He rolled his eyes. "What did he do *this* time?"

"He's the one who warned us." Another boy stepped up.

"About what?" Taylor droned.

"That you're a killer," the boy replied. Taylor furrowed his brow, staying still.

"Did he?" Taylor stated, remembering the conversation he had had with Kaleb at lunch. "I can't do anything without him screwing something up," Taylor muttered to himself.

"So," the first boy piped, eyes wide. "Did you do it?" he asked. "Did you really kill a girl?"

"Think whatever you want." Taylor sighed. "I'm the only one who cares about the truth anyways." The first boy's eyes widened even further.

"So you did?" he asked, causing a stir in the classroom. Taylor looked the first boy in the eyes, making him fairly uncomfortable.

"Think of it this way," he started. "If I had killed someone, *Gerrit* wouldn't have been able to tell you."

The whole murder ordeal lasted throughout the rest of the day, and Mr. Thompson had even been called, but there was no answer. Taylor had been called up to the office for questioning, and an officer had been there for witness, but with no proof or body, there couldn't be a prosecution. Once Taylor had explained that it was just a silly rumor gone too far, he was released back to class, and all charges dropped.

It would take awhile for the students to stop whispering about him as he walked down the halls, and the rumors would grow into elaborate stories later on down the road, but seeing that the office had let him go, the students soon settled down around him; albeit a bit quieter than before.

Kaleb did his best to destroy the rumors, and he gave Gerrit a good scolding for spreading such lies, bashing it into his head that he and Taylor had been talking about something completely different. In the end, Gerrit gave in and offered his apologies, promising to stop spreading the rumor. Kaleb accepted this as enough of an apology from his friend, knowing it was the best he could get, but forgetting one vital thing from their agreement. Gerrit had agreed to stop spreading the rumor, but he never agreed to anything about telling the truth either.

"Hurry up, Kaleb. C'mon!" Gerrit called to his friend from the hallway before sweeping away from the door frame and leaving for practice. Kaleb nodded to himself, reminding him of practice. The guys had all been excited to have their captain back, and even coach Abernathy seemed pleased to have Kaleb around to corral the boys when he needed it. Something about the whole thing, though, just didn't sit right with Kaleb.

Practice was done differently than from before, and when he tried following through, Kaleb would be quickly corrected. The inside jokes were abundant between the boys, along with the war stories of their previous games and how hard they had worked for the win. Being banned from the team by order of coach Abernathy really put a damper on things, but it was the lack of contact from his friends that really set him apart from the rest of the boys.

He was exhausted by the end of the day, which didn't leave much room for Taylor's sessions. The blonde was obviously irritated with Kaleb, and not even his little surprises helped to lessen the blow of his sudden absence. Aside from this, his body wasn't ready for such rigorous training after being away for so long. His sore muscles rippled through his entire body, and he tired out much quicker than the rest of the team.

His back and shoulders had it worse than anything else, almost to the point of worrisome. At one point, Kaleb had gone to the nurse to have himself checked out, but she did little to nothing, and found even less. Now, Kaleb wanted to ask someone else. He straightened his jacket as he approached, slowly making his way to his teacher.

"Mr. G?" he asked. The alchemy teacher turned to face his student. "I have a question for you... Maybe a few," Kaleb told him.

252

"Taylor again?" the teacher asked, used to several meetings about the blonde by now, but Kaleb shook his head.

"No, it's something else."

Mr. G smiled, hopping up to sit on his desk. "Ask away," he said with a sweep of his hands.

"Well," Kaleb rubbed the back of his head. "It's my back," he started. "It's been aching ever since I started football again."

Mr. G shrugged. "Not out of the ordinary," he said. "After all, you did miss quite a bit."

"Right," Kaleb said. "That's what I thought too, at first... " Mr. G looked to Kaleb expectantly.

"But then...?"

Kaleb sucked in his lip. "It's right where my crest is," he admitted. "And it won't go away, no matter how much I ice it."

"Ah," Mr. G looked to the ceiling. "Now you're talking." He leaned forward, readjusting his seat atop his desk. "How is it hurting? Describe it for me."

Kaleb shuffled his feet, thinking of how to do so. "It's like I've pulled a muscle or something," Kaleb said. "Only, it's warm too, like a fever."

Mr. G furrowed his brow, looking to the floor in thought. Then he motioned for Kaleb to turn around, waiting for his student to rid his shoulders of his jacket before pulling back his collar to take a peek at Kaleb's crest.

"It does seem irritated," Mr. G mumbled.

"That's what the nurse said," Kaleb told him. "She couldn't help me, though."

Mr. G sighed. "Something is obviously bothering your soul. Has anything changed since it started?" he asked, gently patting the teen's shirt back into place.

Kaleb shrugged. "To be honest, I haven't really felt like I belonged since I got back," he admitted. "It's like I'm out of place, or something. You don't think that's all that it is, do you?"

Mr. G crossed his arms. "Could be," he told him. "If the feeling's strong enough. I think there's more to it, though."

Kaleb sighed. "I don't know," he mumbled.

"Well, I figured you would have had a better idea about it after your homework assignments," Mr. G told him.

Kaleb furrowed his brow. "You didn't give me any homework over this," he said, earning a look from his teacher.

"Yes I did," Mr. G said, looking Kaleb right in the eye.

"Over soul crests?" Kaleb asked. "I was in the hospital then." Mr. G nodded.

"Right, I sent your homework home with Gerrit."

Kaleb blinked. "Right," he mumbled. "Gerrit." He shook his jacket back over his shoulders and started for the door. "Thanks, G, I'll see you later."

Kaleb marched down the halls to the locker rooms in search of his friend. He had never received any homework while in the hospital from Gerrit, nor from any of his other friends. In fact, Gerrit had told him that he didn't have any homework from any of his classes. He had explained to Kaleb that the teachers agreed to let the students settle down from the excitement of the accident before handing out any more work, and stuck to verbal lectures and movie days while Kaleb was gone.

With his silver tongue, Gerrit would sell bread to a baker, but after years of friendship, Kaleb figured lying to be out of the question, and took his word for it, commenting on how ridiculous, but lucky, that was. The most disturbing part of all this was that Gerrit had gotten away with it without Kaleb or any of his teachers noticing. Kaleb's grades hadn't dropped either, concerning him further about how this was done under the radar.

Gerrit was already dressed and ready to go when Kaleb found him in the locker room. He was laughing and joking around with Jason and Daniel, whipping each other with their shirts.

"Hey, captain!" Daniel called, getting a face full of both Jason's and Gerrit's shirts.

"Hurry up, Kaleb," Gerrit laughed. "Coach is gonna wring your neck if he doesn't see you out on the field." Kaleb's face stayed serious.

"Can I talk to you?" he asked quietly.

"Can it wait?" Gerrit asked. "Practice is gonna start."

"What did you do with my homework?" Kaleb kept his eyes locked on his smaller friend, who became perplexed.

"It's your homework, man, I didn't do anything with-"

"When I was in the hospital," Kaleb interrupted. Gerrit scoffed, but Kaleb wouldn't let him speak. "Don't lie to me."

Gerrit huffed, looking away in irritation. "Can't you take a gift?" he muttered.

Kaleb furrowed his brow into an incredulous scowl. "What gift?" he accused. "Lying to me?"

"Getting your work done," Gerrit explained. "Besides, we couldn't risk losing you from the team for good. Same goes for everybody else here."

Kaleb dangerously lowered his voice. "What did you do, Gerrit?"

The smaller athlete grinned, sliding a finger over the bridge of his nose. "We've got a whole system set up," he whispered. "Nobody on the team has to worry about grades ever again- not with my nerds doing it for them."

Kaleb's eyes widened in disbelief. "You're paying people to do the work for you?"

Gerrit began frantically shaking his head, denying Kaleb. "Not paying; they're doing it of their own free will." Kaleb's face darkened with a sudden thought.

"As long as they don't want bruises, am I right?"

Gerrit shrugged. "How am I gonna pay for it when I don't have any money?" he asked. "This way, everyone wins."

Kaleb was near his boiling point. Rage bubbled deep within his gut, but he controlled himself while in the presence of the team. "You need to *stop this*," he hissed. Gerrit's face dropped, both confused and offended.

"Why?" he asked. "I've got a good thing going here, and it helps everybody!"

Kaleb gripped his fists at his sides. "This is wrong, Gerrit!" Kaleb whispered harshly. "Whether you'd like to believe it or not." Kaleb took a breath, trying to keep himself from screaming at his friend. "If you don't stop it, I'm turning you in myself," he warned.

"Kaleb-"

"Do it!" Kaleb shoved away from his friend, and marched over to his locker to change, completely livid with the situation at hand.

Chapter 16

Kaleb blew a great big yawn as he walked down the hallway. Being game day, he figured he'd be more excited, like he usually was, but today, he couldn't care less. He was exhausted, and the morning rush to the first class of the day didn't help to wake him up much either. Daniel came bolting through the hallway, being chased by Jason, and nearly ran into Kaleb, who stopped just in time to let them dodge past him. His sudden stop caused another person to bump into him from behind, but the two running boys had passed, and Kaleb was walking along again. He caught sight of Taylor, who was glaring at his direction and waved to him.

"Hey, Tay-"

The blonde brushed past him to gently kick a pair of glasses on the floor just as they were about to be crushed by an unsuspecting student. They slid to safety with a small click as they tapped the wall. Taylor bent over and retrieved the glasses, handing them to a girl on the floor.

"Here," he said. The girl looked at him with wide eyes, accepting the glasses with a small thank you, then watched him leave.

"Are you alright?" Kaleb asked, kneeling to help the girl pick up her books.

"I'm fine," she said quietly, not looking at him.

"Heavy, huh?" Kaleb nodded to the books with a smile, but the girl shook her head.

"You stopped, and then those boys knocked me down, so, I guess I just lost my balance." The girl gripped her books tightly to her chest. "Thank you," she mumbled, running away.

"Wait," Kaleb grabbed hold of the sleeve at her elbow. "I'm sorry about that," he told her, letting go of her sleeve. The girl nodded to him, assuring him that it was alright, then hurried away to her first class. Kaleb watched her go, still dumbstruck at her response. She had been knocked over because of he and his friends, and she didn't even bat an eye. It didn't bother her. It bothered Taylor, though. Kaleb rubbed the back of his head, worried of how Taylor would react around him later.

The blonde was already irritated with him for all of his missed tutoring lessons, but now with the idea of Kaleb being a jerk again, and proof of him doing it in front of him, Kaleb knew Taylor would have a few choice words for him later. Or even worse, no words at all. Kaleb sighed, lifting himself to his feet again and started towards class again.

Taylor had been quieter than usual lately, reverting back to his old ways from when he was living with his father. He was short with Kaleb, and usually snipped at him rather than spoke to him like he used to. He was obviously bothered with him, but Kaleb felt that there was something more to the blonde's new mood, and instead of talking it out, he clammed up, hiding his thoughts and emotions deep within himself.

What was worse; Kaleb had caught sight of a fresh bruise on Taylor's shoulder as he was getting dressed that morning. When Kaleb asked him where it came from, Taylor shrugged him off, leaving the house for school.

Kaleb didn't want to bother Mr. G with questions about Taylor *again*, feeling that he had overwhelmed the man with news of the blonde ever since he moved in, though the teacher never acted the way Kaleb felt. He tried to think of ways to speak with Taylor all morning long, bothered by how difficult it was turning out to be. With football now back in Kaleb's life, there was disturbingly little time left for anything else. By the time the two had class together, Kaleb was still a blank slate, but he wanted to speak with Taylor, if only for a moment; so he awkwardly walked up to the blonde reading at his desk.

"Taylor?" he asked, receiving a glare. "Don't give me that, man," Kaleb breathed. Taylor dropped his eyes to the open book in his hands.

"What do you want?" he muttered.

"Just wanted to talk," Kaleb said, rubbing the back of his head. Then, with a sudden thought, "That girl was alright," he blurted. "To be honest, if it wasn't for you, I wouldn't have even noticed she had tripped." Taylor turned a page, still reading through his book. Kaleb sighed, looking for something else to say.

"I know it's a long shot," Kaleb started. "But... Would you mind coming to the game tonight?" Taylor's eyes left his book, looking up at the jock from beneath his brow. "You don't have to," Kaleb told him. "I know it's not your thing-"

"I have work tonight," Taylor said, looking back to his book. "I wouldn't be able to see all of it."

Kaleb's gaze dropped. "Oh," he said. "Okay." Kaleb backed away from Taylor's desk, shoving his hands in his pockets. He trudged back to his seat behind Taylor and sat down to wait for class to begin, more disappointed than he realized.

Class went on as usual, nothing exciting, nothing new. The storm outside did manage to catch his attention, though Kaleb merely kept a wary eye on the windows every now and then. Kaleb barely registered the lessons, still mostly exhausted from his training, and still thinking of how easily Taylor had brushed him off. As the day finished, and the pre-game practice had finished, Kaleb tagged along with the guys to grab a bite at Tammy's before their battle. He smiled enough to fool himself and his friends into thinking he was alright, and by the time he had put in his order, he had tricked himself into having a good time.

"I have a question for you," Kaleb said abruptly.

"It's not math, is it?" Jason quipped, earning a few laughs.

"Nah," Kaleb smiled. "It's something serious... Kind of a game, really."

The boys each grinned in turn, turning their attention to their captain as he leaned up against the table in his seat. "If you could describe me in one word, what would it be?" he asked. The grins around the table broadened, snickering at him.

"That's easy," Daniel said. "Awesome." Jason shook his head, denying the other boy.

"That's not it, it's Captain." More disagreements.

"Legendary."

"Fast."

"Ladies man!"

"That's two words, dumbass."

"Guys, guys, I've got it." Gerrit waved his hands to calm the group. "King."

A roar of agreement resounded around the booth, paired with banging fists and hooting that was quickly hushed by an irritated Tammy dropping by with the next round of orders.

"Tammy, you look awful," Kaleb said, noticing her tired face.

"Now, Kaleb!" Tammy scolded. "You don't ever say that to a woman, you hear?" Kaleb gave an apologetic smile.

"Sorry, Tam," he said. "It's just, you look worn out, is what I'm trying to say."

Tammy held a finger to her temple, leaning against the booth. "It's been a long day," she sighed.

Kaleb pulled out an empty chair from a nearby table. "Have a seat, Tam," he offered.

"Yeah, Tammy," Daniel chipped in. "Take a break."

"We can handle ourselves," Jason said through a mouthful of burger. Tammy looked to each boy in turn, settling on Kaleb, who was still holding out her seat.

"You've earned it," he told her. Tammy sighed, flinging her hands to the air.

"Alright," she said. "But no more orders until I get back up." The boys agreed, smiling at her as she dug around in her apron. "Do you mind if I smoke?" she asked, receiving several shaken heads and lit up, leaning back in her chair as she took in a long drag from the butt. "That's better," she breathed, tapping Kaleb on the shoulder in gratitude.

"You boys ready for the game tonight?" Tammy asked, earning a series of shouting and table banging. "I'll take that as a yes," she grinned. Kaleb pushed his plate of fries to her, allowing her first choice before sharing his food with her as they spoke privately.

"You all better win it for me," she told them. "I don't think I'll be able to make it and be your good luck charm tonight."

Kaleb shrugged. "That's alright, Tammy," he told her. "But you'll be missing one amazing show."

Tammy shared his grin, apologizing for her absence. "Once you get old, you'll understand," she explained.

Kaleb tapped his plate with a fry. "Hey, Tammy?" he asked, turning the woman's head. "If you could describe me in one word, what would it be?"

The older waitress chuckled. "What brought this on?" she asked. Kaleb shrugged.

"Just something I thought I'd try," he reasoned.

Tammy ticked her head, shrugging as well. "I guess I'd have to go with popular," she answered. "Although, considerate is a good one too." She puffed on her cigarette, looking to the ceiling in thought. "Good-kid would be two words, wouldn't it?" She looked to the dark boy and grinned. "This is harder than it sounds, isn't it?"

She chuckled, bringing a smile from Kaleb. The group finished their meals and paid, waving Tammy goodbye as they ran and jumped and played merry, and by the time they had pulled into the freshly prepared field, the boys were completely pumped up, ready to win this game too.

The opposing team, the Birdview Hawks, was a worthy opponent indeed. By halftime, the Riviera Trouts were worn out from all of their blocking and defending. The Hawks were vicious, and played with great strategy, keeping the Riviera boys on their toes. Kaleb managed to throw a few good balls to Gerrit, who weaved his way to the end zone for the score, and even Max and Jason had helped to gain a few touchdowns for the team, but there was no denying their exhaustion.

Kaleb wiped the sweat off of his neck, wishing he could remove his helmet and do the same for his face. He trotted back to the team, glancing at the crowd cheering for them in the stands. The usual folk had shown up, parents of the teammates, hard core fans who supported the booster club, and the chearleaders and their families, all surrounding the other fans who had come to back the team up with their screaming. One person, though, stood silently watching, off at the end of the bleachers, away from everyone else. Kaleb peered through the sweat in his eyes, but he knew that stance, that quiet demeanor, and that hoodie.

Kaleb smiled at Taylor, raising a hand for a tentative wave. The blonde gave a single nod, pointing to the team to tell Kaleb to get his butt back in the game. Kaleb's grin grew, and he hurried back to the huddle, obeying Taylor's orders. He took another look at Taylor just as he joined his team, seeing the blonde wiggle his two fingers at him, telling him to walk along. This triggered a devious thought, making Kaleb wonder if he could actually pull it off.

"Guys," he said, gathering the attention of his teammates. "Follow my lead, alright?" He turned to Gerrit. "Eyes open."

Gerrit nodded, as confused as the rest of the team, but just as compliant. The players left for the field as Kaleb stayed behind to talk to the referee for a moment, thanking him for doing such a good job. The man smiled at Kaleb, patting him on the back as he wished him luck, then sent him to the line with the rest of his team. The boys had already lined up, readying themselves for another play when Kaleb stood up behind them.

"Reff wants us back five yards," he shouted after taking the ball. The two teams broke from the line to regroup, wondering how they had missed the call. Kaleb's eyes caught Gerrit's as he walked along the field, warning him before he threw the ball. Gerrit snatched the ball from the air, and ran straight to the end without a single opposing player in sight to chase him. As Gerrit passed over the last bit of powder, a buzzer blew out, alerting everyone of another touchdown. Kaleb threw his hands to his helmet.

"I can't believe that actually worked!"

The other team began rushing around the referee, complaining for an explanation and wanting an error, but Kaleb's trickery was completely legal, and the touchdown counted towards the Trout's score. The team whooped for joy, slapping Kaleb on the back and congratulating him on his cleverness before running back to the sidelines to huddle up. Kaleb grinned back at Taylor, shrugging his arms out wide as he walked back to the team. Taylor shook his head at the jock, smirking at him for actually walking the ball to the score.

"Hope it was impressive enough."

Taylor climbed aboard the bus to Carter, a grin still trying to escape from his lips. Kaleb had taken his words literally, and walked the ball to the other end of the field, scoring for his team. Taylor was just as surprised about it as everyone else- especially when the Trouts were allowed to keep the points- but what set Taylor off in a round of smothered snickering was the fact that Kaleb had listened to the blonde's off-hand comments about the game.

Taylor shook his head, still unbelieving of the jock. He watched the stadium fade from view as the bus drove away, wondering how late it would be before he made it back home. The sun had dropped from sight long ago, and it was already pitch black without the help of overhead lights. He had planned on being home much sooner than this, but the game had taken what was left of the blonde's evening. Taylor had wanted to stay angry with him, but seeing the disappointment in Kaleb's eyes when Taylor told him that he wouldn't be coming to the jock's game stayed with him throughout the day, even during work. Once he had reprogrammed his client's computer, Taylor waited at the bus for River Hill, but sat through his stop and got off at the game instead.

Now, Taylor was on his way home, fighting off little chuckles that snuck their way to his throat as he thought back to the last half of the game. He switched busses in Carter, then hopped off at the stop in front of Tammy's Diner. He tightened his scarf as a chill made its way down his spine, then started forward towards the Evans home. It was difficult to navigate in the dark after he left town square, but once he made it to the neighborhoods with their lit porches, it was easier to see what was in front of him. As he unlocked the front door and made his way inside, he could already tell, something was out of place.

Vance and Kaleb were no where to be seen, but Trish sat quietly at the dining room table biting her nail, her worried gaze staring off into nothing as she tapped her tea mug with her finger.

"Miss Trish?" Taylor startled her from her thoughts, bringing her back to reality.

"Oh, Taylor." She smiled a tired smile as she got up to greet him. "How was your day?" Taylor loosened his scarf to hang it up, never taking his eyes off of Trish.

"Fine," he said. "What's wrong?"

Trish shook her head. "Oh, it's not..." She stopped herself and sighed. "No, it is," she told him. "Kaleb's upset and there's nothing I can do about it." Taylor gave her a queer look.

"He won the game, didn't he?" he asked, confused.

"He did? Oh-" Trish stopped herself again. "Don't mention it to him, alright?"

Taylor nodded, though still confused. Trish patted him on the shoulder before heading to the kitchen. "We saved your dinner for you," she told him. "Kaleb hasn't eaten either." She paused for a moment, then looked at him. "Think you can try?"

Taylor shrugged, entering the kitchen to retrieve the reheated meals. Trish gave him another tired smile as he left, bothering Taylor greatly. Seeing her like this was definitely not a good thing. Whatever was bothering Kaleb was bothering her too; and an unhappy Trish was equivalent to a widespread depression.

"Hey, asshole," Taylor muttered as he lightly kicked open the door, his hands preoccupied with their dinner plates. "Your mom told me to get you to eat."

Kaleb was lying on his back in his bed, face buried beneath a pillow, unmoving until Taylor entered. His body tensed at the blonde's words, pushing the pillow deeper over his face.

"Did you hear me?" Taylor said. "C'mon, get up." He plopped down at the desk, setting Kaleb's plate on the edge closer to the bed. Kaleb stayed put, not daring to take the pillow away from his eyes.

"I'm not hungry," he muttered.

"Tough," Taylor told him. "You're scaring your mom," he went on. "I can't bring back a full plate, and there's no way I can eat them both. So eat up." Kaleb swallowed.

"I'm scaring her?" he asked. Taylor nodded, unseen by Kaleb.

"C'mon, man," Taylor said, digging into a roll. He sighed when Kaleb remained in bed, eyes still covered with the pillow. "What's going on with you, anyway?" Taylor asked. "Shouldn't you be celebrating?"He stopped there, remembering what Trish had asked of him. Kaleb's mouth flickered.

"She didn't tell you?" he asked.

Taylor swallowed his bite, looking curiously at Kaleb. "Tell me what?"

Kaleb stayed still, thinking of how he would reply before removing the pillow and sitting up. Taylor's breath stopped in his throat when he saw the red eyes and tear stains. For once, Kaleb refused to look Taylor in the eyes when he spoke, rather looking to the floor instead.

"You were right," Kaleb whispered. Taylor looked to Kaleb, confused and shocked at the same time.

"Right?" he asked quietly. Kaleb kept his gaze to the floor.

"About us," he said. "About everything. They were nothing but a bunch of cowards." He dropped his head to rub the back of it. "And I was one of them."

Taylor blinked, still confused by the jock's words. "What do you mean?" he asked softly. Kaleb kept his head down, his hands still on the back of his head until he slid them down the side of his neck to look up at Taylor.

"I quit," he said, barely audible. "I quit the team."

Taylor's eyes widened, completely shocked. "Y- You- *what*?" He stammered over himself.

"I quit," Kaleb repeated, slowly dropping his eyes to the floor again. "I had to… I couldn't stay there anymore." Taylor leaned closer in his seat.

"Why?" was all he was able to manage.

Kaleb returned his gaze to Taylor's, looking him in the eye before speaking. "I could never stand behind anyone who values the score over morals," he said. Taylor was taken aback by this, looking to Kaleb for more answers.

"You're gonna have to elaborate on that for me."

The Trouts were overjoyed with their latest victory, and though they were worn out from the game, they cheered themselves on during the bus ride home, all the way to the locker rooms to shower and change. Kaleb reveled in the water pouring down onto him, enjoying his first shower after his first game since coming back.

"Where'd you come up with that move, cap'n?" Jason piped.

"Yeah!" Max chipped in. "I mean, *walking* the ball? Who would've come up with that besides you?"

The boys shared a laugh, waiting for Kaleb to speak. "Believe it or not, it was Taylor's idea," he answered.

"Who?" Dylan asked.

"Tommy," Kaleb told him.

"*Tommy*?" The boys all gathered in denial, claiming their captain of false truths, but Kaleb held steady.

"We were talking about it one day, and he just said to walk it."

"Why were you talking to Tommy?" Daniel asked, disgusted.

"He's not that bad, guys," Kaleb defended.

"Yeah, and I'm passing math with my *own* brain," Daniel snickered, patting Gerrit's shoulder with a nod. Kaleb glared at his friend, who merely shrugged, then viciously scrubbed his head with soap. Kaleb finished with his shower and toweled off to dress. Gerrit came up beside him, rubbing his head dry with a towel just as harshly as when he had cleaned it.

"I thought I told you to stop it," Kaleb mumbled, looping his belt.

Gerrit shrugged, pulling his shirt over his head. "He couldn't have played if I did," he excused, pulling on his jeans as well. "What's the harm in helping out the team? I thought you wanted to help people."

Kaleb shook his head, glaring at his friend. "I warned you, Gerrit. If you don't stop, I'm turning you in right now."

Gerrit slammed his locker door shut. "Then *do it*!" he challenged. His outburst caught the attention of the rest of the team, leaving Kaleb and Gerrit the center of attention in the middle of a fight.

"Don't make me do this," Kaleb warned quietly.

"You don't *have* to do anything!" Gerrit told him, widening his arms. "If you were my real friend, you wouldn't even joke. Shit, you'd have helped!"

Kaleb stared angrily at his friend, silently stewing at the excuses Gerrit had thrown at him. He shook his head. "You knew it was wrong from the start, that's why you didn't tell me," Kaleb growled. "Last chance, Gerrit, give it up!"

Gerrit furiously stepped up to his friend, never taking his eyes off him. "Fuck you," he said, challenging Kaleb to take action. Kaleb stared right back at the smaller boy and dropped his jacket on the bench, then started to move past Gerrit towards coach Abernathy's office. Gerrit, however, grabbed a fistfull of Kaleb's shirt and shoved him over the bench and onto the floor, wrestling with the great jock for dominance.

The other boys screamed and shouted out of fear, disbelief, and awe as the the team captain and his best friend fought each other on the locker room floor, banging against the lockers and sliding under benches as they struggled with each other. It was a matter of seconds before coach Abernathy had come running in and pulled the two apart, screaming at them for answers.

"Do it!" Kaleb shouted, wiping at his sore chin.

"Do what?" Abernathy demanded. Gerrit and Kaleb never took their eyes off one another, and after a few moments of silent glaring, Gerrit spit at Kaleb's feet, giving him his answer. Kaleb breathed out a disappointed breath, eyes still locked with Gerrit's.

"Coach," Kaleb started. "There's something you need to know."

Abernathy held open his hands. "Well go on, Nancy!" he said. "Office is that way." Then he looked to Gerrit. "You too, Sally!"

Gerrit stayed put, watching Kaleb before moving, then angrily made his way to Abernathy's office. Kaleb snagged his jacket from the floor, then followed after, slipping his arms into the sleeves as he walked. Once the door was closed and the three had settled, coach laced his fingers over his desk and demanded an explanation. Kaleb glanced at Gerrit, who wouldn't even look at him, then turned back to his coach.

"Gerrit's got a scam going on," Kaleb explained. "He bullies other people into doing the team's homework so that they can play on the field." He paused for a moment. "I can think of a few people he might have done this for, but it's not definite evidence."

Abernathy sat quietly at his desk, comprehending what Kaleb had just told him. After a few minutes, he turned to Gerrit, looking him up and down. Gerrit kept away from eye contact, angrily pouting in his seat.

"You came up with this?" Abernathy asked, receiving nothing from Gerrit. "That's brilliant." Both boys looked at their coach.

"What?" asked Kaleb. Gerrit's scowl melted away.

"It's perfect." He pointed to Gerrit. "Good work, Ford. Surprised *you* came up with it, but still. Good work." Kaleb stood from his seat.

"Shouldn't you report him?" he asked. "He could get kicked out for this!"

"Which is exactly why I'm not going to," Abernathy said firmly. "We barely got by with you gone, Evans, what in soul's name would we do with half the team missing?" Coach shook his head. "We can't, and we won't. Not with championships so close."

Kaleb slammed his fists down on the desk, forcing himself to his feet. "That's ridiculous!" he screamed.

"Sit down, Evans!" Abernathy scorned.

"Seriously, dude," Gerrit piped in. "Everyone else is on board with this, why aren't you?"

Kaleb whipped his gaze between the two men. "So, you're telling me that the whole team is in on this?" he said, disbelieving.

"What's the problem, Evans?" Abernathy snipped. "I said it was alright, that should settle things enough for you."

"Yeah," Gerrit agreed. "Listen to coach."

Kaleb glared at the two. "You are beating people senseless in order to play a stupid game," he said, slowly raising his voice from a dangerous growl, to a sudden scream. "IS THAT PROBLEM ENOUGH FOR YOU?!" Coach Abernathy jumped from his seat.

"SIT YOUR ASS DOWN, EVANS!" he screamed back. "If you don't like it, you can leave!" He jammed his finger towards the door behind Kaleb as he said this, keeping his enraged eyes locked onto Kaleb's. "Just know, you'll be running laps 'till you're fifty tomorrow morning!" Kaleb stared back at his teacher, just as angry as him.

"No," Kaleb said quietly. "No need for that." Kaleb slipped his team jacket off his shoulders and plopped it down onto Coach's desk. Abernathy's anger turned to shock as he held steady in his stare down with Kaleb, then back to anger as the teen turned around and left the room.

"Evans!" Abernathy shouted after him. "Don't be stupid, Evans!"

Kaleb ignored him, grabbing his things from his locker and locking it once he had finished.

"You're throwing everything away!" Abernathy shouted, standing in the doorway of his office. The rest of the boys stepped aside as Kaleb marched out of the locker room, mostly silenced by the scene playing before them save for the whispering of their concerns at their captain's sudden exit.

"KALEB!"

The door swung shut on the screaming teacher's words as Kaleb left the locker room and made his way towards the exit. The bitter wind nipped and blew at him as he pushed through the double doors, but he trekked on, ignoring the cold as he walked on without his jacket. He thought about how important that jacket had been to him, to the school, the town- everybody. More than just a simple leather jacket, it was a symbol of success in such a proud town that valued the game more than anything.

Kaleb was giving up on all their hopes and dreams of him ever becoming a Hall of Famer. There would be no trophy or plaque with his name engraved on it, no sixth captain patch for his jacket, no new designed patch for his achievements. He wouldn't be the town legend anymore; not for six years of being captain, at least. He would be known for quitting right at the finish line. This was the end of his five year reign over the field, and the rest of the town would simply have to accept it.

All the years he had spent devoting himself to the game, all the times he spent sitting with the coaches as they designed new plays, every second he sweat training harder than anyone until he dropped, every day he ran through bringing everyone together for the game, and making it worth every moment; every record, every play, every *friend*- all of it. All of it was wasted, thrown away within the last ten minutes.

Any chance of receiving a scholarship was down the drain as well. While his academics were on par with the best, only scouts for teams came looking for gifted students, on the prowl for the best of the best. Kaleb had every chance of being scouted for any college of his choosing, easily proving to be the best and most loyal player on the field, but after tonight, his loyalties would need to lie elsewhere. There was no chance of him returning to the team again, not after what he had seen.

He was disgusted by the people he had once looked up to, had once befriended, and finally, he could see what Taylor had seen all along, and it sickened him. Oh, wouldn't he get a kick out of this when he found out. Kaleb could hear the snark in his voice now, telling him how he had been right all along, and how foolish Kaleb had been for siding with the dumb jocks in the first place.

Kaleb bit his lip, already growing irritated with the blonde, but already agreeing with him. Whatever Taylor threw at him, Kaleb felt he deserved it wholeheartedly. Taylor had been right all along, and Kaleb had been foolish enough to think that he could change Taylor's opinion about them with a few silly games. Oh, what a fool he had been.

Another harsh wind gripped at Kaleb's bare arms as he walked up to his front porch and fit his key into the lock. Once he had swung the door open, he stopped, catching sight of his parents sitting together on the couch. They were pleasantly watching a nature show, cuddled atop each other like a pair of lovesick teenagers before Trish turned to see him standing in the doorway.

"Hi, honey," she said, getting up to greet him. "Where's your jacket?"

Kaleb froze. He was instantly reminded of his parent's achievements, and how proud they were of him when he had made his way down the path of success, and his failure crashed down over him in one fell swoop.

"Kaleb!"

Trish rushed over to her son, reaching towards him to wipe away his tears but Kaleb retracted from her touch. Vance followed close behind his wife, looking to his son for any way of helping him. Trish raised her hand to her son again, trying to comfort him and find the source of his tears at the same time, this time making contact with his cheek, forcing his eyes from off the floor, and onto Trish.

"Please don't be angry," he whispered, looking to his mother with pained eyes. Trish looked back at him with overwhelming concern, and wrapped her arms around her son, holding him close as he sobbed into her shoulder and hid his face away from his father, who laid a hand over his back.

"Please don't be angry."

Taylor lie awake in his bed for most of the night, thinking of what Kaleb had told him. About Gerrit's homework scam, how it worked and how neither the team, nor the coach had cared, and most of all, how Kaleb had quit the team because of it.

"I could never stand behind anyone who values the score over morals."

Kaleb's voice rang in Taylor's ears all night long. He rolled over to his side, staring at the wall as he thought. Kaleb had been so miserable when Taylor had seen him. It was so different from his usual, cheerful self. It bothered Taylor to no end, seeing him so broken down because of his friends; the people he had trusted. Kaleb's disappointment with them radiated off of him, spreading to Taylor, who had despised them all along.

Taylor remembered the look of defeat in Kaleb's eyes as he apologized for his friends, telling the blonde that he realized how Taylor had been right to be hateful of them all along, and it sent his stomach tumbling over itself. He had never meant for Kaleb to be so brought down like this, and he had never even thought it possible until today. The hurt Kaleb had shown burned through Taylor like a lit match, and he couldn't get the vision out of his head no matter how hard he tried.

Taylor ran a hand through his hair. He had never seen Kaleb so disappointed in all the time he had known him. What was worse, though, was that he was disappointed in *himself.* He had apologized to Taylor countless times, telling him that he had never intended to turn out to be like the jerk that Taylor tended to stay away from. He told him how sorry he was for trying to make Taylor like his friends, and how he had never thought that they would stoop so low.

No matter how he looked at it, Taylor couldn't find any faults in Kaleb. As much as he hated the team and its players, Kaleb was a genuinely good guy. He didn't stand on the same level as his friends, not in a million lifetimes. How Kaleb even considered himself to be one of them was inconceivable to Taylor. Rather than joining in with the rest of his friends, and accepting the coach's decision to continue threatening people without question, he left.

He left.

Kaleb left behind more than just football. Considering how important it was in such a small town, Kaleb gave up a lifetime. He wouldn't be known as Kaleb the captain anymore, nor ever again. His future was now a blank slate, no longer drawn out as the king of this town. Kaleb had thrown away his title, his legend, his *friends*- all in the name of doing what was right.

Taylor couldn't give up that much even if he was paid for a lifetime. He rolled over to his back, staring at the ceiling and wondering how Kaleb was feeling now. He was sound asleep below Taylor, lost in whatever dreams that captured him for the moment, but when he awakened, how would he react to the whole situation? Would he sleep on it and change his mind? Would he go crawling back, begging to be let back on the team- back with his friends?

Taylor shook his head, denying that answer. Kaleb would never do such a thing. He had made his decision, and he would stand by it, no matter what. His loyalty was strong, but his morals were even stronger.

"I could never stand behind anyone who values the score over morals."

Taylor rolled onto his side, closing his eyes to try and sleep. When this didn't work, he rolled back onto his back and tried again. He was still restless, and opened his eyes to huff at the ceiling. He leaned over the railing to peek at Kaleb, sleeping soundly in his bed. Seeing Kaleb perfectly fine satisfied the blonde into believing that he was alright, then rolled away from the railing onto his back. Taylor took a deep breath, and let it out slowly, closing his eyes to relax.

Taylor opened his eyes to find Kaleb rising up to meet his lips. Golden skin soon covered porcelain as Kaleb draped himself over Taylor's body, and the blonde's skin rippled with excitement as the older man's hands touched him in a rabid, hungry nature. The darker man ground his hips against Taylor's, sinking lower into the silky sheets as their kiss deepened.

Their tangled bodies electrified one another, sending magnificent shocks of pleasure throughout their entire being. Fire swept through Taylor's veins as they clung to each other, desperate for the next wave that followed each touch. Kaleb pulled away from the intoxicating kiss to Taylor's jawline, lining his lover's neck with the warm mark of his lips. The blonde slid his fingers through Kaleb's dark hair, bringing his lips back to Taylor's mouth, instantly inviting him inside as the sensation of his touch quivered his soul.

"Taylor…" Kaleb breathed, sucking at the blonde's ear and temple. *"Taylor…"*

Chapter 17

"Taylor!"

The blonde's eyes popped open to find Kaleb staring back at him, sending Taylor flying back and slamming into the wall behind him.

"Jeez!" Kaleb blurted, jumping back as well. Taylor instantly curled over himself, hiding his face in his sheets, and other things that needed hiding as well.

"Are you okay?" Kaleb asked, watching the blonde rub the goose egg from the back of his head.

"I'm fine!" Taylor called beneath his arms.

"You sure?" Kaleb did *not* look convinced.

"Yes, I'm fine!"

"You were moaning in your sleep."

"I'm sure!"

"'Cause I can-"

"*Go away!*"

Kaleb recoiled from the sudden outburst, but left his friend alone as he wished. "Breakfast will be ready soon," he informed as he retreated through the door. Taylor felt a slight ping of guilt for his harshness towards his roommate, but he was more concerned with his current condition than anything else. He glared between his legs, still hunched over in his bed, willing the problem to leave.

"Go away…" he pleaded, though nothing would be done about it unless he got up and took care of it himself. Taylor huffed, irritated with his body and confused as to *why* he would even *have* such a realistic dream with another *man*- more specifically, *Kaleb*- or even why he would have this problem in the first place. Taylor peeked through his arms in search of any wandering eyes that may fall inside the room, then carefully made his way down the bunk. He checked the hallway just as carefully before bounding into the hallway bathroom and locking the door behind him. Taylor sighed, pressing his back against the door before doing anything. He had never been comfortable doing anything like this in his own house- let alone someone else's- but it needed to be done.

Taylor grabbed a hand towel from the cabinet and bit down hard onto it while he worked his way out in the bathtub, trying to think of things that excited him to make it go quicker. He thought of Laura Kline, the gorgeous red-headed supermodel that posed for *Think-Tech*'s magazine and her radiant green eyes. The smooth, copper skin and exquisite indentations in his muscles, he thought of his lips and how good they had felt on his skin, and how his large, warm hands knew exactly where to-

"Hun-Nuh!" Taylor denied in the towel, viciously shaking his head. "HUN-NUH!"

He squeezed his eyes shut, mumbling to himself between the towel.

"Boobs, boobs, legs, boobs, babes-"

Taylor repeated this over and over to himself until the job was done, then cleaned up any remaining evidence that he had ever even been there in the first place. He shivered away the last remaining feelings the dream had left with him, then splashed some cold water on his flushed face, hoping to restore himself to normal. He took a good long look at himself in the mirror, slowing his breathing and telling himself to relax. After a while, Taylor was satisfied with his level head, and left the bathroom for breakfast.

"Hey, Taylor." Kaleb waved, sending Taylor's stomach over itself. "Feeling better?"

Taylor whipped around and marched back to the room. "Forgot to change!" he called, still too embarrassed to even look at the other boy just yet. As he dressed, he mentally prepared himself for another attack from Kaleb, telling himself to relax and never think of it again because he would *never* tell Kaleb about his adventures in his mind- or anybody else for that matter. Taylor huffed, slapping his cheeks before leaving the room for another go at the breakfast table.

Kaleb didn't greet him this time, but stared at him, concerned and confused at the same time. Taylor offered a curt nod in greeting before sitting down at the table.

"Are you alright, dear?" Trish asked. "You look like you've seen a beast."

He growled in the other man's mouth as his beastly muscles pressed up against his-

Taylor coughed, reaching for his drink to clear his throat. "I'm fine," he croaked, avoiding eye contact. The blonde stared directly onto his plate as Kaleb sat down next to him, looking at the blonde curiously. "Looks great," Taylor said to Trish, digging into his meal. The family enjoyed their breakfast peacefully, already planning their weekend together. By the end of their meal, Taylor had mostly gotten used to Kaleb's presence when Trish had a sudden thought.

"We're going coat shopping," she stated. All three men looked to her when she said this.

"What?" Kaleb said. Trish gave a curt nod.

"Yep, coat shopping," she repeated. "It's about time you got a new one anyway."

Taylor grinned at his plate. "Have fun," he muttered, thankful to be given some space between he and Kaleb for the afternoon.

"Oh, no," Trish stopped him. "You didn't think that you could get out of this, did you?" Taylor looked to Trish, trying to find an excuse to evacuate.

"I don't need…"

Trish gave him a death glare that could easily scare away an angry hippo. "If I recall correctly," Trish started. "I don't think I've ever seen your coat." She crossed her arms. "Now, I know work has been busy, and you're always home when we get back," she cocked a brow. "But I've never seen you wear a coat." She tapped a finger to her jawline. "So where is it?"

Taylor tried to sink away into his chair, wishing he could melt away from her intense gaze. Even the other two men were silenced by her, and it was more evident now than ever who really ran the house.

"Taylor?"

He flinched, suddenly realizing what Bekah meant about feeling in trouble at the use of her name. "I outgrew it," Taylor said, taking a sip from his glass as he averted from her stare.

"When?"

"What?"

"When."

Taylor ran a hand through his hair, still unable to look Trish in the eye. "... Last year..." he mumbled, barely audible to even himself.

"Mm-Hmm," Trish noted, sighing exasperatedly. "We need to go shopping because my two *idiot boys* don't know how to keep warm." She stood up from the table, tapping Vance's shoulder for a kiss goodbye as she did.

"Come along," she said lightly, though the threat was there. The three men shared a look with each other, sighing at the woman they all loved- and feared- so dearly.

Taylor had to sit uncomfortably close to Kaleb as they drove to Carter, sitting in the middle of the cabin again because of his size. He kept his eyes forward, watching the road as they drove, but he couldn't stop his flinching every time Kaleb moved. Once they were parked, Taylor stretched his arms high over his head to rid himself of the tension that had built up in his shoulders, and to keep from looking at Kaleb who was watching him oddly.

As they entered the store, Taylor bypassed the main entrance entirely, and began browsing the clearance section; though Trish was quick to grab him and drag him to the more 'fashionable' coats.

"Don't do that." She slapped Taylor's hand away from the price tag. "You're one of my boys now, you don't worry about silly little things like that." He and Kaleb caught a glance between each other, knowing there would be no stopping this woman.

"Here, try this one." She held up a red, wool mass and slipped it over Taylor's shoulders, instantly disagreeing with the style judging by the look on her face, and replaced it on the hanger.

"Ooh!" Trish's eyes lit up. "Kaleb, what about this one?"

Taylor was used to shopping with Trish from all of the grocery runs they had done together, but this time was different. Instead of shopping for essentials for the house, now they were shopping for something far more enticing: clothes. Taylor ran a hand through his hair, catching Kaleb rubbing the back of his head from the next aisle over. They loved Trish, they really did, but this was a woman thing, and it didn't excite them nearly as much as it excited her.

Trish carefully inspected each coat on several other racks, holding up many different choices for the boys to choose from, and decided on which ones to hold on to by the expression on her face when she saw them. When asked how they felt about it, the boys offered simple answers to appease the woman, but she could see right through their facade and replaced the coat on the rack in search of a new one. After about half an hour of searching, Kaleb ended up with a smooth, black leather jacket that fit nicely over his broad shoulders, and Taylor... Well, Trish was still looking for Taylor's. She tapped her chin, searching for the 'right one' while the boys sat on a nearby bench to wait for her.

"Sorry about this," Kaleb muttered. "You know how she is."

Taylor shrugged. "When you think about it, it's not a bad thing," he mumbled back, watching Trish instead of Kaleb. "Just means she cares."

Kaleb thought this over, agreeing with him almost instantly. He paused a moment before speaking again, knowing he was walking into dangerous territory.

"Are you okay?" he asked, making Taylor tense. "You've been acting kind of weird all morning." He rubbed the back of his head. "And then, you were sleeping weird, too..."

Taylor looked to his fingers, fiddling with a rubber band he had found from the floor. "I'm fine," he said quietly. "It was just a dream." Kaleb nodded, accepting the answer and letting the interrogation end. Away from the boys, Trish thought for a moment, then slowly turned to a displayed mannequin, the wheels in her head turning at the sight of it.

"Taylor," she called, still looking at the mannequin. "Come here, dear." Taylor dutifully obeyed and stood expectantly beside Trish, waiting for her to shove another jacket onto him. She slid a muted black coat over his shoulders, keeping a close eye on how it looked and fit. Taylor inspected this one as well, noticing how warm it was, and how soft it felt. The cut was simple, but hard edged, later to be described as a pea-coat, but for now, it was just nice to wear. Trish buttoned up the front of the coat, wrapping the two front pieces over one another, revealing to Taylor that the collar could be adjusted so that it covered his chin and nose if he wanted. With his silver scarf around his neck, the look completed Taylor, making Trish smile victoriously.

"Perfect," she muttered, looking to Taylor. "How does it feel?" Taylor shrugged, offering a polite smile.

"It's nice," he told her. "I like it." This time it was true. Trish's smile widened, completing her victory in finding the 'perfect coat.' She hung the coat back on the hanger and handed it to Taylor, smiling the whole time. Kaleb regrouped with the two, ready to leave with them, and headed towards the check out counter with Taylor.

"Where are you two going?" Trish called, making the boys turn around to face her. She cocked a brow to Taylor, fists at her hips. "If I had known that was your style, I'd have bought you more clothes a long time ago."

Oh, no.

"A few ragged t-shirts and some jeans won't hold you over forever."

Oh, *no.*

She turned around, heading for the men's clothing section.

"Come along."

Kaleb and Taylor shared a pained look, then hiked their coats over their shoulders and followed the shopping crazed woman; off to buy Taylor some new duds.

Both Taylor and Kaleb wore their new coats out of the store, and once the cold air hit them, Taylor was grateful for the new addition to his closet. The others, however... Trish had gone wild in there. She grabbed several different t-shirts and pants and vests and flung them all at Taylor, having him try them on one by one for her to look at. Kaleb sat through Taylor's dress up experience, offering a few words of encouragement when his mother prompted an answer out of him, but otherwise left Trish to play doll on her own while quietly figuring out how they were going to fit all of Taylor's new clothes in Kaleb's tiny closet; a task that was going to require some expert maneuvering indeed.

When they arrived home a little more than three and a half hours later, Vance was only slightly surprised when they returned with bags in each hand, offering a sympathetic smile to the two as they walked through. The boys hurried off to their room, telling Trish they would organize the new things in favor of helping with lunch, but plopped down exhausted on the bed once the door had closed shut.

Taylor kept his face buried in the covers at the foot of Kaleb's bed, not wanting to move for the next century. How women could shop like that and still have energy to do more amazed him. Bubbie scratched at the door, wanting to be let in, but the blonde simply didn't have the energy to move. Kaleb sighed and got up to let the dog hop on his bed with them. Having experience over years of shopping with his mother left Kaleb with slightly more energy.

Bubbie snuggled close to Taylor's side, happy to see his friend had come back, and nuzzling him to see if he was alright. Taylor groaned, keeping his head in the covers as he stretched a tired hand to pet his furry friend, calming the dog enough to realize his human wasn't hurt.

"He really loves you," Kaleb chuckled, falling back to his bed. Taylor grunted a reply, trying to fight off sleep and failing. "Go ahead," Kaleb offered to Taylor, reading his mind. "She wears me out too."

Taylor grunted in reply, but didn't stir. He was too far gone, barely able to register anyone else's presence, and his long night overcame him. Taylor fell asleep right there, stretched out at the foot of Kaleb's bunk, face still buried in the covers and his arm still draped over his dog. Kaleb gave a little chuckle, amused by the blonde's exhaustion, and he stretched out over his pillows as well. He lay there for a few more minutes, catching his breath before setting to work on the closet like he had promised his mother.

He managed to clear out more space in his small closet after deciding that he didn't need to hang on to his older clothes, and bagged up the shirts he had never worn that year, or the two years previous. The ones he found with rips or tears, he threw away, not wanting to donate ruined clothing.

The more he threw out, the more he realized how badly Taylor needed this. As overbearing as his mother could be sometimes, he couldn't help but agree with her on Taylor's wardrobe this time. All of his things fit nicely in a tiny drawer at the bottom of Kaleb's cramped closet, and most of them were considerably worn out. This prompted Kaleb to throw out more, leaving him with only what he was sure to wear and making more room for Taylor. Kaleb still had at least half a closet full of clothes when he was done, but it was half a closet more for his friend, satisfying Kaleb for now.

He had left the tags on Taylor's clothes in case anything needed to be done with them, but the leftover shopping bags were being put to good use holding Kaleb's old clothes. He began cleaning up, gathering the bags he would later donate and setting them aside in a neat pile. As he got up from the floor, he stopped, hearing a familiar, unnerving sound. Kaleb turned to the source of the noise, finding Taylor whimpering in his sleep. Kaleb paused, wondering if he should wake his friend, only to remember how badly the reaction he received was last time.

Kaleb rubbed the back of his head, wishing he could help. As eerily silent of a sleeper as Taylor was, it was even more disturbing to hear him like this. Whatever nightmare plagued Taylor leaked through his lips, making Kaleb wish he could do something about it, and hoping beyond hope that it wasn't memories replaying Taylor's awful father. He sighed, knowing that the moody teen would only become angry with him if he intervened, and set forth to bringing the donation bags to the front of the house, leaving Taylor on his own to fight off the dreams.

"*Seven* times?!" Bekah was astounded by this, and her astonishment sent Taylor hissing like a snake trying to shush her.

"Keep it down!" he whispered harshly.

"Sorry," she said, still amazed. "*Seven*?"

Taylor ran both of his hands through his hair, cradling his head in the crook of his elbows as they reached the back of his head. "I can't go to sleep again," he muttered, almost scared. "Kaleb has been on me about the 'nightmares' all weekend- he hears it! Oh, fuck!" Taylor buried his head deeper into his arms, wishing he could melt right through them and dissolve into the earth.

"Well," Bekah grinned wickedly. "It's better having him pound you like this than like before." She snickered, physically jumping away from her computer when Taylor whipped his head up to snarl at her.

"Rebekah, I swear on my soul-"

"I'm sorry, I'm sorry!" she snickered, holding her hands up as she settled back into her seat, muttering "seven" under her breath. Taylor ran his hands through his hair again, ending up back inside his arms.

"I can't even look at him anymore," he admitted. "It's too embarrassing."

Bekah pushed her glasses further up her nose before resting her hands in front of her. "So he doesn't know?" she asked seriously.

Taylor shook his head. "Of course not. I'd die before then."

Bekah shrugged. "Well, he *is* an attractive guy," she offered, after having seen a glimpse of him a few times before. "You don't have too much to worry about."

"You don't understand," Taylor said, bringing his head up to hold his forehead against his fingers while he looked to her. "Something like this has never happened before."

Bekah shrugged again. "So? There's a first time for everything."

Taylor looked straight at her. "I mean nothing like this has ever happened before *period*." This caught Bekah's attention. "No one in River Hill has ever thought about this kind of stuff, and everyone's match is someone of the opposite gender," he explained. "There's no record of this ever happening here. There's no record of it happening in *history*." He shook his head against his fingers. "There's something *wrong* with me."

This lit a fire in Bekah's eyes, and she slammed a fist down onto her desk, sending her to her feet and her chair flying.

"There is *NOTHING* wrong with you!" she shouted, scaring Taylor away from his screen. "Just because you're different- just because you've found something new, that doesn't mean you're defective!" She gripped the desk, turning her knuckles white. "Don't you *ever* tell me that there's something wrong with you because you're scared of what you've found!"

282

Taylor stared at his friend, eyes wide at her sudden rage, and silenced by her words. Bekah stared right back at him, keeping the fire in her eyes until she could sit down again, and the flames were smothered with angry tears threatening to leave her.

"You're not the only one," she huffed, rubbing away the sensation of threatening gravity. "There are others." Taylor blinked, finally able to find his words.

"What?"

Bekah reached her slender fingers over her keyboard, pulling up a link to inspect it. "I've heard about people like you," she replied, turning to look at him. "You're not alone." Taylor looked away, leaning back in his chair. "Even if there weren't people out there," she went on. "You still wouldn't be alone."

Taylor caught eyes with his friend, then offered a grateful smile to her, small as it may be. "Beck," he started carefully. "You know they're just dreams, right? I mean, it's not like we're in love or anything, and we sure as shit aren't soul mates."

She shrugged, holding her shoulders high as she leaned away. "A girl can dream, can't she?" she said slyly, "I mean, you do." She snickered, earning a lovely roll of the eyes from Taylor.

Kaleb rushed towards Mr. G's classroom, once again in search of answers. All weekend long, something had been bothering him, and he couldn't quite put his finger on what it was exactly. He could easily ask his parents any questions about soul crests, but he felt a bit more privacy through his teacher instead. Aside from this, Mr. G specialized in biological alchemy; specifically crests and their nature, so the teen felt he would find better clarity from him.

He hadn't even waited for school to start, heading straight for his teacher while everyone else was eating their breakfast in the cafeteria. Kaleb was on a mission. His soul was unsettled, and this time he couldn't blame it on the team. When he arrived, he knocked on the door before entering, pleasantly surprising his teacher of his presence.

"Kaleb," Mr. G smiled, scrutinizing his new threads. "Where's your jacket?"

Kaleb looked down at the new leather that replaced the old, remembering his eventful weekend. "Oh," he muttered, shaking his head. "Doesn't matter." He looked to his teacher. "Got a minute?"

Mr. G closed his grade book then laced his fingers over it. "More than one," he joked. Kaleb grinned, reaching up to rub the back of his head. "How's your back?" Mr. G offered.

"Huh? Oh." Kaleb shrugged. "Oddly enough, it got better over the weekend…" Mr. G leaned in from his seat.

"But…?"

" … But now, something else is bothering it." Kaleb held his hand to the back of his head, leaning against a nearby desk. "It's a different kind of feeling this time around."

Mr. G spread his hands. "Care to elaborate?" he asked.

Kaleb pulled back his lips in thought. "It's like…" He looked to the window for answers. "Like I need to do something." Then he looked to his teacher. "Like when you know you've forgotten to do something until right before you need it. I feel like I'm… *Missing* something."

Mr. G pointed. "How's your crest?"

Kaleb shook his head. "The swelling's down, it's back to normal." He ticked his head. "But the tingling…"

"I see." Mr. G bridged his hands over his mouth. "Do you notice a difference around different locations? Certain people, maybe?"

Kaleb's eyes flicked. "Kind of, yeah."

Mr. G dropped his hands. "How so?"

Kaleb thought for a moment, trying to remember the feeling and how to describe it. After a few moments of silence, Kaleb spoke again.

"I want to help them," he admitted, not looking at anything in particular. "I want to… I want to make them know something. I want them to feel it, just by me standing there."

A knowing light flickered behind the teacher's eyes and he got up to settle himself against his desk, rather than behind it. "Feel what, exactly?" he asked, listening carefully to his student. Kaleb took another moment to find the right word.

"Wanted," he finally said with a moment of clarity. He looked to his teacher, realizing how cheesy he sounded and began rubbing the back of his head. "Can I ask you something else?"

Mr. G smiled at Kaleb, tickled by his bashfulness, but nodding to allow Kaleb to speak. "Why are you a teacher here?" This paused the man, surprising him at the sudden switch. "You're qualified to be a college professor, right?" Kaleb asked. "Be a real alchemyst, even." He looked to his teacher. "So why are you stuck here teaching a bunch of kids?"

The man thought, smiling as he came up with an answer almost instantly."Because of you," he smiled.

Kaleb was taken aback by this. "I haven't been here as long as you have." he told him, confused.

"Quite right," Mr. G grinned. "I've been teaching longer than you've been alive, kid." He chuckled. "Do you know why?" Kaleb shook his head. "Because I *love* it," he said simply. "I love alchemy, I'm amazed by it, even after all these years, it still excites me." He smiled down at his hands. "So I teach it, hoping to spread that excitement on to someone else, and then, hopefully, spreading it on from there." He looked up to Kaleb, offering a shrug. "Someone like you."

Mr. G held up a finger. "It has been my life's goal to make each generation passionate about learning, and by teaching it for twenty years so far, I think I've done a fine job." He shrugged, proud of himself. "It's up to them whether they teach it to the next generation or not."

Kaleb smiled at this, realizing how clever his teacher's thought process was.

"Now *I've* got a question for you," Mr. G said, holding up a finger again. Kaleb looked to him, waiting for him to ask.

"Why'd you quit the team?"

Kaleb stiffened. He stared at his teacher, trying to figure out *how* he had learned of this when he hadn't even told anyone about it yet.

"You wouldn't give up your jacket so easily," Mr. G answered. "Not unless it was important." Kaleb swallowed, looking to the floor, suddenly ashamed of himself all over again.

"So," Mr. G crossed his arms. "What happened?"

Chapter 18

Mr. G was furious. Absolutely furious. Even more so because Kaleb had decided to keep quiet about it, thinking that the rest of the school board would feel the same about Gerrit's scam as the rest of the team did. For the rest of the week, inquiries were made to each member of the team, specifically Gerrit and coach Abernathy. It didn't take long to find the 'nerds' in question, and after a short interrogation, every one of them confirmed Kaleb's side of the story to the authorities.

The Trouts were dropped from championships without a proper teacher to coach them. Abernathy was suspended until further notice, and he would have been fired, had he not won the school championship games twelve years in a row. Gerrit was pending a trial with the school board over whether or not he would be allowed to stay in school. After a few rough days of fighting back, Gerrit was given a three-strike warning on account of his football skills. The verdict sickened Kaleb, growing to hate the influence the game had over people even more.

The rest of the team had turned their backs on Kaleb, shunning him from their inner group for ratting out his best friend and ruining the team. At least, in their eyes, that's what he had done. Gerrit had stopped speaking to Kaleb, and as far as he was concerned, Kaleb figured it to be a good thing. They both needed time to cool off before speaking again, lest they fall to their fists again. Still, there wouldn't be any hiding from him come the new week. Gerrit would be allowed to return to school, and sooner or later, the two old friends would see each other again.

What bothered him most, though, was that not only was he being avoided by his friends, his team, and anyone who supported the team- most of the students in the school included- but Taylor had been skipping past him as well. During their tutoring sessions, the blonde would pull away from him, and find any reason to cut their lessons short when Kaleb offered more help. At home, he busied himself with the multitude of books that filled the house, or spent his time playing with Bubbie and Skitters rather than sitting down and talking with Kaleb.

What was worse, he didn't know if this was because of the team's situation, or because of the blonde's nightmares. He figured Taylor would be pleased with the team in disarray, but he could never tell with him. As far as his dreams went, he had been having them each night, moaning in his bed just as the sun would come up. Kaleb didn't need the use of his alarm because of this, but that wasn't necessarily a good thing, and every time he tried to bring it up and allow Taylor to talk about it, he would clam up and find some excuse to run away.

Kaleb sighed, rolling a pencil along the desk in his room and staring out into the grim sky. Another shower was on its way, and from the look of things, it would be a rough one. A knock on the door alerted him of Taylor entering the room.

"Kaleb?" he called quietly. Kaleb stayed in his seat, facing the window, but offered a wave over his shoulder to allow entrance. Taylor closed the door behind him, but stayed near it. He ran a hand through his hair, trying to think of how he wanted to approach the ex-jock.

"Something you wanted?" Kaleb asked, more bored than angry. He had gotten used to this, much to his disappointment. There was hesitation in the younger man's voice, taking a while before speaking.

"Are you okay?" Taylor asked finally. Kaleb blinked, turning to face the blonde. He stood fidgeting by the door, obviously uncomfortable, but making an effort to comfort Kaleb. This was new to him, and to Taylor too, judging by the way he kept holding his hair.

"Yeah," Kaleb said quietly, still watching him to try and figure the boy out. "I'm okay." Taylor ran his hand through his hair again- a nervous tick, Kaleb had learned.

"It's just been kinda crazy this past week," the blonde muttered, then gave a nervous chuckle. "You've got a lot of balls to do something like that in a town like this." He was still so quiet.
Kaleb looked to the floor. "Yeah," he said, reaching up to rub the back of his head.

"For the record," Taylor started. " … I think you're doing the right thing… Not a lot of people can do what you did."

Kaleb looked away. "I dunno," he said. "You were pretty good at pissing people off and pushing them away." He chuckled. "Someone had to take your place."

Taylor quieted, looking away. "Kaleb," he blurted, suddenly facing the older man. He tried to continue his speech, but his mouth was left open like a fish. He looked away and tried again, this time grabbing the back of his shirt and pulling it over his head.

Kaleb blinked, surprised at the sudden movement. The blonde popped out from beneath the fabric, holding it tightly in front of him. He looked Kaleb in the eyes for a moment, trying not to be nervous, then turned slowly to present his crest. Kaleb's eyes widened at this, stunned by Taylor's leap of faith. After their last fumble in sharing their crests, Taylor was taking a huge step forward; especially when he could still feel the memory of the pain that had come from Kaleb's touch.

Kaleb rose from his seat, carefully walking over to see Taylor's crest easier, making the tensed teen tighten even further. The darker man placed his finger tips at Taylor's elbows, releasing a small gasp from him from the sudden contact, but relieved to know where the other man's hands were. Kaleb was just as frightened as he was about touching. Taylor swallowed, trying not to let his shivers escape him as he allowed Kaleb to look at his soul crest.

There, centered on his spine, was a pair of vines intricately wrapped over one another. The two major vines met in the middle to twist around each other on the bottom in a delicate spiral, while the top part of those same vines curled into each other, forming the top part of a heart. Two more vines wrapped around the major ones along the outer edges of the curves, dangling to join the spiral at the bottom, but curling upwards at the top to hold a circle. Five more circles were strategically placed at the tips of the vines, completing the crest.

Taylor turned his head slightly to speak to the older teen behind him, still looking to the floor. "You said… You said you knew all of your friends' crests…" He turned his head away, looking to his clenched shirt. "I don't know you to be a liar."

Kaleb stared at the being before him, realizing that he was offering his friendship after so long, and when everyone else had abandoned him. Taylor was sending Kaleb a ray of hope in his darkest hour, and it terrified him to do it, making it all the more real.

Taylor fidgeted in Kaleb's fingers, turning his head occasionally before making up his mind and nodding to the man behind him, allowing him to touch it. Kaleb stilled his breath, not wanting to hurt the blonde again. He kept his fingers in place on Taylor's elbows, debating whether or not he wanted to risk it, but if Taylor could find courage, Kaleb could too. A tentative hand left Taylor's elbow, still unsure of touching the sensitive mark, and hovered above Taylor's skin. Just as Kaleb gathered his wits enough to carefully lay his hand down, a crack of thunder stopped him, surprising both boys from the sudden intrusion and breaking the spell.

They separated, blowing out their held breaths as they settled back into normal. Taylor was quick to put his tee back on, and Kaleb checked out the window, rubbing the back of his head. Taylor gestured to the window, noticing the nervous tick.

"You gonna be okay?" he asked, remembering the chutes.

Kaleb nodded. "I'm fine inside," he replied. "I just…" He rubbed the back of his head, chuckling slightly. "It's not the rain I'm afraid of, but more of flooding."

"Flooding." Taylor stared at him. "You realize you live in a town *surrounded* by water, right?" Another chuckle left Kaleb, this one less nervous.

"Funny how that works."

Taylor couldn't stop it. A snicker escaped his lips before he could have any say of it. That snicker grew into a chuckle, which morphed into a laugh. Kaleb's laughter grew just as gradually as Taylor's, and they ended up laughing together at his silly phobias as the rain began tapping on the window.

"You know what we haven't done in a while?" Vance suddenly asked. "Camping. We should go camping again." This brought a series of curious looks from each person at the dinner table.

"I thought it was too cold," Trish said, taking a sip of her tea.

"Well, they've got their coats now," Vance rebuttled. "And we haven't done something really fun in a while. We need some fun around here. Besides, the nights are perfect for a bonfire."

Kaleb grinned. "I'm in," he piped, giving an encouraging grin to Taylor, who shrugged.

"I'll just get in the way," he muttered.

"Nonsense," Trish mumbled, taking a forkful of salad.

Vance jerked a thumb at his wife. "What she said," he grinned. "C'mon, haven't you ever been camping before?" Taylor had a sudden grand interest in his dinner. "No!" Vance exclaimed, completely astonished. "Never?"

Kaleb elbowed the blonde playfully. "C'mon, come with us. It'll be fun." He grinned. "We'll show you how it's done."

Taylor ticked his head. "If you say so," he muttered.

"It's settled then," Vance said, straightening and using his manliest voice for dramatic effect. "We shall have a Man Journey!" He then dropped his shoulders and quickly switched back to normal.

"Next weekend."

Back in school. Oh, what a joy. Taylor had given up trying to avoid Kaleb all together. As embarrassed as he was, it wasn't Kaleb's fault for Taylor's brain losing a screw, so there wasn't a reason to punish him. Not after all he'd done for him. Aside from this, Kaleb had been outcasted from his friends and anyone else in the school who supported the team. The people who had once parted ways to let him pass now stepped aside so as not to be near him. The ones who had high fived and shaken his hands now gave looks of scorn and disgust.

As far as Kaleb went, he was a trooper about it, brushing off their cruelty as he moved on to his next class, but Taylor could see how it really affected him. His smile wasn't as bright, and his overbearing optimism was smothered down to polite advice. He was quieter than usual too, hardly ever saying a word unless he was prompted, and his laugh was almost nonexistent. The light in his eyes had dulled, making Taylor want to hit someone.

Kaleb had done the right thing, and he was being punished for it. It bothered Taylor to no end, and it forced him to change his mind about running away. He couldn't overload it, however. Taylor needed to start with babysteps, allowing Kaleb to adjust to this new normal before he began spending more time with him, otherwise it would be pity. Walking to school with him that morning would have tipped the scales in that favor.

Taylor packed up from his seat in the cafeteria as usual, leaving for his first class when the bell rang. The morning crowd crammed and jostled each other as every student made their way to class, laughing and chatting as they went. Taylor did his best to be invisible, keeping away from the blocked paths filled with students standing in the middle of the hall to talk and keeping to the walls as best he could. He pushed his way through the Alchemy hall to get to his math class, deciding to skip the cafeteria from now on and just write in front of his classroom instead. Ahead of him, in the distance, Kaleb towered over the rest of the students, making a path of his own. He caught sight of the blonde and offered a wave. Taylor nodded, returning the greeting as he continued forward, but Kaleb's eyes had moved past him, and were becoming panicked.

"Behind y-"

Taylor was slammed from behind, his backpack flying off somewhere along the lockers as he tumbled forward. Another blow came when a pair of feet jumped onto Taylor's back, effectively crushing his soul crest. Taylor screamed in torcherous pain as a sudden rush of infuriated electricity burst from his back and over his body from beneath his skin, stabbing him over and over again with millions of splintered thorns pressed at every nerve in his body. He tried to breathe, but his lungs failed him, along with his eyes, ears and motor functions.

He could vaguely hear someone shouting at him, spewing hateful, blaming words at him as his beating continued with brutal kicks, shoving him against the lockers. He knew that blow was loud, not because of the noise, but because of the vibrations his body had made on contact with the cold metal, sending each nerve into oblivion.

Taylor's eyes rolled into the back of his head as he tried to make right of what was in front of him, but daggers along his temples blurred his vision, sending him into blindness. He fought off the darkness as best he could, but the promise of no more pain was far too enticing. The kicker had been dragged away, still screaming and spitting at Taylor, but the pain remained, jolting poison through his body with every beat of his heart.

A new set of hands were on him, touching his face to make him hold still and make sense of things, but failing miserably against the burning in his throat. The new hands were speaking to him now, shaking him away from the darkness, but no coherent words could be heard through the ringing in his ears. The hands shook him again, demanding he do something, but what, he didn't know, until they reached over to roughly slap his ribcage from behind.

Air scraped through Taylor's throat into his lungs, making him wish he had never learned to breathe in the first place. He was suddenly very cold, and his quivering fingers before him only convinced him of this idea more. The blurred vision began to fade away, showing the head of the Alchemy department kneeling in front of him, trying to shake more air into his lungs. Taylor's hearing was still muddy, and the ringing intensified as his breaths were restored, helping to clear away the confusion. The teacher had looked up abruptly, jumping up to stop whatever was happening behind him.

"Kaleb, stop!" Mr. G pulled Kaleb out of the fight as another teacher snatched away Gerrit, and he instantly whipped him around to scream in his face. "KALEB!"

The angry teen tried to resist, but his teacher's ferocity overpowered him. "Stop it!" the man hissed. "You have more important things to worry about!"

Kaleb seemed to awaken from this, and looked to Taylor when his teacher nodded to the teen lying face down on the floor. Kaleb's heart stopped, suddenly remembering why he had beaten Gerrit, and instantly dropped to his knees to help in whatever way he could.

"YOU *FUCKER!*" Gerrit screamed, still being dragged away by the teachers as spittle dribbled down his chin. "IT'S ALL YOUR FAULT! YOU DID THIS!"

Kaleb wanted to rip him apart for attacking Taylor so violently, but the blonde needed him here more.

"Taylor-" He was breathless. "Taylor, can you move?" He reached to flip the younger man onto his back, but was stopped by Mr. G.

"Don't," he said, pulling back on Taylor's collar. "Shit," he hissed, already feeling the fever from the unhappy soul. From what little he could see, Taylor's crest looked horrible after such a vicious beating. Mr. G lifted the boy's shirt from his waist, seeing thick, red spider veins radiating from the crest, wrapping sporadically across the young man's back, torso and arms.

The crowd watched, completely shocked from the scene and tried to get a better look at the body on the floor, but they were shooed away by several teachers, trying to control the area.

"I'm fine," Taylor mumbled, sweeping his arms to try and rise. "I'm fine." His voice trailed off in pain.

"Don't you dare," Mr. G ordered, noticing Taylor's arm movements. "Try and wiggle your toes for me." The blonde complied, showing slight movement from his shoes, as much as it pained him to do so. "Well, at least we know his spine isn't broken," the teacher muttered to Kaleb, trying to offer solace to the panicked teen.

"Is he gonna be alright?" Kaleb asked, trying to control his shaking- out of fear or anger, Mr. G couldn't decide. The teacher grimaced, not liking the situation one bit.

"Let's see if we can get him to the nurse."

Kaleb followed him through the open door into his classroom, grabbing a large, thick white sheet that normally covered projects that needed dark environments. When they returned to roll the blonde onto the sheet, they found him a little ways away, leaning heavily against the lockers and trying to make his way down the hall nearly falling over his knees.

"I'm fine," he insisted, sounding terrible.

"Shut up." Mr. G forced the blonde to be caught in the sheet as he tripped him forward. They carried on once Taylor was secure, making sure the blonde was off his feet for the two stronger men to drag him safely to the head office. The nurse was already waiting for them outside the principal's office, accompanied by Mrs. Hilton who ushered the men inside to lie Taylor down on one of the cots.

Kaleb was forced to leave, having to make a statement about what he had seen, and what he had done afterwards- earning himself a week's suspension due to violence. Gerrit had been carted off with the school's policeman, Officer Seymour, to the local detention center to clear up all of his newfound trouble, as well as to keep him separated from Taylor and Kaleb, who wanted nothing more than to tear his face off. Gerrit would be allowed to go home after all the paperwork was done, but Kaleb needed to stay with Taylor, and try to figure out what all had happened in such a short time.

It had only lasted a few seconds, it all happened so quickly that Kaleb had to actively think to remember what had happened. Gerrit had seen Taylor, he had been glaring at him as he walked down the halls to his first class, but then he snapped, and charged forward to shove Taylor to the floor and jump on him. He struck quite a few hard kicks to Taylor's back and abdomen, screaming profanities and blaming him for changing things before Kaleb managed to catch up and tackled Gerrit off of the blonde. After that, Kaleb's memory went black. He couldn't remember anything between then and when Mr. G had pulled him away. He didn't want to.

Kaleb had turned into the very same monster that Gerrit had, and it had been triggered by the attack on Taylor. Kaleb thought back, wondering why Gerrit had waited so long to attack in the first place, when he realized the look on his face when Taylor nodded to Kaleb. That was when Gerrit had snapped.

Kaleb held his head in his hands at the sudden epiphany of Gerrit's hatred. He didn't blame Kaleb for their fight. He blamed *Taylor*. Suddenly, "ruining everything" and "changing things" suddenly made sense, and Kaleb's mind was clear. His grip behind his head tightened, making Kaleb curl over in his seat and bury his face in his lap. Kaleb stayed this way for a while, not bothering to move when people passed by. The alchemy teacher came forward to give Taylor's backpack to Kaleb, but decided to offer comfort when he found him huddled up. Mr. G sighed as he sat down next to the huddled Kaleb, keeping his hands on his knees as he spoke to his student.

"We've called your parents," he said, folding his hands as his elbows slid to his knees. "Your dad was with a patient, but your mom was able to come. She'll be here to pick Taylor up soon." He looked to his student. "You can go with him if you'd like. Though, honestly, I don't see anywhere else you *would* go." Kaleb didn't stir, still hiding under his arms.

"Tell me the truth," Kaleb muttered. "Gerrit did a lot of damage, didn't he?"

The teacher sat quietly, thinking of the proper answer before speaking. "When the slightest ill-intended touch can send you reeling," he started. "I highly doubt a kick to the crest could be a good thing." He scratched his temple. "I take it those two don't get along?" Kaleb shook his head as best as his knees would allow. "Wonderful."

Kaleb lifted his face from his knees only to hold his head over them. "Does it make a difference?"

Mr. G ticked his head. "You know how when you were little, and your mom would wash your back in the bath?" Kaleb waited for his teacher to continue. "It never hurt when someone you cared about touched your crest, am I right?" Kaleb nodded. "That's because, in a way, your souls bonded. Not in the way of mates, but in finding companionship. It reflects the love you feel for them." He thumbed his nose. "The same rule applies for those that we don't care for. Only, in a rivalry. It reflects the negative feelings that person feels towards you."

Kaleb looked away, thinking of the murderous look Gerrit had in his eyes. "How bad is it?" he asked. The teacher took a breath before speaking.

"It'll be a few days before he's up again," he admitted. "That much is for sure."

"But he *will* be back up again, won't he?" The older man quieted, not knowing how to answer this question. "That's what I was afraid of," Kaleb muttered.

"I can't answer that for you, Kaleb," Mr. G said quietly. "I can't control what happens." He looked to his student. "I'm sorry I can't give you anything more than that."

Kaleb's gaze dropped to the floor, silenced by this. "Kaleb," the nurse called quietly. "Can you-" She stopped and came out of the room Taylor was in, closing the door behind her when she saw the rush of people coming towards her. "He's asleep," she said, shaking her head. "I'm going to need Kaleb's help, but for now, it was all I could do for him."

"Do what, Charlotte?" Mrs. Hilton asked. The nurse fidgeted, pulling at her fingers before opening her mouth to answer, but caught sight of Mrs. Evans coming in through the door.

"Where is he?" Trish demanded. "Where is Taylor?"

Mrs. Hilton came forward to speak with her while Kaleb began rubbing the back of his head, turning away to hide the bruise on his face courtesy of Gerrit. Trish snapped her attention to her son, snatching his chin and jerking his face for inspection. She cocked a brow at him, expecting an answer. The look of defeat plastered on Kaleb's face dropped his mother's hand, and she turned her attention to the teachers.

"What happened?"

Mr. G stepped up to inform her of what he had witnessed that morning as calmly as he could. Mrs. Hilton pinched the bridge of her nose as she listened, offering her apologies when the alchemy teacher had finished, and promising reprimandation.

"Where is he now?" Trish asked. Charlotte the nurse piped up now, still worried with what she had to admit.

"I gave him a sedative," she confessed. "He was in so much pain-" She stopped short, turning her face away as she smothered her mouth with her hand.

Trish cocked her head, confused. "They have those in school clinics?"

Charlotte shrank, but told the truth. "I used my own."

Mrs. Hilton stepped up next to the nurse. "I ordered her to."

"Clara!" Charlotte tried, but Mrs. Hilton kept her gaze strong as she looked to Trish.

"I threatened her with her job. I take responsibility. Mrs. Fiddlestone was just following orders."

Trish studied the woman before her, realizing that this illegal activity could easily get the nurse banned, and what the teacher was doing to prevent it from happening. Trish laid a hand on Mrs. Hilton's shoulder. "Thank you," she said quietly, silently promising safety to the both of them. Charlotte breathed a sigh of relief, then turned the conversation back over to Taylor.

"He won't be waking up any time soon," she informed. "However, you should still be careful when you move him. Try and keep any stress off his back; keep him as flat as you can." She shook her head. "He wouldn't open up to me, so there wasn't much I could do."

Trish nodded, following the woman to Taylor's closed door. From outside, Kaleb could see a glimpse of his friend lying face down and shirtless on the small cot, his damaged arm draped over the side to dangle down to the floor. The ice pack on his back covered his crest, but not the rest of the ugly, red scars that bulged from his skin. Kaleb turned his head away, not wanting to see the inflicted damage, but the memory was there, plaguing his mind with the image of painful marks spreading over the small man's back and arms. Mr. G clapped a hand on Kaleb's shoulder, comforting his student as best he could.

"Kaleb," Trish called quietly. "I need your help, honey." Kaleb took a breath, then left to obey his mother.

They didn't want to bend the boy in fear of worsening his condition, so they used Mr. G's sheet as a makeshift stretcher and carried him out to the truck. It was obvious with one look that he wouldn't have fit in the front if he were to lie down, so Mrs. Hilton held Kaleb's end of the sheet as he climbed onto the bed to guide the blonde in carefully. Kaleb sat beside Taylor, cautiously covering the shirtless boy with the sheet to shield him from the cold, then made certain nothing would cause him harm before setting himself down to ride next to him. Trish did her best to drive smoothly, and slowed over every major bump in the road, looking back to Kaleb every few seconds for reassurance. It took them an eternity to get home.

When Trish finally pulled into the driveway, she grabbed Taylor's things and hurried towards the back of the truck, hissing in pain the entire way.

"What's wrong?" Kaleb asked, noticing one of the wrists on her sleeves was suddenly bleeding.

"It's nothing, dear." She waved him off. "One of the patients bit me, I'm patched up, don't worry."

Kaleb shook his head. "You can barely handle a backpack, let alone a body." He denied her access to Taylor. "You're either going to hurt yourself more, or drop Taylor. Neither are preferable."

Trish dropped her hands to rest on her hips. "Well, what do you suggest, Kaleb?" she barked. "You and I are the only ones here."

Kaleb knelt down to Taylor, quietly fiddling with his fingers as he decided on what to do, then gently hoisted him up to his chest, resting the blonde's head on his shoulder. Taylor's breathing was ragged and weak on Kaleb's neck, making him freeze. He soon realized it was the pain that made the boy struggle, and not Kaleb's efforts. He cradled Taylor's thighs beneath his arms to slightly wrap his skinny legs around Kaleb, careful not to touch anything higher than his waist to avoid the marks hidden beneath the sheet. Taylor's arms remained at his sides inside the sheet, leaving it to Kaleb to lean back in order to hold the lifeless body close to his chest. Instead of walking to the end of the truck, Kaleb dragged himself over to the end and stretched his feet down to the ground, making sure not to jostle the weak body he carried.

Trish ran ahead to unlock and open the door, doing the same for the bedroom after chasing the animals to the backyard- the last thing they needed was a jumping dog and tripping cat. Kaleb stepped gingerly towards the bedroom, listening for any sign of stress from Taylor. As he entered his room, he slowly knelt beside the edge of his bed, Trish hovering beside him to help flatten the blonde alongside it, and remove the sheet. With only his legs covered by the comforter, Taylor was left to recuperate on his stomach.

"I'll go get some oils." Trish got up to leave.

"Take care of yourself first," Kaleb said, stopping her in the doorway. "You won't be any good to him with shaky hands."

Trish looked to her son for a moment, then nodded agreement, and left to rebandage her soaking wrist. Kaleb turned back to Taylor, rubbing the back of his dark head. Not knowing what else to do, he replaced the ice pack over the blonde's swollen crest, not wanting to see it as much as wanting to heal it. He stared at Taylor's face, taking guilt in the condition he had fallen in. If Gerrit had any sense, he wouldn't have blamed the blonde for the battle between he and Kaleb, and Taylor wouldn't be lying in this pain now.

He brushed blonde bangs away from his burning forehead, feeling the fever rising even now. Kaleb sighed, wanting to go help his mother bring her herbs and oils, but knowing he'd get in the way. He made himself stay, deciding that Taylor didn't need to be left alone at the moment, and waited for his mother to return. A slamming fist on the door changed his mind, and the rage he had felt before started to boil deep in his gut. He could hear Gerrit screaming on his lawn, cursing his mother, and demanding he see Taylor to "finish the job." Kaleb bolted out of his room and marched to his porch, towering over Gerrit, and effectively silencing him.

"Stop it," Kaleb growled, dangerously calm.

"Kaleb-"

Trish was waved off, silently ordered inside the house. Their home was being threatened, and as a man of the house, it was his duty to protect it. Kaleb's eyes never left Gerrit's, the fury in them raging behind a stern face.

"Where is he?" Gerrit demanded. "I know you have-"

"I said. Stop. It." The rage built up, sending eerie fire through his eyes. "You invade my house, you disrespect my mother, and worse of all," Kaleb said, his dark voice still and steady. "You beat my friend into oblivion."

Gerrit scowled at Kaleb. "*I'm* your friend, Kaleb," he hissed. "Not that piece of shit."

Kaleb shook his head slowly, never taking his eyes off of Gerrit's. "You and I have a very different definition of '*shit.*'" Kaleb straightened, making himself grow taller and wider. "Get off my lawn. And don't come back."

Gerrit stared back at him in disbelief. "You're picking *him over me?*"

Kaleb said nothing, staring back at the smaller boy with hate-filled eyes. Gerrit shook his head, still disbelieving.

"He's got you so messed up, Kaleb. Wake up already."

Kaleb remained silent, waiting for him to leave. Gerrit became enraged when he saw that he couldn't talk his friend out of a bad decision, choosing his enemy over him.

"Fuck you!" Gerrit screamed. "You're gonna regret this, Kaleb! You're gonna come crawling back when he screws you over, you stupid *son of a bitch!*"

"GET OFF!" Kaleb roared, scaring not only Gerrit, but his mother watching from inside as well. Gerrit had finally broken Kaleb's control, and he was paying the price for it now. Gerrit stumbled over himself, skipping back in shock from Kaleb's sudden outburst. He was still glaring at Kaleb as he backed away, retreating to his house across the street. Kaleb stayed glued to his spot on the lawn, watching Gerrit until the front door had slammed shut.

Kaleb stayed for a moment longer, watching the door for a few seconds. He had so many fond memories of running through that door, racing Gerrit up the stairs to play in his room. His parents were hardly ever home, leaving the two boys free to do whatever they pleased all the day long. They had so many adventures together, conquering alien kingdoms, killing savage beasts, and eventually rescuing the damsel in distress away on their pirate ship. As they grew older, their interests developed into sports and girls, and on more than one occasion, Gerrit would sneak away one of his father's magazines for them to gawk over, planning imaginative deeds for each model displayed on the pages.

For as long as he could remember, Kaleb and Gerrit had always been there for each other. They picked each other up, shared their secrets, and when Gerrit was especially lonely, Kaleb would invite him over for dinner to avoid eating at an empty table. Gerrit always knew how to put a smile on Kaleb's face, no matter the heartache. Now, with him being the source, Kaleb knew it would take a lifetime before Gerrit could bring happiness to him again.

Kaleb turned from the lawn, walking up the steps and in through the door. Trish stood to the side of him, searching his face for clues on how to comfort him. He sighed heavily through his nose, holding his stern face, but placing his hands on her waist to rest his head on her shoulder. Trish returned the embrace, wrapping her arms tightly around his neck. No words were spoken, and none were needed. They simply stood there, holding one another as they bid farewell to their oldest, and dearest friend.

Chapter 19

Floating in the darkness had almost started to become second nature to Taylor. He lay in a sea of shadows, wondering how he had gotten there again, when a light at his back caught his attention. It was a warm, welcoming light that felt like silk spreading across his skin. Taylor turned, deciding to follow the light, and found himself pressed against a soft wall. He tried opening his eyes, finding this to be the most troublesome part of escaping the darkness. After a few more tries, he succeeded in peeping through a single slit, seeing a blurry image at his side.

Taylor tried to call to the image, finding it difficult to open his vocal chords to speak, and managed a groan. He blinked, clearing the image enough to reveal Trish lightly rubbing little circles across his back. Taylor tried to speak again, uttering a quiet moan before getting out her name.

"Shh," she cooed, dipping her fingers in a vial. "Taylor, dear." She brought her freshly dipped fingers to his burning back and resumed the circling. "Everything is going to be alright." Taylor's eye was far too heavy to keep open, and it drooped repeatedly.

"I..." he tried. "I keep trying to... To wake up, but... I just... I can't..."

Trish hushed him again. "It's alright, dear," she assured him. "Don't fight it, just go to sleep." Taylor's eyes drooped again, far too heavy to raise again.

"But..." A hand gently caressed his cheek, hushing him again.

"It's alright," he heard. "We'll be right here."

"How's he doing?"

It was the first question to leave Vance's lips as he entered the door. Trish shook her head.

"It's bad, dear," she mumbled. "Kaleb's with him now, but he hasn't woken up."

Vance rid himself of his warm layers and washed the bus ride off of his hands in the kitchen sink, then started towards the boys' room, with Trish following close behind. As Vance neared the room, he immediately saw the damage, and turned away, holding the back of his head.

"Gerrit did this?" he asked Trish quietly. She nodded, peeking over Vance's shoulder at her son.

"Best not to bring it up right now, dear," she told him. "For the moment, just focus on Taylor." Vance nodded to his wife, understanding, then entered the room.

Kaleb was sitting on the floor next to Taylor, gently dabbing a cold, wet cloth over one of the nasty veins on Taylor's wrist. As he noticed his father, he dropped his gaze to his duties on Taylor's skin, ashamed of what his friend had done.

"How's it coming?" Vance asked, leaving a hand on his son's shoulder as he sat down next to him.

"It helps," Kaleb mumbled, nodding to the wrist. "It's slow, but it helps." He dipped his head. "It was down his hand when I started."

Vance looked to his son. "This morning?" he asked, receiving a nod. Vance looked out the window, seeing the setting sun and the barely touched plates of food at his side that were left for Kaleb's disposal. He sighed quietly, but pat his son's back, reassuring him.

"You did good, kid," he said. "Let me take over and go eat with your mother."

Kaleb shook his head, keeping his eyes on his work. "I'm alright," he said. "You just got home, you should-"

"Kaleb."

Vance was quiet as he placed his hand back on his son's shoulder. Kaleb paused, not wanting to leave, but knowing his father was right. His legs were numb from sitting there all day, and his stomach was rather displeased with him with the combination of stress, worry and lack of nourishment. Still, he sat there, looking at the painful marks on Taylor's light skin, and it sent a heavy stone to the center of his gut.

"Let me help," his father said, gently squeezing his shoulder. Kaleb looked to the floor, giving in to his father's request, and left his room to find his mother.

He knew this woman, but for the life of him, he couldn't see her face. Her blonde hair swayed with her walk as she stepped toward him. She smiled a sad, caring smile at him, and he recognized the curve of the lips. Taylor reached out to his mother, trying to call out to her but finding he had lost his voice. She was too far, out of reach from his stretching fingers, and the more he chased after her, the more she evaded him. His fingertips barely missed her fading form, and as hard as he tried, he still couldn't see her face.

She was fading quickly, and her face was a blank mask that soon covered her smile as well, leaving her expressionless. Taylor stretched as far as he could, trying to reach his mother before she could fade away for good, and with one last effort, he jumped after her, wrapping his arms around her frame and falling through her as she disappeared, dropping to the darkened pitts below them.

Taylor screamed as he fell, but his voice was still locked inside him, and he was left soundless as he sank into the darkness. He fought and struggled against it, trying to find the light again, but the black was far too strong for him, and resistance was impossible. He was swallowed up, enveloped in the sea once more, lost in the waves until he could find his way out again.

Taylor didn't bother opening his eyes this time. It was too much of a struggle, and it sapped him of much needed energy. His ears, however, could do the work for him. He heard the shuffling of feet as someone neared him, kneeling down at his side and wringing water into a pan. He flinched at the sudden coolness of a wet rag draped over his back, gasping slightly at the change.

"Taylor?"

It was deep, resounding voice that put him at ease. A large hand gently traced its fingers over his forehead, peeking at his eyes from beneath blonde hair.

"Sorry, kid," the voice whispered, dropping the fingers away. Taylor tried to respond, tried to tell the voice that he was trapped, and begging for help. He was being held captive in the darkness, and its heat burned through him like a flame to paper. He was desperate to escape, he only needed that hand's help to pull him out; to free him from this heated prison, but the blonde's voice was caught as well, trapped beneath boiling rivers of muck that soiled his mouth.

A cough was all that escaped, sending his body into torcherous tremors that splintered along his skin. He groaned, whether aloud or not, he didn't know, but the hand returned to his face to try and comfort him. Something painfully cold and wet pressed itself to his lips, seizing his mouth in one fell swoop. He wanted it out, wanted it gone; off of his tongue and out of his body, but no matter how hard he tried, the piercing cold returned, replaced with a new one.

"C'mon, kid," the voice pleaded. "Take it."

Taylor coughed the intruder away, resuming the merciless shocks beneath his skin. His body began to shake, quivering from the effort it took to fight whatever it was the hand was shoving down his throat, and he began to fall back into the darkness. Taylor begged and pleaded, fighting as hard as he could to stay aloft, but it was useless. He sank deep into the shadows, drowning in the inky black that consumed him.

"Bubbie."

Kaleb whispered harshly, trying to get the dog down from his bed. The shepherd remained at Taylor's side, refusing to move. He had been sitting with Taylor ever since that morning when he escaped the backyard and rushed in, his instincts screaming at him that something was wrong. Since then, no matter what the family did, the dog simply refused to leave Taylor's side. Skitters had joined Bubbie in his protest, claiming the pillow next to Taylor's head, but at the moment, she was busy eating her breakfast, and not stationed at her post guarding Taylor's hair.

Kaleb sighed, giving in to the dog's wishes, and sat down on the floor next to Taylor. He resumed his efforts along Taylor's arm, making slow progress towards his elbow. Bubbie watched, nuzzling his head softly down against Taylor's other arm. After a while, the dog sniffed at Taylor's spider veins, inspecting them for his own before licking one.

"Stop it."

Kaleb waved his rag at Bubbie, making him pull away. He stared at Kaleb for a moment, then returned to Taylor's arm.

"Stop," Kaleb ordered, shooing the dog away again. This happened a third time, and when Kaleb went to shoo him away, Bubbie snapped at Kaleb, giving an annoyed whine.

Kaleb eyed the dog, staring him down and trying to figure out his infatuation with licking Taylor. True, it was an affectionate gesture, but he was adamant about it, to the point of fighting Kaleb. Bubbie dropped his stare from Kaleb, satisfied that he wouldn't be interrupted again, and set to work licking Taylor's wounds. Kaleb frowned, but allowed it, figuring the dog wanted Taylor back on his feet as much as the rest of them.

Skitters had returned from the kitchen, and hopped onto the foot of the bed, crawling delicately to the pillows and plopped down in her previous spot. She sat watching the two males tending to Taylor, curling her tail as they worked. Eventually, she grew tired of watching them and decided to bathe, careful not to bump into anything-Taylor specifically. Kaleb shook his head, chuckling at the animals.

"Can't beat the love between a boy and his dog," Kaleb thought. He spent most of his time each day sitting next to Taylor, having more of it than usual after being suspended from school. Gerrit was also suspended, though his would last much longer than the week that Kaleb was banned. His bruised face had almost cleared, but he didn't pay much mind to it. He was more focussed on caring for Taylor's wounds rather than his own. Kaleb froze when he heard a mumble from the blonde, stopping Bubbie as well.

"Taylor?" Kaleb tried quietly. The mumble repeated, and the boy's brow crumpled slightly over his eyes.

"Klb…" he tried, his eyes far too heavy to lift.

"I'm right here," Kaleb assured. "What is it?"

The blonde's fingers shook with effort, trying to raise his arm to reach out, but not having the strength. "Kalb…" Taylor tried again, still struggling. Kaleb took the shaking fingers in his own, softly holding them down on the bed.

"Don't try to move," Kaleb said. "I'm right here, what do you need?" There was a slight movement in Taylor's fingers, as though he were trying to grab hold of Kaleb's hand in return.

" … 'm stk…" he tried, quivering his fingers again. " … Cn't… Can't…"

Kaleb squeezed Taylor's fingers lightly. "Don't worry about it," he assured. "Just go to sleep." Taylor whimpered denial, obviously hearing Kaleb's words.

"I dn't… 'm stuck…" His voice became strained. "Dn't wnna… Go bck…" He was panting from his efforts.

"It's alright, Taylor," Kaleb said. "I'm not gonna leave, just go back to sleep." Taylor huffed, trying to catch his breath.

"Kalb…" His fingers twitched under the bigger man's hand. " … Hlp m…" Kaleb drew closer, hoping his ears hadn't heard him right.

"Help…" Taylor tried again, confirming Kaleb's worries. Taylor tried to speak again, but he drifted away, slipping back to sleep in Kaleb's hand.

Bubbie sniffed him, listening for any sign of life from Taylor, then resumed his position nuzzling his arm to find where he left off. Kaleb reached back to rub the back of his head, sighing. He squeezed Taylor's fingers, wishing he *could* help the blonde, but not knowing how to pull him out of his comatose state. He released his head, returning to the rag in the pan. This was all he could do for now.

Vance entered the master bedroom to find Trish in the bathroom, unwrapping her wounded wrist. He stood in the doorway, watching his wife clean the bite marks around the stitches, careful with her movements. He sighed, rubbing the back of his head as he walked in behind her.

"Was he sick?" Vance asked. Trish shook her head.

"Just a disagreeable patient," she said, turning to him. "He thought he was a dragon." She chuckled. "He was just coming out of anesthesia, dear. Otherwise harmless." Vance stepped forward as she spoke to take his wife's wrist, cradling the tiny limb in his large hands as he carefully inspected the damage.

"As long as I don't have to worry about you too," he said softly, placing a gentle kiss over the bend. Trish smiled at her husband, not having to say anything to show her appreciation. Vance knelt down next to his wife, caring for her wounds while she sat watching. As he latched on the clip to hold the wrap in place, he looked up to Trish and smiled.

"I'm turning into a big softy," he muttered. Trish grinned at him, running her fingers through his hair.

"You like it better that way anyways."

He cocked a brow. "First our boy, then the kid, and now you," he shook his head. "I'm next in line for an injury. Maybe then I can take a break from worrying."

Trish clicked her teeth, displeased with his words. "Don't say stuff like that," she said. "Besides. You'd still worry about us." Vance ticked his head, patting his wife's hand.

"Like I said," he muttered. "I'm a big softy."

Vance took over for Kaleb while he got something to eat. Vance had taken a few days off from work knowing that his patients could wait for him, but Trish and her herbs were needed at the hospital, helping more than just a handful of people. Kaleb checked the fridge, grabbing an apple, and not seeing much else that he wanted. His diet had decreased considerably over the last few days, to the point of frightening his parents, but he simply wasn't hungry. He knew it wasn't healthy, the stress and worry would catch up with him eventually, but for now, it fueled him.

Kaleb decided to make himself a cup of tea as well, irritated when he reached for the empty tin of blueberry. He thought back to the day he had introduced Taylor to the drink, letting him sample from his last cup, and had considered the idea of letting him keep it if the blonde liked it. He rubbed the back of his head and sighed, picking out the ingredients for lemon tea instead.

News of Gerrit's actions quickly spread across the town like wildfire, now putting him in the position to be gossiped and whispered about. Starting such a violent attack in the middle of the school was no way for a respectable person to act, regardless of their status or reason.

Kaleb could only imagine the ruckus this had caused in the school, wondering who the students blamed more for this; Kaleb or Taylor. No doubt, by now, everyone knew of their connection, and paired the two together in the situation. What made it worse; he had overheard a conversation between his father and Mr. G the night previous, discussing his plans to press charges on Gerrit and have him expelled from school, whether the Evans family agreed or not.

Now, for the first time in ages, Kaleb dreaded going back to school. There was nothing there for him anymore, and he knew that if someone made a smart remark about Taylor, his nerves would get the better of him, and he'd snap. The dagger eyes and venom tongues he could handle, but speak ill of someone he cared about when they couldn't speak for themselves, and he couldn't control himself. His loyalty worked against him in that way, and now, it frightened him. Kaleb finished his apple and sipped at his tea, heading for his room.

"The way you dote on him, I doubt I'd need to take off from work," Vance muttered, not even seeing to know his son was there behind him.

"We need at least one doctor in the house," Kaleb replied, sitting at his desk. "I'm not there yet." Vance ticked his head, agreeing with his son, but keeping his attention on dabbing at Taylor's arm. "With an injury as serious as this, wouldn't he be better off in a hospital?" Kaleb asked, taking a sip of his tea.

"Normally, yes," Vance answered. "Soul crests are different, though. They need people they're comfortable with, so we tend to send our crest patients home with a doctor." He ticked his head again, holding up two fingers. "And in this house, we have two. Besides-" he paused a moment, dipping the rag into some fresh, cold water and rose his eyes to his son. "Would you really want him gone?" Kaleb shook his head, rubbing the back of it. "Didn't think so," Vance muttered, returning to Taylor's arm.

The veins weren't so angry anymore, though they hadn't gone away either. After two days of rest, the bright red marks had dulled in color, and thinned slightly, but the only clear spot on the blonde's body was the arm the family had been working on for the past two days, and the small section that Bubbie had been working on. Bubbie was relentless on Taylor's other arm, licking the irritated veins that stretched over his skin, and snipping at anyone who tried to stop him, making slow progress.

Taylor's fever had remained as well, keeping the poor boy in a constant state of baking from the inside out. His body refused to release him from slumber, and whenever he tried, he was left in the pitiful position of panting and whimpers.

Kaleb looked away, tapping his cup in thought. "Are those going to stay behind?" he asked quietly. Vance sighed, inspecting the ugly marks.

"Can't really say," he answered truthfully. "Depends on how he heals, I suppose." He shrugged. "If it was fairly traumatic, I suppose so, but." he looked to his son. "I don't really see him being that scared of Gerrit, do you?"

Kaleb looked away again, not knowing how to answer thanks to the smaller athlete's torment to Taylor for so long before then. If Taylor had to keep those terrible veins along his skin for the rest of his life, Kaleb worried the disfigurement would bring more pain to him along the way.

Vance dropped the rag into the pan, giving up on Taylor's arm for now, and removing the ice pack on the boy's crest. The tangled set of vines imprinted on his spine was battered and bruised with a brutal black base, surrounded by red, puckered skin around the outer edges of it, revealing its irritation.

Vance sighed, dabbing the moisture the sweating icepack had left behind, then closed his eyes as he gently placed his hand over the boy's crest. Kaleb flinched, waiting for the freezing rejection, but his father remained motionless as he watched him touch Taylor's crest. Vance furrowed his brow, sucking in his lips at his attempts, and eventually pulling away.

"He won't open up," Vance muttered, replacing the ice pack. "Not enough, anyways."

"How did you do that?" Kaleb asked, shocked by his father's actions.

Vance looked to his son, confused. "Do what?"

"*That!*" he stressed, pointing. "How did you touch him without-" He pulled his hand back, biting his knuckle as he stared wide eyed at the crest.

"It's a treatment," Vance offered, trying to answer his son without knowing the question. "You have to allow people in for it to work, though. Taylor's too clammed up."

Kaleb thought back to what the school nurse had said about Taylor not opening up to her either. "He's not a very open person," Kaleb said, his excitement dropping. Vance agreed, picking up the rag and handing it to his son.

"Might as well," he said, knowing Kaleb would waste his break in the room again. "I'll get him some more ice chips. Maybe you'll have better luck keeping him hydrated." He left the boys to heal on their own, taking Bubbie with him to relieve the dog's bladder. Kaleb carefully settled down in his seat next to him, peeping over at the work Bubbie had done. He would never admit it out loud, but Taylor loved that dog more than anything else alive, and from the healed section of his arm, it was clear that the bond between them was equally shared.

Bond.

Mr. G had said something about bonded souls to him at the school. He had said that souls could share a bond even when they weren't mated, and the stronger the relationship, the stronger the reaction. Kaleb peered at the icepack, thinking back to when his father had touched it and not gained any ground- either for good or bad. His fingers twitched at the memory of touching Taylor's crest, unnerving him at the thought of hurting the boy even further if he tried touching it now.

"You care about each other whether you realize it or not."

Mr. G's words echoed in his mind, making Kaleb rethink his relationship with Taylor. It had been months since they had first touched, and their friendship had only grown since then. Kaleb thought back to how scared Taylor had been when he revealed his crest, working up the courage to allow Kaleb's touch, and realizing how difficult that must have been for the blonde. Still, he had chosen to befriend Kaleb, comfort him in a way, when he was down on his last leg. Sharing crests was something that was shared between strong bonds, and it was not to be taken lightly when someone as shelled up as Taylor offered the chance to share his soul.

Kaleb licked his lips, taking a deep, nervous breath as he slowly removed the ice pack, eyeing the crest fearfully. He paused, still too nervous to move, then he leaned forward to hover over the blonde's head.

"Taylor," he whispered. "Don't be scared." He bit his lip, trying to take his own advice. "I'm gonna try something. You just have to trust me." He lowered his voice even further to barely a whisper. "Please." The blonde lay still, not reacting to Kaleb's words in the slightest.

Kaleb took another breath, sitting back in his previous spot as he readied himself. He rolled his fingers, preparing them to touch Taylor's crest, then reached out to hold them above the blonde's spine. Slowly, he carefully placed his fingertips along a vine, reeling back at the sudden chill that raced through his fingers. Taylor remained silent, unmoved by Kaleb's attempts. With this in mind, Kaleb tried once more, sliding his fingers softly over the vines before lowering his palm down flat over Taylor's back.

Taylor took a sudden, deep breath, his body surprised at the sudden coolness that spread throughout his skin, while Kaleb focused on keeping his hand still. His fingers tingled at the sensation of the vines, sending shivers through his hand, up his arm and down his body, but the most incredible reaction was the change in the wounds. They withered at Kaleb's touch, moving around the pale skin and shrinking into the crest the longer he held his hand over it. Kaleb couldn't handle the chills any longer, and ripped his hand away, revealing what he had done.

Taylor released the pent up breath quietly, still asleep through the ordeal, but breathing more evenly now. The spider veins had faded to a soft pink, and most of the smaller ones had disappeared entirely, leaving the larger ones to hold root. The dark, ugly bruising around his crest had faded to a pale purple, and the red around the vines were gone completely. Some color had returned to his face, making his sickly white skin return to its original light shade. Kaleb reached up to Taylor's forehead, searching for the fever that had plagued the blonde for days now, and finding it broken.

"Taylor?" he asked, breathless from his endeavors. The boy remained silent, sleeping peacefully for the first time in days. Kaleb shook his hand, readying for a second round to rid the blonde of the rest of the veins, but as he lay his hand down, the reaction was much simpler. The wave of ice never crashed over them, and the shivers were nearly nonexistent. All that remained of the previous sensations was the tingling in his fingers, barely even climbing into his wrist. Kaleb bit his lip, worrying if he had done something wrong, and leapt to his feet in search of his father.

"Abba!" he called, standing in the doorway. The urgency in his son's voice sent Vance scrambling down the hall to help.

"What is it? What?" Kaleb stepped aside to let his father see into the room, eyes widening at the sight. He looked to his son, pointing. "Did you...?"

Kaleb rubbed the back of his head. "I thought I might try it, so I did, and there was this huge reaction and now it won't work anymore and-"

"Kaleb, Kaleb!" Vance had to stop his panicked son before he could talk himself blue. "Kaleb, calm down." He looked back to Taylor, then to his son again. "*You* did that?" Kaleb nodded, afraid to speak again if he wanted to keep breathing. Vance held his hands to his forehead, completely amazed. "Wow," he muttered. "I've never seen that before." Kaleb's heart stopped.

"Did I do something wrong?" he asked, being shushed down by his father again.

"I mean I've never seen a reaction that fast," he explained. "I was gone, what, *five* minutes?" He whistled. "I've seen years-long mates who've had to work harder than that!"

Kaleb blinked, confused. "So, he's okay?" he asked. Vance nodded. "I didn't break him," he stated, earning a chuckle from his father.

"He's not broken." He kneeled down to closer inspect Taylor's wounds. He placed his hand on the boy's crest again, closing his eyes to determine a diagnosis. "Yeah, he's still healing," he said, removing his hand. "Just slowly."

Kaleb scratched the back of his head. "Then, why did it happen so fast?" he asked. "And why is it so slow now?"

Vance shrugged. "I have heard studies about stuff like this. Something about built up intentions or something like that, I can't remember." He turned to his son. "Let me see if Trish can pick up some of those documents and we can figure it out from there." Kaleb nodded as his father neared him, patting his shoulder with a smile. "You did good, kid," he grinned, then left the room, calling to his son from down the hall. "I'm going to go tell your mother."

Kaleb sucked in his lips, not knowing how to handle the situation. He decided on sitting back next to the blonde as he had for the last couple days. He was still healing, according to Vance, so if it would help any, Kaleb would lay his hand over Taylor's crest, treating him like his father had shown him for as long as it would take.

Chapter 20

Taylor smiled at the gentle touch of someone playing with his hair, and slowly opened his eyes. There sat Kaleb staring back at him, a small smile on his face as well. The larger man's hand traced down from his blonde hair to caress his cheek, rubbing his thumb over smooth skin. He stared lovingly into Taylor, soaking in the sight of him alive and well in his hands. Kaleb leaned down, staring deep into his eyes as he drew closer to Taylor's face, and placed a gentle, chaste kiss over his closed lids.

Taylor opened his eyes to find Kaleb at his bedside, asleep atop his golden hand along the edge of the bed, with the other draped over the blonde's back, leaving something else unseen touching Taylor.

"Kaleb?" he whispered. "Kaleb," he tried again, then, "Hey, asshole." The bronze boy stirred from his slumber. He instantly awoke, sitting straight at the sight of the smaller boy.

"Taylor!" He quickly pulled his hand away to rub the two of them together. Bubbie popped his head up at Taylor's side, his tail already going crazy. "How do you feel?" Kaleb asked, then quickly snatched a cup of mostly melted ice and held it up. "Thirsty?"

"Who's playing with my hair?" Taylor asked, Kaleb looked up, instantly shooing away Skitters. She looked at him, indignant of his rude intrusion, then got up to stretch and leave. The boy was awake now. Her job was done.

"Sorry," Kaleb said, sheepishly. "Guess she thought you needed a bath." Taylor blinked, trying to push away his dog with his other arm while still lying on his stomach.

"How long have I been here?" he asked, feeling too drained for it to be an eight hour nap. Kaleb rubbed the back of his head, looking away.

"Three days? Maybe four, it's too early for me to think right now."

Taylor sighed, raising his arms to push himself up. "What are you doing?" Kaleb jumped, trying to stop the blonde.

"I've been lying here for four days," Taylor said simply. "I'm pretty sure I need to take a leak."

"Oh," Kaleb bit his lip, rubbing the back of his head and sticking far too close for comfort while Taylor sat himself up along the edge of the bed. Kaleb had to repeatedly push Bubbie away from Taylor, deciding he would take the dog outside once he got a chance. He stood, and held his hands out for Taylor to grab onto, but the blonde pushed them away and tried to stand on his own.

"Shit!" Taylor mumbled, trying to pull himself out of Kaleb's chest and arms after his knees buckled beneath him.

"That's why I'm here," Kaleb said, helping the boy stand as straight as he could. Taylor looked up at Kaleb, clinging to his forearms to keep from falling.

"You're just as bad as your mother," he said, shaking his head.

"What?" Kaleb asked, but Taylor was already taking his first few baby steps towards the door. They slowly made their way out the door and across the hall as best they could with Bubbie trailing after them, then stopped in the doorway.

"What's wrong?" Kaleb asked, receiving a cross look from Taylor.

"It's bad enough that you had to pretty much carry me all the way here just to piss; don't make it any worse."

Kaleb huffed at this, looking down the hall. "Fine, but leave the door unlocked." He compromised. "Just in case."

Taylor closed the door in his face, leaning against the sink and wall as he took baby step after baby step towards the toilet. He didn't trust his legs to stand, no matter how much he leaned against the wall, so he begrudgingly sat to finish his business, irritated with his weak body.

Kaleb took this chance to remove the dog, and rushed him outside as quickly as he could, much to Bubbie's displeasure. He was leaning against the wall across from the door waiting for Taylor when he had finished, and was quick to offer his help once he saw the door opened again. Trish was in the kitchen getting ready for work, but had come around to lean in the hallway to see the commotion, and instantly spurting forward when she saw the blonde head leaving the bathroom.

"Taylor!" She rushed down the hallway to the boys. "Taylor, dear, are you alright?"

"Mom, you're making it harder to walk," Kaleb said, trying to gently push her hands away while holding his arms out for the blonde to grab onto.

"Sorry," Trish breathed, pulling away for a split second before returning her hands to Taylor's face. "How do you feel?"

Taylor gave a small, polite but tired smile while trying to pull his head out of grasp. "I'm fine, Miss Trish," he said. "But I probably need to get back to bed." Trish quickly pulled her hands away.

"Yes, of course!" She turned to retreat down the hall. "I'll go make you some tea!" Taylor grimaced, not wanting to revisit the bitter drink so soon, and especially not now when he had finally gotten back on his feet.

"I'd drink it for you," Kaleb offered. "But you haven't had anything for a few days, and she's probably going to fill it with stuff you need."

Taylor sighed, nodding his head. "Fine. Let's just go."

The boys made it back to the room, setting Taylor on the edge of the bed. Kaleb had stopped him from leaning against his back, but after a snarky complaint of not wanting to stay on his stomach anymore, Kaleb gathered up every pillow in the room to cushion Taylor's back, and had him lean back very, *very* slowly. He also placed the ice pack behind the blonde, making sure it sat in place atop the pillows.

"So," Taylor started. "What happened?"

Kaleb stared at him in disbelief. "Seriously?" he asked. "You don't remember?"

Taylor shrugged, wincing at the movement. "I remember getting hit from behind. After that, everything goes dark." He ticked his head. "I do remember feeling it, though," he muttered, running a hand through his hair. Kaleb's gaze dropped to the floor, not daring to meet with Taylor's. He didn't want to have to explain to Taylor that it was

Gerrit that had beaten him, and he certainly didn't want to tell him that it was *his* fault it happened either.

"You've got that look again," Taylor said, breaking Kaleb from his thoughts.

"What look?"

Taylor's face fell. "The 'something's bothering you' look," he said flatly. "Why don't you want to tell me what happened?"

Kaleb turned away, cursing his open book nature. He rubbed the back of his head. "It was Gerrit," he said quietly. "He came after you because of me."

Taylor sighed, looking away annoyed. "Figures," he muttered. Kaleb looked to the blonde, confused.

"You're not upset?" he asked. Taylor's face crumpled.

"Why would I be? It's Gerrit. You think I'm surprised?"

Kaleb turned away, closing his eyes in anger upon hearing how lightly he said this, as though it were *normal*.

"What about me?" Kaleb stated.

"What *about* you?" Taylor asked.

"Nevermind." Kaleb leaned his head against his fingers.

"Okay," Trish hummed, walking through the door with a fresh, steamy mug, and stopped short when she saw Taylor sitting up. "What are you doing on your back?"

Taylor shrugged, quickly coming up with an excuse. "How else am I going to drink your tea?" Smooth. Trish cocked a brow at him, but settled with the answer and carefully handed the mug over to Taylor.

"You might want to sip it off the spoon at first," she warned him. "It's hot, and I don't want you actually eating or chugging anything just yet."

Taylor took the mug with both hands, setting it down against his lap. "Thank you, Miss Trish." Trish smiled, absolutely giddy at the blonde's resurrection.

"I'm going to go wake your father," she hummed, practically skipping out the door. The boys shared a look, happy for her joy, but hiding a snicker at her expense. Kaleb pointed to the mug.

"You should probably drink that before it gets cold," he said. "Herbal tea doesn't taste that great after it's cooled."

Taylor looked down at the cup, sucking in his lips and tapping the mug before confessing. "I can't pick it up," he muttered. Kaleb couldn't stop his snicker from escaping.

"It's hot."

And heavy. Taylor left that part out. Kaleb shook his head and got up for his closet.

"Here."

The darker man snagged a jacket from a hanger and bundled it in Taylor's lap, cradling the mug safely from spilling.

"Just hold it in your lap and drink from the spoon like mom said." Kaleb told him. "This should at least keep it from tipping over."

Taylor made a face at the mug in his lap. "Thanks."He carefully dipped the spoon into the mug and lifted it to his lips, blowing before taking its contents, and instantly grimaced. "Yeah," he groaned. "I definitely don't like grass water." Kaleb chuckled, pleased that his friend was able to be his normal self so soon after waking.

"Aw, crap," Kaleb mumbled. "I forgot to ask how long it's been."

"Three days," Vace answered, holding up his fingers as he walked through the door. "Going on four." He yawned, scratching the back of his head. "You couldn't have waited a few more minutes? Couple hours maybe?" Trish smacked her husband's shoulder, leaning in to bid her men farewell.

"I have to go to work, but if you need anything, just send me a chat, okay?" She pulled Taylor's head up for a surprise kiss on the forehead. "I'm glad you're okay," she told him, still holding his face. Once she had released the blonde, she kissed the other two men, giving Vance a particularly sweeter kiss, then left the room.

"Gross," Kaleb muttered.

Vance crossed his arms. "Has to be done, son," he said. "Unless you want us to-"

"Enough!" Kaleb stopped him before he could delve further into what he *knew* would disturb his son for hours and tossed a book at Vance, effectively chasing him out of the room. "Go back to bed, pervert!" Kaleb called, hearing a tickled chuckle escaping down the hallway.

Taylor shook his head, taking another sip of tea. He stopped, sniffed his spoon, then sniffed his skin. "Why do I smell like mouthwash?"

"Oh," Kaleb chuckled sheepishly. "Mom put her oils on you. They're pretty effective." He wiggled his fingers to bring Taylor's arm up for a whiff. "I guess she gave you peppermint- and lavender too, that one's pretty decent."

Taylor gave his arm another sniff. "Could be worse," he muttered, then looked to Kaleb. "Shouldn't you be getting ready for school?"

Kaleb sucked in his lips, rubbing the back of his head as he turned away."I'm not allowed," he mumbled. Taylor gave him a scrutinized glare.

"'Not *allowed*?'"

Kaleb kept his hands along the back of his head, keeping his gaze to the wall. "I sort of got kicked out for the week."

Taylor's laughter surprised them both, but he quieted as quickly as it escaped. "How did Little-Miss-Perfect get suspended?" Taylor snickered. Kaleb looked away, tapping his fingers against the back of his neck.

"I beat Gerrit to a pulp."

319

Taylor's snickering ceased, looking straight at the darker man. "Seriously?" he asked quietly. Kaleb nodded, looking at the floor, then lifted his gaze to meet the blonde's.

"He won't be coming around here anytime soon."

Taylor kept the stare for a few moments before retreating to his mug. "Sorry," he muttered.

"Don't be," Kaleb replied. "It's not your fault."

Taylor turned an irritated glimpse to him. "Then why did you pound him?" he asked. Kaleb sighed, shrugging his head.

"I finally saw him for who he really was," he answered.

Taylor's gaze ran back to his mug, suddenly unnerved by keeping eye contact with the older boy now that he realized the fading dark mark on his face *wasn't* a shadow. He took another sip from his spoon, finding it easier to raise the mug now that it was only half full, but a mournful cry from outside stopped his movements.

"What was that?" Kaleb mumbled. The sound repeated, triggering the blonde's memory.

"Where's Bubbie?"

"Oh!"

Kaleb bolted up and ran out of the room to let the dog back inside the house. A few seconds later, a black and white blur bounded onto the bed, wiggling with excitement, and sniffing Taylor excessively to find any extra wounds.

"Easy, easy!" Taylor muttered, fighting off a grin as well as the dog. Kaleb returned a few moments later and sat down at the bedside again, shaking his head at the shepherd.

"He hasn't left your side for days," he said. "Almost bit me a couple of times when I tried to pull him away." Taylor paused his affectionate scrubbing long enough to hold the dog's face to his own.

"Good boy," he cooed.

"Hey!" Kaleb complained, earning a smirk from the blonde.

Taylor shook his head, trying to rid himself of the feeling but giving in to a yawn all the same. "You've got to be kidding me," the blonde snipped.

"You've still got some healing to do," Kaleb offered. "I'm not really surprised to be honest. Besides," he took the smaller boy's mug and sniffed it. "Looks like you were drugged."

Taylor glared at Kaleb. "You knew that from the start, didn't you?" he accused. Kaleb held his hands up, shrugging away from the boy.

"I can neither confirm nor deny this accusation."

The blonde's glare intensified. "So I'm going to have to kill you *and* your mother," he growled, releasing a chuckle from the darker man. Taylor huffed, closing his eyes to the ceiling. "I don't want to go back to sleep," he grumbled, blindly pushing at Kaleb's arm. "Keep me up."

Kaleb shook his head, denying the blonde. "No can do."

"Asshole," Taylor griped, turning his head to look at him. "I'm not lying on my stomach again."

Kaleb shrugged. "Alright, your choice," he sighed. "Just keep off your back." He paused for a moment. "In fact, let me take a look at it real quick."

Taylor gave Kaleb another glare before he leaned forward over his knees, dropping his head to the covers in compliance to the darker man. The larger veins had almost drained away, receding into Taylor's crest little by little, and losing color by the minute. All of the smaller veins had vanished completely, and the bruising behind the vines were barely blue now, not even reaching much further past the outer edges of the blonde's crest.

"Still got a little ways to go," Kaleb mumbled, letting the boy rise back up. "But better. Much better." Taylor scratched his temple, closing his eyes as he spoke.

"You're not going to watch me while I sleep, are you?"

Kaleb pulled back into a stretch. "Nah," he lied. "I thought I might catch some Z's myself."

Taylor glared at him. "You're not planning on sleeping *up there*, right?" he asked, pointing to his own bed. "'Cause, to be honest, I'm afraid you might kill me."

Kaleb scoffed. "I'm not *that* big!" He crossed his arms, nodding to the bed. "Besides, this old thing's a lot stronger than it looks."

"Whatever," Taylor sighed. "I'm on the edge anyway, so if you fall through, I think I'll be safe." He scooted down from his pillows, carefully rolling to his side after throwing a pillow at Kaleb's face. The darker man grinned, but with a careful inspection of the top bunk, his lips turned in for him to bite them instead.

"You know what, I think you're right," he admitted.

"Told you," Taylor remarked, settling in on his side, with Bubbie snuggling close to his stomach. He reached over and slapped the empty side of the bed near the wall, closing his eyes as Bubbie set in beside him. "It's your bed anyway," he mumbled. Kaleb bit his lip, fiddling with the pillow in his hands.

"Nah, you take it," he said. "I'm not real good at sharing beds."

Taylor furrowed his brow in his pillow. "That explains the bunk beds," he muttered, then waved a hand over his shoulder. "Whatever." He dropped his hand over his dog. A small smile escaped Kaleb's lips as he watched the blonde settle in for sleep, then reached up for the comforter on the top bunk and dragged it down to curl up on the floor.

"What *are* you doing?" Taylor asked, eyes still closed and unmoved from his spot in bed.

"Shut up and go to sleep," Kaleb ordered, flinging the blanket over his long legs.

"You're an idiot," Taylor murmured. "There's a couch for soul's sake."

"Yeah," Kaleb settled into his pillow. "But how am I going to hear you asking for help when I'm all the way in the living room?" Taylor snorted.

"You really are worse than your mother."

"Thank you."

Kaleb closed his eyes as he found his comfort spot on the floor, trying to ease his mind for sleep, but was pestered by festering thoughts. What he had been dreaming about when Taylor had startled him awake was now free to bother him, with plenty of silence to fuel his mind. Still, it was just a dream, and he was tired from all his efforts, so he shook his mind clear of unnerving thoughts, and settled into the pillow to sleep like the rest of the household.

Taylor's rehabilitation went on for the next two days, quickly re-adjusting to life back on his feet, despite Trish's efforts to keep him tied to the bed. By the end of the next day, he could walk on his own again, and was eating with the family at the dinner table. The veins had disappeared completely, and the only evidence of Taylor's adventures with Gerrit was a small, fading bruise that wouldn't last much longer. His appetite had returned, and with two ravenous boys in the house, it was hard to keep up sometimes; though Kaleb would often sneak bigger portions onto Taylor's plate when he wasn't looking. As they finished their dinner, and Vance was gathering the dishes, he put on his best, broadest smile as he announced his weekend plans.

"Ready for that camping trip?"

Trish nearly choked on her tea, charging after her husband for even uttering such an idea.

"The kid's back on his feet, we'd already planned on going, and the weather's going to be perfect, so why not?" Vance argued. "Besides, Taylor's never been before, you don't want to take that away from him, do you?" Trish glared at her husband, knowing how she hated the way he phrased that question. "It'll be big-boy-bonding time," he smiled. "Like always."

Kaleb and Taylor shared a look between each other, and silently agreed to make a break for the bedroom before they could be involved in the argument. Vance was on his own in this fight. As they closed the door behind them, Taylor stopped in the middle of the room.

"Oh, shit," he muttered, scrambling for his backpack and pulling out his laptop.

"What's wrong?" Kaleb asked, watching the blonde set up the equipment with blazing speed.

"I'm in for a lecture of my own."

"Should I leave?"

"Ye- no." Taylor turned to him. "Actually, you just might save my ass."

Kaleb shrugged, sitting down on the bed. "Okay?"

Taylor typed furiously over his keys, pulling up his website and instantly receiving a chat request. His screen was soon filled with a nicely dressed woman. A nicely dressed, very irritated woman. She cocked a brow at Taylor, glaring at him from beneath her brow and tapping her finger on the table.

"So you *do* exist," the woman muttered. "And here I'd thought you were dead." Her eyes tightened. "At least that would have been the case if it were six months ago."

Taylor ran a hand through his hair. "Sorry, Beck," he said, growing puzzled. "Where are you?"

The woman looked away, growing even more irritated. "I'm at a coffee shop," she grumbled. Taylor squinted.

"Did you curl your hair?"

The woman's face darkened with a scowl. "No changing the subject; where have you been?"

It was here that Kaleb decided to lean into sight.

"Hi there." He waved. "I'm Kaleb."

The woman blinked, astonished by his sudden appearance. "I see," she muttered, looking to Taylor, who held a finger out to the darker man.

"I've been sick all week and he's here to vouch for me," Taylor explained.

324

Kaleb held up a hand. "I vouch."

"Oh really?" the woman sassed, eyes on Taylor. "He's also here to keep me from yelling at you, I take it?" Taylor began scratching his temple, looking away. "He wouldn't have stopped it. You're just lucky you caught me in public," she growled. "You better thank your lucky stars for that."

"Believe me," Taylor mumbled to himself.

"I'm sorry," Kaleb interjected. "But I didn't catch your name."

The woman flicked some bangs off her glasses and settled back into her seat. "You can call me Nekko."

Kaleb's eyes widened. "*You're* Nekko? Like, Hacker Nekko?"

"Has the boy wonder been talking about me?" she grinned.

"W- uh, no, it's just, I've seen your posts," Kaleb admitted. "I knew you were one of his fans, but I didn't think you two-"

"Can we focus, please?" Taylor interrupted, not wanting to talk about his writing.

"Sorry," Kaleb mumbled. "Nice to finally meet you, Nekko." She dipped her head.

"And you as well, Kaleb."

The golden man crossed his arms over the side of the desk. "So what loser stood you up?" He nodded to her outfit. "Because he obviously missed out."

Taylor looked astoundedly at her. "Are you... Are you on a date?" he asked, disbelieving. The woman huffed, crossing her arms.

"I was *gonna* be," she muttered, nodding to Kaleb. "Caramel Prince was right. Pansy never showed." She took a sip from her coffee and started playing with her scarf.

Kaleb was mulling over his new nickname, but Taylor couldn't take his eyes off her soon enough to join. He had never seen Bekah dressed up like this before, and it was a weird experience to be seeing it now. She had always been wearing her striped sweater and kitty hat, save for the few discussions they'd had in their pajamas. Now she looked like a new kind of beautiful in her seat.

Her skin glowed in the light, fresh with a light layer of makeup that had hardly ever been applied. She had indeed curled her hair, a drastic change from her normally straight line locks, and her kitty hat was nowhere to be seen. She wrapped a soft, red scarf around her neck that complimented her open brown sweater and lacey white blouse, and a delicate chain dangled across her shimmering chest, bearing a simple heart pendant.

"His loss," Kaleb muttered.

She ticked her head, grinning as she lifted her drink. "I know." She took a sip from her drink before humming out to Taylor. "Where's the next chapter?" she asked, nodding to the blonde, who held up a hand.

"I just told you I've been sick all week."

"Ah," she cocked a brow. "But if I know you, and I know I do, you've been squirreling away extra stories since the last time you posted." She readied her cup for another sip, eyes locked on Taylor. "Two weeks ago."

Kaleb rubbed the back of his head. "You *have* been scribbling a lot," he mumbled. Taylor scowled at the both of them.

"This is a conspiracy," he said. "I should have known better than to put you two together."

"Yeah, yeah, Blondie," Nekko waved. "Just get the journal, would you?"

The 'Blondie' turned his frown to Kaleb. "If I get caught in their death match, I'll blame you," he growled, then got up from the chair to sneak his journal out of the living room under the radar of the bickering Evans'. Kaleb chuckled at the moody blonde, settling in for a better position to see the screen.

"He do that a lot?" Nekko asked.

"Do what?" Kaleb turned to her. She pointed at the missing blonde.

"Sass you like that," she said. "Be a jerk a lot?"

"Oh. Yeah," Kaleb grinned, rubbing the back of his head. "But, I don't think he means anything by it. It's just how he is."

A strange look overcame her face. "Right," she murmured, then pushed her glasses up her nose. "Kaleb?" She leaned forward in her seat, crossing her arms over the table. "I need you to hear something and it stays just between us or I'll come down there and rip your throat out myself, got it?"

Kaleb pulled back his lips. "Okay?" He drew in closer to hear what she had to say, locking eyes.

"Kaleb… " She inspected his face, taking a moment to gather her words. "Thank you."

The Caramel Prince became confused. "You're welcome?" he said. "What did I do?"

Nekko flicked her hair from her glasses. "I know he'll never come out and say it," she said. "But Taylor's grateful to you too." She looked to him, square in the eye. "You saved him from that soulless pit, and now I don't have to worry about him."

Kaleb's gaze softened as her words sank in. "I just-"

Nekko shook her head, stopping him. "Don't," she told him. "You have no idea what you've done. Don't play it down."

Kaleb looked to the desk, dropping his eyes from hers. "I did what I had to," he muttered. "I couldn't stand it."

"Same here," Nekko admitted. "But you did something about it."

Kaleb looked to her. "After what I saw before, how could I not?"

She pointed a finger at him. "See, that's why I like you," Nekko told him. "If you were half the jerk you were before, you wouldn't have cared." His eyes widened.

"So he told you-"

"He tells me everything," Nekko said with a grin. "Absolutely everything."

Kaleb sighed, rubbing the back of his head. "Then you know what he must think about me," he grumbled, looking away.

"I did," Nekko said. "Things have changed."

Kaleb looked to her. "He barely likes me enough as it is," he told her. "I'd hate to see what's changed since then."

Nekko chuckled. "Yeah, it was pretty bad," she said. "But he doesn't hate you anymore."

Kaleb smirked at her. "Right."

"It's true!" Nekko rebuttaled.

"I'm guessing he told you that too?" Kaleb snarked, but Nekko shook her head.

"Didn't have to. I can see it."

Kaleb cocked a brow. "Seriously?"

She looked at him, suddenly becoming serious. "We wouldn't be talking right now if he did."

Out of nowhere, the door burst open, and a rushed blonde sneaked in and closed it with his back, staring at the two. He held up his journal for them to see.

"Got it," he muttered. Nekko pointed.

"Type."

"What'll you give me for it?" Taylor bargained.

"If I'm reading your stuff, I'll be too busy to nag you."

Taylor cocked a brow at this proposition, shrugging as he thought it over. "Plotting world domination while I was gone?" Taylor asked, settling down in his seat.

"I was telling him the best way to kill you in your sleep and make it look like an accident." Nekko grinned. Taylor ticked his head.

"Can't kill me yet; haven't finished the story."

Her grin deepened. "That's why you're still breathing."

Again, the door was opened, and instead of a sneaky blonde, it was a victorious father. "Boys," he grinned. "We're going camping."

Trish was still reluctant to let them leave, repeatedly asking Taylor how he felt and warning Vance to take care of her boys. Still, they made it through her mothering and were now riding down a worn, beaten path towards the woods. Vance and Kaleb told Taylor stories of their previous journeys together through the forest, encouraging him to become as excited as they were. After a while, they left the path and drove off-road to dive deeper into the trees. When they finally stopped, they were surrounded by forest, and any trace of mankind was miles away.

The two, more experienced men set up the campsite, teaching Taylor the basics through hands-on learning, and allowing him to follow and watch like a little duckling. They took their time explaining things, how they were done and why, then had him copy what they had already done. Taylor listened and followed as best he could, both out of wanting to learn, and of not wanting to slow down the camp. By the time the tent was up, the fire pit was dug and stocked and the provisions were properly taken care of, the sun was sliding down through the trees, leaving the air cold without its touch. Vance waved the boys over to show Taylor how to light the fire, having Kaleb start it as an example. He had Taylor throw in a bundle of wrapped sage, then handed them each a skewer once it was lit.

"This is how *I* cook," Vance said, shoving a hot dog onto his own skewer and holding it over the fire. The boys copied Vance's gesture, cooking their dinner over the spit as Vance came up with 'life-lessons' for them to remember.

"Always, always, *always* tell a woman she looks pretty," he told them. "Especially when they're not expecting it, because I can guarantee you, it will make her day." He looked to his hot dog over the fire, smiling. "And if you can make her feel pretty when she's not wearing any makeup, then you can bet, she'll be smiling all day long."

Taylor removed his dinner from the fire, thinking back to all the times Kaleb had complimented any girl at school. The students, the teachers, it didn't matter; he would tell them what he found beautiful on them, and they would all smile and blush, happy to be given such a kind word from the king. Before, Taylor had thought it to be simple flirtations, or a way to butter up the teachers, but hearing Vance now, it changed his mind.

Being around Kaleb for the past few months had also altered the blonde's thoughts about it. Kaleb wasn't the kind of man who offered empty words. As they finished their fill of hot dogs and fruit, Kaleb helped Vance drag a large, fallen branch that could have passed for a tree itself to the fire.

"It'll be cold tonight," Vance said. "If we keep the fire going, we should be fine." He grinned. "And if we still have some coals left over in the morning I can put those orange peels to good use."

Taylor was sent to prepare the sleeping bags while the father and son prepped the fire and made sure it wouldn't escape the pit. As he entered the tent, Taylor found it difficult to see anything without the light of the fire, and nearly tripped over a sleeping bag.

"Careful," Kaleb chuckled, coming to the blonde's rescue.

"I'm fine," Taylor muttered. He dropped to his hands and knees to lay out the bags. Kaleb snickered at his blindness, and knelt to grab a water jug from the floor. He strapped a headlamp to it, pointing the bulb towards the water, and switched it on, effectively lighting the entire tent.

"Cool, huh?" Kaleb grinned, seeing Taylor's eyes widen at the trick. Kaleb smacked a cube shaped bag. "Use these on the floor before you lay down the sleeping bags. Trust me. The foam will help." With that, he left the blonde to help his father, and Taylor set to work laying down the padding over the floor before unraveling the sleeping bags.

"Good work, men," Vance rumbled playfully as he entered the tent. "You've done your manhood some good." Kaleb looked down at his lap, nodding.

"Yep." He looked up. "He's happy."

Taylor scowled at the darker man, shaking his head in disgust. "And you thought *he* was bad," the blonde grumbled, jerking a thumb at a snickering Vance. The men turned off the water lamp and settled into their sleeping bags, joking and laughing with each other for a little while longer before nodding off to sleep.

Kaleb's tongue was incredible. He expertly maneuvered around in Taylor's mouth, bringing soft moans as they tangled in each other. Deeper, stronger, longer; the magnificent touch was ecstasy, leaving him wanting more. The blonde threaded his fingers through black hair, yanking their embrace apart in order to breathe, but leaving delicious, hot pants over his lips as they barely grazed over each other. Kaleb took this opportunity to attack the smaller man's neck, leaving a thin, warm layer over porcelain skin that sent his lover into shivers as the darker man blew over it.

Taylor jolted awake, unable to move. He curled tighter into his sleeping bag, thankful for once for the cold, but stopped short when he found himself pinned. Wrapped around his waist were a set of arms clinging to him tightly, connected to a face buried deep into his back. Taylor rose from his bed as best he could, making it up on his elbows and turning to see who it was and why they were grabbing him. He froze when he saw Kaleb, fast asleep and nestled at his waist as though he were cuddling a teddy bear. A lump formed in the blonde's throat, hoping beyond hope that it was cold enough to hide his problem, but finding it *fairly* warm thanks to Kaleb's embrace.

Another body stirred beyond Kaleb, showing Vance's head pop up into sight, squinting away the morning light. His eyes fell on the two boys next to him, noticing the cuddle puddle. Taylor looked to him, wide eyed and unable to give him a plausible reason, but Vance merely sighed.

"I knew it," he mumbled. He poked his son, trying to wake him. "Kaleb."

"Mmrph." The dark man remained unmoving.

"Kaleb," Vance tried again, poking harder and speaking a bit louder this time, but the reaction was the same, if only slightly louder, and more annoyed. The father sighed, snagging his son's abandoned pillow and dropping it over Kaleb's head.

331

"What?!" Kaleb growled, eyes still closed and arms still wrapped around Taylor.

"Wake up, Kaleb," Vance told him.

"Mmrph."

Vance slammed the pillow over Kaleb once more, causing his son to sit up and turn to him. "What?!" he hissed. Vance straightened his face, seeing his son had not noticed his predicament just yet.

"Sleep well?"

Kaleb sighed, rolling his eyes as he turned back to nestle into his pillow, only to find a pair of hips. His eyes rose up to Taylor's, instantly pulling away from the blonde. Taylor couldn't help it.

"I do make a good pillow, but you have your own right there."

Vance belt out an enormous laugh, falling back to his bed to let the air escape his lungs as his son scrambled for an apology before Taylor could slip out of the tent. He followed the blonde to the campfire, rubbing the back of his head.

"I told you I don't share beds well," Kaleb mumbled, but Taylor ignored him, leaning into the mouth of the tent to Vance.

"You said you wanted to do something with these?" Taylor asked, holding up a bag of hollowed out orange peels. Vance grinned, shoving his chuckling down for the moment and exiting the tent to make breakfast.

"Picked up this trick from an old war buddy of mine," he told them, stuffing the shells with dough. Once each shell was filled, Vance wrapped them in tinfoil and threw them into the coals. Vance nodded to the cooler. "Grab the meat for me, will you?"

Breakfast was a delightful blend of orange flavored biscuits and rosemary seasoned hash, making Taylor wonder how such a man who had burned down a kitchen could make such a meal. As the food was close to being finished, Vance dropped a tied up coffee filter into a pitcher and placed it over the fire, brewing himself some coffee that smelled incredible.

"Wanna try some?" Vance offered, pouring him a mug. Taylor took the offered mug, smelling the eye-opening aroma before taking a tentative sip. "If it's too strong for you, you can always add some cream or sugar," Vance told him, but Taylor shook his head.

"It's good."

"What?" Kaleb exclaimed. "You won't drink grass water but you'll drink boiled beans?" Taylor shrugged, taking another sip from his mug. Kaleb turned away, arms in the air. "Unbelievable." This earned another chuckle from his father. The men ate their meal through stories and laughter with Vance poking fun at how Kaleb had been caught as a cuddler and how he had always been one, even as a child.

"It was cold!" Kaleb complained.

"That's what you said last summer," Vance quipped, releasing a snort from the blonde.

"Whatever," Kaleb grumbled, ridding his plate in the garbage.

"Hrm!" Vance couldn't speak with coffee in his mouth. "Let me see your knife." Kaleb dug out his blade from his back pocket, obeying his father. Vance held it up, eyeing Taylor.

"Another lesson for you, kid." He was still watching the blonde. "Take good care of your tools." He switched open the blade, showing Taylor how sharp and clean it was. "Believe it or not, this knife is at least eight years old." Vance reached behind him, pulling out his own knife and opening it. "This one's over twenty."

Taylor inspected each blade, finding not a nick, nor a scratch, and as clean and sharp as the day it was made. Kaleb handed his father an apple as the man pocketed his blade, then sliced the apple in half with Kaleb's knife.

"You take care of your tools, and they'll take care of you." Vance carefully halved the apple as he spoke. "Because you never know where you'll use it next." He smiled, handing a half to each boy before cleaning the blade free of any juices.

Taylor bit down into the apple, considering Vance's words and thinking back to when that same knife had been used to free him of some troublesome tape. Were it not for Kaleb's knife, it would have been much more difficult to remove the binding that was wrapped around his head, and it would have been even more irritating if the blade were dulled. He looked to Kaleb, spying the darker man munching on his apple half, and wondering what else Vance had taught him. Taylor stared down at his apple half, wondering what his *own* father had taught him over the years, and finding it hard to remember.

A rustling in the leaves caught his eye, pausing the blonde's movements for a moment. The rustle repeated, forcing Taylor to rise from his seat to investigate.

"What do you see, kid?" Vance asked, watching the boy close in on the ruckus. Kaleb went to follow the blonde, wanting to see as well. Taylor kneeled beneath a tree, carefully moving aside a few fallen leaves and found a tiny, red bird; frozen on the spot at the sight of the two boys.

"A bird?" Kaleb commented, tilting his head in confusion. "It's a little cold for them to be here, isn't it?" Taylor shook his head.

"It's a cardinal," he explained. He looked up along the tree, finding the crevice he knew to be near. "Go get a box," Taylor muttered, still looking to the tree. "Small and cardboard if you can."

Kaleb ran back to the firepit in search of the requested item while Taylor turned his attention to the bird. It wasn't a baby, but it wasn't fully grown either, and certainly not ready to fly. Kaleb returned with a long, rectangular box that held their sodas.

"Here." He handed it to Taylor, allowing him to work.

"Gimme your knife," The blonde ordered, then sliced off the end of the box to make a small container, and set the rest of it on the ground. Very carefully, Taylor knelt down and scooped up the bird in the tiny box he had created, making sure he never touched the beast, then handed it to Kaleb.

"Don't move, and don't touch," Taylor demanded. Kaleb nodded, watching the blonde climb up the tree and swing his leg over a thick branch. He leaned down to reach for the bird, slowly raising the box tree level to the nest, and slid the bird back home with his brothers and sisters. Taylor slid down the tree and landed quietly next to the darker man, his mouth open in amazement.

"You're a pro," Kaleb gaped. Taylor wiped his hands, heading for camp. "You sure they'll be okay?" the darker man asked, following close behind.

"Yeah," Taylor mumbled. "Cardinals are winter birds. They're bred for this stuff." Kaleb chuckled.

"First Bubbie and Skitters, then those birds- you must be an animal tamer or something." Taylor scoffed, finding his seat next to a grinning Vance. "Where'd you learn all that stuff?" Kaleb asked, making Taylor think for a moment. A smile hid behind his eyes as he recalled his lessons in caring for animals, wild or tamed and opened his mouth to speak.

"From my father."

Chapter 21

Trish greeted the men home with open arms, silently inspecting each boy for any damages as she held them, then sent them off to the showers to rid them of the nature smell. Taylor relished in the water, grateful for its heat as it ran down his body. He stayed a few more minutes than usual, enjoying the feeling of the water for a little while longer before getting out. As he toweled off, he inspected his crest in the mirror, finding nothing out of the ordinary. He nodded, satisfied with his healing then reached for his clothes.

In his haste to get clean, however, Taylor had forgotten to bring his change of clothes into the bathroom with him, and would now have to bolt across the hall hoping Trish wouldn't see his half naked body. He sighed, irritated with himself, then peeked out through the door. With no sign of the woman, or any other soul for that matter, Taylor snuck into the bedroom across from him, leaning against the door to close it.

Taylor sighed, relieved this time, then headed over to the desk chair where his clean clothes had been forgotten. He righted his briefs beneath the towel, as well as his pants, then removed it from his waist to scrub down his hair. Behind him, the door clicked open, forcing the blonde to rip his head out of the towel.

"Sorry!" Kaleb backed into the doorframe and nearly closed himself in the door trying to back away so quickly, effectively banging both sides of his head before succeeding in his escape. Taylor tilted his head, confused at the darker man's sudden surprise.

Taylor had been covered for the most part, leaving only his top half unclothed, but the way the older man had acted, it was as though he had caught the blonde completely naked. Kaleb's curious nature didn't start there, though. Ever since he had woken around Taylor's waist, he had been a bit more skittish around the smaller man than usual. Flinching at any touch, dancing away when they ended up next to each other; he had even been stiff as a board on the drive home from camp, choosing to look out the window instead of talking.

Taylor shook his head, finding it odd that the strange boy would be embarrassed now after all the stupid things he had done in the past. Still, Kaleb was an enigma; never giving a clear answer to Taylor no matter how hard he looked. A knock on the door came this time before Kaleb even dare enter.

"You dressed?" he asked through the door.

"Get in here, asshole," Taylor snarked, buttoning the last button on his shirt. The darker man sheepishly poked his head inside, stepping into the room but unable to keep eye contact.

"I just needed to grab my stuff," Kaleb mumbled, rubbing the back of his head.

"For soul's sake, man, I'm not a girl," Taylor snipped. "It's not that big a deal."

Kaleb shrank, nodding his understanding to the blonde, but still unable to look at him. He snagged his clothes from the closet, then made a quick retreat for the bathroom. Taylor shook his head, wondering what was wrong with that boy.

The blonde started down the hall towards the kitchen, but stopped short when he heard the distressed mewling of Skitters and scratching. He turned in search of the source, finding the noise growing louder with each step he took. He made it to the end of the hall and checked the door leading to Vance's garage, not seeing Skitters after he opened the door, then slowly backtracked, listening for the cat's next round of pleading.

A sudden, loud scratch attack on the locked door to the storage room stopped the blonde as he was passing it. How Skitters had managed to get inside the room puzzled Taylor, unless the door had been recently opened. He tested the handle, finding it turn in his hand, and creaked open the door just enough to let the cat out. Skitters rushed past Taylor's feet, bounding down the hall to the living room and nearly tripping Vance.

"Woah!" he chuckled, turning to find Taylor holding onto the handle. "Hey, why don't you grab something to eat?" he smiled, heading towards the boy. Taylor suddenly felt very cramped as the man came toward him, closing the door and brushing past Vance for some fresh air out of the hallway.

He took a deep breath as he entered the kitchen, sending away his nerves while he searched for a glass. The way Vance had started down the hall towards him made the blonde shiver, feeling the same sense of dread he had felt with his own father. He filled his glass with water from the tap, then downed half of it in one go. Something unsettling was in that room, and the Evans family didn't want him knowing what it was.

"You ready?" Kaleb asked, staring up at the intimidating building with the blonde.

"It's just another day," Taylor shrugged, walking towards the entrance. Kaleb swallowed hard, watching the recovered man before him.

"I sure hope so," he mumbled, following Taylor inside the school. Kaleb held his pockets close to him as they entered the building, staying near his friend as they wove through traffic. A hush fell over the crowd, sending them into a state of whispers while eyes burned through the two boys as they walked, watching their every move.

"Just another day, huh?" Kaleb muttered to the blonde, who merely brushed him off.

Daniel and Jason pushed through the crowd and stood before the two, stopping the friends from entering the cafeteria. Taylor paused, silently waiting for them to speak, while Kaleb tensed, watching his former teammates closely.

"So you're alive then?" Jason griped, arms crossed.

"We thought you were dead," Daniel said more quietly.

"I'm tougher than I look," Taylor told them simply.

Daniel rubbed his arm, looking silently to the floor, while Jason eyed Taylor up and down. "Guess so," he muttered.Jason's glare scrutinized the blonde. "Why are you living with Kaleb?" he demanded quietly. Taylor returned his glare plainly.

"Is it any of your business?" he asked flatly. Jason turned his eyes to his former captain, receiving only a hardened nod of agreement with the smaller man next to him. His eyes studied them, switching between the two men until he finally left his attention on Kaleb.

"You talk to Gerrit?" Jason asked, hardening Kaleb's face even further.

"Not for a while, no," he said calmly.

Jason took a breath, still eyeing his former captain. "That was a pretty shitty thing to do," he said, eyes locked on Kaleb. The former captain opened his mouth to speak but was interrupted. "Gerrit shouldn't have done that."

"We all think so," Daniel chipped in before being overshadowed by Jason again.

"You still shouldn't have beat the crap out of him," he griped.

Kaleb looked Jason right in the eye. "What would you have done?"

Jason frowned, eyes still locked onto Kaleb's. He huffed, looking away for a second before finally answering.

"Probably the same thing."

For the rest of the day, Taylor and Kaleb were surrounded by whispers. Taylor sat through it, unbothered by the gossip, while Kaleb shifted in his seat, constantly wondering what was being said about him, but Taylor's problem was the newfound attention.

A handful of students would walk up to his desk every now and then, asking him if he was alright, if they could do anything for him, or what he could tell them. Their presence was far too cumbersome and strange for his comfort, making him wish he could use his invisibility techniques in real life. The whole ordeal made him rather cranky, and snippy with people by the end of the day.

"Are you alri-"

"I'm fine!" Taylor snapped, making Kaleb chuckle. "This isn't funny," he griped.

"It's hilarious." Kaleb grinned. "You're finally popular."

Taylor hiked his pack over his shoulders. "Whoever said I wanted to be?" he grumbled, marching out of the laboratory in annoyance. "You coming or what?" he called from the hall.

"Go on ahead," Kaleb told him. "I need to see Kara."

Taylor huffed, still marching to the double doors. "Whatever. See you later, asshole."

Kaleb shook his head, finding the blonde's irritation to be humorous, if not charming. He packed up his things and set towards his friend in the Art department, hoping she could give him an answer to his problem.

"You're still here?" Kara asked, wiping her hands clean on a filthy rag.

"It's not that late," Kaleb told her. "Taylor was too annoyed to go past his homework today, so we finished early." Kara nodded, sitting at her table.

"So what brings you to my my station?" she asked, leaning against the table.

Kaleb sat across from her, frowning. "I don't really know," he admitted. "I just haven't been myself lately."

She looked to her friend. "How so?"

Kaleb shrugged. "I don't know. I've been having these nightmares, I guess."

"What happens that makes you so upset?" she asked, making Kaleb quiet. He thought for a moment, wondering how he could explain it to her.

"It's just," he started. "I'm not myself when I have them. What I do is so out of character for me, it makes me wonder why I'm having these dreams at all."

Kara quirked her lips, pondering her friends words. "I don't know what to tell you, Kaleb," she said finally. "The dream world and the real world are two completely separate places. I guess, all you can do is just learn to live with it, and know that that's not what you're really like in real life."

Kaleb sighed, not happy with the answer he had been given. "I guess so."

Kara smirked at her friend, looking up at him from beneath her brow.

"They're only dreams, Kaleb."

Kaleb found Taylor laying upside down on the couch, hanging his feet over the back and holding his head at the cushion.

"Long day?"

Taylor frowned beneath his hands. "You know damn well what my day was like," he grumbled.

Kaleb slipped off his layers and hung them on the rack by the door. "It wouldn't hurt you to be a *little* more social," he said, walking over to lean against the couch. Taylor peeked at him from beneath his arms.

"It's caused me enough trouble already, thank you," the blonde snipped. He sighed, righting himself on the couch and waiting for the headrush to go away before standing to leave. "I need a book," he mumbled.

Kaleb snickered. "That's one way of dealing with it I guess."

"Gets my mind off of things," Taylor told him, searching the line of bookcases around the living room. "Don't you have the latest issue of Richard Kason's Throne Room?" Taylor asked. "I thought I saw it around here somewhere."

Kaleb stepped away from the couch, waving for the blonde to follow him to the bedroom. "I didn't know you liked Richard Kason," Kaleb said, kneeling down next to his desk.

"He's a good writer. It's kind of hard not to."

The darker man retrieved the sought out novel and turned to hand it to the blonde, but a bang in the front room caught them off guard.

"KALEB!" Gerrit shouted, apparently slamming the door against the wall when he entered. "I know you're in here! I just saw you come in!"

Kaleb rose to face the intruder, but Taylor shoved up against him, ramming them into the closet and closing the door behind them.

"What are you-"

Taylor smothered Kaleb's mouth with his hand, stopping the words from escaping. "I don't want to deal with him right now," he hissed.

Bubbie barked at the invader from the backyard, frustrated at the inability to defend the house from outside while the danger barged around inside. Angry stomping charged into Kaleb's room, searching for the owner.

"If you're out with that stupid Tommy, I swear..."

Thudding and clanking resounded against each other as Gerrit ransacked the room, tossing everything in sight out of order, and into chaos. "Stupid son of a *bitch*!"

Kaleb frowned against Taylor's hand and pushed forward to open the door, but Taylor grabbed his hand on the knob, silently pleading him to resist. Kaleb looked down at the blonde, pressed so close to him now thanks to the lack of space, and searched his eyes.

Taylor wasn't frightened, from what Kaleb could see; there wasn't any fear at all. He looked more like wanting to hide a secret than of running away. His eyes were wide with unease, begging Kaleb not to expose the two hidden in the closet, but there was something else as well. The darker man tried to figure out what it was, but was distracted by the sight. For once, he was able to keep perfect eye contact with him, and saw the bright crystals that resided in Taylor's irises, noticing for the first time just how incredibly blue they were.

"Bastard!" Gerrit growled, finally leaving Kaleb's room to search for him elsewhere. Kaleb stared down at the blonde beneath him, still locked behind his hands. Taylor looked up at him in return, waiting to hear Gerrit leave the house before daring to even move. A rage-filled scream roared out in the living room before the slamming of the front door. The two men stayed in the closet for a few moments longer, staring at each other to let their heart beats level out again.

Finally, Taylor lowered his hand from Kaleb's mouth, resting it over his own chest as he looked to the larger man before him. Kaleb's fingers twitched beneath the handle, reminding himself that they were being trapped under the blonde's hand.

"Sorry." Taylor tried to pull his hand away, but had managed to tangle his fingers around Kaleb's, trapping two of them in place.

Taylor kept his eyes on Kaleb's, finding himself as captured as the darker man before him. His breath stopped, still silenced by the attack from Gerrit, but he took a breath to speak, regardless of what his brain told him.

" ... You have really nice brown eyes..."

Kaleb blinked, surprised by the sudden compliment. "I was going to say the same for you," he whispered back. Taylor squinted slightly, looking almost confused.

"My eyes are blue."

Kaleb released a sigh, closing his eyes with a grin. "So they are," he muttered.

"Um..." Taylor crumpled his shirt with his free fingers. "I can't move my hand."

"Oh!" Kaleb released the door knob long enough to free the connected fingers, then opened the door to release the boys. The room was a complete mess. Books were strewn around in the strangest of places, and the comforters and pillows were ripped from the beds and thrown to the ground. Drawers were pulled out from the desk and dumped over the floor, and the chair had been toppled over near the door.

"He doesn't control his anger very well, does he?" Taylor asked, staring at the mess. Kaleb sighed, rubbing the back of his head.

"I really hope he didn't rip any of my books."

The two set to work righting the room again, taking the time to inspect any damages done to their belongings. The books were once again piled around the room in neat stacks, and the beds were made proper, one at a time. The nickknacks in the drawers were gathered and replaced, but one trinket paused Kaleb as he knelt on the floor to pick it up.

"This yours?" Kaleb asked, holding up the broken dog tags Taylor had kept. Taylor reached out to take it from Kaleb, but the older boy retracted to investigate further. "Looks like he broke it." Kaleb said, handing it to the blonde. "We can get another chain if you'd like."

Taylor shook his head. "I broke it at home," he told him. "No need for a replacement." Kaleb gave him a curious look.

"Why keep it then?"

Taylor looked down to the tags in his hand, thinking back to the day he had found it in his pack. "I don't know," Taylor said quietly. "You're right."

Kaleb pulled back in astonishment. "Excuse me, I don't think I heard you right." He grinned. "*What* did you just say?"

Taylor glared at the darker man, turning away from him to drop the charm into the trash, then left the room. Taylor let Bubbie inside from the backyard, greeting the dog as he rushed inside to warm himself back up and to run ahead into the house to smell for any more intruders while the blonde plopped down on the couch, leaning back his head to close his eyes. Kaleb came to sit next to him, watching the boy.

"You forgot this." Kaleb grinned at him, holding up a book. Taylor kept his eyes shut, ignoring the darker man. Kaleb set the book down in his own lap, scratching his head.

"Can I ask you why?" he asked. "Why you wanted to avoid him?"

Taylor sighed, straightening his head to look forward, averting eye contact. "I just didn't want to deal with him," Taylor said. "What good would it do to get kicked out for another week, anyway?"

Kaleb looked to his friend. "What?" he asked, but Taylor snatched the book.

"Whatever," he grumbled. "Do whatever you want."

Kaleb grinned. "You were trying to-"

"Shouldn't you be doing your chores?" the blonde interrupted. "Go feed the cat or something." Taylor flipped open the book to stare intently at the pages, pausing a moment to flip it right-side-up.

Kaleb chuckled, rising to do as he was told. He left for the kitchen, shaking the container to call for his pet, but the silver feline was no where in sight. Kaleb cocked his head over the bar, searching for Skitters, but not finding her. He poured her food into her bowl and laid it on the floor, then left to look for her. The master bedroom was empty, as well as his mother's office, both bathrooms and his room.

"Skitters?" Kaleb called. "Where'd she go?"

"Probably locked in the storage room again," Taylor muttered from his book. "She goes in there every chance she can get."

Kaleb looked to the boy, considering the idea, then checked the door. Out came Skitters, just as Taylor had predicted, running straight for her bowl. Kaleb locked the door again, then made his way down the hall.

"If you knew she was in there, you should have let her out." Kaleb leaned against the couch as he spoke.

Taylor flipped a page, keeping his eyes on the book. "You guys get jumpy when I go near it," he explained. "I mean, good grief, I can't even bring it up without your mother tensing up."

Kaleb stared at the blonde, realizing what he had said to be true, and scolding himself for even thinking they could pull one over on someone as smart as Taylor. He looked to the floor, gripping the couch.

"I'm sorry," he said quietly. The blonde shrugged, still looking to his book.

"Don't be," Taylor said. "If you don't want to tell me, that's your business. I have no right barging in."

Kaleb looked to the boy. "But you do have a right to know."

Taylor grimaced in his book. "If it's your family's secret-"

"It's my secret," Kaleb said quietly. This brought those blue eyes to Kaleb, staring back at him cautiously. "It's mine, and it's about time you know."

Kaleb leaned away from the couch and headed for the storage room once again, while Taylor flipped the book closed and followed silently after. Kaleb was strangely quiet as they neared the locked door, making Taylor slightly nervous. As they approached, Kaleb stretched a hand over the door frame, finding the key hiding atop it, and shrugging to a bemused blonde.

"Sometimes obvious is the best disguise."

Kaleb turned to slide the key through the lock. He paused for a moment, taking a breath before opening the door and stepping through. Kaleb stepped aside to let Taylor in and take in the view, silently watching the blonde as he looked about the room.

It was small, easily turned into an office if needed, and had a light lavender paint to the walls. A loveseat sat in front of a television, sectioning off part of the room to be used as a viewing section. Desks and filing cabinets leaned against the walls, neatly holding picture frames filled with medals from different sections of the military, and different honors to go with them. Certificates hung along the walls next to pictures of Trish and Vance in formal uniform, their status displayed next to them as well, and newspaper articles were preserved in freshly polished frames; one of which bore the picture from the living room that had previously caught Taylor's eye. The blonde looked to Kaleb, finding nothing out of the ordinary with the room.

"Look closer," Kaleb told him, leaning against the couch. Taylor took a few more steps inside, further inspecting the pictures and articles. He picked up one picture displayed on the desk, looking closely at its occupants. Trish and Vance were in the desert again, kneeling with two, small children, smiling for the camera, and holding them close. They were dark skinned, and had black hair and brown eyes. Taylor squinted, finding uncanny similarities.

"Is this you?" he asked, turning to Kaleb who reached out for the picture.

"That's me," he said. "And that's my sister. Twins." Taylor looked to him, astonished by this.

"Where…"

Kaleb shook his head with a sad smile, looking to the blonde. "Little girls and landmines don't mix." He looked around the room. "This would have been her room. If she had made it back with us."

Taylor looked to the floor, running a hand through his hair. "I'm sorry."

Kaleb gave another small smile. "I've shed my tears. What was it you said? 'What's done is done, leave it in the past.'"

Taylor took the picture, studying it again. "Why were you there in the first place?" Taylor asked. "A battlefield is no place for a child."

Kaleb nodded, crossing his arms. "That picture?" He nodded to it. "That was to commemorate the first day we met."

Taylor looked to Kaleb, silenced. The darker man stared back at his friend, staying just as quiet. "If you've ever wondered why my parents look so young, it's because they are," he said quietly. "Dad's around thirty-seven and mom-" He scratched his head. "She can't be more than thirty-six." He looked to the blonde, replacing his arms over his chest. "We met when they were in their twenties, and after my sister died, Trish wouldn't leave me behind."

"What about your real parents?" Taylor asked quietly.

"They had died long before." Kaleb took the picture to look at it as well. "Acane and I needed the money, and helping soldiers kept you from picking up a gun yourself. Abba and Abi took us in right away, and we ran errands for them while they worked on wounded from the war."

Taylor leaned against the couch next to Kaleb. "Abba and Abi?"

"Trish and Vance," Kaleb explained. "Acane told me they were husband and wife, so that's what we called them. Husband and Wife." Taylor glimpsed at Kaleb.

"So that was her name? Acane?"

Kaleb nodded.

"And what about..." Taylor dropped his gaze to the floor, gripping the couch behind him. Kaleb looked at the blonde, watching him struggle, then lightly elbowed Taylor's ribs to gain his attention.

"My name was Kalabne," Kaleb answered. "My name *is* Kalabne." Taylor stared up at the darker man in silence.

"Kalabne Petra." Kaleb turned back to the picture. "And Acane Petra." He lowered his voice. "Akenian orphans of the war." He turned his gaze back to Taylor with a small, tired smile. "Now you know."

Taylor swallowed, not knowing what to do with this information, and there were still so many questions he wanted to ask, but didn't want to press too far, nor did he know where to begin. Kaleb chuckled, rounding the couch.

"Sit down," he said. "It's a long story."

Taylor sat diligently as he listened to Kaleb explain how Trish and Vance *Saunders* had stolen Kaleb after his sister had died, and how they were deserters of the war. The Alterian military refused to let them take Kaleb home with them, forcing the young couple to sneak back to their homeland in secret. When they had returned to Alteria, the Saunders' had to get rid of their old life and start over so as not to be caught, fearing they would lose Kaleb if that happened.

They emptied their bank accounts, changed their names to Evans, and fled their hometown in search of a new city to raise their stolen child. With their parents gone, and no siblings of their own, it was all too easy, but readjusting to life in the colonies was an all too new experience for young Kalabne.

"When I first saw how green it was, I was shocked," Kaleb said. "Plant life is sacred in Akenya because of the lack of water, so gardens were meant for those with money." He chuckled. "So when I saw an empty field as soon as I got off the boat, I looked to mom and asked her if we had landed on a king's land." He grinned and pointed to the back wall.

"That's also why my garden is so big," he explained. "I had found some flowers once and wanted to show them to mom, but when she saw them, she picked them, and I threw such a fit because I thought she killed them. The only way she could calm me down was to tell me that we could replant them- I never knew it was so easy here." He shrugged. "Ever since, whenever we pick something, we plant it."

Kaleb went on to explain how finding River Hill had been a complete accident. The town was so small, it didn't even register on the map. When they passed through the town on their way to another city, they knew this would be their new home. They had to work together to readjust to their new way of living. With no experience as parents, and still thriving in their twenties, the Evans' had to figure out a way to raise Kaleb, as well as make him feel at home when he was so far away from his deserts.

The way they spoke was completely different, leaving Kaleb with a weird speech pattern and a new vocabulary to learn. They had improved their communications back in the desert, but his accent was thick, and strange.

Compliments were oddly given, and insults were also different in this new land. Kaleb never knew when he was being picked on, nor why people became so confused when he would lash out at their choice of words. Somehow, the Evans' always found a way to explain Kaleb's behavior without raising any red flags, and would later teach Kaleb what their words really meant.

"Dad didn't know what to call me when we were in front of people," Kaleb said. "They both would find any other name to use while we were in front of people so that I wouldn't be found out." He shrugged. "It wasn't until we moved here that I found my new name." He looked to Taylor. "Believe it or not, it was Gerrit who gave it to me."

Taylor blinked, stunned. Kaleb grinned, thinking back. "He said my name was too hard, so he just called me Kaleb. After that, I went home and told my parents. I was so excited to have been given an Alterian name from a real-live Alterian boy my age; I demanded that they call me that from then on." He grinned again, scratching his head. "To be honest, I think it was a relief for them."

He stopped for a moment, realizing something. "Come to think of it, I think that's how we became friends in the first place." He snickered to Taylor. "I was the only kid who could pronounce his name right the first time."

"Because everyone tried to call him Jared?" Taylor asked.

"Yeah." Kaleb snickered. "I take it you did too?"

Taylor ticked his head. "Kind of hard not to." He turned back to the Akenian. "What about Trish? Didn't she want kids of her own? No offense."

Kaleb shook his head. "None taken," he said. "But they tried. They tried for a really long time. After about a year, they found out that she couldn't have kids." He looked away. "I was kind of glad when I found out." He started picking at his fingers. "It's a kid thing, of course. I was worried they'd forget about me if they had a baby of their own, but then I saw mom." He softened his voice.

"She was devastated. Wouldn't eat for days and just laid in bed all day. So, one day, I made her a cup of tea and took some crackers from the cupboard and brought them to her." He waved his hands in a passing thought. "It's a comforting thing back in the deserts," he explained. "But I brought it back to her room and got up on the bed with her. I looked her right in the eyes and said, 'Mom, next time my friends come over, you can take care of them too.'"

He grinned in thought. "She told me later that that was the first time I called her mom instead of Abi." He looked to the blonde, taking in air to fuel his words. "After that, mom started having tea with me, and every time my friends came over, she would always chip in ideas for us to have fun."

Taylor readjusted in his seat, finding a more comfortable position. "You said Abi means 'wife,' right?" he asked. "And, what was the other one, Ava? That means 'husband', yeah?"

Kaleb chuckled. "Abba," he corrected. "Ava means something completely different." Taylor looked to him, confused. "It means 'bird heart.'"

Taylor looked away. "That *is* a switch," he mumbled, bringing a chuckle from the darker man. "What other words do you know?"

Kaleb leaned back, scratching his head in thought. "I grew up speaking Akenish, but it's been so long since I've used it fluently that I'd probably mess up a lot if I tried." He ticked his head. "I'm *sure* I have an accent now."

Taylor shrugged. "It's not like I would hear it. Tell me what you know."

Kaleb looked to the blonde. "Like what?"

Taylor shrugged again. "I don't know, like…" He thought for a moment. "Do your names mean something? You and your sister's?"

Kaleb belted into laughter at this, surprised by this question.

"It's not that big a deal," Taylor grumbled.

"I know, I'm sorry," Kaleb wheezed. "I just wasn't expecting it is all." He rubbed at an eye, calming his laughter. "Acane's soul crest was in the shape of a bird with its wings spread open wide, so she was named after it; 'beautiful bird.'" Kaleb grinned. "Kalabne roughly translates to 'curious scholar,' and Petra is just a regular family name; it doesn't mean anything."

Taylor snickered, turning away from the other man.

"What?" Kaleb asked.

Taylor turned back to him. "'Curious scholar?' Your parents pegged you perfectly."

Kaleb grinned at this. "I guess you're right."

"What about your parents?" Taylor asked. "What were their names?"

Kaleb paused a moment, trying to think back to his birthplace, and finding the memory hazy. "I don't remember," Kaleb said. "I guess it's been too long." Taylor looked away, suddenly uncomfortable.

"How about me?" he asked, looking to the wall.

"What about you?"

Taylor turned back to the boy. "What name would you give me? Unless Taylor means something."

Kaleb looked to the blonde, considering the idea, and wondering if he should speak it. A slow grin spread across his face as he decided to answer. "Teahnu."

"Teahnu…" Taylor tasted the name on his lips. "What does that mean?" Kaleb's grin grew wider.

"'Angry white boy.'"

Taylor whipped a sofa pillow out from behind him and slammed it across a giggling Kaleb. "See? There!" Kaleb laughed. "It's the angry white boy!" Taylor smacked him again, wrestling with Kaleb to shove the pillow over the darker man's mouth to close it for good.

"What is going on in here?"

The boys froze, looking up from the couch to find Trish home early from work, and standing in the doorway.

"Hi, mom." Kaleb waved beneath Taylor, who climbed off of the darker boy almost immediately.

"Hey, Miss Trish," he said, feeling the heavy gaze she was bearing down on him. She looked between the two, taking in the situation and making accurate assumptions.

"I'm sorry," Taylor muttered, feeling heavier with every passing second. Trish looked to the boy, then shook her head.

"No, dear," she said. "No need for that." She looked to her son. "I'm just surprised, is all." Kaleb rubbed the back of his head.

"I figured… Since he's living here and everything… And we know so much about him…" He looked to his mother. "Taylor should know. Besides, you trust him, right?"

Trish sighed quietly, closing her eyes and leaning against the doorframe, a small tilt slowly growing over her lips. "Yes," she whispered, opening her eyes to Taylor. "I trust you."

The two looked to one another as they shared this one moment of peace; one relieved to know his honor's value, the other relieved to be rid of the burden of secrets. Trish nodded to the hallway. "Go get cleaned up for dinner," she said. "I'm gonna need some help."

Kaleb jumped up from the couch and bound down the hall, suddenly giddy, and lighter now that he had revealed himself. Taylor followed after, though much more slowly, and walked with Trish.

"I'm glad," Trish said quietly, wrapping around one of Taylor's arms. "He's kept this to himself for so long, I'm glad he could trust you with it." She placed a light kiss on his cheek as they made it to the hall. "Thank you."

Taylor looked to her. "I'm sure Gerrit was…" His words faded as Trish shook her head.

"Gerrit was a good friend, but he also had a big mouth." She giggled. "I guess he still does." Taylor blinked, looking to the woman. "You're the only person he's told." Trish smiled, letting go of his arm as they made it out of the hall. Taylor stayed, watching the woman enter the kitchen with her hyper son drying his hands at the sink.

"C'mon, Taylor, I wanna eat tonight!" Kaleb grinned, turning to his mother. "What are we making?" Trish tapped her chin in thought.

"You know, I have a sudden craving for curry," she said, sending Kaleb's triumphant fist in the air.

Taylor watched the mother and son smiling and playing in the kitchen, seeing firsthand how much they loved one another, regardless of their differing blood. It didn't matter if they were connected in that way, what mattered was the bond they shared then and now, as they grew together. They stumbled and failed, laughed and cheered, cried and comforted; all in the name of family. They had chosen to live the rest of their lives together, and in a way, it was the greatest form of love of all.

Chapter 22

Taylor yawned as he trekked down the hallway through the morning crowd. Being invisible was a little harder to do now that he had become famous, but it was easier to evade people now than it had been before since his fame had died down. He brushed passed the usual idiots who liked to block the middle of the halls with their stagnant conversations and rushed past the lockers, only to bump into another evading person as well.

"Oh!" The girl jumped back in surprise, dropping her books to the floor. "I'm sorry!" she squeaked, as her voice was fairly quiet. Taylor shrugged it off, kneeling down to pick up her books.

"Oh, it's alright, I'll get them," the girl protested. "Really, I'm sorry." Taylor rose, handing her books back.

"No big deal," he muttered. "It's not like we crashed." He recognized her to be the same girl Kaleb had knocked over before. "Not real steady on your feet, are you?" he asked. The girl looked down at her books, shrinking away from his gaze. *"Oops."* Taylor smiled politely. "What's your name?" he asked.

The girl kept her head down, looking to the lockers. "Karen," she said quietly.

Taylor nodded, wanting to get this encounter over with already, but knowing she would be upset if he just left right then and there. He resumed his troublesome smile, suddenly remembering Vance's lessons from camp.

"Nice name," he said. "It's pretty." Karen looked up to Taylor, suddenly blushing.

"Thank you," she mumbled. Taylor nodded to her again as he began to walk past her.

"Oh," he turned. "I'm Taylor." Karen nodded.

"I know," she muttered.

Taylor turned away, waving over his shoulder as he headed for class, cursing his fame with each step. As the day wore on, Taylor dodged the usual do-gooders who wanted to help him in any way they could, and did his best to catch up in his studies after the week he had missed. Kaleb was kind enough to help him finish his late assignments during their tutoring session, making it easier to turn them in faster. Their sessions were longer now thanks to the extra homework, but neither boy really seemed to mind, especially since it taught Kaleb what he had missed as well. After a few hours, they packed up and started for home, talking along the way.

"I'm so sick of people," Taylor griped. "I feel like I've been watched all day."

Kaleb snickered. "That's because you were."

"Huh?" Taylor looked to him, confused. Kaleb looked ahead, grinning from ear to ear.

"Remember that glasses girl that I knocked over a few weeks back?" He turned his grin to Taylor. "She's been watching you all day." Taylor scrunched up his face.

"Great," he grumbled.

"I asked around and found out that she's a first year- and her name is Karen Bickerman," Kaleb went on, grinning to Taylor. "Dude, her dad is *loaded*. He's like a huge sponsor for the school too." Taylor grimaced.

"Is that supposed to make me like her?"

"Nah," Kaleb shook his head. "But it helps." Kaleb's grin grew. "Dude, she likes you." Taylor glared at Kaleb.

"Seriously?" he asked, disbelieving, but Kaleb nodded.

"A blind man could see it."

The blonde hiked his pack over his shoulders. "Too bad. I'm not into her."

Kaleb scoffed. "Cut it out with this whole 'I hate people' thing. She's gorgeous, smart, and insanely rich. What's not to like?"

"How about the fact that she's afraid of her own shadow?" Taylor snipped.

Kaleb shrugged. "So she's shy. A lot of guys like that."

Taylor frowned. "Well I don't," he grumbled.

Kaleb scoffed again, rolling his eyes to the sky. "Don't tell me you're into someone else," he huffed.

"Hurry up, I'm freezing," Taylor growled, making Kaleb stop.

"*Really?*" Kaleb's grin returned. "Who? Who is it, c'mon, tell me!"

Taylor kept his eyes forward as he walked. "It's no big deal," he grumbled. "Besides, it's not like anything's going to happen anyway."

"You never know!" Kaleb said. "Do you think she'll ask you to the dance?" Taylor stopped to look at Kaleb.

"The what?"

"The Girl's Choice dance," Kaleb answered. "They have it every year at the end of Winter." He followed Taylor, who had begun walking again. "So, do you think she'll ask you?"

Taylor frowned, remembering the silly formal occasion. "I don't do dances."

Kaleb groaned, lifting his eyes to the sky again. "You're so anti-social it hurts- it physically hurts!" Kaleb scolded. He jumped in front of Taylor, stopping the blonde to talk face to face. "How about a deal?"

"No," Taylor said bluntly, brushing past the darker man.

"You haven't even heard it yet!" Kaleb said, charging after him.

"Don't have to," Taylor replied. "Every time you say that, you make me do something I don't want to do, and going to the dance would *definitely* qualify as something I don't want to do. Besides, I'm not going to be asked to the dance."

Kaleb came closer to the blonde to speak more quietly. "She might," he tried.

Taylor shook his head. "Not gonna happen," he said, eyes forward. "I wouldn't want to go with anyone else anyways."

Kaleb stopped, watching the blonde walk ahead. "Free lessons. For the rest of your life."

Taylor stopped, turning to glare at the darker man behind him.

"If you get asked, and go to that dance, I'll give you free lessons for as long as you want them," Kaleb said. "No papers, no fun things, nothing. Nothing at all."

Taylor's glare intensified. "Why are you doing this?" he asked quietly. Kaleb kept his eyes on the blonde.

"Because I want you to be happy, Teahnu."

The two boys stared down one another, battling their thoughts alone as the evening sun shined its final rays over their skin. Finally, Taylor turned around and started for home again, leaving Kaleb to stand on his own for a few seconds before chasing after the blonde.

"Let's go work on battery for the bike," Taylor mumbled. "We can do that much at least." Kaleb sighed, nodding his head as he looked to the ground.

"Fine by me."

Taylor sighed as he dropped his book over his chest, connecting Kason's character to Kaleb's sister; a young, strong woman who had died in battle. It had been a while since Kaleb had told him the truth, and ever since, Taylor had been curious to find more. Often times he would sneak into the room while everyone else was busy just to look at the pictures or read the articles, wherever they may be. Now, Taylor wanted to see them again.

The blonde climbed down from his bed and peeked his head out of the bedroom door, hearing Kaleb in the living room watching a dolphin documentary. Trish and Vance would be coming home from work soon, giving him little time to lollygag.

He quietly stepped out into the hall and passed through the door, silently closing it behind him. Staff Sergeant Patricia and Sergeant First Class Vance Saunders stared back at him from their frames on the wall, their crisp uniform and solemn face making them look much more stern than their usual demeanor. Taylor looked away from their stares to instead graze over the room, considering all the stories connected to each item, and headed straight for the photo of Kaleb and his sister.

Taylor picked up the picture again, examining the tiny siblings closer. The resemblance of he and his sister was remarkable, truly exposing them as twins. Their dark skin and brown eyes were the same, and while Kaleb's hair spiked around, his sister's was long, sleek, and beautifully tied over her shoulder.

Their clothing was certainly different from regular Alterian attire, designed to keep them comfortable in the desert, and safe during sand storms. Kaleb's shirt dangled loosely around him to keep the sand from hiding between crevices, and a sash was wrapped around his waist for easy access to protect his eyes and face during a storm. His sister's dress came in layers, covering her chest and arms separately to expose her shoulders. The so-called sleeves tied around behind her, allowing her to flip the back of her sleeves over her head and face like a helmet, and it was thin enough to see through, without the risk of sand blowing into her eyes during a storm.

Taylor peered into the young girl's eyes. They were calm and steady; focused just as Kaleb's were now, but there was a sense of elegance behind them as well, telling anyone who dare look upon her that she had seen the world at its worst, and had lived through it gracefully.

Taylor blinked, realizing how young she was in the photo, and wondering if she had even made it to the age of seven before dying. He rubbed his thumb over the frame, wondering what it was like in such a horrid place, when he noticed something else. He squinted, bringing the picture closer to his face to find freckles over her nose. Taylor switched his attention over to little Kaleb, and found a tiny patch trying to hide over his own nose.

"Having fun?"

Taylor jumped, juggling the picture in the air in efforts to keep it from falling to the ground.

"Didn't mean to scare you," Kaleb chuckled.

"How did you know I was in here?" Taylor asked, placing the picture down on the desk behind him. Kaleb jerked a finger at Bubbie, wagging his tail at Taylor's feet. "I got up to pee and he was at the door."

Taylor closed his eyes in a sigh, embarrassed at being caught, and frustrated with his dog; though staying mad at the beast would be impossible. Kaleb grinned at the flustered blonde.

"So what did you find?" he asked.

Taylor opened his eyes. "What?"

Kaleb nodded to the picture. "You look like you'd found something."

Taylor looked over his shoulder at the picture, turning to pick it up and examine it once more. He looked to the children, flicking his gaze to the Kaleb before him from beneath his brow as he compared the two. He sucked in his lips, then leaned up to inspect the darker man's face closer.

"You have freckles," Taylor muttered, staring him down. Kaleb threw a hand to his face to try and cover the tiny dots barely showing through his dark skin.

"I thought I outgrew those!" He looked absolutely horrified. Taylor snickered.

"You can barely see them, but they're there," he said, finding the darker man's reaction amusing.

"That's not the point!" Kaleb said. "The point is, they're still there!" He ripped the picture from Taylor's hands to find the aggravating dots on his younger face. "I really thought they were gone by now." Kaleb groaned. Taylor shrugged, his small, amused grin still on his face.

"Some people like those kinds of things," he said, leaning against the desk. "I'm sure if you showed it to the girls, they'd go wild." He snorted. "They're suckers for stuff like that."

Kaleb frowned at the blonde. "Good for them, not so much me."

The front door clicked open in the distance, alerting the boys of the Evans' return. "Oh, what a day," Vance sighed. The boys replaced the photo and left the room to greet the adults.

"In there again?" Trish asked, catching them leave the room. Taylor ran a hand through his hair, keeping away from eye contact as he made his way to the kitchen to wash up. Trish scrutinized the blonde the entire way, leaning against a chair as he entered the kitchen.

"Taylor," she said, freezing the blonde. "I'd like to see you after dinner. If you don't mind."

Taylor swallowed, suddenly sick. He nodded, turning on the sink to wash his hands.

"Alright."

Throughout dinner, Kaleb noticed Taylor was quieter than normal. He smiled when needed and kept up with the conversation, but kept his responses short, and quiet. He was tense as well, sitting uncomfortably in his seat while he ate. Kaleb looked to his mother, finding her attitude to be breezy through all this, as though she hadn't noticed, or more likely, it didn't even bother her. The two had been dancing around each other all evening with Trish taking the lead, jerking the conversation around to force the blonde to speak. As they finished their meal, Trish rose from her seat and gently placed a hand on Taylor's shoulder as she walked by him, freezing the blonde as he drank from his glass.

"Help your father with the dishes, please, dear?" Trish said lightly, not even looking back as she walked down the hall. Kaleb shared a look with Taylor, almost as terrified as the blonde.

"You think she's mad?" Kaleb asked, looking to his father.

Vance merely shrugged. "I've been married to that woman for almost fifteen years, and I still don't know what's going on in her head."

Taylor swallowed the lump in his throat. "Got any tips?"

Vance, who looked him right in the eye. "Beg for mercy, and tell her she's pretty."

Taylor dropped his face to the table, smothering a groan.

"Taylor, dear," Trish called sweetly, making the men tense. "I'd like to speak with you, please."

The blonde lifted his head, eyeing the hall despairingly, then left the table with one last pitiful look. "If he dies, I get his stuff," Vance murmured to his son. Kaleb scowled at his father, shoving his hand over the man's face. They rushed through the dishes, eager to get the chore done to go and rescue the blonde if need be. Once the plates were put away, and the pots and pans were dried, Kaleb dashed down the hall as quietly as he could, leaving his father to put away the big stuff while he tried to hear what was happening behind the door of the storage room.

Kaleb tip toed closer, lightly pressing his ear against the door, hearing a child's voice. He pulled away from the door confused, and pressed his ear even closer to the door.

"Come on in, Kaleb," Trish called, obviously hearing this action. He dropped his head, cursing his noisy nature, and stepped into the room. He found Trish and Taylor sitting on the couch watching something on the television.

"Oh, no," Kaleb mumbled. There, on the screen, was Kaleb as an eight year old boy, running around the house with a towel tied around his throat, goggles over his eyes, and Space Captain Rogers' space ship printed all over his pajamas.

"I finally have someone to watch these with," Trish grinned, leaning her head back over the couch to see her son. Taylor smirked away, keeping his eyes off of the darker man.

"I had nothing to do with this," he snickered. Trish huffed.

"You're always in here looking around, I never get to watch these- it just seemed to fit!" she exclaimed. "If you wanted to know more, here's your chance." Taylor rubbed his nose, still smirking at the wall.

"'Scuse me," Kaleb pointed. "Don't I get a say in this?"

Trish laughed. "Oh, honey. Not a chance."

The screen flickered, and Kaleb was sitting at the dining room table with a purple face. "Oh, this is a good one," Trish said, settling into the couch.

"You sure you don't know where the blueberries went?" Vance asked behind the camera. Kaleb nodded, looking at the table.

"Huh." Vance's hand picked up an empty carton. "I wonder where they went."

Kaleb shrugged. "I don't know, Abba." His accent slipped through slightly. "Maybe a bird came in?" His big, brown eyes looked up at the camera.

"Maybe," said Vance. "That must be it."

Kaleb nodded, taking the empty carton to throw it away.

"Hey, Kaleb?" Vance asked. "Abi's gonna be home soon, why don't you go get cleaned up in the bathroom? Make sure we look nice when she gets here?" Kaleb smiled, running out of the kitchen.

"Okay!" he grinned, being closely followed by Vance.

As Kaleb entered the bathroom, be pulled out his step stool and climbed up to wash his hands in the sink, but gasped when he saw his messy, purple face in the mirror. Vance snickered behind the camera as Kaleb turned to look at him with wide, horrified eyes, then burst into tears, slamming the door in Vance's face. Vance turned the camera around to face himself.

"Don't worry kid," he giggled. "This is punishment enough. Once your first girlfriend gets a load of this, we're even."

Trish burst into laughter, with Taylor hiding his muffled snickering behind a hand as best he could.

"I remember that!" Vance chuckled, coming in behind Kaleb.

"What is this, 'gang up on Kaleb' day?" Kaleb complained.

"You were so upset, and then your mother came home and she couldn't stop laughing long enough to punish you," Vance laughed, sitting on the arm of the couch next to Trish. Kaleb buried his face in his hand, groaning his embarrassment into his fingers.

"Oh, now this one's sweet," Trish cooed, tilting her head onto Vance's torso.

Kaleb was older now, around nine or ten perhaps, and he was holding a kitten up next to his face for the camera.

"Who's that?" Trish asked somewhere behind the camera.

"This is the Johnson's cat," Kaleb smiled, cuddling the kitten to his chest.

"Yeah? What's he doing here?" Vance asked, holding the camera again.

"She," Kaleb corrected. "Mrs. Johnson said I could take care of her while they're gone." He scratched her behind the ears as he spoke, leading down to her neck and chest. The kitten mewed, wanting down on the floor to play. Kaleb complied, sitting down on the floor with her as she dashed across the room after the catnip mouse the young boy had thrown.

"She sure is fast!" Vance said, gaining a grinning nod from the boy. "What's her name?"

Kaleb shook his head. "She doesn't have one yet, the Johnson's want her new owner to pick one out for her."

"Yeah?" Trish asked, sitting on the living room couch. "Well, what would you name her?"

Kaleb shrugged, leaning over the floor to play with the speedy kitten. "She likes to run around on her toes a lot."

"Yeah, she does skitter around fairly well," Trish said, confusing her son.

"She what?" he asked.

"Skitter," Vance explained. "That's what she's doing right now." Kaleb turned back to the kitten, grinning.

"That's a good name." He looked to his father. "You think if we tell the owners, maybe they might like it?"

The kitten climbed up over Kaleb's back and onto his shoulder, surprising the boy into a smile. He carefully pulled the kitten down into his arms, rubbing his cheek against hers. Vance turned the camera to view both Kaleb and Trish.

"I don't know, honey," Vance said. "What do you think?"

Trish smiled. "I think it's a fine name," she said. "Thanks for choosing for us, sweety."

Kaleb looked between his mother and father as a brilliant smile began to spread over his face. "You mean-?"

Trish began giggling at her son's happiness, watching the boy joyously cuddle the kitten next to his face.

"Thanks, mom! Thanks, dad!" Kaleb cried. "I promise I'll take good care of her!"

Vance chuckled behind the camera. "Glad you like her, kid."

Kaleb set the kitten down on the floor to play again. "C'mon, Skitters!" He tapped on the floor for her attention. "C'mon, girl!"

As though on cue, the fully grown Skitters hopped up onto the sofa between Trish and Taylor, meowing loudly in demands for food.

"Good idea, Skit," Vance said. "We need popcorn."

Kaleb huffed loudly. "This isn't helping!" he exclaimed, completely ignored by his father as he hurried past him to the kitchen.

"Don't be so embarrassed, honey," Trish chided. "Everyone's done it before, I'm sure of it."

Kaleb simmered at his mother, not daring to fight back with her. He glanced at Taylor, who shrugged at him, offering sympathies through this embarrassment. The dark man sighed, settling down in front of the sofa on the floor.

"That's my boy," Trish said, patting his shoulder.

For the rest of the evening, the family watched each home movie hidden away in the drawer beneath the television, laughing and smiling through every adventure recorded on film. Some of the videos were tricks; pranks being pulled on the adults between Trish and Vance in an all out war for the title of best prankster, while others were commemorative moments, like the first day of school, or in Vance's case, his first promotion. Pillow forts were constructed for bouncy ball cannon fire battles, fighting off Trish who was a girl, and therefore not allowed inside. Trish would have her revenge in a later short when she tossed a bucket of water over her husband's head during a water gun war, effectively dousing the man entirely.

The lights had been turned off halfway through, making the television the only source of light in the room, and sending a movie theater vibe through the evening. Taylor watched the films, captivated by the mischief and affections, thinking back to a time when his own family was just as loving, and smiling at the thought. The night wore on, and the adults had nodded off to sleep on the couch in the dark, leaving Kaleb and Taylor alone to watch the movies for themselves.

"I guess they wore themselves out," Taylor whispered, setting down the empty bowl of popcorn.

"Sorry you had to sit through all of that," Kaleb mumbled, but Taylor shook his head.

"I don't mind when we're having a good time." He looked away. "Sorry your mom set you up."

Kaleb sighed, putting his cheeks to the ceiling. "Yeah, she does that," he muttered. "Guess it's a mom thing."

A small smile tugged at Taylor's lips, agreeing with the darker man. "Think we should wake them?" he asked. Kaleb nodded.

"In a minute," he said, stretching his shoulders in front of him with an evil grin. "A little crick in the neck will serve some justice."

Taylor shook his head, rolling his eyes at the man, then sat up on his knees to remove the video.

"Did your mom ever record you?" Kaleb asked. Taylor nodded.

"Not as much as yours did. She kind of stopped after a while."

Kaleb stared at the pile of videos lined in the dresser drawer. "Does she know how to work a camera?" he asked. Taylor shrugged.

"Probably, I mean, it's been a while, but it's like riding a bike, right?" He placed the video back inside with the others, closing the drawer for the night. "Why?"

Kaleb licked his lips. "What if you were to send a recording of yourself to your mom?" he offered, freezing Taylor. "Instead of the letters, you could talk to her through the camera, and then she could talk back to you."

Taylor stared at the darker man, shocked at the sudden epiphany, and too stunned to move.

"I mean, when was the last time you saw your mom?" Kaleb asked. "Heard her voice? I can only assume it's been way too long, am I right? We have the camera here, we can..." Kaleb stopped, noticing the strangely quiet blonde. "Taylor?"

"I think that's the best idea you've ever had," Taylor said quietly.

Kaleb looked to the boy, silenced by his response. He cleared his throat, rubbing the back of his head. "Guess we better wake them," he muttered, standing. "We'll get it all set up tonight, if you want."

Taylor stood as well, quietly cleaning up after himself and leaving Kaleb with the task of waking his parents. Taylor scurried to the bathroom, checking himself in the mirror and straightening a few things to make sure he looked presentable for the camera. He spied the scar on his cheek, wishing there was a way to hide it, but more than anything, he wanted to see his mother, and to let her see him; even if he *was* imperfect.

He gave up on his scar, then hurried back to the room, bidding good night to the Evans' as he passed them in the hall. He found Kaleb crouched before the television, fiddling with the camera and wires. He switched the light on, surprising Kaleb and causing a pained grunt to escape him as the sudden light attacked his eyes.

"Sorry," Taylor breathed.

"No worries," Kaleb groaned. He poked at the camera a bit more, making sure everything worked right. "It's gonna need a minute. Need to let some juice in before it can boot up."

Taylor picked at his fingers, shifting his weight from foot to foot behind the sofa as he suddenly found himself anxious. Kaleb placed the camera on the dresser, angling it to view Taylor on the couch while still plugged into the wall to charge.

"Let's try this," Kaleb mumbled, standing up to leave. "Just press the red button, and if the light comes on, it's recording. Okay?" Taylor nodded, receiving a pat on his shoulder. "Good luck."

Kaleb left the room, closing the door behind him to give the blonde his privacy. Taylor sat on the couch, shaking his fingers and taking deep breaths to calm his nerves. Finally, he closed his eyes, took one last breath, then knelt forward to press record. He watched the light shine red, signaling success, and Taylor grinned as he pulled away from the camera to sit on the couch.

"Um…" He fiddled with his fingers. "Hi, mom." He waved slightly, offering a small smile. "It's been a while, huh?" He grinned to his fingers in his lap, not knowing what to say.

"It was my friend Kaleb's idea," he told her. "He thought, maybe we could make it work." He looked up to the camera. "I hope it can."

Taylor ran a hand through his hair. "Um…" He really had no idea what to say to her. "I'm going to send a letter with this as well, just in case, but…" He shrugged. "I really hope you get this." He sucked in his lips, leaning forward to rest his elbows on his knees, and dropping his voice to just above a whisper.

"I miss you. And I promise, we'll be together again soon. It's just a little bit longer. " He gave another small smile.

"I love you, mom."

Chapter 23

"That's a great idea!" Bekah smiled. "Why didn't I think of that?"

A smile tugged at the corner of Taylor's lips. "I sent it this morning. Now, all I have to do is wait."

Bekah bounced in her seat, a giddy grin on her lips. "I can't wait- you have to tell me if it works!" she beamed, bringing out the smile from her friend. Bekah leaned forward against her desk into the computer. "This'll tide you over until you see the real thing," she grinned, entirely too happy. "How close are you?"

Taylor shrugged, crossing his arms over the desk. "To be honest, I've been focussing more on school than work." He ran a hand through his hair. "After everything's that happened, I've been having trouble keeping up. Even with Kaleb's help." He thought for a moment. "I don't think I've had a job in weeks."

Bekah's eyes went wide. "Wow," she muttered. "Well, you definitely need to keep your grades up. You have one more year left, you'll have plenty of time to catch up. Besides, you're not having to pay the bills anymore, right?"

Taylor nodded, his eyes unfocused. "I guess you're right," he mumbled, then looked up, changing the subject to her. "How's the application coming?"

Bekah groaned in her seat, rolling her eyes so far back into her head, she plopped back into her chair.

"That bad?" Taylor asked.

"College applications are hard enough as it is, but doing it overseas is just ridiculous," she grumbled.

As close friends as they were, their age was the only thing that pulled them apart. Rebekah was a year older than Taylor, already sitting through her final year of high school and waiting to leave for Lori. The chosen school: Aislea University of Technological Arts. It was their plan for her to be a scout; checking out the school, learning the tricks, making connections and rating professors before Taylor could catch up to her the following year.

One of her most important duties, however, was to look after Taylor's mother. That responsibility had never been given by verbal form; it was a simple fact that Bekah ordered herself to follow, with or without Taylor's consent.

"By the way," Bekah said. "Don't fill out your application as a 'returning student.'" She covered her eyes. "I thought it meant high school to college, but I was *so* wrong."

Taylor snickered at his friend. "How you managed to make it this far is a mystery to me."

She removed her hand to glare at him. "I'm going to laugh when you have to go through this," she growled. "And when you ask for help, I'm going to make you *beg* for it."

Taylor ticked his head. "If all goes according to plan, you'll be in Lori. You won't be able to see me go through it."

Bekah sucked in her lips, sliding her eyes to the wall. "I knew that," she muttered.

He shook his head. "Dork."

She sighed, pushing her glasses over her nose. "I need to get a tan before I go." She slid up her striped sleeve to peer at her pale skin. "I should ask Kaleb what his secret is." She rolled her sleeve back down over her arm.

"How about the sun?" Taylor quipped, earning another glare from his friend. He shrugged away, looking to the wall. He hadn't told Bekah about Kaleb's secret. It was, afterall, a secret. No matter how close Bekah was, no matter how much he trusted her, Taylor couldn't tell her about Kaleb's heritage. Kaleb had trusted Taylor at the risk of pulling their family apart, and there was no way he would betray that. A knock on the door took their attention.

"Perfect timing!" Bekah beamed. "We were just talking about you."

Kaleb shut the door behind him, cocking a brow at the woman in the screen. "That's never good," he snarked, earning a scoff. "Sorry," he said to Taylor, leaning back to look at him. "I just needed to grab a book."

Taylor shrugged his hands. "No big deal," he muttered. Bekah leaned in closer to the screen.

"Hey! Prince Carmel!" she called, turning the golden man from his pile of books. "How'd you keep your tan?" Kaleb frowned.

"What?"

She rolled up her sleeve again, showing it to the camera. "Everytime I try and get some sun, it goes away within a week." She dropped her arm to show her face. "So how do you keep your tan?"

Kaleb looked to Taylor, who shook his head slightly. A smile hid behind his brown eyes, seeing his faith in the blonde bearing fruit before him.

"You wanna know my secret?" Kaleb grinned, looking mischieviously to the woman on the screen.

"You have one for me?" She straightened in her seat.

Kaleb leaned over the desk, waving a finger at her. "C'mere," he whispered, effectively drawing her closer into the screen. He held a hand up next to his mouth to whisper his answer. "I'm just that sexy."

Taylor snickered at the answer given, as well as the flustered reaction Bekah had performed. "That's not what I wanted to hear!" she yelled.

Kaleb shrugged, grinning as he walked away from the computer. "All I can give you," he breezed as he left the room, waving his book high over his head. Bekah huffed at him, glaring at the blonde as soon as the door shut.

Taylor cocked a brow at her. "Don't blame me for this."

Bekah shook her head, rolling her eyes away from him and quieting as she gathered her thoughts. "How are the dreams?" she asked quietly.

Taylor sucked in his lips, leaning forward in his chair again to speak quietly. "Still there," he replied just as quietly. "Not as frequent, but…" He looked away. "I still have them." He rubbed his nose. "It's getting easier to be around him, though. It's not so awkward anymore."

She nodded, still turned away. "I'm glad," she murmured. "Because he is *seriously* hot."

Taylor scowled at his friend. "Beck-" he complained over her giggling.

"You should show him off more often," she snickered.

"You have a problem, you know that?" Taylor grumbled.

"Do I hear a hint of *jealousy*?" she sang obnoxiously.

"Rebekah!" Taylor growled. "You're taking this too far."

She snuffled out her snickering, waving her hands in retreat. "Alright, alright, I'm sorry." She chuckled. "But that doesn't change my mind about keeping him around."

Taylor scowled at her. "I told you, we're not-"

"No, no, not like that," she interrupted. "I didn't mean in a dating sense, I meant as a friend." She smiled at him. "You should keep him around."

Taylor gripped his straps tightly as he walked down the sidewalk, barely noticing anything else around him. He had been pulled aside by Mr. Finnigan after class again, and what he had to say was most definitely not what Taylor wanted to hear. Now he was walking home, drowning in his thoughts, not even noticing the world around him. He was planning; plotting out every move from that second to the next year, trying to figure out a way for him to right what had been wronged in as little time as possible.

"Taylor!" Kaleb called from the distance, but the blonde was so lost in his thoughts, he kept on walking. "Taylor?" Kaleb caught up with him, catching his shoulder to turn him, but surprising the boy into a small, gasping jump.

"Sorry," the darker man apologised, scrutinizing the blonde. "Are you alright?"

Taylor nodded. "Yeah, I'm fine."

Kaleb frowned. "You sure?"

"Yes, I'm sure. Why?" Taylor huffed.

"Because you missed our session," Kaleb answered. Taylor blinked, having completely forgotten about tutoring.

"Oh, sorry," he said. "I guess I forgot."

Kaleb's frown deepened. "You never forget," he muttered, peering into the blonde. "Your face is all red, did you-"

A chill in the air blew past them, ruffling whatever bang snuck out of Taylor's beanie, and piercing his cheeks, reminding him of the cold.

"Yeah, that." Kaleb sighed heavily. "You should cover your face."

Taylor dutifully unbuttoned his collar and readjusted it so that it rose high over his neck and covered his nose, then set off for home once more, now hiding behind his coat.

"What's wrong, Taylor?" Kaleb asked.

"I said I'm fine." Taylor's voice was muffled behind his high collar. "Just drop it."

The two boys walked in silence from then on, both worrying about something completely different. As they approached the Evans house, Gerrit could be seen riding his bike in his driveway, and started pedalling over to the boys once he caught sight of them.

"Hey, Tommy," Gerrit sneered, circling around them. "Thanks for the toys." He looked to Kaleb. "You don't get to play." The two kept a wary eye on the rider, saying nothing yet.

"Go inside," Kaleb mumbled, then stepped in front of Gerrit's bike, allowing Taylor to go safely inside the house while Kaleb stayed behind.

Taylor needed to calm down, he needed reassurance that things would be alright, he wouldn't be able to breath right unless that was promised. He shed himself of his layers as soon as he stepped through the door, then ran to the bedroom in search of his lockbox.

Counting his money helped him plan, planning helped calm him down, and he really, *really* needed to calm down. Taylor closed the door behind him as he entered the room, then knelt down at the edge of the bed, finding old habits to die hard. He pulled away a few stacks of books near the wall, reaching down under the bed in search of his lockbox, and feeling nothing. He dropped to his hands and knees to peer beneath the bed, finding it empty. Taylor's breath caught in his throat, and he began to frantically shove aside books, hoping to find the lockbox hidden behind the stacks, but leaving himself in a big, panicky mess.

Taylor turned to the bookshelf beside him, ripping the books away from the shelves, still coming up empty. His breathing now was far too panicked, and he was coming to the point of hyperventilation the longer he searched, still unable to find the elusive lockbox. He gripped his hair, panting much too quickly as he tried to think of where his lockbox may be, and if Kaleb might have taken it.

Taylor shook his head, finding the idea to be ridiculous. Kaleb wasn't a thief, and he had nothing against Taylor any longer. Gerrit, however, had plenty of reasons to hate the blonde. Taylor's mind was reeling, remembering when the angry boy had ransacked the bedroom in search of Kaleb, and connecting the idea of robbery.

"Thanks for the toys."

"Go inside."

Kaleb stood in front of Gerrit's bike, allowing the blonde to safely enter the house while Kaleb stayed behind to talk.

"You like it?" Gerrit grinned, waving his hands over the handlebars. "Just bought it last week." Kaleb began walking towards Gerrit's house, leading the boy away from his own. "I also got a mini-fridge for my room, it's so cool. There's other stuff, but you gotta do something before you can see them." Gerrit rode along around Kaleb, circling him as they drew closer to the athlete's house.

"You never have any money," Kaleb muttered.

"Sure I do."

"Then why was I always the one to buy your burgers?"

Gerrit scoffed at this. "I didn't have money *back then*," he snarked. "Thanks to Tommy, I could get as many burgers as I want."

Kaleb glared at his former friend. "What are you talking about?" he asked in a low voice. Gerrit stopped and roughly dropped his bike in his lawn, digging something out of his pocket.

"Dude was loaded," Gerrit said. "He's good for that much at least. This was with it." Gerrit handed over a plastic badge broadcasting Taylor's picture. "Had to use a screw driver to get it open."

Kaleb's eye widened at the border pass in his hand. "You didn't!" he hissed, whipping his eyes to the athlete.

"He deserved it!" Gerrit defended. "I was gonna share it with you, but you still haven't said you're sorry, so your loss."

Kaleb stepped up to the smaller boy. "Do you have any idea-"

"GERRIT!"

Taylor burst out from the front door, roaring with rage as he charged barefoot across the street.

"Taylor, no!" Kaleb blocked the blonde from attacking, literally lifting him off the ground from the force of impact and efforts to keep the two apart, while Gerrit howled with laughter at the sight of this.

"I'M GONNA KILL YOU! I'M GONNA FUCKING KILL YOU! YOU BASTARD!"

Taylor fought against Kaleb, kicking and screaming and clawing away at the darker man, but he was too strong for him, and Taylor ended up stagnant in his charge to battle.

"Get out of here, Gerrit!" Kaleb screamed, growling at the athlete to scare him into compliance. The small boy scoffed at the two, scowling at the scene they were making and waved them off, turning to retreat inside his house, all the while being threatened by the enraged Taylor that Kaleb dragged across the street. As soon as they were close, Kaleb threw Taylor inside the house and slammed the door shut, locking it for second measures.

"YOU FUCKER!" Taylor whipped his venom over to Kaleb as soon as he was released, cursing him for letting the incorrigible athlete escape, but the dark man grabbed hold of Taylor's shoulders hard, shaking the blonde as he screamed.

"ANOTHER WEEK!" Kaleb shouted. "You said so yourself, getting suspended would be pointless!" His grip tightened as he drew closer to growl in Taylor's face. "And assaulting him on his own property would land you in jail!"

"It doesn't matter anymore!" Taylor spat back. "I'm stuck here anyway!" He ripped out of Kaleb's grasp, backing away to scream at him some more. "I can't get out without that money, I can't get out without that class- I'm stuck here for good!"

"What are you-"

"Finnigan said so himself, I'm done for!"

"You can still-"

"No!" Taylor's breathing was far too erratic. "Don't you get it? I messed up! I'm screwed!" He began pacing with wide, wobbly steps. "I've missed too much, I can't do it! It's taken me this long to save up a few hundred papers, now I have to start all over- and I can't do that if I'm stuck in extra classes!"

Taylor grabbed fistfulls of his hair, trying to cover his eyes at the same time. "I can't do it! I can't get out! I'm stuck here! I can't-"

Kaleb rammed forward and wrapped his arms around Taylor, the blonde simultaneously throwing his arms around Kaleb's neck on contact to hyperventilate into his shoulder. Taylor shook beneath the stronger man's arms, trying to steady his breathing, and clinging tightly to Kaleb's broad shoulders for support, having to stand on his toes to reach him. Kaleb rose a hand to rest at the base of Taylor's neck, gripping his shirt and whatever shoulder he could find.

"It's going to be alright," Kaleb said softly. "Whatever happens, we'll get through it."

Taylor closed his eyes, holding as tightly to Kaleb's words as he did his body. They stayed like this until Taylor's breathing had normalized, and his quivering body stood still. Kaleb drew the blonde in tighter, but the smaller boy pulled away, turning his back to the darker man. He held himself, clinging to his arms as he turned his head to nod, refusing to look at Kaleb, then silently walked back to the bedroom.

Kaleb watched him go, silently wishing he could do more to comfort his friend. As he heard the bedroom door click shut, he sighed, leaning against the wall beside the front door and closing his eyes. Gerrit would definitely be expelled from school now thanks to his three-strike probation, though Kaleb couldn't bring himself to be happy about this fact. He straightened from the wall to remove his layers and hang them up on the racks next to Taylor's.

In his haste to go after Gerrit, the blonde had raced out of the house without his coat, and had even left his shoes at the front of the house. Kaleb sighed again, looking down at the abandoned articles as he hung his coat, only to have something else catch his eye as it fell out of his pocket. Kaleb knelt to retrieve it, and after giving it a thorough examination, decided to meet with Taylor.

Kaleb went to the kitchen first, grabbing a soda and some crackers from the pantry before heading down the hall to his bedroom. He knocked lightly on the door, receiving no answer, then quietly pushed through.

Taylor lay in his bunk, face down in his pillow and unmoving. Kaleb closed the door behind him, then made his way to his own bed, kneeling over his pillows to sit below the blonde and against the wall, stretching his legs out before him.

"Taylor?" he asked quietly, holding up the offerings. "I know you don't like tea, so I figured soda would work." He gently slid the two items overhead onto the edge of Taylor's bunk, untouched by the frozen blonde. "I also have this for you." He pulled out the fallen item from his coat, tapping his hand with it. "It doesn't look like he did any damage to it."

Kaleb slipped it over on top of the food for Taylor to see once he decided to move again. Slowly, Taylor turned his head, peering through his bangs to find his border pass. He stared at the small pile Kaleb had left on the edge of his bed for a while, saying nothing. Then, he carefully reached for his pass and brought it closer to his face for inspection. He closed his eyes, letting the badge fall over the bridge of his nose and eye.

"You can still use that to get out of here," Kaleb said quietly, having seen the tips of the blonde's fingers as he took the pass. "You still have that much at least."

Taylor kept his eyes closed for a few more moments, taking hold of the badge and gripping it close to his neck.

"You really think I can make it?" he asked quietly.

Kaleb nodded an unseen nod. "Only if you don't give up," he replied softly. Taylor turned his head back into his pillow, still gripping the badge. Kaleb waited in silence for another response from the blonde, sitting patiently on the edge of his bed against the wall.

"I'll be down in a minute," the blonde muttered finally.

"Alright," Kaleb said softly. "Want to keep trying?"

"I'll be down in a minute," Taylor repeated quietly. Kaleb nodded again, accepting the answer, and got up to ready their lessons in the dining room.

"Kaleb," Taylor mumbled, stopping the darker man. " … I'm sorry…"

Kaleb turned back to the door to leave. "Just keep trying, Teahnu," he said. "You haven't failed me yet."

With that, he left the room, allowing the blonde to gather himself on his own. Taylor lay still, holding his pass close to him and finding the strength to rise from his despair. He slid his pass under his pillow, burying it deep within the pillowcase, then pushed up on his arms, leaning back to sit on his knees and turned his head to look at the empty door for a moment.

"…Thank you…"

"Can we skip our lesson today?" Taylor asked in the doorway. "Or, at least postpone it?"

Kaleb looked to the boy, confused for a moment, then remembering what day it was. "Do you mind if I come with you?" he asked. "It's been a while since I've seen Hector, and I could really go for a burger from Tammy."

Taylor looked ahead, avoiding the darker man's gaze. "Sure," he muttered. "Hurry up."

Kaleb hurried out of the laboratory and caught up with the blonde in the hallway, off to see Hector the postman. "Do you think it worked?" Kaleb asked, striding up beside his friend.

Taylor shook his head, uncertain. "I don't know," he muttered.

"What if it did?" Kaleb asked.

"Then I'll watch it in Acane's room," Taylor replied. "And if it doesn't, you'll get your burger."

The boys walked in silence as they made their way towards the post office. Kaleb occasionally turned his attention to his friend to see how he was handling himself, while Taylor kept his eyes forward, watching the horizon as they drew nearer, and keeping a steady pace. Once they entered town square, however, there was a slight change in his steps. He steadily became quicker the closer they came to the office, and by the time it was in sight, he trotted across the street to go inside. Hector was reading behind the desk, propped up comfortably in his chair with the newspaper hiding his face.

"Hector?" Taylor asked, stirring the newspaper.

"Oh!" Hector smiled when he caught sight of the teen. "Hello, Taylor." He noticed Kaleb behind the blonde as he was rising from his seat. "Looks like it's a party today," he chuckled. "Be with you in a moment."

The old postman hobbled into the back room in search of Taylor's mail, calling out to the blonde as usual.

"It's another small one," he said. "It's kind of heavy, though."

Taylor tapped his fingers along his backpack straps, making himself believe it was just his mother returning the camera. As Hector came back with the box, Taylor's heart sank at the sight of the box he had used before, holding the camera safely inside. He offered a polite smile to the postman, taking the box off the counter and leaving for Tammy's diner.

"Aren't you going to open it?" Kaleb asked, following behind.

"It's the same box I used to send it to her," Taylor answered. "She's just returning the camera."

Kaleb paused a moment, watching the blonde quietly head inside for a booth at Tammy's, then hurried after him. "Maybe there's a letter inside," Kaleb offered. "I mean, she *did* get it at least."

Taylor dropped the box onto an empty table, sitting down in the booth. "Yeah, she did," he said, grabbing a butter knife to pick at the seam of the box. "Order your burger."

Kaleb sighed quietly, then sat down across from the blonde, waving to Tammy for her attention. Taylor managed to rip open the box with a jagged slice from the knife, opening the box just as Tammy walked up.

"Hey, boys," she smiled. "How's it going?" The two ignored her, however, in favor of a small card lying atop the camera with a simple message written on it in neat cursive.

"Have Kaleb watch, too."

The two boys looked to one another, then bolted out of the booth, rushing out of the diner.

"What the- hey!" Tammy shouted after them in surprise.

"Sorry, Tammy!" Kaleb called. "Next time!"

They raced home as fast as their legs would take them, not even bothering to strip their coats and shoes as they entered the house, and ran straight for the storage room. Taylor dropped to his knees in front of the television, ripping out the camera from the

380

box and began wiring it to the screen. Kaleb shed his extra layers behind the blonde, dropping to the couch to watch the screen for any sign of movement. Taylor turned it on and looked up before pressing play, wanting to see the fruits of his labor first hand.

There on the screen, was a woman with beautiful blonde hair, and watery blue eyes. She sniffed, smiling at the camera through her tears, and laughing sheepishly at herself for it.

"Hi, Bubbie," she mumbled, offering a small wave. "You've gotten so big." She gave another small laugh, looking away to wipe her eyes. "I promised I wouldn't do this." She sniffed, smiling back at the camera.

"Kaleb." She nodded to him. "If you're watching this, I want to thank you for letting me see my son again." She wiped her cheek. "Oh, I'm Sarah, by the way," she chuckled. "It's nice to meet you."

Kaleb absentmindedly waved at the woman on the screen, momentarily forgetting that she couldn't see him. "You look just like her," he mumbled.

"Taylor."

The blonde straightened at his mother's call.

"You hang onto him," she told her son. "He's a smart one." She chuckled. "I'm glad you have a friend like him."

Kaleb took his eyes off the screen to watch the blonde, who sat unmoving on the floor before the television. Taylor couldn't take his eyes off of the screen. He listened to his mother's voice, studied her face, her movements, noticed every detail he could while she was still there in front of him. He didn't dare take his eyes away. Taylor wanted to reach up and touch her, even if it was just a picture, but he restrained himself, not wanting to look like a sad puppy in front of Kaleb.

As Sarah said her final words and waved goodbye, the two boys sat in silence, letting her voice echo in their ears. Slowly, Taylor turned to Kaleb, looking to the darker man on the couch, and smiled. Kaleb stared back, astonished. It was a real smile; not his usual smothered, hidden glimpse of a grin, but an actual, real life, *happy* smile that lit up his fantastic blue eyes.

"It worked," Taylor said quietly, his smile still shining.

Kaleb smiled back at the blonde, a victorious laugh bubbling in his gut. "It worked!" he laughed, leaning forward off the couch and onto his knees to clap his friend's shoulder. He shook the blonde with excitement, leaping to his feet with fists in the air. "Ha-HA!" Kaleb cheered, then turned to his friend holding out a hand, still smiling. "Gimme your coat, you can send another one right now."

Taylor looked down at his chest, remembering he had left his coat on, and began unbuttoning right away, but slowed as a thought rose up in his mind.

"Hey… Why don't you stick around for this one?"

Kaleb looked to the blonde, surprised by his offer. "You sure?" he asked, receiving a shrug.

"Just for a second. You don't have to. You can just say 'hi' and reply to what she said to you." He kept his eyes on his buttons. Kayleb grinned, eyes shining at the blonde.

"Okay," he said, grin growing. "Yeah, cool."

He took Taylor's coat and set it aside with his own, then sat down on the couch next to the blonde, rubbing his knees in anticipation. Taylor pressed the record button and sat back on the couch.

"Okay, go."

Kaleb smiled broadly to the camera. "Hi, Miss Sarah." Kaleb grinned, offering a small wave. "I'm Kaleb, and I'm glad it worked. We should meet for real some time."

"And, you're done," Taylor snarked, smirking at the darker man's reaction.

"Fine then," Kaleb snipped, crossing his arms and looking back at the camera. "Keeping your mom all to yourself- I see how it is!"

He grinned at the camera, waving goodbye and lightly elbowing Taylor in the ribs before leaving. He stayed a moment, absentmindedly listening as the door closed before realizing he was invading, and turned to make his way down the hall to let the dog inside. His curiosity got the better of him, however, when he heard Taylor chuckling behind the door. Kaleb turned back to hover his ear over the wooden barrier.

"Yeah," he heard through the door. "That was Kaleb. And yes. He *is* like that. *All* the time. He's so weird, sometimes," Taylor went on. "And he tells me the strangest things- he says I have a stalker," Taylor scoffed. "Apparently, this girl I helped has been watching me. According to Kaleb, she's in love with me. Unfortunately for her, I'm not interested in dating."

Kaleb dropped his eyes to the floor, remembering what he was doing, and quietly turned away from the door. His spirits were heavier now, not as light as they had been before, making Kaleb wonder what was wrong with him. He let Bubbie inside from the cold, smiling at the warm welcome the dog gave him as he entered the house. The boy knelt down to rub the dog's neck, receiving kisses along his cheek from Bubbie. Kaleb chuckled, pushing the snout away from his face.

"Good to see you too, bud."

Chapter 24

"I guess that'll do it for today." Kaleb stretched in his seat, his long arms reaching high over his head. "If you want to work on more later, we can."

Taylor nodded, already packing up his extra credit and homework. "We'll see."

The two packed up and left the laboratory for home, locking up behind them as usual. Taylor looked around the hallway while Kaleb fiddled with the lock, seeing each poster and banner boldly expressing the excitement of the Girl's Choice dance coming soon.

"I'll never understand the appeal for dances," Taylor mumbled.

Kaleb followed his gaze to a banner. "It's a lot of fun, actually," he said, starting down the hallway. "If you would just give it a shot." Taylor grimaced.

"Loud, hot, and full of people. People I don't even like." He shook his head. "No thanks."

Kaleb rolled his eyes as they pushed through the double doors. "You're so weird," he muttered, then turned to the blonde. "What if your girl asked you?" He grinned slyly. "Would you go then?"

Taylor frowned. "Girl?"

"Don't give me that." Kaleb shoved his shoulder. "That girl you were telling me about."

Taylor looked away. "Oh. That."

"'Oh. That.'" Kaleb mocked in a bulky voice. "You're just *so* excited."

Taylor glared at the darker man. "I'm just not into that stuff, alright?"

"So you *wouldn't* go if she asked you?" Kaleb grinned.

"I'd rather we do something else," Taylor answered. Kaleb jumped ahead, stopping in front of the blonde.

"But if that's what she wanted to do," Kaleb looked him in the eye. "Would you do it?" Taylor frowned, brushing past the older boy. "C'mon." Kaleb followed after him. "It's just a simple question."

Taylor shrugged exasperatedly. "I don't know!" he huffed. "Maybe."

Kaleb grinned. "She must be some girl."

Taylor looked away, scowling. "I don't really care what we do," he muttered. "I just…"

"Like being around her?" Kaleb offered, sending the blonde into defense mode.

"I don't even know why I'm telling you this!" Taylor complained, bringing a chuckle from the darker man.

"Because we're friends," Kaleb answered. "And I'm good at mind tricking you into giving me what I want."

Taylor glared at Kaleb, unable to deny this truth. "Let me guess," Kaleb went on. "You want to spend all of your time together, that's a given." He grinned at the blonde. "You also can't stop thinking about her." Taylor scowled forward, not daring to look in Kaleb's general direction. "You want to know everything there is to know about her, and what you already know isn't enough."

"Is there a point to this?" Taylor snipped, gripping his straps against a cold wind.

"You've got it bad," Kaleb chuckled.

"How is it that you know this stuff anyways?" Taylor barked. "Guys like you don't ask these sort of questions."

Kaleb pointed a finger. "Guys like me don't major in alchemy and hobby in chemistry either," he grinned. "Guys like me are rough and tough football players who don't know how to spell their own name."

Taylor hiked his pack. "Whatever," he grumbled. "It's not like you're an expert."

Kaleb shrugged. "True. I may not be an expert but I do know what it feels like to want someone."

Taylor scoffed. "You? The king?" He frowned at Kaleb. "It wouldn't take you long to get her."

Kaleb ticked his head, smiling. "And yet, I'm still chasing."

Taylor looked to the darker man, surprised by this. "You mean you-"

Kaleb shrugged, walking ahead of the blonde and stopping his words. "To be honest," Kaleb said quietly. "I'm scared to tell you about it." Taylor stepped up next to him, with Kaleb keeping his eyes forward. "I'm scared to tell anybody, but…" Kaleb pocketed his hands, looking to his moving feet and smiled. "If you can do it, Teahnu, then I guess I can too."

Taylor looked away, his lips a thin line. "You shouldn't have a problem with getting the girl," he told him. "Like I said, you're the king. You can get whatever you want. I'm sure she'd ask you to the dance anyway."

Kaleb tilted his head. "I've made an offer," he said, the wind biting at his cheeks. "Doesn't look good, though."

As they walked through the park, a body could be seen waiting at the bridge leading to the Evans house. Brown hair and a long, flowing skirt blew in the wind, making the girl huddle closer to her body for warmth.

"Karen?" Kaleb called, turning the girl. She straightened when she saw the two, trying to straighten her disheveled hair before they could reach her. "What are you doing here?" Kaleb asked. "It's freezing." His eyes popped when he noticed her books. "Have you been here since school let out?"

Karen's wide eyes looked to him, struggling for an answer, but was too distracted by the blonde next to him to spit it out.

"Are you alright?" Taylor asked, eyeing the silent girl.

"Yes!" she blurted finally. "Yes, I'm fine." She pulled her hair back from her face, still trying to manage it in the wind. "Um," Karen looked to Taylor with large eyes. "I was…" She looked away, too shy to speak any further. "What I mean is, I…" She squeezed her eyes shut, marching past the two and away from the bridge. "Oooh!" She growled, stopping to huff at the sky, and turning to and from the boys a few times, bouncing on her toes before finally marching back to Taylor.

"Will you go with me?" Karen asked. She looked away, nervously twirling her hair. "To dance? Go dance? With me? I mean, go, with me. At the dance, you, me, us together. I mean you don't have to, it's just that; well I thought-"

"Sure."

Taylor stopped her before she could pass out there in front of him, earning two pairs of shocked eyes on him.

"Really?" she asked.

"*Really*?" Kaleb muttered.

Taylor shrugged. "Go home and get warm. I'll see you at the dance."

A bright smile exploded over Karen's face. "Alright! I'll see you there." She turned to leave, waving to the boys with her smile still glued to her face. The two returned the gesture, waving goodbye to her for as long as she would look at them.

"I thought you didn't want to go," Kaleb said quietly, still watching the beautiful brunette walking away.

"It took a lot of balls to ask. Why ruin it for her?" Taylor answered, also watching her leave. Kaleb looked to the ground.

"I guess you're right," he said quietly, then turned to resume their journey home. Kaleb gave a smile, still looking to the ground as they walked.

"That was cool of you," he said softly. "Doing that for her."

Taylor looked away. "It wasn't just for her," he said, gaining the darker man's attention.

"It wasn't?" Kaleb asked, looking to the blonde. Taylor stared ahead, walking forward towards home. "You had a reason too?" Kaleb pressed, making the smaller boy frown.

"You're the one who offered free lessons."

"Aww," Bekah cooed. "You've got an admirer."

Taylor huffed at her, giving a tired glare. "It's not that big a deal," he sighed. "I just went because she asked me." Bekah shook her head.

"There's more to it than that, I can tell." She grinned wide. "Besides, someone *likes* you. That's a change from before, for sure."

Taylor cupped his jaw, holding his head up with a lazy hand. "Yeah, I guess," he mumbled. Bekah's grin subsided, and she looked to her friend curiously.

"What's wrong?" she asked gently. Taylor shook his head lightly.

"I don't know. I think…" He looked behind him to make sure the door was closed, then turned back around to sigh at the desk.

"Kaleb and I were talking today," he muttered to the desk. "He said he…" The blonde looked away, running a hand through his hair. "He said he was chasing someone." Taylor sighed. "I know what I'm going through is just a phase, but…" He looked away. "For some reason, I haven't felt right ever since he said that- and he looked so…" Taylor rubbed his eyes. "The look on his face when he said she didn't like him back is still in my head."

Bekah crossed her arms over the desk, studying her friend's eyes. "You really like him, don't you?" she asked quietly. Taylor whipped away from the computer.

"I don't know- I don't know!" He held his head in his hands, bending his elbows over his knees. "I mean, why would I?" Taylor asked. "He's- he's a *he*, and I'm not-" He groaned into his hands. "I figured I could change my mind if I went with her."

"No you didn't," Bekah said. "You're not so easily swayed."

Taylor held his position over his knees, staring at the floor.

"Why did you *really* agree to go?"

He closed his eyes into a sigh, staying that way for a few moments. "He wanted me to," Taylor answered quietly. A knock on the door straightened the blonde, turning to find Kaleb in the doorway.

"Dinner's ready." He paused when he saw the strained look on Taylor's face. "You okay?"

"I'm fine," Taylor replied, turning to his friend in the screen. "See ya, Beck." She waved goodbye, watching the two for as long as she could before the screen went black.

"You sure you're okay?" Kaleb asked. Taylor brushed past the darker man in the doorway, avoiding eye contact as he walked away from Kaleb.

"I'm fine."

A crack of thunder jolted Kaleb awake, a small gasp escaping his lips. He sighed away the excess air, relaxing into his pillow and rubbed at his eyes with his palms. Up above, he could hear the rustling of Taylor's moving body, then felt the sinking in his bed as a foot touched down.

"Sorry," Kaleb mumbled, looking to the blonde. "Didn't mean to wake you." Taylor said nothing, but drew the covers up over his legs. "What are you-?" Kaleb turned to him. "I'm fine, really…"

Taylor remained silent as he plopped down on the pillow next to Kaleb, closing his eyes to sleep. Kaleb eyed the stubborn blonde, sighing back down into his pillow.

"You realize you're going to be either pushed off or wrapped up later, right?"

Taylor didn't stir.

"All right," Kaleb shrugged, turning his head to close his eyes. Another crackle went by, making Kaleb open his eyes again. He looked down to his chest, biting his lip.

"Is this how you handled things that scared you?" Kaleb asked quietly, looking to the blonde. "You know, sticking close to someone."

Taylor kept his eyes closed as he answered. "I got used to doing things on my own," he uttered simply.

"What about before?" Kaleb asked. "I mean, when you were a kid. Did you crawl in bed with your mom or something?"

Taylor opened his eyes, looking to the ceiling. "When I was upset, or something bothered me," he started quietly. "I would curl up on the bed, and she would come up behind me." His mouth quirked. "She didn't even have to say anything. She'd just hold me until I felt like talking again. Then, we'd end up talking all night long."

Kaleb smiled softly to the bunk over him. "That sounds nice. Your mom sounds pretty cool." He fiddled with his fingers. "She looks like she really loves you too…" He looked away to the wall, afraid to ask.

"So why did she leave?" Taylor asked for him.

Kaleb looked to the blonde, suddenly uncomfortable, then looked to the bed, his hands, anything to keep from eye contact. Taylor rolled to his side, eyes on Kaleb as he reached for his hand. Kaleb flinched when the blonde took his fingertips, but turned to Taylor as he put the darker man's hand on his cheek, pressing his fingers over the small crevice engraved in his face.

"You wanted to know how I got this." Taylor kept his eyes on Kaleb's as he felt the scar, silently waiting for the blonde to continue.

"It was a bottle," Taylor answered, dropping his gaze. "It must've been cracked or something, because it broke when he swung at me." He shook his head, accidentally brushing Kaleb's finger's off his cheek, then looked to the darker man. "He was angry because I did it. I sent her away."

Kaleb stared at the blonde, stunned.

"I couldn't stop it," Taylor said quietly, shaking his head. "She wouldn't let me." He frowned at the bed. "She would always shove me away- I just couldn't keep watching her get hurt." He kept his eyes down and away from Kaleb's. "The only way I could get her to go was by promising that I would come right after her, and that I would run before things got too dangerous." Taylor sucked in his lip. "He found out after she left, and blamed me."

Kaleb furrowed his brow. "He shouldn't have," he said, causing Taylor to look up at him.

"It wasn't all his fault; he was angry," Taylor told him. "He had every right to blame me." Kaleb's face darkened.

"No matter what you did, no matter why you did it, there is never a reason to be beaten bloody."

Taylor stared up at the darker man, unable to find a rebuttal.

"A man like that has no right punishing you for protecting your family," Kaleb said, just as quietly.

Taylor shook his head. "He wasn't always like that," he defended. "Before the war-" he looked away. "I always had a good time with him."

Kaleb studied the blonde, seeing the change in him. "What was he like?"

Taylor peered up at Kaleb, finding no scorn in his face, but curiosity. "He was a lot of fun," Taylor said. "He and I would always hang out together when he wasn't working at the garage, and even then, sometimes he would have me come over and help just to hang out." The blonde smothered down a smile. "He had the worst dad-jokes, too." Taylor sucked in his lips. "One time, he told me that he wondered where the sun went all night long, and then it *dawned* on him."

Kaleb snorted. "That's awful," he snickered.

"I know," Taylor grinned. "That wasn't even the worst of it, either."

"I'd hate to hear the rest of them," Kaleb chuckled.

Taylor rolled to his back, grinning slightly. "He also had this thing about sugar." Taylor rolled his eyes. "He had a *huge* sweet tooth," he said, looking to Kaleb. "Whenever we went out, he would buy us two desserts when I couldn't make up my mind, and we'd share them together." He turned his head back to the ceiling. "Mom got so mad at him for that, but he'd always give her a kiss and say the same thing." He suddenly lowered his voice in imitation. "'Sarah, life's too short to be healthy all the time.'" Taylor's grin lowered as his thoughts wandered. "I guess he was right."

Kaleb's grin dwindled as well, and was about to say something when Taylor took a breath.

"It'll work," he said, mostly to confirm it to himself. "We're too stubborn not to let it." Kaleb looked to the bunk above him, chuckling.

"Yeah, I believe it."

Taylor awoke wrapped in the arms of Kaleb, his dark head nestled on the blonde's shoulder and chest, sleeping peacefully. Taylor stared at the darker man for a moment, taking in the sight while trapped on his back. He looked to the ceiling, closing his eyes to feel the warmth emanating from the body that clung to his side and stomach, and taking pleasure in the comfort that it brought him. The two had stayed up all night talking about Taylor's father, and had ended up falling asleep together in Kaleb's bed. Now, Taylor waited for Kaleb to wake, pretending to sleep himself in order to stay in his arms if even for a moment longer, and hating himself for it.

The alarm went off, doing its routine job to alert the boys of another morning for school. Kaleb groaned, burying his face into Taylor's shoulder. "Go away," he mumbled. The alarm was relentless, however, and screamed shrilly for Kaleb to come and turn it off. He sighed, heating Taylor's chest with the warm breath, and he rose to turn it off. Taylor remained motionless, keeping his eyes closed as Kaleb noticed the position they were in, and heard him sighing again, rubbing the back of his head as he sat up.

"Taylor," Kaleb whispered, softly tapping the blonde. "Taylor, get up."

Taylor took a deep breath as he opened his eyes, further selling the idea that he was just waking up. "What?" he mumbled, making a small chuckle come from the darker man.

"We need to get ready for school," Kaleb whispered, playing along.

"Okay, but I have one question first," Taylor whispered back.

"What?" Kaleb asked. Taylor looked him right in the eye.

"Why are we whispering?" Straight faced.

Kaleb's mouth quivered into a grin. "Because it's too early for talking," he answered quietly. Taylor nodded.

"I see," he whispered. "When do we start talking again?"

Kaleb gave him a coy look. "You said you only had one question."

Taylor stared back at him. "I do. *Another* one." His straight face was beginning to waver as Kaleb's grin grew with his chuckling.

"Smart ass," Kaleb said, breaking the whisper battle. "C'mon."

The two boys readied themselves for another school day, taking turns grabbing things from the closet to get dressed. Trish had left breakfast for them on the kitchen counter, and Vance left half a pot of coffee for Taylor, which he gladly accepted. Once they had eaten, and Taylor had locked Bubbie in the backyard, they were off. Winter was coming to an end, but the air still clung to the chill that came with it, holding on for a few more weeks to come.

Kaleb yawned, blowing a cloud of steam around his face as they walked along. A dark grin spread over him as an idea sparked, and he blew out another wave of hot air from his mouth.

"I'm a dragon, raaah!" he hissed, his tongue sticking out as well. Taylor shook his head.

"You're an idiot," he corrected, but Kaleb shook his head.

"Nope! I'm a dragon! Raauhg!" There goes his tongue again.

"Dragons don't flick their tongues out like lizards," Taylor snarked, sending Kaleb's tongue rolling back into his mouth. He ticked his head, flicking his tongue in and out and twitching his head every so often. Taylor shoved the 'lizard' off the sidewalk, sending him into a fit of laughter as he righted himself next to the blonde.

"You're pretty hyper for someone who didn't get any sleep last night," Taylor noted as they entered the school.

"Guess I'm just in a good mood," he grinned, rolling Taylor's eyes.

"It's too early for that," he muttered, earning a chuckle from Kaleb. They made their way to the cafeteria for their morning rounds; Kaleb meeting and greeting with the people who were beginning to talk to him again, and Taylor finding a quiet table to write in his journal. They were stopped, however, when a perky young blonde stepped up to them with a smile.

"Good morning, Kaleb." the girl smiled.

"Morning, Candice," he returned. Her smile broadened as she stepped closer to him, completely ignoring Taylor.

"Do you have a date for the dance?" she asked, wiggling her shoulders as she walked.

"Can't say that I do."

Candice's smile widened even further.

"You do now." She whipped around, her long, yellow hair barely missing Kaleb as she waved a hand high over her shoulder. "I'll see you there!" she sang. Kaleb and Taylor shared a look, silently noting every detail of what had just happened. Kaleb shrugged.

"Guess I'm going to the dance," he said. Taylor looked away, trying not to bite his lip.

"Is she-"

"No," Kaleb answered. "She's not the one."

Taylor gripped onto his shoulder straps. "Don't you want to wait and see if she'll ask you?" he asked, not looking at the darker man.

"Too late for that," Kaleb said. Taylor turned to him.

"She already has a date?" He scoffed. "She works fast, doesn't she?"

Kaleb snickered at his friend. "Looks like neither of us will be going with who we want." Kaleb shrugged, leaving Taylor on his own at an empty table. He watched Kaleb leave, all playfulness now gone since seeing the pesky blonde steal away his friend.

Taylor was quiet for the rest of the day. For the rest of the *month* actually. The days passed by quickly, filled with Candice popping in on Kaleb's conversations to drop hints about what she would be wearing, what kind of flower she liked, how many dances she knew, and it was all far too annoying for Taylor to stick around and listen to. He had grown to dislike Candice, not only for her pushy demeanor, but also for butting in on his time with Kaleb outside of home. He realized this to be a ridiculous reason to not like her, but it changed nothing. Kaleb was his friend before he was her date.

As annoying as she was, though, Taylor used some of Candice's questions to his advantage, and planned what he would do with Karen should the need arise. She was useful for that much at least. Still, whenever Candice would come around, Taylor would sneak away before he could become too irritable, leaving Kaleb alone with the flirtatious blonde for his own pleasures. He did his best to keep his mind busy, anything to keep him from imagining her leaning up against Kaleb, touching him, laughing at his jokes- he would end up slapping his hands over his face in frustration at how irritatingly jealous he was being over a man who wasn't even interested in him in the first place.

Now Taylor was walking to the bedroom alone while Kaleb was stuck in a conversation with Candice over the chat in his mother's office. He plopped down on Kaleb's bed, stretching over the foot of it to rest an arm over his tired eyes. Bubbie came panting in and hopped up to lay next to Taylor, giving his arm a small lick before laying his head down. Taylor blindly patted the dog, giving a scratch when he was done. He stayed like this for a while, eventually dozing off for a few minutes and waking up to find Kaleb leaning back in his chair, eyes covered as well.

"Sorry," Taylor muttered, stirring the darker man. "Didn't mean to take your bed."

Kaleb shook his head. "No worries." He stood to sit next to the blonde, stretching out next to the pillows with his legs hanging off the edge of the bed. "Easy fix." Kaleb grinned under an arm.

Taylor turned his head back under his arm. "You tired too?" Taylor asked, earning a grunt from his darker counterpart.

"She can talk up a storm over absolutely nothing," Kaleb complained. "I'll be happy when this is all over and done with."

Taylor frowned, looking to him. "I thought you liked this stuff."

Kaleb scoffed. "I like the dance part, not the plan part. Candice is making it much more difficult than it needs to be."

Taylor stared at Kaleb, perplexed by the strange boy.

"Sorry she bugs you," Kaleb muttered, surprising the blonde.

"She doesn't-"

"Don't give me that," he interrupted. "You run off any chance you get. Besides, it's not like you were a big people person anyways."

Taylor looked away, frustrated with himself for even thinking he could hide his irritation from Kaleb.

"Hey, Teahnu?" Kaleb tried. "Can I ask you something?"

He had begun to call Taylor this name more often. Privately of course, but more and more over the past month, and it was starting to grow on the blonde. Taylor looked to his darker friend, waiting for him to speak. Kaleb's face was serious under his arm, staring straight up into the bunk and not daring to look anywhere near Taylor. His mouth twitched, wanting to speak but not knowing what to say.

"Well, are you going to ask me or what?" Taylor sassed, making Klaeb look away.

"No, nevermind," he said quietly. Taylor thinned his lips, wishing he hadn't been so snippy with the darker man.

"Didn't mean to scare you off," he muttered, looking to the bunk.

Kaleb looked up to the bunk as well. "It's not that, it's just…" He sighed. "It's not important."

Taylor furrowed his brow, still staring up. "What's wrong?" he asked quietly. Kaleb shook his head, eyes locked above him.

"Nothing's wrong."

"Bull shit," Taylor rebuttaled. "You're usually cracking jokes right about now, and bugging me about stuff I think is stupid."

Kaleb huffed, closing his eyes into a small smile. "There's no fooling you, is there?" he asked, eyes still closed. He sighed again, slowly opening his eyes to the bunk. "It's not a big deal," he said softly. "I don't really want to talk about it anymore." Taylor frowned to the bunk, then rose on his elbows to turn to the darker man.

"When you do, come to me," he said sternly, forcing Kaleb to look at him. "What else am I here for?"

Kaleb stared at the blonde, silenced by his words. Taylor stared right back, keeping eye contact with the darker man. He was serious about wanting Kaleb to talk with him. He may not be able to do anything about what was bothering Kaleb, but Taylor could at least be an ear for him when he needed someone to listen. Troubled or not, Taylor would listen to anything Kaleb had to say.

The creak of the front door didn't stir the two, but when Trish called to them, Kaleb broke his gaze to answer her. Taylor laid back down, dropping his arm over his eyes again as he sighed.

"You're on your own!" Vance shouted, retreating somewhere to the other side of the house.

"Boys?" Trish poked her head into the bedroom with a quick knock. "C'mon, let's go." She waved to hurry them along.

"Are we eating out?" Kaleb asked, sitting up.

"Sure, but we need to get to the shops before they close," Trish answered, freezing Taylor. Kaleb, however, didn't understand just yet.

"The grocery stores stay open late, don't they?"

Trish grinned, leaning further into the room. "We're not going grocery shopping." Her grin grew. "You need something nice for the dance, right?" She popped out of the door, not seeing the pained look Taylor was clinging at or the horror dripping from her son's face, but continued on, calling to the two boys as she walked down the hall. "Come along, you two!"

"Oh, no."

"Not again!"

Chapter 25

Finally, the night the entire school had been anticipating had arrived, and everyone was excited for the chance to let loose and have fun. Everyone, that is, except for Taylor. He sighed as he buttoned up and tucked his shirt into his jeans, eyeing his hair in the reflection of the window. Trish would be dragging him off to the bathroom any second now, saying she had plans for him ever since breakfast that morning. He huffed, slipping his smooth, black vest on and buttoning it up. He was having trouble with his tie when a knock on the door tensed the blonde on the spot.

"Relax, it's just me," Kaleb chuckled. Taylor turned to find Kaleb looking him over. His purplish shirt was unbuttoned at the top, allowing the girls a good show of his collar bone, and flustering the blonde.

"Here." Kaleb walked forward to reach out for Taylor, but the younger boy took a step back, still fiddling with his tie. "You're wearing it wrong," Kaleb told him, waiting for the blonde to allow his help. He unbuttoned the cuff of Taylor's sleeve, then pulled it up to his elbow. He folded it in half two more times, transforming the formal, white shirt into a charming, casual party look.

"You looked like a busboy like that," Kaleb explained, rolling up Taylor's other sleeve.

"Thanks," Taylor muttered, sitting on the bed to get out of eyeline with Kaleb's perfectly tan chest. He fumbled some more with his tie, earning another chuckle from Kaleb.

"When was the last time you wore one of these?" he asked, kneeling to take the black strip from the blonde's hands. Damn, he smelled good.

"I've never had a reason," Taylor mumbled, catching sight of his chest again.

"I can tell," Kaleb grinned, tightening the tie around Taylor's neck. He looked up to study the blonde, the wheels in his head turning. Taylor stared back at him, too scared to say anything to Kaleb with him being so close.

Without a word, Kaleb reached up to Taylor, running both of his hands over the blonde's head. He started at his forehead, tracing his fingers over the top of Taylor's head and around to the back, feeling every soft strand in between. Taylor closed his eyes, allowing Kaleb to run his fingers through his hair, and secretly taking note of every feeling to remember later. The large, warm hands stopped at the nape of Taylor's neck, opening the blonde's eyes as they pulled away. He looked to the darker man for answers, but Kaleb merely stared back with a content look.

"I have always wanted to do that," he admitted quietly.

Taylor gave him a confused look. "Why?"

Kaleb shrugged. "I don't know." He looked to the blonde. "You do it all the time." He grinned sharply. "At least, you do when you're uncomfortable."

Taylor stared at the darker man, wishing there could be some distance between them and wanting to run a hand through his hair now. He looked away, tucking his tie into his vest.

"Whatever," he mumbled. Kaleb looked away as well, standing to let the blonde up. He tilted his head as he examined the blonde, looking at the style.

"That tie might be too much, actually," Kaleb muttered.

"It won't be when I'm through with him." As if on cue, Trish stepped through the doorway. She locked eyes with Taylor, grinning at the unwilling blonde and waving him over to follow her to the bathroom. Taylor sighed, frowning at the ceiling.

"Why am I doing this?"

Kaleb snickered. "You can tell her no. Just be ready to get mind fucked, because she'll end up getting her way anyways."

Taylor glared at him, smacking his chiselled chest as he walked out for the bathroom. Trish grabbed him as soon as he entered and spiked his hair up for him, turning his flat, blonde hair into a new, sharp style. When he caught Kaleb's attention with it, Taylor wanted to melt into the floor. Kaleb's eyes searched him further.

"That... Actually looks good," Kaleb admitted, inspecting the blonde's gelled hair. "Like, *really* good."

Taylor looked away, pocketing his hands. "I look like a boy band," he muttered, making sure Trish was gone before speaking. Kaleb shook his head.

"I like it. She was right, too; the whole look works." He smiled at Taylor. "You look good."

The blonde turned away, having to pull his hand away from his head when he tried running it through his hair. Kaleb's compliment was too much for him, he needed to get out of there. "Let's go," he muttered, not so self conscious anymore. Kaleb liked the way he looked. That was enough.

Karen's long brown hair was held back with a simple hair-pin, allowing her dark locks to fall over her shoulders and down her back. Her white and pink flowered dress was a simple cut with thick straps hugging her collarbone and shoulders, flaring out at her hips to her knees beneath a pink, satin belt. She wore simple white sandals that made her half an inch taller, and her hands were covered in dainty, lace gloves that cut off at her wrists. A single, gold necklace held a tiny, white gem just as her neck connected with her shoulders for the finishing touches of simplicity that added to her beauty. All in all, she looked like a lovely young woman. Candice, however, was another story.

Candice's blonde hair was tied tight on the top of her head, flaring out from the bottom of a bun. Her dress was barely a dress at all; more of a red, silky tube sock cut in the back to expose her swirling soul crest between her shoulderblades, and her butterfly tattoo at the base of her spine. Her matching red heels were at least four inches tall, making her almost reach Kaleb's eyes when she stood next to him, and her large, hoop earrings dangled around her cheeks for a few seconds longer when she moved her head.

She didn't give Kaleb the chance to present her corsage. Her bright red lips smiled broadly when she saw him, and she tapped over to him as quickly as she could without tripping over her shoes, waving her hands around her for balance as she drew near him. Once she wrapped her hands around his arm, she dragged Kaleb off to the dance floor, leaving him waving to the other two behind him.

Taylor shook his head at her, glaring at the disappearing duo, and cursing the blonde woman for taking away the one person he felt comfortable with in this crowded shit-hole. Karen looked up at Taylor, fiddling with her gloved fingers for a moment to try and think of what to say.

"Um…" she started, gaining the blonde's attention. "… You look really nice." She waved a finger around her head. "Your hair too." Taylor offered a polite smile.

"You don't have to-"

"No, no," she interrupted him. "I mean it. I can see you this way. I mean- I can see your eyes this way."

Taylor kept his smile up as he stepped closer to Karen, channeling his inner flirt and wondering what Kaleb would do in this situation. "So," he said, slipping on her corsage. "What would the lovely lady like to do first?"

Karen blushed, smiling to the ground. "You wouldn't mind if we got something to drink, would you?" she asked. "I'm not ready to dance yet."

Taylor plastered his smile on his face, determined to keep it on the entire night, and offered an elbow to her. She smiled shyly back, taking his arm as they walked to the food bar together.

They mostly spoke through the night, trying to hear each other over the roar of the crowd and the pounding music. Neither of them really cared for the dancing part, but the music helped to keep Taylor collected, occasionally tapping his foot along with a song that also played on his headphones or any other song that caught his fancy. He laughed when he was supposed to, responded quickly, and kept his smile on his face no matter the situation.

After a while, a slow song came on, and Karen shrank into her shoulders, nervously looking to the floor. Noticing the change, Taylor slipped her cup from her and set it down next to his on the table, then took her hand to guide her to the dance floor.

Taylor gently placed Karen's flowered hand on his shoulder and cupped the other in his own, just as Trish had taught him, then swayed with her through the crowd. Karen's blushing was uncontrollable as she smiled to the floor, trying to hide her flushed cheeks from her date. Her hair fell over her face, further hiding her from sight. Taylor stopped dancing for a moment, tilting her head up to face him. Then, he took off her glasses, and brushed back her hair behind her ears.

"There," he said as he nestled her glasses back over her nose. "Now I can see you."

Karen smiled to the floor, but quickly looked up at Taylor, trying not to hide again. They resumed their positions on the dance floor, this time Karen laying her head on Taylor's chest as he guided her around.

Karen squeezed Taylor's hand, drawing herself closer into his chest as the song came to an end. She looked up to him with wide eyes, biting her lip.

"Taylor?"

Before he could reply, she stretched on her toes and pressed her lips against his, dropping a quick, light kiss on his lips before sinking back to the floor. Her grip on his hand tightened in fear as she studied his completely stunned face. His smile had gone, and he was looking to her with shocked eyes, his mouth slightly parted in efforts to make words, but none came. He had no experience with turning down girls- he had no experience with girls *period*. He certainly had never seen Kaleb do it either. Taylor was stuck.

Karen's face crumpled as she twirled away from Taylor's grasp, running away as quickly as she could through the crowd.

"Karen," Taylor called, following after her. "Karen, wait."

She had managed to make it to the hall, clicking down its length towards the exit.

"Karen!" Taylor had caught up with her, lightly grabbing her elbow to turn her around. "Karen, please."

She kept her gaze down, refusing to look at him as tears streamed down her face to fall to the floor. "I'm sorry," she whimpered. "I shouldn't have-" She sniffed. "I thought-" She covered her face with her gloved hands, unable to speak anymore. Taylor sighed, rubbing his hands down her shoulders.

"You're a nice girl, Karen," Taylor said softly. "I'm just not interested in a relationship right now."

Karen cried into her hands, leaning forward to Taylor's chest, who begrudgingly held her close as she sobbed into him.

Kaleb kept an eye on Taylor as much as he could, watching him whenever Candice would allow his eyes to wander. The moody teen was laughing a lot, and smiling too, seeming to be having a good time with Karen, but Kaleb wasn't the only one watching Taylor. His attendance did not go unnoticed by the other students, the girls especially. Around him, Kaleb heard the whispers and gossip already brewing around the blonde and the wallflower; girls whispering about his sudden change of appearance and wondering if it was because of the girl he sat with now.

"Is that Tommy?"

"It's Taylor."

"He's so hot!"

"Look at how cute they are!"

"He dressed up just for her, how sweet!"

"Do you think Keith will get mad if I ask him to dance?"

"He's Karen's date, don't you dare!"

Kaleb grinned at the gossip, already snickering at the reaction he would receive when he would tell the blonde later. Candice went on dancing around him, rolling her butt against him as she shimmied to the music, and smiling at him when she turned her head. Kaleb danced along as best he could, not really caring for her choice of movements and limiting his reactions to keep from touching her inappropriately- which she made severely difficult.

Candice was a machine, dancing from one song to the next without even a breath in between. Kaleb did his best to keep up, using his energy reserves he had learned to build up from years of football, but when a slow song came, he would have been lying if he said he wasn't relieved. She cuddled up close to Kaleb, wrapping her arms around his neck and smiling up at him. "It's about time," she grinned.

Kaleb kept his hands high, gripping both of his wrists behind her back and around her waist instead of letting his hands fall over her rump like many other couples had. Candice sighed contently, laying her head on his chest to close her eyes. The darker man took this moment to catch his breath, closing his eyes and letting his mind wander as well while they swayed to the music.

"Hey, Candice?" he asked.

"Hmm?" She kept her head pressed against his chest.

"I have a game for you," he replied, earning a grin.

"What kind of game?" she asked seductively.

"Nothing big, it's pretty simple, really," he brushed off. "Just answer me this: if you could describe me in one word, what would it be?"

Candice pulled her head off of him to look up in his chocolate eyes, a deep grin stretching on her far-too-large lips.

"Hot."

She giggled into his chest, resting her head back down on him with another content sigh.

"Oh my soul, look how cute they are!"

"He's showing her how to dance!"

"Aww!"

Kaleb looked up to find Taylor holding Karen close to him, dancing with her the same way Trish had taught him from before. Karen was obviously smitten, smiling happily to the floor in efforts to hide her blushing face from Taylor.

"Oh, she's so cute!"

"Look, look, look!"

Taylor stopped the dancing long enough to brush Karen's hair from her face, smiling down at her and muttering something that made her smile outshine the stars, and sent the whispering girls into a frenzy of "awing." Kaleb stared at the two, unable to take his eyes off of them. Karen gently laid her head on Taylor's chest, her smile still on her face. Kaleb gripped his wrists, inadvertently tightening his arms around Candice. She smiled, tightening her arms around his neck, then lifted her head to greet him with a kiss. His attention, however, was misplaced. She turned to find what had taken her date away from her, and scowled when she saw the same couple Kaleb had been eyeing all night long.

As the song came to an end, Karen looked up to Taylor, asking him something. When he looked down to answer, she lifted onto her toes to kiss him. The whispering girls squealed with delight, but Kaleb wasn't so happy. Without even realizing it, his face dropped, as well as his hands. He stared at the couple, dumbstruck at the sudden happenings, and slowly growing bitter. Karen pulled away, watching Taylor's face, then ran away as quick as she could in the crowd. Taylor ran after her, trying to catch up between the groups of people.

"Oh, no!"

"What happened?"

"He doesn't like her!"

Candice glared at Kaleb, turning her attention to the retreating couple, then huffed at her own date, stomping her foot as she charged after the two.

"Candice?" Kaleb was finally pulled out of his trance. "Candice, wait!" He followed after her, the two of them trapped behind crowds of people. By the time they had reached the exit, they found Taylor holding a sobbing Karen in the abandoned hallway. Candice stomped after them, angrily glaring down the couple.

"What is your problem?" she screamed, turning the teary Karen. "You stay away from my man!"

"Candice!" Kaleb grabbed her elbow to pull her away, but the angry blonde ripped her arm from his grasp and charged forward.

"Slut!"

"What are you talking about?" Karen sniffed. Taylor pulled her to the side, trying to put himself between her and the raging woman, but Candice was too quick for him.

"He's been staring at you all night long!" she raged. "He's my date, he's my boyfriend, and he's *not* available, so just lay off!" She shoved Karen roughly, making the brunette stumble backwards.

"Candice, stop it!" Kaleb shouted, but Taylor stood up instead, blocking her from Karen.

"Knock it off," he warned, his dangerously low voice more threatening than angry.

"Don't defend her!" Candice hissed. "That whole innocent flower act is just that- an act!" The angry woman glared at Karen. "She's really a boyfriend stealing slut!"

"Candice!" Kaleb shouted, finally getting her attention. "What are you doing? I'm not your boyfriend!"

"Oh, yes you are!" she yelled, eyes growing wider by the second. "What do you call this past month then, huh? All the time we talked together?"

Kaleb held out his arms. "Conversations!" He looked her right in the eye. "I only went with you to the dance because you asked me to, nothing more."

Candice's face morphed into a furious scowl. "You want that *pig* over me?"

"Candice, you're being-"

"No!" she screamed. "Fuck you, Kaleb Evans!" She turned to Karen. "And fuck you, you fucking slut!"

"Stop it, Candice!" One of the whispering girls from the dance floor piped up.

"Yeah, you're being a bitch!" said another. The whispering group wasn't so quiet anymore, having followed everyone else out into the hallway to see if they could comfort Karen in her hour of need.

"Karen didn't do anything!"

Candice reached over to one of the girls to rip her drink from her hand, then tossed it over Karen's top, staining the white bodice to a dingy brown. Karen shrieked at the attack, backing away to stare down at her ruined dress. Candice threw the empty cup to the ground.

"That's what you get, bitch!"

"CANDICE!" Kaleb rushed forward to help Karen in anyway he could, separating the two girls with his own body while Taylor stepped up to the bitchy blonde.

"You shouldn't have done that," he muttered, towering over her. Candice's eyes went wide, both from fear and rage as she growled at Taylor, backing away from him and threatening him. Taylor said nothing, merely backed her away from the scene until she finally stomped her foot and huffed away, screaming in anger as she left. Taylor watched her leave through the door back to the dance before turning back down the hall. Karen was a blubbering mess surrounded by the trio of whispering girls, and Kaleb was off to the side watching, rubbing the back of his head.

Taylor looked between Kaleb and Karen, putting the evidence together, and realizing Karen to be the girl Kaleb had been talking about for the past month. The distress on his face now confirmed it, and from all the conversations he and Taylor had had together, it all seemed to add up perfectly. Now, with Candice's outburst, and the fact that Kaleb had been watching her all night, Taylor was certain of it.

He stopped for a moment, catching his breath while his heart put itself back together. Kaleb looked over to Karen, looking like he wanted to die right there for causing her so much pain, and it broke Taylor's heart all over again. He took a breath, trying to find the strength to use his legs again, and trying to keep his face stone cold. All the times Kaleb had told him about this girl, all the times a smile had been brought to his face because of her, all of the *advice* Kaleb had given him on how to treat Karen, it all piled up in Taylor's gut, weighing him down on the spot.

"Can I ask you something?"

Taylor closed his eyes on the memory of Kaleb's momentary depression, wondering if it was Karen he was going to ask Taylor about. *Knowing* that it was Karen he was going to ask about. Taylor cursed himself for his blindness, wishing he could have seen the signs sooner. The timeline added up perfectly; after she had asked Taylor, he remembered seeing Kaleb's face. His bright smile and joking manner were lost on sight.

The blonde swallowed hard, trying to dispel the knot in his throat as he also remembered how Kaleb had thanked him for being kind to Karen, accepting her

408

invitation even when he didn't want it. His broken heart was pounding against his chest, copying the angered pulse of his aching soul crest that seemed to want to burn through his skin. He finally looked up, taking a breath to calm his broken body, and forced himself to move.

The blonde sighed, walking past Kaleb and up to Karen, gently pushing through the crowd of fretting girls. She didn't dare look up at him. She kept her head down low to hide her red, wet face behind her hands. Her glasses were slipping from over her fingers and would fall at any second, so Taylor carefully removed them from her face. He unbuttoned his vest and slipped it off his shoulders, placing it over hers.

"Here," he said quietly, gently taking her hands from her face to slide them through the sleeves. He buttoned it back up for her, hiding the ugly brown that splattered over her breasts. Karen looked up to Taylor, her swollen face filled with wonder. Taylor kept his eyes on his fingers as he worked the buttons, ignoring the whispering girls around them. If Kaleb really cared about this girl like he did, and it was Taylor's fault that he couldn't get to her, then Taylor would at least take care of her for the night. That much he could do. He looked to Karen when he had finished, offering her glasses back to her and a small smile.

"Do you still want to dance?" he asked softly.

Karen looked to him for a moment before shaking her head. "No, you've done enough." She was trying to smile. "I'll chat my dad and have him come pick me up." She sniffed, slipping her glasses over her nose. "Thank you, Taylor."

He nodded, deepening his painful smile. "No problem."

Karen was ushered away with the whispering girls, off to find a computer to call her father, leaving Kaleb and Taylor alone in the hall.

"That was cool of you, Teahnu," Kaleb muttered, shattering Taylor's spirit.

He turned to his darker friend, his fake smile still in place. "You ready to go home?"

Kaleb gave Taylor a strange look, but nodded anyway, leaving silently with his friend. Neither of them said anything for most of the walk home. Taylor was too busy patching up his bruised heart, and Kaleb was preoccupied trying to figure out what all had happened that evening. After a while, Kaleb noticed the strained look on Taylor's face, still haunted by the smile the blonde had given him before. He rubbed the back of his head, looking to the moon above.

"I promise it's not normally this crazy," he said. "Dances are usually a lot more fun."

Taylor shrugged, keeping his gaze low. "They had fun. Right up until the end."

Kaleb chuckled at this response. "I guess you're right."

Taylor sat shirtless, fresh out of the shower and hunched over his journal in his bed, his headphones blaring over his ears as he wrote. It had been a while since he needed to use them to lift his spirits, but now, even the music wasn't helping. His fingers felt the smooth texture of the journal, thinking of how he felt when Kaleb had given it to him. Taylor huffed, growing irritated with himself for making the heartache worse, and shut the book with a thud, tossing it to the end of his bed. The blonde ripped off his headphones and left them to dangle around his neck as he curled up in his bed.

Taylor had been like this since the dance the night previous, claiming to be feeling sick in order to avoid contact with the Evans'- which was mostly true. Kaleb's sorrowful face was still burned in Taylor's memory, making the truth all the more painful. Karen was the mystery girl Kaleb had fallen for, and Taylor was the one who had taken her away from him. The blonde knew he would never be able to be with Kaleb from the start, and now, with the truth laid out in front of him, it stung too deep for Taylor to go back to normal so soon. The worst part of it, though, was that he had caused Kaleb unintentional harm.

Stealing Karen away from him so swiftly had to have been painful, and pretending to be alright with it had to have been even worse. Taylor closed his eyes as he imagined Kaleb feeling the way he did now, and wanted to bury himself under a rock for it. He wouldn't wish this pain on anyone; least of all the person he cared most about. A small knock quietly creaked open the door, followed by footsteps that entered the room.

"Taylor?" Kaleb asked. Taylor remained unmoving, closing his eyes to the wall and pretending to sleep, not wanting to deal with the darker man at the moment. Kaleb drew closer to the bed, climbing on his own mattress to rest his chin on Taylor's bunk.

"Teahnu."

Taylor's heart shivered at the name.

"Please talk to me," Kaleb asked quietly. "What else am I here for, right?"

Taylor stayed, keeping his back to the darker man.

"I know when you're faking, Teahnu, give me some credit."

Taylor furrowed his brow. Of course Kaleb would know. Still, he remained motionless as he continued to ignore the man he cared for. Kaleb sighed, spotting the blonde's irritated soul crest. He reached a hand up to try and calm the angry crest, but as his fingers touched Taylor's vines, an icy blast shot through the both of them. Kaleb was thrown off the bed and to the floor, while Taylor rolled over in his bed, muffling his pained screaming into his pillow.

"What the fuck?" Taylor growled, glaring at the darker man on the floor.

"I'm sorry- I-"

"Get out!" Taylor hissed, shoving his face back into his pillow to groan out the pain. Kaleb stood up, closing the door behind him and holding his fingers close to him. He marched down the hall, panicking at what had just happened. Taylor had rejected him again, just as he had the first time they touched.

The dance had been his idea, and he was the one who had forced Taylor to go, so it would be all too easy to blame Kaleb for their misadventures with Candice. Kaleb paced in the front room by the dining room table, trying to figure out what to do next when he decided to ask the one person who knew Taylor better than anyone. Kaleb charged forward to his mother's office, setting up the computer. He searched Taylor's website for Hacker_Nekko, sending a chat request as soon as he found her. She rejected his advances three times before answering him, showing up on his screen a few seconds later.

"Look, Bookworm, I don't know y-" Her irritated face turned into surprise when she saw it was Kaleb, and she suddenly became worried when she saw the look in his eyes. "What's wrong?"

Kaleb looked away, rubbing the back of his head. "I don't know what to do," he admitted. "I think Taylor's mad at me because of the dance, but he won't talk to me, and when I tried to touch his crest, he-"

"Woah, woah, wait-" Nekko stared at him with large eyes. "You *touched* his crest?"

Kaleb dropped his shoulders. "It looked irritated, and I was trying to help-"

"How could you even think that was a good idea?" she hissed. "*Especially* after last time!"

Kaleb bit his lip, looking away. "Actually…"

Nekko scrutinized the darker man. "What did you do?"

He shook his head. "I never told him this- but, remember when he was sick?"

She nodded.

"Did he tell you why?"

She frowned, shaking her head. Kaleb sighed, rubbing the back of his head.

"My friend Gerrit attacked him. My *old* friend." He looked away. "Beat him within an inch of his life." Nekko's eyes widened, turning away in disgust.

"His crest was in really bad shape," Kaleb went on. "They didn't think he'd make it out without a few scars." He rubbed his forehead. "My dad's a doctor, and he taught me a healing trick that didn't work for anybody else; Taylor kept on pushing them out. I thought I might try it, and when I did…" Kaleb looked to the desk. "Dad said he'd never seen such quick healing before. Said it had something to do with pent up intentions or something like that." He looked to the woman in the screen. "Taylor woke up the next day."

"So you thought you could do it again," Nekko stated quietly. She sighed, looking to him. "Don't try without asking anymore," she ordered. "You know how private he can be."

Kaleb nodded, gripping his still frozen fingers.

"As far as the dance thing goes, I'm in the dark," she said. "What happened?"

Kaleb went on to explain the night and events leading up to the debacle, emphasizing the fact that it was Kaleb's idea to go in the first place.

"And this Candice chick thought you were cheating on her?" Nekko asked, but Kaleb shrugged, shaking his head.

"I have no idea, she's nuts."

Nekko blinked, fitting the situation together like a puzzle with too many pieces. "I don't think he blames you for the fight," she said finally. "He's not the type of person to blame you for something someone else did." Kaleb looked away, realizing that happened a lot around him. "You're never gonna know unless you talk to him yourself, though."

"He won't talk to me."

"Give him some space."

Kaleb looked to the woman in the screen, but she waved away his worried face.

"You're gonna have to if you want to get down to the bottom of it," Nekko explained. "And you *definitely* need to make up for touching his crest."

Kaleb closed his eyes into a sigh, dropping his head to stare at the floor.

"Just give him some space," Nekko repeated. "He'll come around." She looked to him. "And if he doesn't after a few days, poke him with a stick. A little nudging into the conversation should do it."

Kaleb chuckled, giving a small smile as he looked up to her. "He's lucky to have a friend like you," he told her.

"Stop it." Nekko waved. "We had our sappy moment last time, don't you know we only do that once a year?"

Kaleb chuckled at her, feeling slightly better. No wonder Taylor spoke with her every day.

"Oh, can I ask you a favor?" Kaleb asked. Nekko crossed her arms over the desk, leaning in to hear what he had to say. "Can you *not* tell Taylor my username?" He sucked in his lips as he looked away. "If he finds out who I am, he'll kick me out of the site."

Nekko grinned at him, snickering in agreement. "Don't worry. Your secret's safe with me."

<u>Final Chapter</u>

"I really need you today, Taylor," Miss Hart said, tapping the blonde's shoulder. "We've got a new recruit and I need you to fill her in." Taylor nodded, agreeing to his duties as president.

"I guess we'll be going to the club first then, huh?" Kaleb asked, referring to their lessons. Taylor hiked his pack higher over his shoulders, leaving the classroom without a word. He made the excuse of needing a different book from his locker in order to convince himself to stay away from Kaleb, giving him time to think of how he would skip talking to him at Miss Hart's technology club.

He still hadn't forgiven himself for not realizing sooner, and he was still patching up his heart to the fact that the one he cared for didn't care for him. As much of a long shot as it was, Taylor couldn't help but imagine what it would be like if he and Kaleb were together. Now, that flicker of a thought was snuffed out, leaving the blonde to pick up the pieces. He unlocked his locker, switching out his books and slipping them into his pack. He zipped it back up and shrugged it onto his shoulder, heading back to the classroom to teach. When he arrived, he stopped in the doorway, staring at the new member speaking with Miss Hart.

Karen stood facing the teacher, her back to Taylor, but with a point from Miss Hart, the young brunette turned to find Taylor staring at her in the doorway. She shrank into her shoulders, brushing her hair behind her ear before walking up to him.

"Here," she said quietly, presenting Taylor's folded vest inside plastic wrapping. " We had it cleaned, so you don't have to worry about any stains."

Taylor accepted the fabric, nodding his thanks to her. She looked to the floor, fiddling with her fingers.

"Is it true?" she asked. Taylor became confused.

"What?" he asked, making her look up to him.

"Are you and Kaleb fighting over me?"

Taylor looked to her, unable to speak for a moment. He glimpsed around for the darker man off at the other end of the room, frowning when he noticed him look away quickly. Taylor sighed, catching her eyes and shaking his head.

"No, we're not," he answered softly. Karen nodded, sucking in her lips as she looked to the floor.

"Good." She took a breath, returning her gaze up at him. "I know you're not ready for a relationship," she said quietly. "But would it be alright if I joined your club and be your friend?"

Taylor's eyes widened for a moment, surprised by this request. Karen looked up to him with large, expecting eyes, silently waiting for an answer. He offered a small, polite smile, then nodded agreement with her. She gave a small, shy smile in return, turning to the class.

"So, where do you want me to sit?" she asked.

Taylor looked to the ground, running a hand through his hair. "Why don't you go sit with Kaleb," he told her. "He can help you out."

Hopefully this would shine a light on the darker man, and his chances with the younger woman would sky rocket. Taylor could do that much for him at least.

His plan backfired, however, because she continuously asked Taylor questions. Kaleb was of no help in the technical field, and he would request the blonde's help as well, making it difficult to stick with his avoidance plan. He did his best to walk about the room, helping the other club members with any problems they had and giving Kaleb and Karen plenty of time to talk amongst themselves, but it didn't take either of them long to call for him again.

Kaleb watched the blonde work, teaching each student individually where they needed help, and explaining it masterfully, making even the most confusing acts sound simple. Privately, he was impressed with Taylor and how he handled himself. Supposedly, the blonde wasn't good with socializing, and in a way, that was true. However, here, he was in his element.

Taylor was able to speak freely, communicating with the people in the room easily, and openly speaking to anyone who would listen. Truthfully, Kaleb enjoyed this part of the technology club the most. Seeing Taylor so comfortable talking with people made Kaleb feel like his friend was beginning to open up, giving hope for the future.

Beside him, Karen hummed in frustration, sucking in her lips as she stared at her computer, once again stuck on a problem.

"Do you know how to do this?" she asked, looking to Kaleb. "I don't want to bother him again."

Kaleb grinned. "You're not bothering him; it's his job to help."

She bit her lip, unconvinced. Kaleb took a closer look, recognizing the problem instantly.

"Here." He took her laptop, taking his time in showing her how to work it. "You know where I learned it?" Kaleb asked. He looked to Taylor at the other end of the room, turning back to smile at the shy girl. "He's not a bad teacher."

Karen sucked in her lips, twirling an end of her hair between her fingers. "I just don't want to bother him any more than I already have," she said quietly. "He's been so nice to me, I don't want him to think I'm too pushy."

Kaleb chuckled. "Believe me, that's the last thing he'd ever think of you."

She looked away, still playing with her hair. "Um…"

Kaleb leaned in to hear what she had to say.

"Are you…" She glanced at him from beneath her glasses. "Are you and Taylor alright?"

Kaleb looked to her, confused. "Why do you ask?"

Karen shook her head. "Nothing, nevermind." She looked to the blonde, questions still bubbling in her mind. "He's acting so different," she mumbled. Kaleb's eyes dropped to the floor, pulling himself back to sit properly in his seat.

"Compared to what, exactly?" he asked, keeping his eyes away, although her eyes stayed on Taylor.

"It's just… He was so much happier at the dance."

Kaleb rubbed the back of his head. "He's in teacher zone right now," the golden man excused. "He's more focused on his work. There's no need to worry."

Karen studied Kaleb, spying his sudden discomfort. "Have you talked about it? Since it happened, I mean?"

Kaleb turned to the brunette, caught off guard by the question, but he looked away, chancing a peek at the blonde. "I've been giving him space." He turned back to her with a smile. "Besides, we were more worried about you than anything else."

Karen furrowed her brow, looking worriedly to the darker man. "I think you should talk," she said quietly. "I don't want to step on your toes or anything, but I think it'll help get things back to normal." Kaleb searched Karen's face, seeing her genuine feelings through her eyes.

"You really care about him, don't you?"

Karen blushed, pulling away from Kaleb and busying herself with her work on her computer. "I think we should get back to work." Her voice wavered with embarrassment. Kaleb couldn't help but smile at her, letting it drop just as quickly. His eyes dropped to the floor, sighing quietly as he faced his computer.

"I'll take that as a yes."

Taylor dropped his head into his book to loudly groan in frustration.

"You're doing good, just take a breath," Kaleb encouraged.

Taylor huffed into his book, then lifted his head just enough to rest his chin on the table to glare at the scientific equation that plagued him. He shook his head. "Nope," he said simply, dropping his book.

"Alright." Kaleb flipped the page. "Let's take a break from the math part and talk about elements. How about potassium?"

"'Kay," Taylor droned.

"Now you're getting it!" Kaleb grinned, snickering at the glare he received from the blonde.

"Not funny," Taylor mumbled.

"It's a little funny," Kaleb chuckled. "What number?"

Taylor sighed, lifting his head from the table. "It's number nineteen," he huffed. "It's also a metal."

Kaleb looked to his friend. "What about its atomic mass?"

Taylor grimaced. "I don't know, man, thirty-nine something."

"You can do better than that," Kaleb scolded, earning another glare from his counterpart. Taylor looked to the ceiling, digging deep through his memory for the answer.

"Thirty-nine point oh-nine."

Kaleb smacked the blonde's shoulder in congratulation. "See? You know this, you just need to take it one step at a time."

"That's too slow," Taylor grumbled.

"Get's you from A to B," Kaleb quipped.

"Whatever." Taylor sighed into his hands, stretching over the back of his chair and staying there for a moment. Kaleb looked to the blonde, thinking of how he would approach the conversation ahead, and biting his lip ahead of time for it.

"Hey, Teahnu…"

The blonde tensed at the name.

"About the dance… And everything after it…" Kaleb sighed, rubbing the back of his head.

"The fight wasn't your fault," Taylor told him, still stretched over his chair with his eyes closed to the ceiling. "Candice is nuts."

Kaleb laughed a bit, thinking back to how he had described the angry woman to Nekko. A huge weight was lifted from off his shoulders with Taylor's answer, making Kaleb relax a little.

"I hope you had fun, at least," Kaleb said.

Taylor shrugged. "Karen's not much of a people person either, so it worked out alright."

Kaleb grinned, looking to the table. "You sure were smiling a lot," he noted, tensing the blonde again.

"Yeah," Taylor mumbled. "I just thought she'd have a better time if she wasn't worrying about why I don't smile." He quirked his mouth. "I thought my cheeks were going to fall off. Being polite is too much work."

Kaleb chuckled at his friend. "Well, you warmed up to her pretty quick."

Taylor quieted, opening his eyes to the ceiling. He sat up, running a hand through his hair to face Kaleb. "If I had known, I wouldn't have said yes," he told him.

Kaleb gave him a queer look. "Known what?"

Taylor frowned to his paperwork. "Karen," he said simply. "I didn't know you liked her. Otherwise, I wouldn't have said yes."

Kaleb stared at the blonde, speechless. After a while, he furrowed his brow. "Has this been bothering you ever since the dance?" he asked quietly.

Taylor ran a hand through his hair, looking away. What he heard next was, to say the least, unexpected. He turned to find Kaleb laughing in his seat, his thunderous bellows growing gradually louder as it bubbled up from his gut.

"*That's* why you've been upset?" Kaleb wheezed, falling back into his uncontrollable laughter.

"What in soul's name is wrong with you?" Taylor asked, watching the giggling Akenian.

"I- I thought-" Kaleb stopped for a moment to take a deep breath, steadying his laughter to speak. "I thought you were mad at me for making you go." He smiled. "Turns out, you were worried about *me* the whole time." His smile broadened. "And all for nothing!"

Taylor's eyes widened. "You're not upset?"

"'Course not!" Kaleb chuckled. "Even if Karen was the one, I wouldn't blame you for her *liking* you. That's way out of your control."

A flame sparked behind Taylor's eyes as rage instantly overwhelmed him. "What the fuck?" he yelled, standing from his seat to loom over a wide eyed Kaleb.

"What-"

"You're not into Karen? Fine!" Taylor towered over Kaleb in his seat. "Absolutely perfect- no skin off my back! But if you're going to go on about this mystery girl, and mope around because she doesn't like you, then go do it somewhere else!" Taylor was furious; all that worrying over nothing. "I'm done worrying about you- butch up and go after her! I can't watch this anymore!"

Kaleb stared up at the angry blonde, silenced by him. Taylor glared back down at him, fighting the urge to run out the door screaming. He couldn't do this again. He couldn't stand the heartache from seeing Kaleb's face soften when he spoke about her, couldn't stop the hurt from attacking him when the darker man smiled to himself- no doubt thinking of her, and most of all, he couldn't stand the jealousy over this invisible girl any longer. If Kaleb finally nabbed the girl of his dreams, and if it meant having to go through that pain all over again, Taylor wanted it to be fresh. He wanted it now rather than later.

"Okay," Kaleb said quietly, unblinking as he stared up into Taylor's angered eyes. "I'll do it."

Taylor straightened, still glaring down at the darker man. "You're going to tell her?" he stated. Kaleb nodded slowly.

"I'll do it today." His voice was so quiet.

"Fine," Taylor growled, then dropped down into his seat, picking up his book to flip through the pages. "This problem here," he grumbled, pointing to it as he turned to his tutor. "What about this-"

The darker man had leaned forward to snatch the blonde's lips with his own, silencing Taylor with a heavy kiss. Just as quickly as it happened, Kaleb rushed back to his seat, looking straight down at his paperwork, but Taylor was stuck in place, not sure what exactly had happened. Kaleb chanced a peek at the blonde, looking away quickly when he saw Taylor staring back at him with wide, blue eyes.

"I don't- I mean, you- Um…" Kaleb stumbled over his words, rubbing the back of his head as he tried to figure out what to do with his eyes. "You don't have to- I was just- It's okay if you don't…" He huffed, biting his lip as he looked away. His blushing spread only over the tips of his ears and nose, now broadcasting the usual invisible freckles through his dark skin.

"… Say something," Kaleb asked, peeking at Taylor.

The blonde blinked back to reality. That actually happened. Kaleb had really kissed him- the proof was still cooling on his lips. Taylor looked down to his book, trying to find his breathing pattern again. He *liked* him.

"… You kiss like a pansy."

Kaleb popped his head up, excitedly turning to the blonde with a great smile that was instantly smothered with Taylor's open book shoved into his face.

"Now help me with this problem, asshole."

Taylor held the book in place over the darker man's face until Kaleb could take it from him, then snatched Kaleb's book to use instead. He busied himself with finding the right page, trying not to notice the pleased smile the Akenian was giving him. The darker man smiled down to the book, complying with the embarrassed blonde, but couldn't help but smile broader at Taylor's flustered state when they caught each other's side glances.

"Alright," Kaleb chuckled. "This is how it works."

"Come on!" Kaleb had finally cracked. "I've been good all afternoon, at least talk to me about it."

Taylor hiked his pack on his shoulders, eyeing the darker man that jumped in front of him. "You want to know here?" he asked, looking around the neighborhood.

Kaleb shrugged, walking backwards to face the blonde. "There's no one around," he rebuttaled. "I'm dying here, just, give me something."

Taylor scanned the area, ensuring it to be abandoned before making eye contact with Kaleb, who smiled at him. "How long has it been?"

Taylor looked away, considering his answer. "I don't know," he mumbled. "I didn't realize it at first, but, after a while, I sort of grew into it." He looked away, keeping watch along the empty sidewalk. "I tried to stay away, too." He glimpsed up at Kaleb, shaking his head. "Didn't work out too well."

Kaleb's eyes lit up as he thought back to the sudden avoidance Taylor had given him around the time he had quit football, smiling to himself. "You've kept it to yourself this whole time?" he asked, walking beside the blonde now instead of in front of him.

Taylor peered up at him. "If we're gonna do this game, we're going to play fair." He cocked a brow at Kaleb. "You answer."

Kaleb grinned down to his feet, agreeing with the blonde. "I guess, I started noticing you after you got hurt," he answered sheepishly. "I thought I was so worried about you because you were my friend, but-" He stopped, biting his lip as he looked down to his feet.

"What's wrong?" Taylor stopped as well, turning back to him.

Kaleb looked up to him, still biting his lip. "It's about your crest," he said quietly. "I healed it." He looked down to the ground. "I healed it by touching it. That's why I tried again the other day; I thought it would work again."

Taylor studied the golden man, eyeing him as he stared back at the blonde, silently begging forgiveness. "How exactly did that work?" he asked. Kaleb shrugged.

"Dad said it was a treatment, and nobody else could get through to you, so I thought I'd try it. When I laid my hand on you, most of your scarring had disappeared by the time I took my hand off." He looked to the ground for a second before returning his gaze to the blonde's. "If I had kept it on longer, you probably would have healed sooner, but... It felt really weird... I couldn't keep it up."

Taylor cocked a brow at him, letting the information set in, then turned to walk up the yard. "I guess I should thank you, then."

Kaleb smiled slightly, rushing to match pace with the blonde. The two strode up the walkway towards the Evans house, waiting to speak more until after they stepped inside.

"So..." Kaleb met eyes with Taylor as they dropped their things off at the racks. "What now?"

Taylor looked away, embarrassed to keep his eyes on Kaleb's. "That's up to you, I guess," he said, walking to the kitchen to put some space between them. "I mean, it's not like I can make you do anything you don't want."

"Same goes for you, Teahnu," Kaleb told him, following him to the kitchen. Taylor grabbed a glass from the cabinet, suddenly needing a reason to remove the lump in his throat. Kaleb leaned up against the sink, peering down to his fiddling fingers.

"Can we... Can we try again?" he asked, looking up to the blonde.

Taylor was close to crushing the glass by now. "Try what?" he asked, already knowing the answer.

Kaleb looked to him for a moment, locking eyes with the blonde before leaning forward to try and brush his lips against Taylor's. The smaller man stopped breathing, closing his eyes to allow the darker man access to his lips, but was stopped when they heard someone coughing in the back room.

Kaleb and Taylor froze, looking to each other just inches apart. The cough repeated, pulling the two boys from each other in search of the intruder. Kaleb took the lead, searching Trish's office and the bathroom before trying the master bedroom. He jiggled the handle, finding it locked.

"Don't come in, I'm sick," a raspy voice called from inside.

"Mom?" Kaleb asked. "You sound terrible."

Another coughing fit echoed from the room. "Thank you, dear, that's exactly what I wanted to hear," Trish sassed, making her son rub the back of his head.

"Have you eaten?"

"It's just a twenty-four hour bug, honey, I'm fine, don't worry about me."

"Not gonna happen," Kaleb told her. "I'll find the key if I have to. This door better be unlocked by the time I'm done cooking."

A small chuckle came from behind the door. "Yes, sir," Trish giggled weakly. Kaleb sighed, turning back to face Taylor, and shrugged. He pat the blonde's shoulder, leaning in to sneak a silent kiss over his lips as he passed to the kitchen. Taylor stood in place as Kaleb left him in the hall, touching his lips lightly once he was alone to make sure he wasn't hallucinating. He dropped his hand, turning from the hall to leave for the bedroom, and quickly set up for a chat with Bekah.

Her face showed up in his screen with a soda in her hand, coming down from her mouth after a swig. She scrunched up her face, looking to the boy confused.

"What's with the face?" she asked. "You look like a frittering school-girl that just got asked out."

Taylor's smile stretched over his face, making Bekah's eyes widen.

"No," she muttered, broadening Taylor's smile.

"No!" she smiled back, slamming her hands on the desk in front of her and squealing in excitement. She shot her fist straight up in the air, laughing victoriously.

"*Yes!*"

Writer's Block:
<u>*The Second Chapter*</u>

The two pulled away gasping, finally returning proper air to their lungs after such a vigorous attack. Kaleb smiled as he pressed his forehead against the blonde's and he lowered their hands from the wall to their sides.

"Man enough for you?" he breathed.

"Shut up," Taylor replied, just as breathless. Kaleb chuckled, closing his eyes as he began nuzzling his nose against Taylor's.

"I've wanted to do that for a long time," Kaleb muttered. "I just didn't know you wanted it, too."

Taylor sighed, closing his eyes as well. "We're going to have to work on our communication skills," the blonde mumbled. "We've been missing out on too much already."

Kaleb chuckled, capturing Taylor's lips for another kiss, this one sweeter and softer. "Deal," he whispered with a smile.

"Boys?"

The two opened their eyes.

"Oh, shit!"

Author's Notes

Not everyone has a crazed father who tries to strangle them in their sleep, but ... IDK, BRO. In all honesty, though, I had a completely different reason as to why I wrote the way I wrote, and added in what I added in. The answer is simple: awareness.

In my few years here on earth, I've seen plenty things that go unnoticed. I've been blessed to have such a widespread, supportive and loving family who would do anything to help me succeed in this life, and pick me up whenever I've fallen. There are others out there though, that don't have that luxury, and unfortunately, I've seen that as well.

For years, I had seen too many people in the News with smiling pictures being the only thing left of them after their recent suicide because of bullying, or because of their sexual preference. This fear hit all too close to home for me as each of my friends discovered themselves through the years, and I wondered what life would be like without them.

I wanted to tell them how much better life is with them in it, how much I loved and adored them, no matter how different they were, or how society thinks they should act. I wanted to let everyone know this, regardless of their situation, be it in finding themselves, or finding themselves in a hopeless situation.

I've seen the effects of bullying. I've seen friends running for their lives out of their own homes because of their enraged father. I've seen families ostracize their own kin after pulling through the fear of coming out. I've seen the displeasures of alcoholism ruin too many good things in this life, and I've seen the desperation the effects of war has had on the ones closest to me.

I've seen all of this and more up close and personal, because it is real, raw life, and that is exactly what I wanted to write about. *Life.* It doesn't matter if you live in an alternate world where you know for sure who your soulmate is, or in the real world where true love isn't as easy to spot. If you're hurting, laughing, crying, or even dying; you're living.

I know words are small, but used correctly, they can have a huge impact, and I'm hoping that impact will be a change for the better, if even for one person. Everything I have written, I have written purposely, and with a message to go along with it.

All you have to do, is see it.

---

www.ingramcontent.com/pod-product-compliance
Lightning Source LLC
Chambersburg PA
CBHW020845090426
42736CB00008B/242